DISCARD

The LAST PALACE

The LAST PALACE

Europe's Turbulent Century in Five Lives

and One Legendary House

NORMAN EISEN

CROWN
NEW YORK

GRATEFUL ACKNOWLEDGMENT IS MADE TO REPRINT FROM THE FOLLOWING:
Otto and Martha Petschek letters, Marc Robinson and Eva Petschek Goldmann
Collections, Petschek Family Archives.
Dulcie Ann Steinhardt Sherlock unpublished memoir and other materials, courtesy
of the Steinhardt Family Archive.
Excerpt(s) from *The Journey: An Autobiography* by Cecilia, Countess Sternberg,
copyright © 1977 by Cecilia Sternberg. Used by permission of The Dial Press, an
imprint of Random House, a division of Penguin Random House LLC.
All rights reserved.
They Broke the Mold: The Memoirs of Walter Birge, copyright © 2007 by
Virginia N. Birge.
Resistance and Revolution by Rob McRae. Montreal: McGill-Queen's University Press,
1997. Print. http://www.mqup.ca/resistance-and-revolution-products
-9780886293161.php.
"The Velvet Revolution and Me," copyright © 2014 by Robert Kiene.
"Prague Diary" by Shirley Temple Black, *McCall's*, January 1969, pages 74, 75, 91, 93,
94, 95. Originally published in *McCall's*® magazine. All rights reserved.
Shirley Temple Black's forthcoming autobiography and other materials, courtesy of
the Black Family Archive.

PHOTOGRAPH CREDITS
Title page, 175, 212: Nat Farbman/The LIFE Picture Collection/Getty Images;
11: Courtesy of The Archive of the Czech National Bank; 25: Eva Petschek
Goldmann and Marc Robinson Collections, Petschek Family Archives; 39: Marc
Robinson Collection, Petschek Family Archives; 82: Personal Archive of Ján Semka;
99, 126: © CTK—Photo 2018; 132: Courtesy of Alexander Toussaint; 163, 241, 338:
Courtesy of the author; 237: Courtesy of Jan Hájek and Miroslav Hájek; 257: Arnold
Newman/Arnold Newman Collection/Getty Images; 303: © Fernando Rondon,
courtesy of the Black Family Archive.

Library of Congress Cataloging-in-Publication Data is available upon request.

ISBN 978-0-451-49578-5
Ebook ISBN 978-0-451-49580-8

Printed in the United States of America

Book design by Lauren Dong
Map by Laura Hartman Maestro

9 8 7 6 5 4 3 2 1

First Edition

To my mother, Frieda, my wife, Lindsay, and my daughter, Tamar,
who helped me find my way around Prague—
and everything else

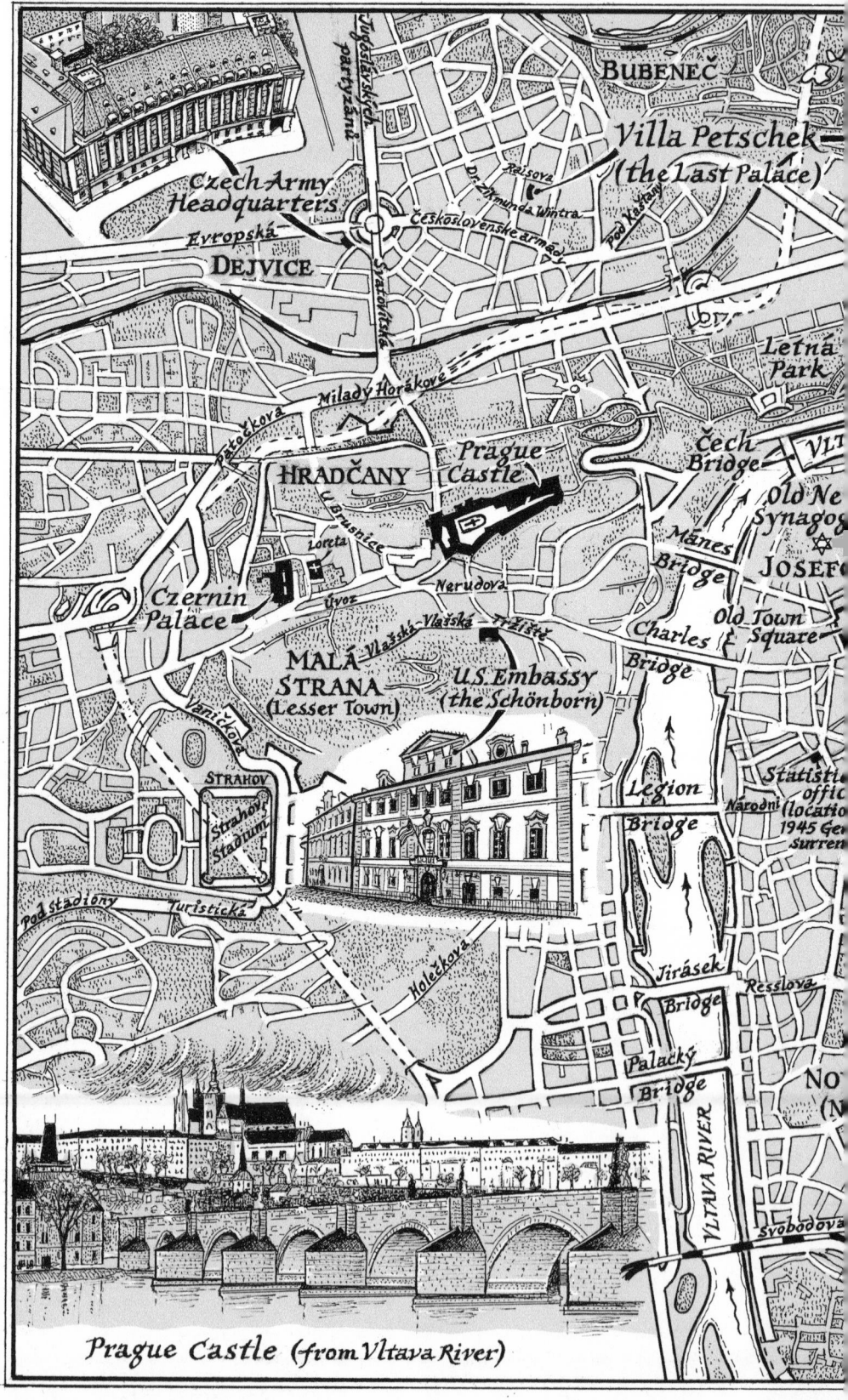

Prague Castle (from Vltava River)

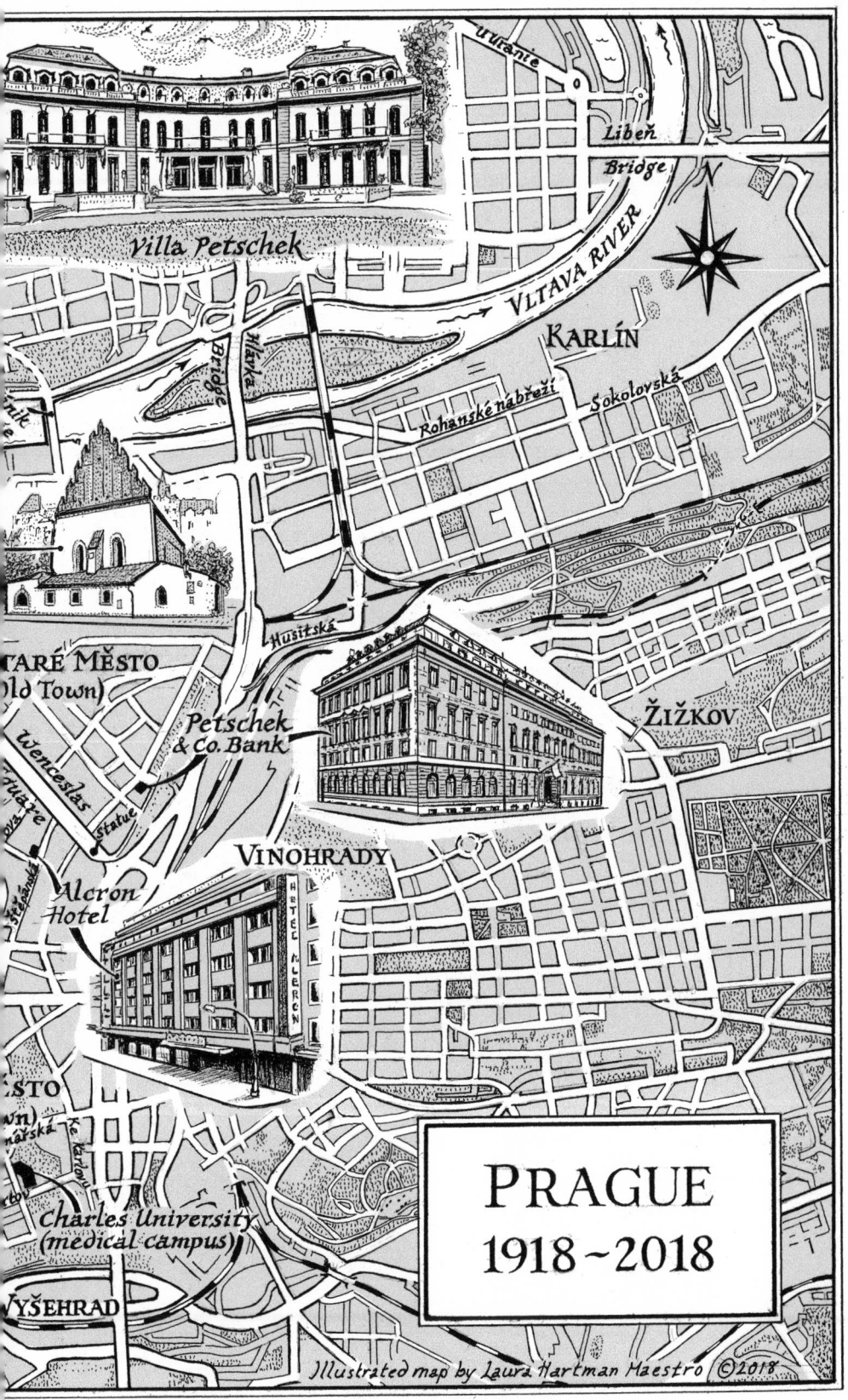

PRAGUE
1918–2018

Illustrated map by Laura Hartman Maestro ©2018

Contents

Author's Note

THE STORY TOLD IN THIS BOOK IS BASED PRIMARILY UPON THE diaries, letters, and other papers of the main protagonists, many of which have never before been made public. Additional details have been furnished through my interviews with their direct descendants and others who knew them, as well as other historical research.

Quotations serving as dialogue are drawn from correspondence or other materials, as detailed in the endnotes. There is one exception: my mother's story is substantially based upon more than a half century of my conversations with her. These are reconstructed from memory, including quotes attributed to her.

I thank the families of those who lived in the palace for providing me extraordinary cooperation. Without their generosity, the full story of Otto Petschek's palace—secret for so long—could not have been told.

The American Ambassador's Residence in Prague has been called the last palace built in Europe. . . . He knew now why he felt so fond of the Ambassador and his wife, so safe in the Residence, and so subtly reluctant to leave.
He was frightened of Europe.

—JOHN UPDIKE,
"Bech in Czech," *The New Yorker,* April 20, 1987

PROLOGUE

Over the Atlantic Ocean; April 10, 2010

I PICKED UP THE HEAVY WHITE RECEIVER OF THE PHONE BESIDE my seat and asked the operator to place a call to my mother.

I listened in as he opened a line and dialed.

"Hello," she answered with her distinctive Eastern European lilt.

"Frieda Eisen?"

"Speaking."

"Will you accept a call from Air Force One?"

"Yes," she replied, sounding excited but skeptical.

"Hi, Mom," I said.

"Oh, Nachman," she exclaimed, calling me by my Yiddish name. "I thought it might be President Obama!"

"No, it's just me."

"That's good, too," she said, laughing. "What are you doing on Air Force One?"

"I'm traveling with the president. To Prague."

"What? Why?"

"He has asked me if I will take over as ambassador there."

"Whose ambassador?"

"Ours, of course. The United States."

I waited for a cry of delight. My mother had been born in Czechoslovakia and immigrated to the United States from there. She sang me some of my first lullabies in Czech and Slovak. She venerated the father of the country, its first president, Tomáš Masaryk; his successor and protégé, Edvard Beneš; and their most brilliant modern successor, Václav

Havel. And she took great pride in my own accomplishments as a first-generation Czech-Jewish American, most recently my job as a White House lawyer. I thought she would be thrilled that I would be representing the United States in today's Czech Republic.

Instead, the line was silent.

"*Maminka?*" I asked, using the Czech diminutive for mother. "Are you there?"

"Yes," she answered, clipping the word short, her voice suddenly flat.

"What's wrong?"

"Nothing."

"You don't sound very excited."

"Hmm."

"Mom, what is it?"

More silence.

Finally she spoke.

"I'm scared."

"Of what?"

"That they will kill you."

I was stunned.

"Who will?" I asked.

She paused before answering.

"You know what happened to us there."

In 1944, the Nazis deported my mother and her family from their small town of Sobrance to a ghetto, and then to Auschwitz. There her parents, most of her other relatives, and almost everyone she knew from her village were murdered. She had survived, eventually making her way to the United States and starting a new life.

I knew that her scars had never completely healed. But she loved and longed for all that she had lost, and I had been sure that she would see the president's offer as I did: vindication. Coming full circle. An American success story.

I said as much.

"I couldn't bear it if anything happened to you," she whispered.

I silently cursed myself. I should have seen this coming. But I had been so caught up in my own excitement that it hadn't occurred to me that she might react like this.

I had learned from our lifetime together—the hard way—that arguing with my mother was not effective when her anxieties flared. I had another idea.

"Mom, guess where the ambassador lives?"

"Where?"

"Otto Petschek's palace."

"Ohhh," she gasped. "Really?"

My mother may have been the poorest Czechoslovak Jew and Otto Petschek the richest. Otto and his family were famous among their fellow Czechs—the local equivalent of the Rothschilds or Rockefellers. Their Prague home was a Beaux-Arts masterpiece that conjured Versailles, with more than one hundred rooms—so many that no one seemed to agree on an exact count. It was chockablock with antiques, old-master paintings, rare books, and other precious objects that Otto had collected and that remained in the house. The mansion spread out across a lush garden compound the size of an American city block. Erected after World War I, it had been called "the last palace built in Europe"—a final monument to a gilded era that definitively ended in 1938.

My mom thawed a little as we talked about the palace—enough for me to seize the moment.

"Mom," I told her, "we would love it if you would come with us." My wife, Lindsay, and I had agreed that we wanted Frieda to join us in Prague.

"Come with you?"

"Why not? There's plenty of room. We would wait on you. You wouldn't have to lift a finger. You would be coming home."

She was silent again.

"I will think about it," she said finally. "So, tell me, what's the food like on Air Force One?"

⌣

AFTER returning to the States, I flew to LA to visit my *maminka*. I wanted to tell her about the trip, put her mind at ease, and convince her to move with us.

She hugged me tightly, pressing her head into my chest. Her embrace was still strong even though she was approaching ninety. Never much more than five feet tall, she had, it seemed, grown shorter—maybe even since my last visit, only a couple of months before. But in her face I could still see the beautiful girl smiling in surviving photographs from 1945 Czechoslovakia. Her complexion remained clear and fair, though now seamed with fine lines. She had begun dyeing her hair a pale blond, instead of the brunette shade that she had pulled off well into her seventies, and she patted it back into place when she finally released me.

We sat together on the sofa and she held my hand in hers. It was veined and mottled on top, but her palm was no less soft than it had been when I was a child. I told her that Prague was beautiful, as she had always said. I had been to Prague Castle with President Obama, and he had introduced me to the current Czech president, Václav Klaus. I had even managed to catch a glimpse of the Petschek house, though I hadn't made it inside—drape measuring by future ambassadors was frowned upon. Its façade seemed to justify the superlatives, though, its turrets, balconies, and putti running the entire length of the block.

This time, my mention of the palace failed to distract her. "Nachman. You are so good at your White House job. Why do you have to leave?" She carried my business card around with her in a little plastic sleeve to prevent wear and showed it to everyone she met. And she loved the nickname that the press had bestowed upon me, the Ethics Czar. She liked to tell people, "It is the only time a czar has ever been good for the Jews!"

"I don't *have* to leave. It's a promotion," I replied.

"What do you know about diplomacy?"

"Mom, the president says I am going to be a great ambassador."

"Well," she replied, "if you don't mind my saying so, this is no time to send an amateur." Europe, she felt, was in crisis. Right-wing nationalism, with its hatred of Jews and other minorities, was stirring, and so was the Russian bear. My mom, still damaged from the century's great upheavals, saw everything through that lens.

Her suspicions extended to the sitting Czech president. She had loved Havel but cared little for his extremely conservative successor: Klaus was a climate-change denier who embraced Russia. He ridiculed Havel's slogan "Truth and love will prevail over lies and hate," and mocked Havel and his acolytes as *pravdoláskaři,* idolaters of "truth-and-lovism." My mother felt that the US-Czech relationship had deteriorated badly during the Klaus years, and she blamed him, along with others.

All that bore no resemblance to what I had just seen with my own eyes. The Czechs had greeted Obama rapturously. He and the Russians had just signed an arms-control treaty at Prague Castle. They were on good terms. President Klaus had welcomed me warmly. Jewish life was flourishing all over Prague, and I saw no signs of anti-Semitism whatsoever. I imparted all this to her.

"Nachman, listen to me. You went to Prague for twenty-four hours with the president of the United States. You don't know Europe like I do. It hasn't changed that much."

She argued her position ferociously. Even in her late eighties, she was a formidable debater—as smart as anyone I knew. Her apartment was stuffed with books and periodicals, and she haunted the library. She pulled a sheaf of highlighted and underlined news clippings from her purse with a flourish and pressed them into my hands.

I told her that if things were as bad as she said, she should be glad that I was going back to her country to help.

"My country? Does my country even exist anymore, Nachman?" My mother had taken the 1993 division of Czechoslovakia into two nations hard. She had been born in the eastern part of the country, now Slovakia, but had also lived in the western part, now the Czech Republic, where I would be serving. She had deep emotional ties to both and still called herself Czechoslovak.

"Come on, Mom. All you ever talked about when I was growing up was your country. You love the place!"

"Nachman, it's a mistake to love a country. It can't love you back."

"Look, we are going to Prague—it's settled. We want you to come with us."

She blinked back at me, exasperated.

"Mom, it's a triumph for our family."

"No, no way. That door is closed. I left, and I am not going back."

"Not even a visit?"

"My doctors won't permit it."

"Have you even asked them?"

She sighed loudly and I knew I had scored a point.

"We will see."

⌣

ALMOST eight months passed before I actually left the White House for my job in Prague, in January 2011. Seemingly everyone I met with to prepare mentioned the palace where I would be living, saying with good-humored envy that it was the most beautiful ambassadorial property owned by the United States anywhere. Often they would recount its outlandish legends: that Otto Petschek had honeycombed it with hidden compartments and passageways, in one of which he had concealed a fortune in gold; that after the Germans had swept into Prague, it was the scene of wild Nazi bacchanals, the officers and their mistresses cavorting in its Olympic-sized indoor pool; that the United States had acquired the immensely valuable mansion and grounds after the war for free, as a gift involving a Czech general and his future American daughter-in-law; that Cold War–era listening devices were still to be found secreted inside its paneling and in its chandeliers; and on and on.

Curious, I made inquiries, but verifiable facts turned out to be surprisingly scanty. I confirmed the basic chronology of Czech-Jewish ownership and German occupation followed by long American possession. I received a short guide to the palace that included some basic historical information, mostly about how Otto Petschek and his family had used the place, and I stumbled across a few other documents to the same effect. But I could confirm none of the wildest rumors.

The less I found out, the more I wanted to know. Who were the people who had lived in my future home—and what was their experience of the tumultuous past century? That history didn't belong only to the palace. It was my family's story, too. The people who had lived there had driven, and been driven by, forces large and small that had shaped my mother's homeland and the first part of her life—and eventually brought her to the United States. And now the zeitgeist was bringing our family back to Prague.

There is a Yiddish saying that I often heard from my mom: *"Az men est chazzer, zol rinnen uber den bort"*—"If you are going to eat pork, let it run down your beard." And that's what I decided to do while living in Prague: dig into the palace's story and let all that history flow over my beard.

⌣

THE eight-month lag in taking up my post also gave me plenty of opportunities to work on my mom and get her used to the reality of my new job. I knew that I was making progress when I overheard her telling people, "They took us out of there on a cattle car and my son returned on Air Force One!"

There was another promising sign as well: she started giving me advice about the job. She and my late father had abided by a strict moral code in our family business, a hamburger stand. When I paid her one last visit before departing for Europe, she urged me not to forget their three rules, even though I would now be occupying a mansion. "Always do the right thing, Nachman. Always be loyal." "And," I joined in, both of us laughing in anticipation at the final line, "always serve the best hamburger you can!" By the time I, Lindsay, and our daughter, Tamar, had touched down in Prague on Monday, January 17, 2011, my *maminka* had at least agreed to pay us a visit once we settled in.

Then I made the mistake of telling her about the swastika.

I phoned her at the end of my first full day in the Czech capital, placing the call from the library of Otto Petschek's palace. Flames crackled in the fireplace as I dialed Los Angeles.

My mother wanted to know everything. I recounted the flight and the way our motorcade had swept us from the airport into the city. I described how Prague's gleaming ultramodern glass-and-chrome office buildings butted up against tall, brutalist Iron Curtain–era apartment blocks. Medieval monasteries stood next to Bauhaus dwellings, and elaborately detailed art-nouveau mansions nestled among whorled rococo churches.

"And the Petschek house?" she asked.

We had approached it down a long avenue. From a distance, we saw a pink exterior wall patrolled by policemen garbed in black. As we came closer, the house rose into view. It was a span of alabaster masonry reclining on a green lawn among a bower of trees. Round windows seemed to emerge from behind the fence to meet our gaze, steadily staring back at us from beneath a mansard roof of green oxidized copper and black slate.

We turned in to the compound. Passing through an ornate iron gate, whose black bars bisected golden pomegranates, we crunched up a gravel driveway. At the head of the drive, about a hundred yards from the entry, stood the palace. Its extended façade and jutting rectangular wings were richly ornamented with rusticated stone, grilles, and statuary, so complex that it could not be absorbed all at once. As the motorcade slowly proceeded up the driveway, the building's shape kept shifting, too; somehow it looked entirely different than it had from the street. By the time we pulled up to the portico, a tall porch supported by Tuscan columns, we could no longer see either end of our new home.

In front of the pillars, and every bit as firmly planted, was Miroslav Černík, the majordomo, beaming. Pigeon chested, silver haired, and in his early sixties, he looked more like an ambassador than I did. He greeted us and led us inside. The rooms were a blur of cool stone walls and warm, elaborately carved wood paneling, gleaming silver, and richly colored tapestries and oriental rugs. Exiting onto a patio overlooking acres of orderly gardens, we turned to take in the rear of the palace; I saw that it was built in a curve, the whole massive neobaroque structure bending in a pronounced concave arc. That was why the house had seemed to be moving as we came up the drive.

My *maminka* loved hearing every detail. "Nachman, imagine that— Otto Petschek's palace is your starter house!" It was true; I had grown up in apartments, and that's all that I had lived in ever since.

In my enthusiasm, I leaped ahead to tell her about the most dramatic moment of the day.

In the oval receiving chamber at the front of the house, before one of the floor-to-ceiling windows, stood a French antique table. Mr. Černík came to a stop in front of it. Like everything else in the palace, it was opulent: the top was cherrywood with scalloped edges, the russet grain of the surface inlaid with a darker wood. Curved legs sharply tapered downward to points, each shod with a metal hoof that matched the shining brass bumper framing the table's edge.

"Please look under here, Mr. Ambassador," he said, pointing to its underside. I crouched down on all fours and ducked beneath the piece. Craning my neck and peering up, I spotted an old paper label. It was the size of a large commemorative stamp. Its surface was yellowed and faded, slightly warped and bubbled from the paste that had been used to affix it many years before. It bore a serial number and an illegible signature scrawled in ink in an antique hand. There was also a symbol rubber-stamped on the label, which was hard to make out.

I moved closer and squinted in the dim light, and the image jumped into focus. It was a stylized black eagle, with extended wings, its head turned to the left. It was clutching a wreath in its claws. The garland encircled a tiny, sharp-edged swastika. Černík said that similar traces of the Nazi occupation were hidden all over the palace.

"Mom, can you believe it? And now *we* are living here. How amazing is that?"

Chilly silence.

"Mom?"

"There are swastikas in the house?"

Shit.

I tried to undo the damage. "Mother, don't think of it that way." I reminded her that we would be transforming the palace into a Jewish home. We would be keeping kosher, observing the Sabbath, putting up mezuzas on the doorposts. What better revenge on Hitler than that? She needed to come see it for herself.

"Why would I want to visit any place that the Nazis liked?"

"Come on, Ma, don't say that—it's a beautiful house."

"What if I found a swastika in my room?"

"I will scour your room. Hell, I'll scour the whole palace before you come."

But she was unmoved.

To me, the swastika was dark evidence of our family's triumph and a fascinating historical artifact—a signpost to the past. It made me wonder again about my predecessors: Who were they? How had they ended up here? What had the past century—the tornado of historical forces that had whipped through my mother's homeland—looked like to each of them through the windows of this very palace?

But to my mom, the Nazi symbol was no beguiling relic. It did not provoke curiosity. It evoked visceral trauma, a sinister weight that she would always bear. The harder I worked to persuade her otherwise, the more implacable she became.

Best to change the subject. Desperately casting my eye about the palace's library, with its thousands of volumes belonging to the original owner, their spines catching the firelight, I asked her the first thing that came to mind. "What do you know about Otto Petschek, Mom?"

"Ah," she sighed, "Otto Petschek! The Czechoslovaks were the cleverest people in Europe—and the Jews were the smartest people in Czechoslovakia. And Otto? He was the best of them all. He had everything: talent, money, education. But he was an optimist like you, Nachman, and optimism can be a very dangerous thing in Prague."

Part I

Otto (standing) with his brothers and cousins in the palace gardens.

1

The Golden Son of the Golden City

Prague, Czechoslovakia; Spring 1924

IT WAS SHORTLY BEFORE DAWN. ON THE HILL ABOVE THE OLD Town, just north of Prague Castle, a thirty-nine-year-old man awoke in his small yet elegant house. It was one of the little villas that speckled the Bubeneč neighborhood; rural not so long ago, it had become the most fashionable district in the city. He slid his feet into his slippers, inserted his arms into his robe, and cinched the belt. He moved carefully, so as not to wake his wife, whose slender form was rising and falling beneath the covers. Gingerly opening the door to the terrace, he stepped outside.

Every morning, Otto Petschek greeted the rising sun, now stirring below the horizon. His butler, who was wearing a swallowtail coat and a striped vest, would join him in the soft blue light and set down a coffee service with his white-gloved hands. Today, with practiced efficiency, he poured out a cup, handed it to Otto, and returned indoors. Otto felt the coffee's warmth radiating through the delicate Meissen china, which was intricately patterned with pink flowers and gold leaves. The set had been a gift for his wife, Martha. After eleven years and four children together, it still delighted Otto to see her face light up when he brought her beautiful things.

Otto sipped his coffee and gazed out at the view. Although he lived near the center of Prague—a city that had been built up for a millennium, with new construction perpetually squeezed in and layered on—a remaining slice of wilderness sprawled just behind his home. His parents and then he had accumulated multiple plots over decades, stitching them together into a single, rambling, five-acre parcel. He studied its contours. The terrain was partially obscured by the darkness still cloaking the ground, but he knew it by heart, practically down to the last leaf. He had spent years walking the individual tracts, visiting on weekends, attending family celebrations, even proposing to Martha here. Old trees reared up, tall and shaggy. Hedges ran among them, stands of flowers, swaths of lawn. In the distance, Otto could hear the clop-clop of horses' hooves, the day's first carts delivering produce, ice, and milk to his neighbors' homes.

Farther behind him and this unformed tangle of land, to the east, was the heart of Prague: the city center where Otto was born, the synagogue where he was bar mitzvahed, the schools where he was educated, the business that he had helped build. He was a model citizen of the Czechoslovak capital. Still, every morning he looked to the West: to Germany, for language and literature; to France, for art and architecture; to England, whose business acumen he respected; and across the Atlantic to the United States, whose energy he embraced, grateful for its role in creating the fledgling Czechoslovak state. In the predawn haze, if he squinted he could imagine the curvature of the earth beneath his huge expanse of land and trace its arc, a vector connecting him to each of the nations he admired.

Music was likely running through Otto's head. It was his first great passion, and he remained an intense classical aficionado, a sustainer of Prague's German Opera, and an ardent Wagnerian, admiring the composer's heroes and their appetite for daunting challenges. Perhaps this morning he heard the low thrum of strings that launched *Das Rheingold,* the day stirring like the instruments, the tones spreading like the sun.

While listening to his invisible orchestra and watching the dawn rise day after day over his sprawling, overgrown property, Otto had formed an idea about what to do with his land.

He would build a palace there—one that would compete with any other in the city. It would be huge, more than one hundred rooms, the entire length of a city block. Its façade would marry the mathematically elegant columns of ancient Greece and the muscularity of Roman sculptural forms with the golden ratios of Italian Renaissance architecture and the majesty of the French baroque. He would render the march of Western civilization in stone, marble, and brick, right up to the present—bowing the façade into a sharp, ultramodern curve, a dramatic contemporary flourish that would distinguish his creation from every other palace in a city stuffed with them.

It would be a residence befitting his status as a leading banker and industrialist in the new democracy, the perfect home for his beloved Martha and the children they shared. And it would be an embodiment of the twentieth century's brilliant future—the new era of peace and prosperity ushered in after the war to end all wars.

Otto's reveries were interrupted by stirrings in the villa behind him. The sun was fully up now. Martha and the children had begun to rise, and the staff were commencing their day's work.

As he turned his back on the sunlit yard and reentered his home, he hummed to himself, drafting elaborate plans for his palace in his head.

⌒

THINGS had always come easily to Otto. He was born in 1882 to Isidor Petschek and Camilla Robitschek, scions of two of the most prosperous Jewish families in the Austro-Hungarian provinces of Bohemia and Moravia. He was the first child of his generation, and the Petscheks anticipated his arrival no less eagerly than a nation would await the birth of royalty. On October 17, the musical wail of the plump infant was heard for the first time inside the family town house in Prague's center. Otto was delivered at home, cleaned by the midwife, and presented to his mother. Isidor and his brother, Otto's uncle Julius, inspected the baby in Camilla's arms closely. Their stern demeanors concealed the affection they felt as they studied little Otto's marked Petschek features: a large cranium, broad forehead, and stubby nose.

Three generations occupied the same sturdy house, stacked on top of one another in a Petschek layer cake. Otto was taught there by a tutor through age six—a naturally confident child. In short pants, a jacket, and a floppy black cravat, he was brought before Isidor and Julius to do his sums. He stood at attention in the parlor, and the numbers flowed out of him. Otto took after his father, Isidor, square headed and handsome, albeit without Isidor's luxuriant goatee. Uncle Julius was pear-shaped and balding, with a long, drooping mustache, and his mass often settled into one of the parlor's overstuffed sofas. The brothers were pleased with Otto's talent. They were financiers, making loans and buying and selling shares of coal mines and other companies, and expected great things from Otto in the same line of work. Otto was a born showman, which is perhaps why he enjoyed these performances so much. If he seemed a little *too* fond of the spotlight, well, the brothers believed they would expunge that in due time.

Young Otto's gifts extended to music. It was everywhere in Prague. Recitals, concerts, symphonies, opera—melodies poured into the streets, flowing through the city as freely as the Moldau (or as the Czechs called it, the Vltava) River. Song also swam within the walls of the Petschek town house: when the extended family gathered, the horse-drawn carriages often pulled up to Stadtpark Street filled with hired musicians. Family members dressed in their finest, the men wearing tails, the women high-necked gowns over their corsets. Although the family was Jewish, the high culture of the Austro-Hungarian Empire and neighboring Germany was every bit as much their religion. Several family members performed with the professionals, singing or playing the piano.

Some of the children fidgeted on the edges of settees, faces scrubbed and hair plastered down. But young Otto was transfixed. He begged for piano lessons and was soon perched before the keys, his fingers mastering the spellbinding meter of Schubert, Chopin, and Schumann. With his parents, he visited the new German opera house that opened in 1888. Wagner's *Die Meistersinger* inaugurated the building, and his other works were performed in the seasons that followed. Otto stared up at the whorls of its neobaroque ceiling as the sounds washed over him, sparking a lifelong adoration of the composer. Otto loved Mozart and Beethoven, too, both of whom had created and conducted in Prague— and all the other German-speaking masters. He amazed his family by coming home from musical performances and stretching his own fingers across the ivory keys, playing solely from the fresh memory of the show he had just seen.

Otto found beauty everywhere. Liberated from the confines of the family dwelling as he began attending school, Otto wandered the city wide-eyed, studying the rhythms in the stucco, marble, and plaster lining the city streets, amalgams of centuries of European building. "Music is liquid architecture; architecture is frozen music" went the saying attributed to Goethe, a venerated authority in Otto's German-speaking home. The Old New Synagogue and the other medieval buildings were baritones, deep in solid stone. Renaissance monuments, such as the Royal Summer Palace, were sopranos, trilling. Saint Nicholas Church and the Wallenstein Garden, baroque giants, were tenors. To some, the juxtaposition of these styles seemed discordant. But to Otto, the cityscape was a harmonious chorus.

Prague's admirers cherished its idiosyncratic façades and knew them as well as their own faces. There were details that less-practiced eyes missed: a bawdy fresco here, a secret passageway leading to an ancient grotto there. Residents of the city had long formed a cult that worshiped its beauty. They preserved the history that gave the façades life: extravagant legends, unwritten secrets, legacies of seers and oddballs. Parents and grandparents whispered tales to their children of the clairvoyant founder of the city, Princess Libuše; the miracle-working priest, Nepomuk; Rabbi Löew and his golem; and a thousand others—pointing out the dwellings where they lived and walked.

All great cities have their guardians, but Prague's were particularly fierce in their devotion. These Praguers, the ones who did not forget, who always observed, who passed down the city's lore from generation to generation, were the Watchers of Prague.

Otto was one of their number. But he was not content to only observe. He did not know how yet, but like the operatic protagonists whom he admired, he fully intended to make his own heroic mark on the city that he loved.

∿

IN 1892, at age ten, Otto graduated to university preparatory school, "gymnasium," spending the next eight years immersed in the classical liberal-arts curriculum. He clambered from Europe's roots, Latin and Greek, to its treetops: contemporary literature, science, and mathematics. The course of study was intended to instill the Enlightenment's faith in reason and progress, and in Otto's case, it succeeded. But Isidor and Julius made sure that Otto's exposure to Athens and Rome, Paris and Vienna, did not come at the expense of Jerusalem. They had been raised in an Orthodox home and, although they had become more liberal, they still had Otto study Jewish law, lore, and history in daily religion lessons.

In 1895, his clear voice rang out in the Old New Synagogue as he chanted his bar mitzvah portion in well-practiced Hebrew, marking his ascension to Jewish adulthood. His head bent low to read the tiny calligraphy in the Torah scroll, his hand guided a silver *yad* right to left along the ancient Hebrew script. The notes of his cantillation floated high overhead in the dim light among the five-ribbed Gothic vaulting. (The fifth rib was purely decorative, to avoid forming a cross.) In the attic above, the golem slumbered, legend had it—ready to arise again if needed to protect Prague's Jewish community. Below, its newest member confidently led the service. He had grown taller, become lean, but still had his marked family looks, a shock of black hair above his high forehead. His father and uncle, bulkier versions of the young Otto, flanked him on the bimah, while his mother and her sister Berta, now married to Julius, peered at them through slits in the foot-thick walls that separated the women from the men.

In the years following his bar mitzvah, Otto learned that not everyone in his city and the lands surrounding it was equally fond of his tribe. Czech nationalism was surging: the reassertion of Czech language and identity almost three centuries after the Slavic Bohemians and Moravians had been conquered by the German-speaking Austrians. The Petschek family enthusiastically supported the current Austro-Hungarian ruler, the benign, long-serving Franz Joseph. He was known for his warm relations with his Jewish subjects throughout the vast span of his empire, stitching together dozens of nationalities across Europe. Indeed, Uncle Julius served him as an *Oberfinanzrat,* a financial counselor to the empire.

But ethnic Czechs resented the centuries of Habsburg domination over Prague and the lands around it. The nationalists, dissatisfied with their fragmentary representation in Franz Joseph's parliament, wanted self-determination or independence. As the new century approached, a vocal minority of Slavic nationalists began to focus their ire on culturally German residents of Prague, with Jews prominent among their targets. Anti-Semitic pamphlets titled "Pro Lid" ("For the People") circulated, slandering the Jews for their assimilation of German language and culture. Bigots marched to demand the boycott of Jewish stores, stomping down the streets and chanting *"svůj k svému"* ("each to his own"), resulting in the failure of many of those businesses.

Worst of all, some among the nationalists revived the ancient slander that Jews killed Christians to procure blood as a secret ingredient in Passover matzo. An itinerant Jew, Leopold Hilsner, was falsely prosecuted for ritually murdering a Gentile woman. Throughout the period, there were anti-German and anti-Semitic riots and street fighting in Prague, with Jews beaten, their store windows smashed, and the stock looted. Jewish homes and synagogues were attacked and destroyed as well, until Franz Joseph sent his army in, marching through streets littered with broken glass to restore order.

The fin de siècle waves of anti-Semitism made Otto's father and uncle nervous. They had fled to Prague to escape a pogrom, and still it haunted them. They grew up in Kolín, where their father had acquired land cheaply from the townspeople, then resold it at a substantial profit to the government for a railroad. In 1876, an angry mob gathered in front of their home. The family looked out cautiously from behind the curtains, wondering if they were going to be violently attacked. They decided to flee, settling in Prague and quietly succeeding as passive investors who stayed out of public view. The Petscheks were not eager to have to up stakes again.

With all the idealism of a seventeen-year-old, Otto took a more optimistic view. The Petscheks were not only Jewish; they were Austro-Hungarian, Bohemian, German-speaking Praguers. Surely anti-Semitism was guttering out—a periodic eruption on the fringes of society. After all, a non-Jew, the Czech nationalist Tomáš Masaryk, the leading defender of Hilsner, was against the blood libel. A philosopher, writer, and publisher of a liberal newspaper, the forty-nine-year-old Masaryk, his stare fierce behind his pince-nez, was a formidable champion of the Jews. The nationalist ranks included many others who welcomed Jews—and even some Czech Jews themselves (though Otto was not among them). Otto believed that the empire was not going anywhere and that the Petscheks were securely embedded in it. Franz Joseph had even offered to elevate them to the nobility, although Julius and Isidor had declined. They preferred a low profile, informed by the cautious Jewish philosophy of *sha shtil*—hush, be quiet.

Otto felt no such compunction. A new century was coming, and at its dawn, in 1900, he would graduate from gymnasium and continue his education. He wanted to train as a conductor. He was musically gifted and temperamentally suited for the job, commanding and joyfully unrestrained. He had seen the great conductors of Europe, and he admired them—for the most part. He once wrote to his parents, "10 days in Vienna and no Wagner, only rubbish! As if Mahler did it to spite me!" If he were a conductor he could program whatever he wanted, whenever he wanted it.

Julius and Isidor forbade that career. Music was a hobby, not a profession. They had other plans for the eldest Petschek son: Otto would study law, as they both had, and then enter the family business. Otto's exuberance made his father and uncle uneasy, and they hoped that professional studies would sober him up. Perhaps they had overindulged him. Supervising one of the largest fortunes in Prague wasn't supposed to be romantic; no one ought to mistake the pits and shafts of a coal mine for a box at the opera. Should Otto find legal scholarship dry, so much the better.

If Otto resented their dictates—and he must have—he kept his feelings to himself. No indication remains that he complained or attempted to talk them out of it. His was a culture and a home that enforced hierarchy; he was a dutiful son and nephew, and he acceded to his elders' wishes. They sent him to their alma mater, the German-speaking branch of Charles University. Founded in 1348, it was one of the oldest institutions of higher learning in Europe and one of the most distinguished. Charles drew scholars from across the German-speaking world. (Einstein joined the university's Faculty of Arts just a few years after Otto matriculated, in 1911.)

But education in the law did little to contain Otto. The black covers of his textbooks bore intimidating titles: *Verwaltungslehre und Oesterreichisches Verwaltungsrecht Algemeiner Theil*; *Deutsche Reichs- und Rechtsgeschichte*; *Sammlung von Civilrechtlichen Entscheidungen der k.k. obersten Gerichtshofes.* Yet inside their funereal bindings, Otto's underlining and marginalia ignited the pages. An explosion of red, blue, and green ink dazzled the eye. The law was another complex system—like math, music, or Prague's architectural medley—and Otto's imagination was alive to its patterns, intangible but omnipresent. Its rule undergirded Franz Joseph's empire, which in turn protected and nurtured Otto, his family, the Jews, and all its subjects. Law was the instrument of the Enlightenment vision of an ordered, rational society that he had imbibed at gymnasium. He was enthralled.

This enthusiasm was not shared by all his peers. One of his acquaintances described their legal curriculum as "intellectual sawdust that thousands of others' mouths had already chewed up for me." That pessimistic law student was Franz Kafka. Franz and Otto made the journey through the Charles University undergraduate and then doctoral law program in parallel. Otto furiously scribbled notes, hunched over the page, trying to catch every detail, as if he were transcribing a symphony. Franz listened dubiously, his narrow, sharp features cast with anxiety. To him, the intricacies of the Austro-Hungarian legal system inspired terror of unfair, even incomprehensible accusation, guilt, and punishment. That dark outlook was totally foreign to Otto.

Otto's legal education had no discernible effect on his flamboyance. For his parents' twenty-fifth wedding anniversary in 1906, he dragooned the family members of his younger generation to the Petscheks' lush Bubeneč garden. He compelled everyone to dress in the Mozartian finery of the classical era and perform musical selections. Otto's younger siblings and cousins were pressed into service and (over some objections) into costume to make up an orchestra. Otto was the conductor, resplendent in skintight breeches, his long white tailcoat adorned with heavy gold braid. His outfit was topped off by an outrageous powdered wig tied back with a black ribbon. Everyone else's faces in the anniversary photograph wear little joy. But Otto, his feet firmly planted onstage, adored the show.

⌒

OTTO completed his legal studies with a *juris utriusque* doctorate (JUDr.) in 1909, and Isidor and Julius dispatched him to serve a lengthy clerkship in the offices of one of their friends, JUDr. Julius Popper. There the newly minted doctor of law would enjoy no special privileges as the heir apparent. Despite his advanced education, Otto was an apprentice, and the work was hardly dramatic: legal research, writing, even keeping his boss's desk tidy. When that humbling initiation was completed, Otto formally joined the family business. Isidor and Julius trained him in the least-glamorous aspects of their operations—bookkeeping, correspondence, and personnel—and they assigned him to the subterranean recesses of their investments, the warren of coal mines honeycombing northern Bohemia and Silesia, to learn operations there. They brought him to their own meetings as a silent observer, setting a grueling pace:

"I had to go away with Papa and Uncle Julius on Monday and Tuesday. Never have I experienced a week as confusing as the last one. And I was so terribly tired that I managed the incredible, and fell fast asleep for a whole hour on the way back by car from Aussig—we didn't finish in time to make the train and left by car at 9:30. If you consider that the road is bad and full of puddles and that the chauffeur quite rightly made the horn bellow at every curve, you will see that this great achievement must be valued highly."

His mentors were testing him to see whether he would do as he was told. Otto seemed to comply, at least on the surface. He donned the same impassive expression, ramrod posture, and dark three-piece suits as his father and uncle.

There was one area, however, in which Otto resisted their dictates: marriage. Throughout his twenties, his father and uncle, as well as his mother and aunt, had been pressing him to wed. He demurred; he wanted to be in love. (Too much opera, they grumbled.) But when he was serving his apprenticeship with Popper, someone finally caught his eye: his boss's daughter, Martha. She too was a German-speaking, Prague-born Jew. Her father had long been part of the Petscheks' business and social circle. Otto, five years older than Martha, had been vaguely aware of her when she was growing up.

In 1911, she was twenty-three and lovely: svelte, with a smooth, round face and long, elegant limbs. She had a kindness that made people trust her with their secrets; everyone from grandmothers to children sought her out to share their problems. Otto saw her every day when she came to pick her father up for a stroll. She was gentle and affectionate with the aging barrister. One day it suddenly occurred to Otto: "Why not marry Martha?"

For the greater part of a year, Otto attempted to engage her in conversation, to connect. She was polite but always slipped away to accept the whispered confessions of her needy confidants. In truth, Martha found Otto's extravagance off-putting. He made the mistake of disclosing to her that he owned forty-five hats—a ridiculous number. She was interested in people, not things.

But Otto, ever dogged, persisted into 1912—and one night, as they sat in front of the fireplace at her father's home, shadows dancing on her dove-gray dress, Martha relented. She discovered that the same passions bubbled within both of them: music, art, and literature. They set each other's enthusiasms to a high boil, and before long they were keeping company. Martha had a teasing sense of humor, which she deployed with a soft, lilting voice. She made Otto laugh by calling him *Dumme* (dummy). He turned it right back on her, and it became their private pet name.

She poked gentle fun at his Jewishness, too. He was just one generation removed from Kolín's insular Jewish community, where his father and uncle were born and grew up speaking Yiddish. Otto claimed to Martha that he was "a big realist and a Doubting Thomas"—the result of his long secular education. But he flavored their sophisticated conversation with Yiddish words, marked the Jewish holidays, and stopped to say a prayer when he narrowly avoided an auto accident. "It could have turned out bad," he told her. "In such moments where your luck seems to be terribly small, I always have the strong urge to thank someone—God, fate . . . Yesterday as well, I said 'Thank God' from the bottom of my heart, when it was over. Do you laugh at me because of that?" She did—but she soon found that she was sprinkling "Thank God" into her own speech.

Despite her better judgment, she began yielding to his aestheticism as well. He recruited her for the Watchers of Prague, taking her through the city's picturesque streets. They stopped to window-shop, and he made her blush with his sensuous assessments of the curving Moravian porcelain, the delicate Bohemian glassware, and the sumptuous imported fabrics. The city had once been a center for alchemists—"Magic Prague"—but to Otto, the creation of gorgeous objects by human hands was the real alchemy. He tried to woo Martha by buying her the ravishing things. She chastised him for spending so much money. Sometimes she even sent the items back. But she kept a few, too.

One day Martha bought *him* a present: his forty-sixth hat. He teased her that "perhaps it was slightly *too* fashionable," and added, "By the way, I wouldn't mind at all if you took care of the rest of my 'toilette' as well. At least my budget could be smaller then." But his banter belied how delighted he was. Perhaps Martha thought better of her gesture when he dropped her another note shortly thereafter, announcing that her gift had a new companion:

Encouraged by your best present, I bought myself a new green hat yesterday—actually one must say "haaaayut," it looks so Tirolean. Number 47. I look simply charming in it—like the gals in Ischl! When I walk down the street, I'm always afraid that a constable will arrest me for disorderly appearances. But I'll risk it. Enclosed is my latest photograph. Please enjoy with caution! . . . The little children in the street start to cry when they see me. I think you will do the same.

Any pause that this gave her was minor compared to her improvident suitor's next misadventure in their courtship. Otto was on a business trip and realized that he had left a document that he needed at her house. He sent one of his colleagues over to get the papers. The man bowled past Martha's maid, went into her room, and ransacked her desk. Martha came home to find the maid in tears and fired off a blistering letter. Otto wrote back, apologizing profusely. "My Mama always says: 'Born stupid and never learned anything!' If you will pardon me, I empower you to say the same." For all his genius at analyzing systems, Otto could be clumsy in human relations. Martha allowed herself to be placated, but her guard was back up.

Otto remained patient. They visited an overgrown garden adjoining a summerhouse that Otto's parents had purchased in Bubeneč. Otto and Martha headed north from the Old Town, taking the funicular or crossing the art-nouveau Čech Bridge spanning the Vltava on foot. Ascending through Letná Park, they paused at the crest of the hill to look down on the breathtaking sweep of the city below. Along the way, they saw friends and relatives and exchanged nods, greetings, and small talk.

Prague's affluent Jews were starting to move out of the city center, and the extended Petschek family, *feinschmeckers* (connoisseurs), had snapped up plots all over the neighborhood atop the rise. Otto's parents owned several parcels on a single large block of prime Bubeneč land. Their summerhouse sat on the edge of the huge property, but the block was largely vacant. It was a natural garden, open to the entire neighborhood. Patches of bright wildflowers, sparks of crimson and yellow, dotted the hedges and lawn. Otto and Martha, arm in arm, stopped and remarked at the blooms, each one a tiny masterpiece.

They visited the site regularly, watching the foliage change, together growing attuned to the subtle variations in the seasons. As the leaves fell, so did Martha's reservations. Despite Otto's quirks, indulgences, and awkwardness, she could no longer imagine life without him. By October the trees were bare. On October 25, 1912, Otto invited Martha to the garden. His conversation was especially energetic; her repartee sparkled more strongly in response. After their usual stroll, he got down on one knee. He asked her, with a twinkle in his eye, in the teasing tone they used, "Madam, would you like to become a Petschek? Do you want to risk it with me?"

They married in 1913 and honeymooned in Italy. Otto had traveled across the country before and was as eager to show Martha his favorite things—deteriorating ruins, domed cathedrals, and Renaissance arcades—as if he had commissioned them personally for her. He committed images of the trip to memory: of Martha standing in front of the architectural wonders that they visited, each tinted with the rosy glow of his passion for his bride. They spoke Italian to the shopkeepers and hoteliers and to each other—they would revert

Otto and Martha, circa 1913.

to it for the rest of their lives whenever they didn't want the rest of the family to hear their secrets.

Returning to Prague to live with Martha's family, Otto resumed his work as a full partner in the business. Now that his apprenticeship was over, he thrilled to the "romance and tragedy" of banking, as one of his American books put it. But he strained not to let it show, further assuming the serious mien of his mentors, even starting to accumulate some of their bulk. They rewarded him by dispatching him to meet with business partners and inspect investments around the Continent in 1913 and 1914. It was the last flush of peace, when a child of Europe could roam freely across her every inch, from Saint Petersburg to Scotland, Aachen to Athens. Otto made trip after trip, living out of his portmanteau. For traveling companions, he acquired a collection of thick crimson Baedeker guidebooks. Between meetings, on trains, and in his hotel rooms, Otto studied the shiny pages, then looked up to admire the real thing. Whenever he had a spare minute, he slipped off and gorged himself on culture, devouring the ornamentation on the palaces, churches, and theaters he visited, storing it all away for future reference.

Otto drank in the Continent's beauty but yearned for home and Martha. He poured his feelings into long letters to her, corresponding daily, sometimes twice a day. "It's FLOWING," he would write of his love for her—scrawled on thick sheets of foolscap bearing the letterhead of the Hotel Imperial in Vienna, the Continental in Paris, or the Grand Hotel on the North Sea in the Netherlands. He sent her gifts from all the great cities of Europe, too: a fifteenth-century miniature of a praying saint, antique red Venetian glass, small incunabula with intricately worked ivory-and-silver covers. She wrote or telegrammed back, good-naturedly chiding him for how much money he was spending on her, signing off with "HRDLS," their secret term for kisses.

In February 1914, Martha gave Otto a present in return—the finest one of all: a child. They named their boy Viktor. He was the spitting image of Otto, dark hair dusting the distinctive family cranium. Viktor was a cheerful baby, and a hungry one. Privately, Otto and Martha nicknamed him *der Hund* (the dog), as a nod to their son's affectionate nature and strong appetite.

It was a joyous time—and it was about to end.

⌒

IN that summer of 1914, things in Europe started spiraling into calamity. The catastrophe began with the June assassination of the heir to the Austro-Hungarian throne, Franz Ferdinand, by radical ultranationalists in Serbia who objected to Austrian interference in their affairs. Otto worked long days side by side with his father and uncle to assess the deteriorating situation, known as the July Crisis. The three huddled, poring over the daily newspapers from Prague, Vienna, and Berlin, piecing together bits of information gathered from their business colleagues, debating the accuracy of rumors traded at the Prague stock exchange.

Would war come? Their anxiety wasn't just about business. Otto had completed his compulsory service as an officer in the emperor's army, but his three younger brothers (Paul, Fritz, and Hans, twenty-eight, twenty-five, and eighteen, respectively) all held commissions in the reserves and would be expected to fight if war broke out.

On July 28, 1914, Austria-Hungary declared war on Serbia. Each side's allies jumped into the fray, and within two weeks all of Europe was battling for the first time since the defeat of Napoleon. Prague, too, was in the grip of war fever, although the Czechs, in their resentment of three centuries of domination by the Austrian throne, were as a whole less enthusiastic than their Croat, German, and Magyar counterparts. Otto rallied to the cause of Emperor Franz Joseph and the monarch's ally Germany, the Central Powers. Otto's language and culture were German, the core of his business was in Austria-Hungary, and the family venerated Franz Joseph. Otto's brothers would serve as officers in the emperor's military as Otto himself had done. So he embraced the pan-Germanic alliance with Kaiser Wilhelm II.

At first, Otto was encouraged by the results of the war in the east and reassured by his cheerful brother Paul's letters. The next-oldest Petschek was working as an artillery spotter, using the family limousines (complete with chauffeur) to drive around the front lines, estimating where the Austrian shells were striking. As far as Otto could tell from those and other missives, the newspapers, and the constant flow of information from business colleagues, the Germans and the Austrians seemed to be making progress on the eastern front (even if things seemed somewhat bogged down in the west). Paul's letters described the disarray and retreat of the Russian armies in 1915, fueling Otto's hopes that the war would soon be over. Otto ran a fund-raising drive for medical assistance to the soldiers and was decorated with the Red Cross medal for drumming up a large sum. Martha assisted him and also received a silver medal, which she proudly pinned on her bosom.

But 1915 came and went; the war dragged on. By its third year, 1916, even Otto had grown disillusioned. The units from the Czech lands suffered the highest casualties in the Austrian army. Otto saw the wounded men in the Prague streets: a pinned-up sleeve where an arm was lost, a crutch compensating for a missing leg—or, worse, more and more families wearing black armbands to signify a dead father, brother, or son.

Now the Petscheks waited daily for bad news. Every telegram that arrived brought a burst of anxiety. Hans's battery was hit, but he escaped harm. Paul was not so lucky; he was injured in battle, hospitalized, and then assigned to a desk job at the War Ministry in Vienna. Worst of all, Fritz's nerves broke under the stress of the front, and he was discharged, coming back to Prague with shell shock. He wandered the halls of the family business, writing his name in the air over and over again. No one was safe, no matter how high in society; even the emperor, Franz Joseph, after an extraordinary run of sixty-eight years on the throne, was felled by illness and the strain of the war. He died in November 1916, another blow for his subjects. Julius had been the emperor's longtime counselor, so the Petscheks' grief was especially deep.

It was a trial for Otto's confidence—the first time in his life that he had faced true adversity. But he refused to give in. To Isidor and Julius, to the world, it may have looked like a stalemate, chaos, an unpredictable muddle. But Otto, as if listening to the instruments tuning up before a symphony, thought he could make out the bars of the next movement. Peace was coming. When that happened, he believed, Czech coal would power the reconstruction and skyrocket in value. Now, while the fog of war still clouded the energy market, was the time to corner it.

The exact reasoning underlying his calculation is murky; his letters to Martha suddenly become cryptic in 1916, referring to people and events elliptically, and even in code. His correspondence hints at a heresy: the West was going to win the war, and the Czech lands of Bohemia, Moravia, and Czech Silesia were going to end up aligned with them. The Allies had declared their war aims to include self-determination for central Europeans living under foreign domination. Since 1914, Masaryk—the very same professor who had distinguished himself in fighting the Hilsner blood libel—had been pushing for that outcome as an exile, zigzagging from London to Paris to Moscow to the United States. Otto was far from a Czech nationalist. Nevertheless, he seems to have concluded that an autonomous, Western-oriented Czech polity would offer enormous economic opportunities, and coal would drive them forward.

Whatever his logic, Otto argued to his partners that they should go all in, aggressively buying up coal and related assets in the Czech lands, expanding their position as much as possible. The older Petschek men stared dubiously back at him—his father: implacable, shrewd, with his flattop and his piercing eyes; Uncle Julius: ponderous, less keen, stroking his mustache, and trying to understand. Otto argued for his vision. He knew every major mine, had seen the operations, talked to the miners, and visited so often that he could walk through blindfolded. Now was the time to acquire majority positions, take control of the boards, and move into active management.

Otto had found an outlet for his restless optimism: investing in the coming peace. His mentors, always more cautious, stalled. Uncle Julius was in particular being a "schlmiel" and "won't listen to anything anyone says," Otto reported to Martha, though he admitted, "I am a little nervous and crazy . . . I feel like a woman in her eighth month! At least, this is how I imagine it must feel." But he pressed ahead, writing his "dear only Dumme" that he was holding a big meeting to try to convert his father and uncle. He would need to present facts and figures supporting his position. He enlisted Julius's teenaged children to help him draw up accounts. "They are sitting around the dining room table . . . doing arithmetic with great concentration. They are working with great enthusiasm and it is a pleasure to watch them," he reported to Martha.

Whatever reluctance the two older men may have felt about his bold strategy—objections based on business considerations, danger, or patriotism—they grudgingly yielded to Otto's calculations regarding the enormous upside. Referring to his success, Otto exulted to Martha that "the child is born and does very well!" During that freezing winter of 1916–17, when coal was at a premium, heating homes across the city, the tiny flecks of soot flying out of chimneys and mingling with the whirling snowflakes, Otto embarked on an acquisition spree. To accommodate the new activity, Otto expanded the family's Prague operations: "Much to Papa's and Uncle's surprise I furnished a whole office now . . . two rooms with 5 new secretaries . . . I also created a new system in the writing-office." The staff soon ballooned to thirty-six people, requiring the partition of existing offices to fit everyone in, although not all the Petscheks shared Otto's architectural vision. "Papa was very surprised when he saw the men building a wall today," Otto continued to Martha. "I really have to leave before Papa comes back, otherwise he'll kill me."

And leave Otto did. He constantly traveled, spending days and nights visiting sellers and making deals. As a result, he saw even less of home than he had when he was crisscrossing Europe before the war. He missed Martha and young Viktor, now a friendly and curious three-year-old. The child's parents bestowed more nicknames on him; besides the *Hund*, they also called him the *Bursche* (boy) or Viky. He made them laugh with his first efforts at speech; coming into the bedroom one morning and unable to see either of them, he proclaimed, "No Mama, no Papa here."

Otto apologized to his son for his constant absences, writing, "My dear Burschischi [little boy], Papa has a lot of work . . . that's why he can't come for your birthday . . . When Papa comes to Viky again, Papa will bring the parcel. Papa sends you and Mama many kisses . . . Bye! Bye!" Martha likely winced—she knew her husband meant well, but gifts were no substitute for his presence. That remained a sore spot between them. She was not shy about telling him what she thought, and her letters could be lacerating. But in the end, they always patched up their quarrels, Otto signing off his notes of apology, "A thousand and more kisses, I love you madly."

In his missives to Martha in 1917 and 1918, Otto alluded to his business maneuvers and the external events that would decide his big bet, pointing Martha to the news that would determine their fate. The American entry on the side of the West in 1917 supported his wager; the subsequent collapse of the West's ally Russia threatened it; and it fluctuated with all the other unpredictable swerves of that year, the battlefield tides ebbing and flowing, and his fortunes with them. Living conditions on the home front worsened as well: restaurants and theaters closed early; hotels were blacked out; tobacco, then coffee, and finally meat became unavailable. Otto's brothers, per his request, sent their rations of butter to Martha and Viky so that they would have a supply. Periodic strikes and riots erupted among a Czech public tired of war and of their Austrian Habsburg masters.

Through it all, to outsiders, Otto seemed impassive, even forbidding. He had by now fully adopted the stoicism of his mentors—time and the pressure of the war years applying the final hermetic layer that sealed away his true personality. But to Martha, he divulged his grand plans, his soaring hopes, and his wrenching anxieties:

I finally concluded the business here. It really tortured me for four whole days . . . It's as if I had to decide today whether to dress for warm or cold weather tomorrow. That depends on tomorrow's weather, but I have to decide today. Do you understand? I believe that, after four days, I made the right decision. Rudi [a colleague] always says that I'm never satisfied with myself. Today I am, a little. Whether I have the right to be, the future will tell. Bye bye, my angel, love me as much as I do you!

When they were both in Prague, the couple snatched moments together at the beginning or end of the day. When they were apart, letters and telegrams had to do—sometimes three or more within a span of twenty-four hours. Often they ended with an instruction from Otto to destroy the document, lest his pro-Western orientation leak out: "Rip up the letter immediately and throw it into the toilet-bowl!"

By 1918, Martha had perhaps grown *too* close to Otto, seeming to absorb his bouts of stress. Her energy ebbed, and a nagging cough deepened and lingered. One morning she was unable to get out of bed. The family doctor feared that it might be tuberculosis. An anxious Otto rushed back to Prague. Specialists couldn't agree on a diagnosis and decided to send her to a sanatorium in Semmering, in the Austrian Alps. Otto hoped the clear air, careful diet, and peaceful atmosphere would cure whatever ailed her.

MARTHA's absence unexpectedly triggered in Otto the obsession that would come to dominate his existence: building.

Before she fell ill, they had decided that it was time to move out of their downtown apartment. They were planning on having more children after the war (they were hoping for a girl next and had already picked out a name, Eva). Their existing home had also grown too small to accommodate all of Otto's purchases. They needed more room. They had found it in Bubeneč, on a plot of land that held romantic associations for the couple as it overlooked the wild garden where Otto had proposed. It already contained a structure, a relatively modest, two-story neoclassical villa.

With Martha away, Otto took over acquiring the property and readying it for them. To his dismay, the little villa, so charming on the outside, was badly neglected within. One room "was so wet and humid that water was dripping down the walls." In another walled-off space, "there were two loads of horse manure." But he told Martha not to worry. He would make it "as clean and dry as a dance hall." It would be his latest gift to her and the largest yet.

For help, Otto turned to one of the master builders of Prague, Matěj Blecha. The fifty-seven-year-old engineer, a self-made Bohemian country boy, had shaped the eclectic cityscape that Otto loved, helping construct everything from art-nouveau apartments to a celebrated cubist street lamp. Blecha might not ordinarily have bothered with a remodeling job, but Otto was a customer worthy of cultivation. Blecha started by planning a central heating system to dry out those damp walls and winterize what had been a summer dwelling.

Otto, curious, asked to see the technical sketches. He was fascinated. The furnace, the snaking conduits, the calculations of heat—it was another beguiling system (and, like Otto's expanding empire, it ran on coal).

Before long, he was poring over blueprints and throwing out ideas on remaking the house and its grounds. "I'm having the garage turned into a garden-room on street level. Blecha calls it a *'salla terrena.'* The costs, *nebbich*," he informed Martha, using a Yiddish term roughly meaning "poor me." He later wrote her that he had designed a set of pillars for the house, sending along a drawing of his handiwork and also describing a newfound landscape-architecture project:

> Now that the wall has been taken away and the canal which ended in the garden has been rerouted . . . I want them to make the big flower bed between the entrance gate and the entrance from the street smaller and make the paths wider, so that it will look more like an entrance drive. Also, I want to put a seat in the bushes that used to line the old wall, facing Mama's garden. Do you agree?

Another letter advised his frugal Martha that he had been "very imprudent" and enumerated a bevy of new furnishings for the house that he had picked up in Vienna; despite listing eleven items, he concluded, "[O]ne can't buy anything right now . . . *voilà tout!* [that's all!]" Martha wrote back, urging restraint. Otto responded by bringing the house plans on a visit to the sanatorium. He walked her through them, pointing out each of the details. In the end, she let herself be charmed, as she so often was by his extravagant presents. They were hard to resist.

He left with her blessing, and an additional specification. They decided that they would share a bedroom—a daring undertaking in their day, when husband and wife typically had separate rooms. It was so scandalous that Otto was apparently embarrassed to present it directly to the maids and other staff who were starting to set the place up for Martha's return. "Please arrange through Mama," he wrote to his father, "since I *nebbich* can't demand it directly."

Otto was in a rush to complete the little villa. A series of delays held matters up, provoking him to joke with Martha, "Hold me or I am going to jump out of the window." But at last he was able to tell her that "Bubeneč has been finished" and "the villa has really turned out to be very beautiful."

As she packed to leave the mountain sanatorium, Martha surely believed Otto's building mania had passed. In fact, it had barely begun.

THROUGH the summer and fall of 1918, the US entry into the war proved as decisive as Otto seems to have predicted—the New World was coming to the rescue of the Old. Otto was thoroughly sick of the conflict, joking to Martha, "What is the difference between war and hemorrhoids? One is fed up with war all the way up to the neck." Otto had "high hopes for peace." He believed that the Czech campaign to secure the support of America for autonomy (and with it, his gamble) was looking promising— Otto was pleased that the Czechs were giving the US president, Woodrow Wilson, the assurances he desired.

By 1918, those representations were being made personally to Wilson in Washington, D.C., by Tomáš Masaryk, with the same vigor and eloquence with which he had fought the blood libel during the fin de siècle spurt of anti-Semitism. The avuncular philosopher with the enormous white walrus mustache repeatedly lobbied his fellow academic, Wilson, for the creation of a Czech state in confederation with their closely related Slavic neighbors, the Slovaks. The two professors bonded, providing the final bit of impetus to years—indeed, a lifetime—of Masaryk's quest for national freedom and self-determination. On October 18, 1918, the new state of Czechoslovakia declared its independence with the full support of America. The proclamation, written by Masaryk, was termed the Washington Declaration.

The inclusion of Slovakia seems to have come as a surprise to Otto (who had not invested there) and to many others. That Austro-Hungarian province adjoining Bohemia and Moravia was more rural, less educated, and historically and culturally distinct. The Slovaks were predominantly Catholic, fervently so, as opposed to the more secular Czechs, who had lapsed into skepticism and modernity. The contrast was equally dramatic between the two regions' respective Jewish communities, Otto's (and even more so, Martha's) modern sensibilities contrasting sharply with the Chassidic ultra-Orthodoxy of the Jews just to the east.

But the languages of the two neighboring lands were quite similar, and each was majority Slavic, so their marriage was anointed with the ideals of pan-Slavic nationalism. There were many other affinities as well, including the fact that Masaryk himself was half-Slovak. Joining with his neighbors gave Masaryk more heft with the Allies, so Czechoslovakia it was. France and others joined America and signed on, too. That was thanks in no small part to the hard work in Paris of an aide of Masaryk's—a young Czech journalist and academic whose dry, even mousy demeanor concealed a shrewd, calculating mind. His name was Edvard Beneš, and he would loom large in the life of the new country—and of Otto.

A few weeks later, on November 11, the war formally ended. When the peace treaties were concluded, Otto had won his bet. The Americans and the French insisted on the recognition of Masaryk's new country. Germany, Hungary, and Austria grudgingly complied (though the latter was losing 70 percent of its economic capacity). The new Western-backed state of Czechoslovakia was a reality, becoming the tenth-largest postwar economy. The Petschek family holdings skyrocketed in value, establishing them as central figures in the Czech economy. They were the single largest holders of brown coal in the region, and they controlled almost half its trade in Europe. Otto was the King of Coal.

But it would be five more years before the monarch could begin thinking about a palace worthy of his throne. The expanded family holdings were vast, and managing them demanded all of Otto's time. His father's health faded, and in 1919, Isidor died. Otto missed him terribly; for all his severity, Isidor had cherished Otto and acted as a buffer when Uncle Julius and the rest of the extended Petschek *mischpoche* (family) got on Otto's nerves.

That happened with more frequency now that Otto had assumed his father's role as the de facto leader of the family concern. He converted the offices that he had so laboriously built out into a full-fledged private bank, Petschek & Co., its main business managing the family's ever-growing empire. They expanded their holdings in Czechoslovakia and across Europe, taking positions in paper, glass, pharmaceuticals, pulp, chemicals, and more, even investing across the Atlantic, in the United States. Otto insisted on making room for his brothers, Paul, Fritz, and Hans, back from the war. Julius resisted, but Otto felt that his uncle "didn't realize that young people arose around him who were eager to work and to take responsibility . . . that the children he carried in his arms became equal men." So Otto won places for the three, sidelining Julius. Otto was, however, no more gentle with his brothers than his mentors had been with him. He loved the younger boys, but exacting tutelage was the only way he knew.

Otto and his brothers were loyal veterans of the Austro-Hungarian army and viewed the breakup of the empire with varying degrees of bitterness. They were no Czech nationalists, barely speaking the language. (To the great amusement of his children, Paul once found a button on the ground and, rushing to the woman who had lost it, told her in his broken Czech, "Excuse me, but we have eaten this button.") But the new country appealed to Otto, with his liberal education, as an archetypical Enlightenment idea: that disparate peoples and territories could be stitched together virtually from scratch into a cohesive, functioning whole, around ideas of political, personal, and market freedom. Otto seems to have preferred that virtue in its most unadulterated form, at least when it came to economics, adorning his home with no fewer than seven busts and portraits of the pro-business, libertarian prime minister Karel Kramář and maintaining ties to the conservative Austrian economist Ludwig von Mises.

Czechoslovakia leaned heavily on Otto in those immediate postwar years. Establishing a new country, even a prosperous, resource-rich one, was chaotic. When there was a run on the Czechoslovak currency in 1921, Otto propped it up, the Petschek bank buying crowns to help end the panic. He bore disproportionate responsibility for maintaining labor peace as well. With outright ownership of the mines, he had to deal with the fractious leadership of the miners, including some Communists inspired by the new Bolshevik regime in Russia. They lacerated him and the other mine owners as exploiters. He was buffeted from the right too. In periodicals such as *Shield of the Nation,* right-wing Slavic nationalists and populists attacked "the Jewish power of billions, which immediately with the help of the press took control of the uninformed people in our new state" and claimed that "the disgraced [Austrian Habsburg] nobility were immediately replaced by a new nobility a thousand times worse ... Weimann, Petschek, Bloch, etc." Another conservative publication complained, "Where these Jews send coal, there it is. Where they do not, there is none. Two Jews, Petschek and Weimann, control the lives of 14 million people in the Czechoslovak Republic." The anti-Semitism was not confined to words; there were sporadic eruptions of violence in both the Czech and the Slovak parts of the country in 1918 and beyond that had to be put down by the authorities, in episodes reminiscent of the 1890s' looting.

Otto brushed off the extremists on both the left and the right. The new country was led by Masaryk, who had made his name defending the Jews and who was a formidable champion of liberalism. He was described by the ever-modest Soviet leader Lenin as his "most serious ideological antagonist in all of Europe." Masaryk's right hand, Beneš, was equally dedicated to promoting democracy and resisting anti-Semitism, leading some Jews to joke about changing the traditional Yiddish invitation to say grace, "*mir viln bentschen*" ("we want to pray"), to "*mir viln Beneš*" ("we want Beneš").

Otto had occasional dealings with President Masaryk and more frequent ones with Beneš, to the point where the anti-Semitic press claimed that the foreign minister was taking Petschek bribes. The reality was simpler: their minds worked alike. Both were Enlightenment thinkers, believers in systems and in reason, convinced that their prodigious intellects and work ethic could solve any problem (with a little help from the benign deity on which they both relied). Beneš dined with the magnate, asked Otto to aid the Czechoslovak state financially, and otherwise sought his support. He even encouraged the Petscheks' patronage of the German opera as part of bolstering the German minority in the multi-ethnic state.

The two men shared a deep affinity for the new League of Nations promoted by Wilson and the postwar international order—the European and American alliance advocated by the American president. Otto even acquired a palm-sized version of the Covenant of the League that he could carry in his pocket. The freedoms that it guaranteed could be messy. But he had faith in them.

What little spare time Otto had he spent with his family in their villa. By 1920, Viky had been joined by a younger sister. Otto and Martha named her Eva, just as they had agreed to during the war. In 1922, the growing family welcomed twin girls, Ina and Rita. Otto played with the children in the Bubeneč garden where he had courted their mother. He had snapped up more pieces of it as they became available. He could certainly afford it; he had more money than he knew what to do with. By 1923, he owned or had options on five contiguous acres—virtually the entire block.

That year, Otto's artistic energies reignited. His business was more or less in order, and so was his new country. He took to waking up early, slipping outside, and daydreaming. He looked at the wild landscape, often obscured by the morning mist, and thought back on walking through it with Martha more than a decade before. How much had happened since then—steady turmoil, but it had only served to acquit his optimism. In the intervening years, some of the work he had enjoyed the most was that on the little villa and its grounds.

He wanted to further express himself by manifesting something grand on his land, and ideas began unfurling—to construct a palace, to shape the garden, and to synthesize the two. The vision came in little flashes throughout that year and into 1924. He mulled it over while at work, studying his wineglass at dinner, or staring at the murals from his box at the opera, slowly building it in his imagination.

It would be another gift to Martha, to his heir, Viky, to the three girls, and to their children's children: a tribute to his beloved city of Prague, the prosperous new nation of Czechoslovakia, and the Europe in which they were anchored. His descendants would live there as Praguers, Czechoslovaks, Europeans, and Jews. The palace would be magnificent, and he would fill it with all the little European treasures that he had bought for himself and Martha and acquire many more, traversing the Continent to purchase antiques, paintings, tapestries, and objets d'art with the unlimited funds he now enjoyed. It would not just be beautiful—it would be *good*, expressing his values, his faith in reason and progress, in the new era of history that he trusted was dawning.

These motivations woke him as much as the coffee he sipped on that spring morning in 1924 as he looked out from his terrace. Hearing his family rousing, Otto turned away from the garden, opened the balcony door, and went to greet Martha.

He was ready to begin.

2

THE KING OF COAL

Otto and Viky, circa 1917.

OTTO WOULD HAVE TO TELL MARTHA OF HIS PLANS. HE PRO-crastinated, knowing her well.

She was firmly opposed.

Martha could be remarkably forceful with Otto, though always in private. On one occasion when she took exception to his behavior, she wrote him a twenty-four-page letter criticizing it. He was not known for apologizing or admitting that he was wrong—except with her. But when Otto truly wanted something, even his beloved *Dumme* could not stand in his way. In this case, he was pushing on an open door: Martha adored him; she wanted him to be happy.

Her best rhetorical weapon—arguing that they could not afford it—was no longer accurate. Her remonstrations about Otto's profligacy had never been about mere cash flow, of course; in the Yiddish patter that Otto and Martha shared, their recurring dispute really concerned *ruchneus* versus *gashmeus*: soulfulness as opposed to materialism. Yet by 1924, Martha's long-standing contention that Otto was busting the family budget had lost its force entirely. His successful wager on the Czechoslovak economy meant that they had unlimited sums at their disposal.

It was more, they both believed, than they could ever spend.

So she gave in.

Otto began by reconstructing the sprawling, wild gardens that had attracted him to the grounds in the first place. They had been the scene of his wooing and winning Martha. Now they would be the location into which he would carefully fit their new home—a gem placed into the tines of its setting.

Landscape architecture was a discipline unto itself, with its own venerable traditions: André Le Nôtre's mannered French horticulture; Capability Brown's more natural English style; the rough, untamed German gardens of Franz Späth. Otto knew all three styles well—from the volumes he had accumulated for his library and firsthand from strolls through the great gardens of Europe on his travels. He intended to borrow the best from each of them. He even pored over a book titled *American Gardens,* apparently determined to reflect every pillar of the new transatlantic structure that he believed would protect his country.

For assistance, he turned to the firm that Späth's clan had founded, now in its sixth generation of family management. Though headquartered in Berlin, Späth was a global operation, dispatching explorers in pith helmets and lederhosen around the world to serve clients and collect rare trees and plants. Like Otto, Späth did business internationally, coordinating study trips and exchanges with botanical gardens across the globe. The nursery's highly sought after garden-design division was at the cutting edge of European landscape architecture. What better expression of that ethos than helping to design a Gallic-British-Teutonic landscape presided over by a linguistically German, legally Czechoslovak, culturally European Jew?

Every morning platoons of workers in canvas overalls and caps streamed onto Otto's compound. It was gradually cleared, trees moved and replanted, and heaps of new rich black soil trucked in. Thousands of plants and seedlings were delivered to realize the plans conveyed by Späth's designers, master gardeners, and engineers. The laborers swarmed over the large swath of land, digging, heaping up the soil, leveling it off, and planting everywhere. Otto hired a young Prague-based landscape architect, Mr. Valášek, to supervise the workers. But Otto was there in the morning before he went to work, he came home for lunch to supervise, and he made sure to check in at the end of the day, giving Valášek instructions at each appearance. After years of communing with this stretch of land, Otto felt intimately acquainted with its hidden genius loci—its particular spirit.

Martha must have cast an appalled eye at the unwieldy mess in her backyard. But to Viky, now age ten, it was fascinating. His parents (germophobic after Martha's health scare) didn't allow him to muddle about in sandboxes with his peers because of the risk of polio, TB, and other diseases. So, to the sheltered boy, the torn-up land was a giant playground. He found it much more interesting than his schoolwork. He was clever, but, to the frustration of Otto and Martha, he lacked application. His schoolmasters reported that he was distracted and restless. He had a mischievous streak: spying on his sisters, making jokes when the wet nurse fed the twin infants. The woman retaliated by taking one of her breasts in her hand and squirting him in the face from across the room. It became an instant family legend.

Everyone in the extended Petschek clan was amused, except for his parents. This lack of discipline would not do for Otto's heir. Otto pushed him as he had been pushed, making the boy stand before him and declaim his Latin verbs and other lessons. Otto had planned Viky's education not long after his birth, charting his curriculum through adulthood: Latin at four, followed by other languages at two-year intervals, and layering on math, science, economics, and literature, year by year. But the harder Otto pressed, the worse Viky seemed to do.

To try to get through to him, Otto brought him along on his walks through the construction. All of it would be Viky's, in due course. Viky promised his parents that he would work harder. Still, he grew to resent his father's pushing, and he continued to struggle in school. Otto warned him that if he did not shape up, he would be withdrawn from gymnasium and taught by tutors at home. The sociable boy dreaded that—but severity had been effective for Otto and he applied it at work to his own younger brothers. He was confident that his demanding methods would be good for young Viky.

OTTO intended to be just as hands-on in the design of his palace as he was in constructing his garden. Given his prior experience with the small house, he was aware that he would need help. For his architect, Otto turned to a known quantity, Max Spielmann, who was, like Otto, a Czech-born, German-speaking Jew, and a well-credentialed one, having trained in Vienna and Prague. The family had hired him to build a headquarters for their new Petschek & Co. bank downtown—a massive Renaissance fortress in the style of the Medicis. It was nothing like the home that Otto was contemplating. Otto had novel ideas: a palace that would capture the best of Europe's history while embracing its present and even its future; a dwelling curved like the arc of history; one that would break down the most fundamental distinction in architecture—that between outdoors and in—and possess a lightness missing in Spielmann's other projects. But if Otto had any initial qualms about the architect, he left no record of them.

For his part, Spielmann snapped up the assignment. He was used to dealing with wealthy and demanding clients. He did what *he* thought was best and made them like it. He undoubtedly believed that he could do the same with Otto.

Spielmann rolled out impressive architectural drawings for his patron: each sheet was three feet long and eighteen inches wide. Thousands of finely etched lines saturated page after page, stacked to render the dark roof, spaced to sketch the corpus of the building. The structure was depicted from every possible angle, with views of all four sides of the building, elevations, and cross sections.

Otto studied the depictions. In the French style, the palace sat high above the garden on a plinth, an elevated terrace. Across the terrace was a long façade, ornamented by the pillars and arches of Greece and Rome. The *piano nobile,* the formal floor, for entertaining, was the ground floor, as in Italian and English construction. On the next floor were the living quarters. A basement, an additional upper floor, and an attic completed the five stories. Windows were everywhere, with meticulously depicted panes, the rectangles and squares tiny and perfect on the flat page.

The plans, however beautifully rendered by Spielmann's pen, were thoroughly conventional. They had the flavor of Versailles—a suitable inspiration, given the peace treaties signed in and around there anchoring the postwar order, of which Czechoslovakia and the Petscheks were the beneficiaries. But beyond that, Spielmann's work bore little resemblance to the palace that Otto seems to have envisioned with such precision: a marriage of ancient and modern, the sweeping curve, the unity of internal and external space. Yet Otto approved them. Perhaps he was seduced by the elegance of the drawing, or was simply too new to reading architectural plans to see how far short of his vision the design would fall when it was executed.

Spielmann had little idea of whom he was really dealing with. He appears to have seen only the surface Otto: the sober, black-wool-clad financier. He did not know the chromatic inner Otto, who passionately conducted in powdered wigs and gold-braided topcoats; who identified with Wagner's protagonists and their impossible quests; and who was capable of writing three or four love letters a day about his heart when it was "FLOWING!" for Martha. But Spielmann would meet this man soon enough.

SPIELMANN'S plans were submitted to the municipal authorities and approved in July 1924. The palace's construction began immediately. A second horde of men took the field opposite the landscapers. The crews were like two occupying armies reenacting the Great War, but this time their goal was creation, not destruction. Surveyors, engineers, foremen, and a full excavation team dug deeply to establish the foundation. Across the entire west end of the plot, a rectangular pit started to form. There were trenches everywhere, and the noise of the construction was deafening.

Otto walked among the laborers, asking questions, urging them on. He took to carrying stacks of colorful Czech currency in the pockets of his dark suits, slipping the workers twenty- and even fifty-crown notes. "Pinks" and "blues," the Czechs called them. To workers making as little as 200 crowns a week, extra money was welcome. Otto also brought them beer and cigarettes. The men, some brawny, some wiry, paused to doff their caps, wipe their brows, and have a drink or a smoke on *Herr Doktor*.

The men seemed genuinely to like him. To Otto, their amiability was proof that he was an enlightened capitalist, creating work, sharing the wealth, making the Czech economy hum. He hoped his miners felt the same way. Otto believed that he was providing a public service. Would the miners have jobs were there no coal trade? Would their families be fed? Would the Czech people be warm in winter, or travel on trains, or operate the factories that made the thriving country the envy of the new postwar states that, with it, had joined the League of Nations?

Otto's gift was for comprehending systems. Liberalism—free-market democracy—was the most complex of those that he studied. His library was filled with books in every language assessing it, from critics on the left (the victorious Trotsky) and on the right (the vanquished Kaiser Wilhelm). Although Otto was on the conservative side himself, he was a devotee of the left-leaning English economist John Maynard Keynes, studying all his work, starting with *The Economic Consequences of the Peace*. To Otto, Czechoslovakia was a vast and intricate set of mechanisms, like the inside of one of the pocket watches that he owned. Politics, culture, communities, businesses, people—they were the interlocking gears, complex wheels within wheels, all turning simultaneously. And markets were the mainspring driving it all, producing prosperity for the country with every tick forward.

A very different view of capitalism was taken by the Communist organizers circulating among the workers in his mines. Emboldened by the Bolshevik revolution that had produced the nascent Soviet Union, the leftists believed that the proletariat would eventually rise up in Czechoslovakia, and where better to start than with the soot-smeared laborers straining belowground? For all his reading and his charitable giving, Otto had a blind spot when it came to the Communists, who had a foothold of roughly 10 percent in the Czechoslovak parliament. To him, their attacks were personal, and he hated them. He was not much fonder of the less-extreme Social Democrats, who he felt would ruin capitalism if their supporters (fluctuating between 15 and 25 percent of the voters) let them. When he learned that a family member called herself a Socialist, he was inflamed. She didn't mean it—she just intended to say that she had a social conscience. Well, as a good capitalist, making everyone better off, so did *he*.

But Otto had his limits. He bristled when the city asked him whether he would consider treating part of the garden that he was building as public, allowing pedestrians to come and go through his property at will. It smacked of the Soviet collectivization being overseen by Lenin. The answer was a firm no. Otto held his ground on this point, and the city backed down.

To Otto, the social compact underwritten by the growing Czech economy was exemplified by the scene in his backyard: perhaps the wealthiest man in the country fraternizing with his dirt-smeared landscape crews. They seemed to accept him because of his evident interest in and respect for their craft (though the banknotes, beer bottles, and smokes probably did not hurt matters either). Otto detected no whiff of Communism, nor any hint of anti-Semitism, for that matter. He was confident that those ills would never flourish in the good Czech soil that he was planting.

OTTO did not leave the collection of botanical specimens for his garden to Späth alone. Later that year, on a business trip in Lučany nad Nisou, in the mountains of northern Bohemia, he called on a glass manufacturer, Mr. Fischer. While on Fischer's property, Otto spotted a thirty-two-foot silver fir tree. It was magnificent. On the spot, Otto asked to purchase it for his compound.

No record of the exact conversation survives, but it is not difficult to imagine:

> *Fischer, one more thing—how much for that tree?*
> *I beg your pardon?*
> *The tree, man, the tree—I want to buy that tree.*
> *Why?*
> *For my garden in Prague.*
> *Don't they have trees in Prague?*
> *Fischer, I mean to have that tree—name your price.*
> *But how will you get it there?*
> *Leave that to me.*

Soon after, a team of gardeners were on their way to Lučany with instructions to dig the fir up, wrap its root ball in a huge sack of canvas packed with dirt and sewn tight, get the thing down the mountain, and send it on to Prague via train. Otto was one of the railroad's biggest customers, shipping countless tons of coal yearly. His request was accommodated—the fir traveled like a celebrity, on its own specially commissioned flatcar, to its new home in Otto's compound.

After Otto bought that first perfect tree, he saw them everywhere he went: elms, lindens, chestnuts, and more. Valášek and the landscapers became accustomed to receiving them, roots tightly bundled, trunks extending into splayed branches and leaves, reposing on railcars arriving from all over the Czech lands and even from elsewhere in Europe. Many were giants, their height creating an impression of antiquity in the Eden that Otto was shaping.

⌒

By spring 1925, as Otto awoke and again stepped onto his terrace, a year into the project, the garden was bursting forth. Amid the soaring trees there were blossoms everywhere, coming into bloom daily. The property became a riot of color as about forty thousand bulbs erupted into flower, including fifteen hundred rhododendrons; three thousand hyacinths; and five thousand tulips.

But it was the bluebells that made the most powerful impression. One morning over breakfast, Otto told the family that he had something new to show them. He led a procession down the path from their house to the garden. Martha walked beside him, her white hand nestled in the crook of Otto's stout, wool-clad arm. Viky, now eleven, trying to please his father by imitating his self-assured bearing, and little Eva, five, with short bobbed hair, followed close behind. Bringing up the rear were Ina and Rita, age three, toddling under the supervision of their nanny.

When they came to the bottom of the slope, the trees and shrubbery parted to reveal the giant oval field at the center of the property. Martha and the children stopped in disbelief. Thousands and thousands of tiny bluebells had sprung up overnight, the delicate flowers seemingly hovering inches above the lawn—an astonishing wash of azure filling an acre of land. Viky tumbled down into the field of blue, running in dizzy circles. The three twins (as the girls were called) were close behind, moving in circles of their own, skipping and dodging the small flowers and one another. Giggling, dancing, they followed Viky as he waded into the middle of the field, where they all lay down amid the flowers. They floated on their backs, transported. The gardeners tending the flower beds, the construction workers digging the foundation, the other laborers teeming around the site—all stopped to enjoy the sight of the four ecstatic children at play.

Otto looked at Martha, smiling. She had to admit that it was unbelievably beautiful. The children were delighted. And Otto, too—the joy was visible on his face. Martha and Otto turned back toward their family—happy, for now.

⌣

WORD made its way through the narrow lanes of the ancient city that a new wonder of Prague was taking shape. Rumors and gossip were inevitable—some days it seemed that half the city was laboring on the project. The compound was far from finished; still just a garden with a huge hole in it. Nevertheless, in the spring of 1925, the people of Prague started to show up, doing their best to peer through the fencing. All ages hiked up the hill from the Old Town, strolled down from the Castle Quarter, or rode the tram to the Bubeneč stop and walked the rest of the way: couples arm in arm, grandparents holding grandchildren by the hand, or schoolmates in small clusters, carrying their books in satchels. They were those memory keepers, the Watchers of Prague. They passed the city's oral traditions from generation to generation, not trusting scholars and experts to understand the lived experience of their home. They were assessing Otto's work in progress, and Otto himself, for membership in the pantheon of Prague's legends. The Watchers marveled at the scope of the planting and the explosions of color—the proprietor's painting of his horticultural canvas. If this was just the garden, what would the palace be like when it rose?

Otto felt the gaze of his fellow Watchers upon his work—and him. As he slipped onto his terrace every morning, his own eye was drawn to the western end of the property, where the palace would stand. The foundation had been dug, the cement poured, the channels for plumbing and electric laid. Otto tried to erect it in his imagination. He visualized Spielmann's design at the head of the magnificent landscaping, attempting to conjure this from the two-dimensional page and superimpose it on the metal rods beginning to rise from the ground. Would the planned palace measure up? He took to spreading Spielmann's plans out on the big table in his library, pinning down the corners, and studying every line. He probed the drawing of the palace as one would tongue a sore tooth to see if it was coming loose.

To Otto, it seemed as if it was. Try as he might, he couldn't shake the feeling that what was taking shape at the head of his property was not what he wanted. The long façade was too straight. Where was his curve? Where was the melding of inside with out, the combination of classic and modern? True, Otto had approved the plans. But he was no longer the same man who had signed off on the design a year ago. He had evolved from a consumer into a creator, one of those alchemists whom he had always admired, who magically infused base materials with ideas, bringing beauty into the world. He, Späth, Valášek, and their army of gardeners and landscapers had done that; drawn out the potential of the land; remade it into something exquisite. He had impressed Martha and his family. Prague's memory keepers had taken notice, and others had as well. So remarkable was his passion (and his spending) that horticulturalists would name a new breed of flower for him: *Aster amellus 'Doktor Otto Petschek,'*—a late-blooming perennial that appeared to be an ordinary shrub, until it exploded into hundreds of lavender blossoms with bright yellow centers, when other plants were fading away for the year.

After much deliberation, Otto confronted Spielmann. The architect, undoubtedly accustomed to client jitters, attempted to calm his nerves. One-dimensional plans, even good ones, cannot do justice to a building. Spielmann would create an actual model. If Otto saw what the palace would actually look like in space, he would appreciate it.

Not long after, Spielmann displayed the palace in miniature for his patron. The austere, neobaroque domicile rendered in three dimensions was about three feet long and a gleaming, virginal white, like a Greek temple. Every detail was perfectly formed. The Doric pillars framed the entryway. The flights of stairs led to the palace. To Spielmann, it represented the principles of Beaux-Arts architecture that he so slavishly followed: Symmetry. Harmony. History.

The model persuaded Otto, but not as Spielmann intended. The lack of ornament underscored its cold and severe features. Setting the structure high above the garden on a plinth cut off the palace from its environment—the opposite of what Otto wanted. As for the desired curve, the bend was barely noticeable. It was an expression of Otto's austere exterior, not his inner self. Spielmann hadn't understood him at all.

Otto stepped toward the table. He grasped the model, one hand on each side. Before Spielmann could react, Otto lifted the whole piece. He raised it high above his head, then brought the model of the palace down, whistling through the air, and onto his raised knee. With a sharp crack, it snapped cleanly into two halves.

Otto set the two pieces of the palace back on the table. He calmly angled the halves toward each other, as if the model were hinged at its center.

He told Spielmann that *this* was what he wanted—a curved palace.

The ashen-faced architect agreed to redo the plans before shuffling out, a fragment of his model under each arm.

Spielmann produced new plans doubling the curvature, so that it would look as if the palace were wrapping its arms around the garden. The deflection was extreme—when standing at one end of the central hallway, Otto would no longer be able to see the other end. Per Otto's demand, the new plans also eliminated the elevated terrace that formerly separated the palace from the garden. Instead of the building sitting above the grounds, it was level with them, the better to enjoy the magnificent landscape.

As if all that were not radical enough, Otto proposed another innovation. He didn't want just windows or doors to open onto the outdoors. He wished for the entire ballroom wall facing the garden to be retractable. With the flip of a switch, a thirty-foot section of the façade would sink into the basement, eliminating the separation between the palace and its environs. Otto had been reading his Frank Lloyd Wright, and he sought maximum integration of home and environment. It was a startlingly modern idea, and a first in the Czech lands. (Mies van der Rohe would suggest something similar in the most famous modern house in Czechoslovakia, the Villa Tugendhat—but not for another four years, in 1929.)

To accommodate this novelty, plans had to be drawn and redrawn. The workmen were stopped, started, and then stopped again. The prime building months of 1925 slipped away. By November, well over a year had gone by since the project had commenced, and little visible progress had been made on the structure.

Amid all the back-and-forth, the harried Spielmann apparently made a mistake: he seems to have forgotten to get city approval for the revised plans. Unapproved changes were against the law. They could prove dangerous for the building crew or the eventual occupants. So when the municipal building inspector showed up to check on progress in November 1925, he must have been shocked by the dramatic changes. The bureaucrat issued an immediate order—all building on the site was to cease immediately.

On November 6, the municipality formally notified Otto and his architect that the construction of the villa was "performed without an official permit and with deviations from the approved plans." Otto was directed "to immediately apply for approval of the changes and stop them being carried out in the meantime, until he [received] a building permit."

The right-wing nationalist publication *Shield of the Nation,* which had been so viciously anti-Semitic (and anti-Petschek) in the postwar years, was quick to pounce:

> Building is continuous in the Bubeneč district by the banker Petschek on a grand palace in his park, supposedly without permission from the local government . . . [They] are building a chateau in the Bubeneč quarter as to, allegedly, hide income from the tax services, meaning they have so much money, that they don't know what tax bracket they should declare for themselves . . . The Petschek banking Jews are probably in our time the most powerful banking dynasty in Czechoslovakia.

The matter wended its way excruciatingly slowly through the city bureaucracy—from the building inspector's office, to the city magistrate, to the Prague City Council. Otto apologized, furnished the corrected plans for approval, and promised that it wouldn't happen again. Unnerved, Spielmann swung to the opposite extreme, seeking his patron's advice for every decision, no matter how small. Otto told Martha, "I refused, and told him he should picture things for himself as if I were not there." Otto's patience was running out.

THE winter of 1925–26 was a gloomy season for Otto, and not just because of the short, cold days and the halt in construction. Support for the Communists actually grew in November's elections. The extreme left narrowly missed winning altogether. They ended up just half a percentage point behind the victorious center-right Agrarians, who formed a shaky coalition government that included Otto's preferred party, the conservative National Democrats.

As Otto sat at home and wrote checks to his largely idle workers, about thirteen out of every hundred were Communists, at least if they mirrored recent voting trends. Instead of fading away, they were gaining, and their large bloc did not help efforts to form a lasting parliamentary majority; in the months that followed, alliances formed and re-formed, with seven parties making up three different ruling coalitions. Meanwhile, the half-constructed palace loomed like an ancient ruin in the blowing snow from the tightly sealed windows of Otto's villa.

As the weather warmed in 1926 and Otto resumed his daily predawn survey of the property, he could reflect on a litany of Spielmann's mistakes. Otto had once explained to Martha, "[E]ither I don't love someone at all, or madly!" He certainly did not love Spielmann madly anymore. The architect could not have enjoyed his patron's whims, either, or the modernizing alterations to his rigid conservatism.

Did the disaffected Otto fire Spielmann, or, fed up with his patron's interference, did the architect quit? Perhaps their parting was mutual. But whatever the explanation, Spielmann's signature appeared on only one more set of plans for minor alterations submitted to the municipal authorities early in 1926. After that, he completely vanished from the work. To Otto's credit, he did not exile Spielmann from the family's bank project, or from working for Otto's brothers. The designer went on to build a giant, architecturally orthodox, hideous Beaux-Arts mansion for Fritz and a series of projects for other, less particular Petscheks.

Without the architect, Otto himself could drive the project forward starting in 1926—a conductor at last. To help, Otto kept on the general contracting firm for the project, the Blecha outfit. It was the same one that had helped him reconstruct the small villa in which he and his family still lived. Its head, Matěj Blecha, had died. He had perhaps sunk too much of himself into each of his many projects, hastening an early demise at age fifty-seven—an object lesson to those who loved building too much. The firm was run by his son, Josef, a vigorous builder and businessman who had his father's eclectic spirit—and willingness to accommodate impetuous clients.

In 1926, Otto sat at the big table in his library and continued to scour every inch of the palace design as if he were working on a blank canvas. In front of him were the house plans, big sheets of paper spread flat, surrounded by piles of large architecture and design books. Otto's head swiveled back and forth between his sketches and the books. The massive volumes had little text, just plate after plate of engravings, photographs, and other elaborate constructions.

As he scanned the pages, his means, experiences, and inclinations were liberated for the first time in his thirty-eight years. He could create without limits. All his life he had pursued beauty: the numbers dancing in his head as he did math for his father and his uncle; the music floating in the Prague air; the mélange of ornate edifices on the city's streets; the beguiling wonders of Europe on his journeys; the fragile, precious glass and porcelain he collected; Martha, whose qualities (and person) had so struck him when he spotted her tenderly escorting her aging father on his daily walk. Among the English poets whom Otto liked to read, Keats had famously said, "Beauty is truth, truth beauty,—that is all / Ye know on earth, and all ye need to know."

Otto was chasing both as he pored over his enormous sample books, deep in concentration. His children, curious, would sometimes creep up and peer over his shoulder at the enormous pictures and engravings. The volumes depicted refined city villas and rustic country castles, mountain redoubts with thick walls, and lakeside palazzos open to the sun and air. The tomes were as much of an escape as the Westerns, detective novels, and science-fiction volumes that he liked to trade with friends in his "trashy literature exchange" and read on trains or in bed at night.

Otto's benchmark was Robert Dohme's *Barock und Rococo Architectur*. The three thick red folios were almost as large as keystones. The palaces depicted were beautiful but formidable. They had been designed to impress aesthetically but also to repel the assault of the marauding armies that had swept back and forth across the Continent for centuries. All that was over now, Otto hoped. The future had arrived, secured by the treaties ending World War I signed at Versailles, Trianon, and the other châteaus around Paris.

When Otto met with Josef, he handed over his lists of notes and inspirations. The contractor must have been staggered. Normally so careful, even reverent, with his things, Otto had slashed hundreds of the pages referenced out of his cherished books. He thrust a thick sheaf of them at the contractor. Here was the basis for the cartouches, here for the balcony, this for the library. And Otto didn't want mere imitations. The illustrations, accompanied by Otto's lengthy typed guide, were intended only as jumping-off points for flights of fancy. The palace was meant to *make* history, not to mimic it.

Josef did his best to comply with his patron's manic instructions. A frenzied Otto kept them coming, continually revising the plans in his bold scrawl and slashing lines. He was altering the design as the palace was being built, as its skeleton began taking on form and definition. Each adjustment meant that parts of the building had to be reversed, ripped out, and redone, with government permission newly sought. Additional delays accrued. The workers grumbled. The City of Prague wrote threatening letters, implying that it would withhold approval.

As 1926 wore into 1927, the half-built palace could be mistaken for a half-destroyed one—for ruins. A rumor made the rounds among the Watchers of Prague that Otto had gone to see a fortune-teller. She had, they whispered, read his palm and told him that he would die when he stopped building. That was why, they said, the construction went on and on, why he tore out and remade it constantly. His behavior invited comparisons to the mad builders of Prague: Emperor Rudolf, whose compulsion for architecture and the arts contributed to the electors thinking him insane and deposing him; Count Wallenstein, whose magnificent estate was a symptom of the airs that led to his assassination by Emperor Ferdinand; Count Czernin, who went bankrupt, leaving his sprawling palace unfinished (completed after his death, it was now the home of the Foreign Ministry and its head, Beneš).

The murmurs got back to Otto. He lashed out angrily at this superstition. It was an affront to his veneration of science and reason. He flew into a rage whenever the fortune-teller story was mentioned.

THE rumormongers were not the only objects of Otto's ire. He and Martha began to clash more frequently. She began to recognize that the project had become an unhealthy obsession, and one that was eating into their fortune at an alarming rate. She resumed her warnings about spending. She was not shy when her anger was aroused, nor was he. The children heard shouting behind their parents' closed doors. He refused to budge; she complained, "You don't treat me like an adult"; he replied that she was wrong, and, anyhow, his decisions were "the result of logical reasoning" and had nothing to do with treating her as an adult. "Enough, now," he urged. In an apparent effort to placate Martha, Otto even had another model of the palace built. This one had movable components so that they could plan the construction together and she could see how changes would look. She remained dubious, and their private arguments continued.

The children also came to fear Otto's temper. Instead of peering over their papa's shoulder at his work, they now tiptoed past the room or avoided it entirely. Otto could still be charming when he chose to be. On good days, he played a musical guessing game at the dinner table, beating out a rhythm with his fork and challenging the children to name the tune. But he was increasingly prone to snap at them if they guessed the wrong opera.

Viky, who turned fourteen in 1927, was a particular target of Otto's outbursts. The adolescent became increasingly indifferent to his studies as Otto became more obsessed with the palace. The young Petschek brought home grades that shocked his father. "The Hund again has an omission and other mistakes due to inattention in his Latin homework. Mitzi wanted to invite him to dinner today, but . . . I didn't permit it." When all else failed, Otto followed through on his draconian threat to withdraw Viky from school. Otto felt that Viky had to experience the consequences of his mistakes; he believed that "only taking responsibility can teach growing men and let them enjoy their work. Responsibility shows results and achievements to him and keeps him from being lightminded." Otto was mindful of his duty to mold Viky into shape as he had been molded by his elders, maintaining, "That's the basic way to make useful business members."

Otto hired a series of tutors to oversee the heir's education, but the youth performed even more poorly. Visitors to the Petschek home were startled one day to find Viky standing on a chair loudly proclaiming Mark Antony's speech from *Julius Caesar* in German: *"Römer! Mitbürger! Freunde!"* ("Romans! Countrymen! Friends!," as reordered in Schlegel's German translation), while a professional actor corrected him. It turned out that Otto had commanded Viky to recite Shakespeare as a cure for the boy's mumbling. Otto took control of Viky's social life as well, banishing friends whom he deemed bad influences. On another occasion, Otto—perhaps thinking about his son's pranks and practical jokes—suddenly waved the butler over in the middle of a meal with his brothers and their spouses. Otto told the servant, "Go find Viky and whatever he is doing, tell him to stop it!," precipitating the muffled laughter (undoubtedly mixed with sympathy) of the other diners.

Viky sometimes jotted his father's harsh words in the margins of an English biography of Queen Victoria, apparently as part of practicing that language. "Rogue, blackguard," the boy transcribed, "[g]o up and don't linger about here." Viky asked his father if he could tour the grounds with him, perhaps trying to ingratiate himself, or remembering the pleasure he once took in the giant sandbox. It's "just an unfavorable time to see the new building," Otto replied. Viky recorded his reaction in his childish handwriting: "The day is dismal."

Otto's brothers were not spared, either. He berated the three grown men as if they too were naughty children (apparently forgetting his criticism of Uncle Julius for infantilizing them at the end of the war). Fritz and Paul were genial and tended to shrug it off, but Hans had a temper of his own, resulting in shouting matches with Otto. The brothers and their wives took to calling him "Ottolini" behind his back—a sarcastic reference to the Italian dictator whose ranting speeches had propelled him to power in that country. (In 1927, Europe's nascent Fascist movement was still a laughing matter, and its leading German proponent, an obscure politician named Adolf Hitler, was an ex-convict barred from public speaking.)

Otto even seemed to take his wrath out on the palace. He ripped out planned rooms to provide for more natural illumination. He banished to oblivion the tall staircase for guests entering the palace. Instead there would be a few shallow steps and two entrances into two cloakrooms, to facilitate the arrival of the large numbers of people he expected to entertain. Whether he fully realized it or not, he was compelling form to follow function, just like the Bauhaus modernists whose works were increasingly displayed in the architecture publications that he riffled through for inspiration.

But all that paled in comparison to Otto's forcing an Olympic-sized swimming pool into the design—one *inside* the palace. He tore out the basement to elongate the existing, more modest bathing area. Soon Otto was heaping on additional elements: showers, changing and exercise rooms, a massage chamber. The pool grew in length as he and Josef discarded and revised the plans again and again. It would run 160 feet, almost the full length of the building, and measure 24 feet deep at its lowest point.

Once again, Otto had to go to the city for its official sign-off on the plans. The response was incredulity. Squeezing in a giant pool at this late date, after the foundations had already been laid? The whole building could collapse (as indeed happened with another building elsewhere in Prague not long after, killing forty-six people). A protracted negotiation ensued, and Otto agreed to take substantial remedial measures. Eventually he wrested approval from Prague, agreeing to all the city's conditions. By the time that went through in October 1927, another prime building season had been lost.

⌣

OTTO kept Josef and the men busy through the miserable winter of 1927. The Watchers hurried by the compound, bundled against the cold in mufflers and thick tweed coats, gloved hands holding hats to their heads in the wind—shocked that after more than three years the work still was not done. Indeed, it was not even close, as evidenced by the frigid air whistling through the scaffolding and into the exposed and roofless spaces of the half-constructed palace. Arguing in the Prague pubs, some claimed that Otto had torn it down and rebuilt it three times in the span of as many years. Others scoffed, claiming that he had created and destroyed the palace no fewer than six times.

Still, in 1928, when the weather thawed, the palace finally began to emerge from the ground. A second story now sat atop the first, and work on the third was under way. Progress might have broken another man's fever, but it had the opposite effect on Otto. Now that the exterior was taking shape to his satisfaction (or perhaps was simply so far along that even he no longer dared rip it down to the foundation), Otto turned to the cavernous voids of the interior. He was determined to put his stamp on every centimeter of the raw spaces, planning to insulate the exposed stone, brick, and steel with a thick cushion of luxury and refinement. He ordered paneling for the walls in exquisite woods from Prague's Gerstel & Co., to be painstakingly hand-carved with garlands of flowers and cornucopias of fruit. He traced geometric patterns for the floors, to be executed in Italian marble jigsawed into enormous kaleidoscopic displays. For the ceilings, he would procure dozens of custom crystal chandeliers, fabricated by the venerable Desliles firm in Paris, the designs so beautiful that the owner framed one for display in his office.

Even though the finished interiors existed only in his mind's eye, Otto began furnishing them as well. He and his agents spread out across Europe, bidding at auctions and private sales for antiques, paintings, and rugs—the frenzied culmination of decades of shopping for treasures. On one buying trip to a French château, he was ushered into an extravagant salon, its paneling a pale green frosted in gold, with eighteenth-century paintings of French court life in ornate gilded oval insets. His host offered to sell him some of the antiques that were standing about, but Otto was transfixed by the unusual walls. Legend has it that he asked the man, "Never mind the furniture; how much do you want for the *room*?" Like the trees once shipped home for the garden, the disassembled chamber was soon lying on its side on a railcar, carefully wrapped, and headed to Bubeneč for eventual installation as Otto's music room.

Martha, always nervous about Otto's profligacy, was beside herself. The project that had started years before as a supposed gift for her had consumed her *Dumme*. His temper, her anxiety, the fights, the whispered complaints from his brothers and their wives, the pressure of keeping up a cheerful front—it all became too much. She was aging noticeably, gray streaking her once-raven tresses. Her old lung ailment flared up. She had difficulty breathing, lost weight, became gaunt. Her doctors in Prague and Vienna argued again over what precisely was causing her health issues and ordered her back to Semmering, in the Austrian Alps, where the family had a vacation home. Otto, alarmed, joined to help nurse her. She panicked when her eyesight flickered, went black. She feared that she was going blind. Her husband reassured her, and the episode passed. As soon as she showed signs of improvement, he was back at the palace, building. Resigned, she too returned to his side in Prague.

Then another blow struck Otto—the most unexpected of all.

THE news was most likely delivered on that day in 1928 by one of his brothers. Perhaps it was Paul, the next eldest. With his dark suit, mustache, and high Petschek forehead, Paul was unmistakably Otto's sibling, though his manner was gentler. Did he step into Otto's office at the bank, close the door that was padded in thick, quilted leather (so designed for privacy—an overheard whisper could move markets in the Czech lands), and tell his brother that he had something important to discuss?

Or was the approach made by one of Otto's lifelong employees, entering deferentially, asking if he might disturb JUDr. Petschek, then uneasily explaining what he had discovered?

Maybe Otto even figured it out on his own, as he was going over the bank's and his own accounts and liabilities, flipping through the enormous ledger books, their two-foot-long pages crosshatched with lines and crowded with digits. These charted every *koruna* (crown) coming in and going out. Did the numbers suddenly shift as Otto studied them, checking and rechecking, flashing through the calculations with rising panic, his heart racing, unable to believe it was true?

Whatever the source, the news was shocking.

Otto was out of money.

The sprawling garden; the imported shrubs, flowers, and trees; the building and rebuilding of the palace; the years spent on the project; the finishes, fixtures, and furnishings—they had depleted all his reserves. His capital was gone, sunk into the cycles of construction and demolition, of shopping, bidding, and acquisition. He had insufficient funds to continue paying for it all—for the bills that poured into the bank incessantly. Indeed, he was already in the red from those that had arrived so far, and deeply so—even as more mounted. Otto had once had all the resources in the world, more than he could keep track of. Now his obsession with the palace had brought him to the edge of ruin.

Back home in the little Bubeneč villa, Otto broke the news to Mar-

tha. It was a conversation that she had dreaded since their courtship—
the risk of his extravagance that he had joked about when he proposed
marriage had finally come to pass. Some in the family thought that she
was too soft on him at times like this, too quick to give in. Another person might have criticized her spouse, berating him. But Martha loved
Otto, deeply and unconditionally, in spite of it all. Day-to-day bickering
was one thing; a moment of crisis was entirely different. It surely helped
that, at bottom, she had never cared very much about the possessions;
she would be able to get over losing them.

There apparently were no "I told you so"s when Otto brought the
news to her. Recriminations were set aside as the couple searched,
together, for a solution. Otto and Martha huddled in conference, the
unfinished, unlit palace looming at the end of the property, visible in the
night only as a deeper darkness. They couldn't just leave it there, empty
and incomplete (much as the thought might have temped Martha). In
the Yiddish that Otto and Martha sprinkled into their most intimate
exchanges, it would be a *shanda*: a public disgrace. Otto would never hear
the end of it, the Watchers shaking their heads for centuries to come (as
they still did about Count Czernin abandoning his construction more
than a century before). No, Otto had invested too much in the palace—
and not just financially—to walk away.

He had only one real choice: he had to go to his partners in the bank—
his family—and ask them for the money to finish.

⁓

THE Petscheks gathered to decide their chief's fate in their forbidding
bank building downtown, four stories of heavy rustication and rough-
hewn stone, windows barred to protect the wealth within. They met in
the lush third-floor boardroom, with its dark woods, Corinthian columns, and a conference table and fourteen chairs as gilt edged as the
family's investments. Large portraits of the founders, Otto's papa and
uncle Julius, adorned the walls.

The men filed in one by one: a grim Otto, determined to rescue his
masterpiece; the genial Paul, who now lived in Berlin in an elegant lakeside villa of his own, managing the family's German mines; Fritz, whose
unattractive Spielmann-built mansion was good enough for him; Hans,
the youngest and, after Otto, the keenest. Uncle Julius was there as well,

less spry than in his portrait, with his son, the youngest of the next generation, Walter.

They had never really understood Otto's obsession with his palace, and each bore accumulated resentments against him. Otto considered Julius a "schlmiel" and shunted him aside; frustrated Paul's love life (he forbade him to marry his first girlfriend, a working-class woman who, Otto believed, was a poor match for his younger brother); constantly locked horns with Hans; and treated Walter as if he were still a child and not a man of thirty.

But he was their blood and, despite their bruises, they cared about him. They were not prepared to let Otto's name and credit be besmirched—nor their own. Otto had not been careful in segregating his obligations, and, under Czech law, the partnership might have been liable for some of his debts. The family business had been split once before, when Isidor and Julius's third brother, Ignatz (nicknamed "Uncle Nazi" in the days before that term had other connotations), had gone his own way. That very public and messy rupture still had not healed, and another would have been a disaster.

Still, the other Petscheks didn't make it easy on Otto as he listened to their terms. They would bail him out but put him on a budget. His most profligate days were over. It would be a loan, not a gift. And it would be made on another condition: no more Ottolini-style decision making. The bank would now be divided into equal shares, one for each of the seven members of Otto's generation: Isidor's four children and Julius's three (Walter had two sisters).

Otto fought back against the conditions. He had built the business, driven its growth over the previous generation's hesitations, welcomed his brothers into the enterprise, made room for them, and trained them. He had made enormous sacrifices, giving up his hopes for a career in music, suffering his arduous apprenticeship, working incessantly for decades. The exchange was heated. But the others held firm, united against him.

In the end, Otto was not ready to abandon the home he was building. It meant too much to him. And so he at last assented.

The King of Coal had abdicated his throne to save his palace.

3

PALACE NEVERENDING

THAT NIGHT, OTTO WALKED UP THE STEPS OF THE LITTLE villa and sat with Martha, the unfinished palace ghostly in the distance. He told her the outcome. She did her best to soothe him. Even with the lifeline from his family, he was riven with worry. How was he going to finish the palace on a fraction of the budget? Martha was, perhaps, privately relieved that there would finally be some limits. But she reassured her husband: he would find a way.

Otto went back to his big library table, which was piled high with books and plans. The exterior of the palace was largely complete. If he simply stopped where he was, it could be done within a year, provided there were no more teardowns and no more additions. The inside of the palace, however, was another matter. The second and third floors were unfinished, as were the Roman baths and the rest of the basement. The first floor was the furthest along—the ornate paneling, chandeliers, antiques, and rugs ordered. But many gaps remained, even there. He had a massive dining table seating thirty-four on order, but no chairs.

It was bitter to confront reality after years of creating without limits. But he willed himself forward. He looked again at the sample books stacked in front of him. They were full of trompe l'oeil effects: walls painted to show gardens that didn't exist; forced-perspective galleries— shallow niches that were made to look like long corridors by an artist's brush; and meticulously simulated doors, windows, and balconies, giving an impression of luxury where there was in fact only rich imagination.

He did have an option after all.

He could fake it.

The row of tall marble columns that was to line the second floor? He would instead use metal cylinders, shaped and tinted to look like smooth stone. The paintings to fit into the ovals in the wood paneling for Martha's private salon would be forged in the style of Fragonard and then artfully aged, using heat, to create the *craquelure* that made them seem venerable. The exotic woods on order for the walls of Viky's room would be replaced with plain ones, the grain carefully detailed in yellows and browns to give the impression of rare timber. The fireplaces that dotted the palace? They would be for show only, unable to actually kindle a blaze.

And so the next great phase of Otto's building began, desperate rather than obsessed. Once he got into the swing of it, he found that he was as extravagant in saving money as he had once been in spending it. To fill in the thirty-four missing seats for the dining room, he bought two authentic Louis XV chairs at auction and ordered the Prague woodcarver Emil Gerstel to make thirty-two replicas. (With Otto's typical attention to detail, the angle of the back of the fakes was relaxed ever so slightly to allow diners to recline a bit more.) Exact copies of other antiques in his inventory were fabricated in the same way, expanding the existing collection of furnishings to fill gaps and populate the rooms. Even the china got the Otto treatment, additional settings of the existing pink-and-white Meissen set precisely duplicated by a Czech manufacturer, the only difference the tiny maker's mark on the underside. What guest would be so impolite as to flip a plate over to inspect the inscription?

Otto's greatest legerdemain, however, was reserved for the basement pool. He sent to Italy for a crew of masons with wizard-like skills: able to conjure fake marble, scagliola, in extraordinary colors and patterns. Like magicians designing their tricks, the masons operated in total secrecy. Whenever the workmen stepped away for lunch or a beer, one stood guard at the door. At night they hid their materials—and even their tools—before locking the pool door behind them.

When the Italians packed up and departed, they left a marvel. The enormous swimming chamber, running almost the full length of the palace, was coated in the chromatic scagliola. Dozens of supporting columns lined the walls in stately formation, each a rich blood red, shot through with veins of stark white. Behind the pillars were curved alcoves and niches of yellow, black, and gray, unnatural striations of color swirling. The saturated pillars, walls, and alcoves played against the light green tile of the floors and the pool. The tiles' glaze faded in a gradient down the deep walls of the pool, transitioning to a white floor far below.

Otto surveyed the workmanship. Although it was concealed in the basement, this explosion of color reflected the *real* him. He had come to artifice by necessity but discovered that it could improve upon nature. It could have been kitsch—but instead it had turned out beautifully. Martha had been right: he was finding a way.

By October 1929, more than five years after Otto had begun, the exterior was almost complete. A third floor and an attic had been added, along with a slanting roof of gray slate, topped by copper cladding already oxidizing green. Spielmann's initial, austere design had been richly embellished by Otto with the ornamentation that he had enjoyed as a youth studying Prague's façades. The second floor was punctuated by balconies with ornate black-and-gold grilles, the third by round windows custom designed by Otto—oxen eyes, he called them. Romanesque statues of romping children adorned the parapet, perhaps a symbol of his own offspring celebrated for posterity.

If Otto could maintain this pace, the family would finally move into its new home in 1930. Martha had reason to be hopeful. The construction was at last nearing an end. Perhaps her husband would soon return to normal—just as with the completion of the little villa a decade earlier.

Then came October 29: Black Tuesday. The New York Stock Exchange collapsed, sending shock waves across the globe. Otto had invested heavily in America, so much so that he had planned for the bank to open an office there. He was going to dispatch his youngest brother, Hans, to head it (perhaps to keep their respective hot tempers as far away from each other as possible). In preparation, Otto had been educating himself; his latest batch of American books included a rosy 1929 volume titled *New Levels in the Stock Market*. So he paid attention when the reports of the crash came in that Tuesday from Manhattan. They were fragmentary and unbelievable, like screams from a far-off massacre. Soon the American market had fallen by more than 25 percent in twenty-four hours.

Events on Wall Street caused the already shaky European economy to yo-yo in the months that followed. Otto attempted to keep the Petschek bank on track, working days as long as those at the end of the war. Disaster in America was initially averted—Otto and his partners managed to dodge the losses that wiped out so many others. But the Depression settled in regardless. The Czechoslovak economic miracle that had propelled the country's GDP to the tenth largest globally was heavily dependent on exports. The nation was hit hard when the rest of the world stopped buying.

Otto struggled with his mines and the miners in them. They staged protests, stoppages, and strikes. Increasing numbers of the men were drawn to Marxism. It didn't help that the Soviet Union claimed to be thriving—a workers' paradise. The Czechoslovak Communist Party was led by Klement Gottwald, a stocky young cabinetmaker and member of parliament who made no bones about taking orders from Stalin. He helped organize the labor actions targeting Otto and the other mine owners. Gottwald's square, rough-hewn face was red and sweating as he shouted at his fellow parliamentarians:

> You say that we are under command of Moscow and that we go there for wisdom. Well, you are under command of . . . Petschek, Weimann, Preiss, you are under command of the League of Nations, that is, the company of imperialist predators, you go to get wisdom from Petschek, Weimann, Rothschild, Preiss, to learn how to exploit the working people even more efficiently. We are the party of the Czechoslovak proletariat and our headquarters really is Moscow. And we go to Moscow to learn, you know what? We go to Moscow to learn from the bolsheviks how to wring your necks. And you know that the Russian bolsheviks have mastered that.

When the other parliamentarians finally burst into fits of mirth at his meltdown, he warned them that one day, "you will stop laughing!"

Otto juggled palace invoices as he tried to get by on his reduced cash flow and finish the interiors of his future home, stitching the real and the unreal into a single coherent scheme. Once again, a stack of bills piled up. It was unheard of: a Petschek late on payment. Otto assured his vendors that he would honor the bills. Some irritated creditors even went so far as to file suit to collect. He settled, but the public disclosure of Otto's limitations did little to speed his building efforts.

As he strained to push the construction forward, the world outside his walls slid into economic despair. A shudder went through the region when the greatest of the Viennese financial institutions, Creditanstalt, collapsed in 1931. Otto was on its board, and despite his having done no wrong the crisis weighed heavily on him. This was no mere collection suit over an unpaid plumbing bill; it was an international scandal, wiping out depositors, triggering suicides, and spawning years of headlines, litigation, and investigation. Although it had survived Black Tuesday, Otto's American portfolio too was hit hard by the aftershocks of the global crash. Another blow came later that year when the United States called in all its loans to Czech banks. The Czechoslovak financial sector was in disbelief—America had birthed their country. They were counting on her for help, but what she offered was hindrance.

The Communists continued to vent their rage at Otto—including for the audacity of continuing to work on the palace in the depths of a depression:

> The biggest Czechoslovak capitalist and at the same time one of the largest capitalist vampires on the international scale, the coal-baron Petschek . . . sucks from thousands and thousands of Czech miners in northern Bohemia and has made such a great fortune from the sweat and blood of his Czech and German wage-slaves that his magnificent life and his wasting of tens of millions of crowns for the construction of the most luxurious house in Prague have become an outrageous mockery of the misery and poverty of most of the working population in Prague.

The animus even targeted Otto's children. One day the girls came home from school distraught. In class they had read a poem about the orphan of a coal miner, "Maryčka Magdonova." The verses told of a destitute girl who attempted to gather twigs for a fire on the mine owner's land. "Hochfelder the Jew" caught her and turned her into the authorities. In shame, Maryčka threw herself into a ravine, committing suicide. As if that were not bad enough, the instructor then called on Ina to declaim the lengthy ballad out loud.

Otto's worries were not just on the left. In neighboring Germany, where the family also had large coal holdings, Adolf Hitler and his far-right agenda were rising. Elections in September 1930 increased Nazi representation in the Reichstag from a mere 12 members to a full 107. Herr Hitler now commanded Germany's fastest-growing political party, and its largest save for the Social Democrats. Otto's brother Paul reported from Berlin of Nazi atrocities, of the Brownshirts assaulting Jews in the streets, of anti-Semites in his children's classrooms. He abandoned Berlin in 1931, moving back to Prague. From then on, he, Otto, and the other Petscheks managed the family's German holdings remotely, shuttling in and out of the country as needed.

The Nazi virus soon migrated to the ethnic German areas of Czechoslovakia, including the so-called Sudetenland. After Hitler's election breakthrough, his popularity surged among its majority-German population. Nazi sympathizers formed Czech organizations, such as the *Volkssport*, to advance their views. Otto had always prized his identity as a German Czechoslovak. He was a leading sponsor of the New German Theatre and a myriad of other German cultural endeavors. But now his own fellow Czech Germans were turning on him; the Sudeten German managers and pit bosses of his mines became as sullen as the left-wing miners. Otto was accustomed to being attacked by ethnic Czechs for being too German; now he was also under assault from the country's Germans for being too Jewish.

The worse it got, the harder he worked. As in the darkest days of the war, he sought reasons to be optimistic. At his long library table, Otto's architecture books were now interspersed with studies of Fascism, economics treatises, and dissections of the Depression. Martha came into the library at night and urged him to put out the light and come to bed. But he lingered into the wee hours. He was squeezing every minute out of the day to find a path ahead.

By spring 1931, Otto was physically much altered from the vigorous dreamer he had been in 1917. He looked more like a man of sixty-five than of fifty. He was portly, his once-black hair and mustache now salt and pepper. His internal alarm clock still went off every morning, but he no longer bounded out of bed quite as easily. Martha—his companion in everything—had aged with him. The stress had left her as thin as Otto had become corpulent. Her hair had gone gray. Her breathing as she slept, once so even, was consistently ragged.

During her waking hours, Martha kept a sharp eye on her husband's spending, down to the smallest items. When he needed a new raincoat, he jokingly warned her, "Now you will get mad," before informing her that he had purchased one. She even objected to him spending on her: "My dear Dumme! . . . I didn't cancel the order for your dress, but ordered it instead. Don't scold me! Otherwise I didn't spend anything."

One place that he refused to scrimp, however, was on Martha's bathroom in the palace: pale pink marble floors and walls veined with red (all genuine this time), an elevated tub reached by steps and framed by classical columns of the same highly polished stone, chandeliers dangling from a high domed ceiling, faucets and other fixtures of a special gold alloy that gleamed preternaturally. But for the toilet and bidet, it might have been a Roman temple. It was his gift to her for everything, and she was not so unkind as to reject it. Otto's own bathroom was a large but more utilitarian affair of green tile that would have been at home in any Bauhaus construction. He did sneak in one treat for himself: a custom-built *Tausend Strom Dusche*, a thousand-stream shower, with multiple spray heads on every side. The dials and switches were so elaborate that they looked like the controls of one of the time machines in the H. G. Wells novels that Otto enjoyed, and the knobs required detailed written instructions for proper operation.

In that spring of 1931, in spite of everything, Otto could finally contemplate the imminent prospect of moving into the palace. With its roof in place and the final sculptures and railings affixed, the exterior was at last complete. The interior was close to being habitable, although it would not be completed until after occupancy. One could see traces of its varied influences, from the Bourbon kings who built Versailles to Frank Lloyd Wright. But it was ultimately Otto's imprint on every one of its millions of square inches. He loved the palace even more than he would have if building it had been easy, and must have hoped its progress was a favorable omen for his many challenges in the world outside its walls.

IN June 1931, sun filtered through the trees as Otto walked out of the old villa, arm in arm with Martha. The children trudged in his wake, sad when the door closed for the last time behind them. Otto proudly led them through the elaborate gardens and across the wide lawn toward the massive structure looming in front of them.

To Otto, the building was breathtaking: the vast curving façade like outstretched arms inviting the family into its embrace; the rhythmic punctuation of the brass-framed windows and doors revealing the enormous light-filled spaces within; the treasures of the European millennium that filled them, every country and every art and craft represented, the works of Flemish tapestry weavers and French rug makers, Dutch oil painters and English book designers, German porcelain fabricators and Bohemian glassblowers (not to mention the Prague forgers who had filled the gaps in the collection when the money ran low). Martha had made her peace with the palace and acknowledged its beauty. After all, it was an expression of her Otto—down to the shape of the keyholes.

The children saw something quite different as they crossed the lush green oval. The palace was utterly foreign—nothing like the cozy house that they had grown up in or the ones where their friends lived. The way it curved, like a giant monster reaching out to grab them, was scary. Their fear of the palace's mercurial creator also colored their perception. Eva had tears streaming down her face as they approached.

But it was Viky who loathed the palace most of all. He felt as he entered as if he were marching to an execution. The enormous edifice represented all the obligations that he would inherit as the eldest son. He was crushed by the pressure.

Perhaps intending to please his children, Otto had lowered the retracting wall between the garden and the ballroom. To their young eyes, the fact that a wall was missing, that the outside flowed directly into the palace, that real flowers and birds suddenly became enamel ones in the chandeliers, with bizarre ceramic animals lining the walls, candelabras branching from their heads—was more eerie than charming. In silence, they walked with their parents through the giant rooms, where they were rendered insignificant by the high ceilings and tall panels. They were afraid that they would knock over one of the countless precious objects on display. They passed through the strange curved hallway that ran through the center of the palace, unsettled by how it disappeared at either end. Ascending to the second floor, they were startled by their bedrooms, with sixteen-foot-tall windows, crystal chandeliers, parquet floors, and gleaming gold-plated fixtures. These chambers felt foreign and uninviting, like those of royalty. How they wished that they could move back to their comfortable little house on the other side of the giant lawn.

Otto, oblivious, was as openly delighted with his creation as his children were silently dejected. He immediately began putting the palace to use. He was proud to show it off but also (banker that he was) amortizing his investment—proving to the world that he was undaunted by all adversity. He and Martha hosted elegant dinners in the wood-paneled dining room, Otto in tails and Martha wearing a floor-length ermine cape over her gown, welcoming Foreign Minister Beneš; visiting nobles, with their epaulettes, sashes, and medals; or other dignitaries. They conversed with Otto's brothers and representatives from Prague's business elite beneath the oval paintings of French troubadours serenading deshabille maidens set into the lunettes ringing the room. As planned, the table accommodated up to thirty-four animated diners, their places set with Otto's Meissen (real and imitation), bathed in warm light from the five chandeliers of glittering Czech crystal above.

After dinner, Martha led the ladies to the *Damenzimmer* (women's salon) for coffee and conversation, with its ecru silk panels and a lit vitrine in the wall displaying the rarest of their specimens of porcelain, silver, and glassware. The gentlemen followed Otto to the *Herrenzimmer* (men's salon). It had walls of dark silk and a hidden, built-in, six-foot humidor from which he distributed cigars, the perfume of tobacco permanently lingering. Then the couples reunited in the Wintergarden, with its enormous six-pointed, multihued star set into the floor and its floor-to-ceiling retractable glass wall, perhaps lowered to enjoy the evening if it was a pleasant one. Often the guests retired to the music room for a concert. Two grand pianos faced each other among the flamboyant sea-foam-green paneling, its curlicued edges trimmed in gold leaf—the deep, shining black of Steinways making the wildly colored walls glow all the more brightly. Professional musicians and singers or the most talented family members—sometimes even the host himself—would perform. At some point in the evening, Otto would find an excuse to show off his treasures to the visitors, from the giant thirty-foot Flemish tapestry of Jason and the Argonauts to a tiny early Meissen tea set, with grisaille Chinese cityscapes—among the first porcelain ever fired in Europe.

Afterward, Otto and Martha would see the people out and retire to the library to sit before the fire among the thousands of books, gossip about the evening, and reassure each other that everything would turn out to be just as successful as that night's affair had been.

OTTO eventually discerned his children's discomfort. Martha reassured him that their offspring would grow accustomed to life in their new home, but their adjustment was slow to come. They were ill at ease, and embarrassed to invite their schoolmates over. When they did, butlers served them in white gloves. The young Petscheks did not understand why they could not just have lemonade and cookies on the table, or even on the floor, as at their friends' houses.

To christen the giant basement pool, a swimming party was scheduled for the children. The bathers were led downstairs. Initially overwhelmed by the enormous chamber, they were soon happily splashing about, their cries and laughter echoing in the cavernous space. But everything went awry when Rita, chilled from hours in the water, contracted pneumonia. She recovered, but a shaken Otto drained the pool and declared it off-limits. The episode deepened the insecurity. This, they thought, was confirmation that the palace was unsafe.

Viky found excuses to be elsewhere as often as possible, sneaking off to dance in Prague's nightclubs or attending the avant-garde Voskovec & Werich cabaret show, with its Socialist sympathies. He told people that his father "would have killed me if he knew." The three girls took refuge in one another. Nighttime was the most frightening, the curving central hall disappearing into darkness around the bend, their parents sleeping a block away at its other end. The twins, at least, shared a bedroom. Eleven-year-old Eva was alone. Eventually she abandoned her ornate quarters altogether and moved into a small, simple chamber adjoining the twins' room, originally designed for a nanny.

Preoccupied as he was with events outside the palace, Otto tried to win the children over to the extent that he could. He conducted his musical contests over meals, tapping out the beat of various scores on the dining table, the children competing to guess the composer. He told them the stories of operas, replete with drama. He played tiddlywinks and cards with them and their cousins, amazing one observer who, used to Otto's forbidding mien, was surprised to stumble upon one of the games. "It's relaxing," a slightly sheepish Otto explained—a sentiment not shared by a straining young cousin, Ruth, who, at six years old, was desperately trying to hold her own.

Otto even took all three of his daughters on vacation to the Netherlands, without Martha. Perhaps he thought that it might be easier to connect with them away from the intimidating surroundings of the palace. He escorted them to the beach, on boat rides, and to cafés, where he plied them with tea cakes and other delicacies. He told them tales (including how he had wooed their mother) and joined their games. But it rained throughout the trip, and he had to cut it short to deal with an emergency. His other attempts fell similarly shy. He had been distracted by the palace for too long, and his obsession had left him too prone to sudden swerves of temper and too forbidding a figure. Instead of a bridge to his children, the palace was a barrier.

Those outside the building were no fonder of it than Otto's offspring. The aristocracy and those on the right sniffed that it was ostentatious and vulgar. Those on the left took offense to the cost of the palace, said to be upward of 300 million Czech crowns (well over $100 million today). *Who would build such a thing during the Depression?* they asked. Otto could have answered the rhetorical question—pointing out that he had started it long before, that leaving it unfinished would have helped no one—but any reply would only have stoked the flames of resentment. Even Otto's erstwhile admirers, the Watchers of Prague, murmured against his creation. They were having a moment of resurgent nationalism and felt that the palace was too cosmopolitan. There was not a single *Czech* feature at all, they complained. The architecture critics did not deign to take notice of a banker's pet project and ignored it altogether—perhaps even worse, to a creator, than criticism.

The most stinging blow of all, however, fell when Viky refused to live there any longer. In the fall of 1931, he asked to go to boarding school in England. Martha's maternal anxiety flared. She didn't even like him to overnight with friends in Carlsbad (or as the Czechs called it, Karlovy Vary). Otto was angry—the rejection, and all that it represented, cut him deeply. But he mulled it over and discussed it with Martha, and eventually they assented. They had tried everything they knew to help the boy thrive, and it had all failed. Perhaps a change of scenery would improve matters. Otto would accompany him, making the final selection of schools and settling him in.

And so the palace bid the first of what would be many mute farewells to its original occupants. As Otto and Viky traveled down the driveway toward the train station to begin their journey, the father would have been shocked to know what his son was thinking. As far as Viky was concerned, he would have been glad never to set foot in their home again.

⌣

In early September 1931, Otto was at the office, dealing with his daily stresses—the Depression, the rise of Fascism, the Communists in the mines, his unpaid bills, and his concerns about his son. At nine a.m., just as he was getting started on that day's battles, he felt a sharp, stabbing pain in his abdomen—then another, and another, radiating through his torso. Otto cried out in agony. His secretary and brothers raced into his office, laid him on his sofa, loosened his collar, and sent for the nearest physician.

All morning, his doctor moved in and out of Otto's office as his groans were heard from behind the closed door. Finally, at one p.m., the physician withdrew a hypodermic needle from his bag and gave Otto an injection of opium. The pain at last abated. Otto was carried out on a stretcher, admitted to the hospital, and subjected to a battery of tests: X-rays of his heart, stomach, and intestines; cardiograms; and urine and blood samples.

They found nothing life threatening. Otto had a slightly elevated temperature, which lingered for two weeks. He otherwise seemed fine. After the opium shot, the pain vanished as quickly and mysteriously as it had arrived. Otto tried to return to work after a couple of days, which was met with an outcry from Martha, his brothers, and the doctors. Yielding slightly, he set up a home office on the third floor of the palace. There he replicated his bank routine from early in the morning until late at night, complete with his secretary visiting the house to take dictation. There was too much that demanded his attention. As soon as his fever lifted, he was back at his desk at the bank.

Later that fall, Otto was awakened by the same violent, thrusting pain on both sides of his abdomen. He cried out, startling Martha awake. Fortunately, the children were so far away, in their rooms at the other end of the curve, that they heard nothing. Once more, the pain continued until an opium shot was administered. At four p.m., Otto was again moved to the hospital, where the same tests were repeated, with the same results: no explanation.

Otto returned again to his home office as he recuperated from the October attack, working as long a day as he could. He leaned heavily on a new majordomo, hired away from one of his Prague caregivers: Adolf Pokorný. Otto had been impressed by Pokorný's ministrations and decided that he wanted that at home for himself—and his palace. The tall, balding, silent Czech in black livery was strong enough to carry a grown man from room to room and discreet enough never to mention it. The same skilled, long-fingered hands that provided Otto's injections also gently dusted the banker's collections of rare, fragile glass, polished the silver to a high shine, and operated the retracting wall in the Wintergarden so that Otto could recuperate in the light and air.

Pokorný outfitted a third-floor chamber as a medical office for Otto's physicians and nurses—a one-room hospital. Otto had his bad days, when he could barely walk or had to rest for hours after composing a single letter—the opium syringe was all that helped. But he pushed himself to tolerate the pain, to keep moving, eventually willing himself to walk around the oval in his garden with Pokorný's assistance. By November, Otto was back at the bank, only to be felled by another attack in January 1932—this one more severe than the last. Again, only opiates would relieve the pain. The symptoms were becoming worse, as new, more terrifying ones were appearing. About ten days into the January attack, Otto lost all feeling in his leg. No one knew what to do about the paralysis; thankfully, sensation returned later that day.

And so Otto came to occupy his palace day and night, living and working there for months at a time. It became not just his residence but his refuge. As 1932 and then 1933 unfolded, Otto had long stretches of gradual improvement when he could emerge, returning to his normal life at the bank, only sooner or later to be felled by another attack. The children became accustomed to Otto working at home, though they were careful not to bother him. When he was on the third floor, Martha instructed them to tiptoe past his door on the way to their lessons in the gymnastics room or to see visitors in the guest apartment.

The physicians tried every test but never determined what was causing the pain. But the Watchers of Prague thought they knew. They remembered the fortune-teller's prediction. Prague had its own energies, the universe its own balances, that defied reason. Otto had drawn on them to create his palace, and now the debt was being called in.

Otto dismissed such talk as pure garbage. He believed that science would cure him. One day, a team of movers carried a series of unusual contraptions into the palace. There were giant wheels, metal drums, long pulleys, and skeins of wires, all attached to tall steel frames. There was even a saddle mounted on a steel base. Perhaps the more superstitious among the movers and the house staff stared and whispered among themselves. Were these magical implements to repel the fortune-teller's curse?

The truth was the opposite: Otto had imported pioneering health technology, the very first exercise machines. They were the invention of Dr. Gustav Zander, a Swedish physician. Otto's was the first recorded private use of the machines in Prague. As befits such rarities, the machines were given a room of their own, a white-tiled chamber in the basement. It was termed the Zander Room. Otto applied himself to the machines, straining and sweating, determined to get better.

⌒

As Otto's health was in jeopardy, so too was the Czech economy's. While other nations showed signs of recovery in 1932 and 1933, Czechoslovakia lagged behind. Industrial production fell to almost half its pre-Depression level in 1932 and lingered there in 1933. Social unrest was spreading: now it was not just the miners who were in the streets, but workers of every kind, marching, protesting, and even rioting. Almost a million of them were unemployed in a nation of just under seven million working-age people. As a result, the Communists were gaining strength; their leader, Gottwald, continuing his rantings: "The Czech government . . . stands side by side with the . . . Petscheks, Guttmanns, Rothschilds, and the Czech soldier protects the German coal-baron against the Czech miner—this is the patriotism of the state!"

On the bright side—and Otto always tried to consider the bright side—Gottwald was right about one thing. The banker *could* look to the state for support. The fourteen years since Czechoslovakia's founding had proven that. Masaryk and Beneš had, so far, guarded the core freedoms—personal, political, and economic—that defined liberal democracy and made Otto's functioning possible. He respected the aging philosopher-president. Masaryk had returned the favor, visiting the Petschek bank building in March 1927.

But it was Masaryk's deputy, Edvard Beneš, whom Otto trusted most. The foreign minister had lived up to Otto's high hopes of 1918, proving to be one of the most adroit statesmen in Europe. Beneš had engineered a web of treaties that encouraged trade and ensured the country's protection by a host of allies across the Continent. They were led by France and reinforced by the Czechs' "Little Entente" with Yugoslavia and Romania. Beneš had seen to it that those arrangements were backed by a powerful Czechoslovak army—outnumbering the troops of even the United States in the early '30s, following America's postwar demobilization and turn toward isolationism.

Beneš had also helped lead the fight against Nazi sympathies within Czechoslovakia. Dr. Rudolf Jung, the chairman of the Czech-German National Socialists, had denounced the Jews, embraced Hitler, and demanded a customs and economic union with Germany. The Czech government promptly banned the party, sending Jung scurrying across the border.

Beneš utilized all the tools at his disposal to help the Czech state, and that included his relationship with Otto. The foreign minister came to the palace to ask Otto for a loan for his country. Beneš encouraged Petschek support for the New German Theatre in Prague—a symbol of cohesion in the multiethnic state. And as the situation across the border in Germany continued to deteriorate, Otto was asked to represent Czechoslovakia on a League of Nations commission to deal with the plight of German refugees. In 1932 the Nazi Party had become the largest in Germany, winning 230 seats in parliamentary elections. By January 1933 Hitler was leading a coalition government. As a result, Jews and liberals were taking flight, creating a humanitarian crisis in Czechoslovakia and across the region. The League had formed a commission to address the problem, and the Czech government thought that Otto would be a suitable representative.

Otto mulled the offer. Like Beneš, he believed in the League and had his well-worn pocket-sized charter to prove it. And Otto had compassion for the refugees; an entire department at the bank was dedicated to giving *tzedakah,* charity, and he was helping to house, feed, and clothe those who had run from Hitler. But Otto had German problems of his own that were preoccupying him. The Nazis had called for a boycott of Jewish businesses in April 1933 and soon thereafter passed legislation to drive Jews out of the newspaper business. Could coal be far behind? Paul still commuted in and out of Germany, careful to avoid the Nazi mobs, protected by his status as a businessman—but for how long?

Otto regretfully declined.

THE floodwaters of Nazism spreading outside the palace seeped through the walls in other ways—ones that touched Martha's life and that of the children. The Petscheks' head housekeeper was German, the rigidly efficient Fräulein Fürst. She marched up and down the back staircase, her huge ring of keys jangling at her waist, and her blond braids, wrapped like a crown around her head, immobile. A native of Würzburg, she had been with the Petscheks for years, watched the children grow up, and even traveled with them on vacations. Hers was one of the first basement rooms finished when the Petscheks moved into the palace in 1931, even before some of the upstairs rooms.

Fürst had never been a warm person, yet everyone in the palace had grown accustomed to her iciness. As Hitler rose, they noticed her extra remove. But Fürst still noted household expenses in the giant ledgers and kept a sharp eye on the contents in wine and tobacco rooms just down the hall from her basement office. She still prowled the floors, keeping order.

Fürst was indispensable, particularly to Martha, whom she served as Pokorný did Otto. But she was also, it emerged, a Nazi sympathizer. She was one of the millions of Germans who believed that Hitler was their savior, caught up as they were in the enthusiasm of his rants, the parades by torchlight, and his assaults on the Treaty of Versailles. Although she had once been attracted to the family because of its Germanness, now she was apparently repelled by its Jewishness. One day she announced to a stunned Martha that she could no longer work for them. She delivered the news in her usual frigid style. Soon she was gone—presumably back to Würzburg, a hotbed of Nazi activity.

The children had known Fürst their whole lives and didn't understand why she had to go. Martha explained the best that she could. They took it in stride. Pokorný assumed more responsibility, and soon things seemed back to normal again—as if Fürst had never been there.

⌒

WHEN Otto could go to his bank office in 1933 and 1934, he did. When he had to solve problems while lying flat on his back in a pool of sunlight on the third floor of the palace, he did that, too. He remained fundamentally optimistic, notwithstanding the political currents around and in Czechoslovakia—at least, those near him saw no indication that he took the danger seriously. He seems to have believed that the family would be just fine; it had been since abandoning Kolín for Prague a half century before.

Not all the Petscheks shared his confidence. Some began taking steps to prepare for possible political upheaval: giving their children names that worked in every language, smuggling money out of the country, and considering plans to live abroad. Otto did not think that was necessary. Having invested so much of himself in his palace, he had no intention of leaving it.

Instead, Otto's daily routine embraced his home. He had breakfast on his personal balcony with Martha, overlooking the sprawling garden. It looked as if it had been there for centuries: so peaceful, the morning light playing on the flowers, making the colors glow. He watched the children walk down the drive to the family limousine that would take them to school. Otto did not permit vehicles in the compound—the fumes! So the three girls passed through the main gate, its arch an enormous pergola of roses heavy with huge blossoms, and entered the vehicle from the street, trailed by the scent of the blooms. (Little did Otto imagine how embarrassed his daughters were by this style of travel, or that they instructed the driver to let them off a block away from the schoolhouse.)

After breakfast, Otto walked down to the other end of the curved hallway, his quarters vanishing behind the bend. He entered the ornate black elevator cage and rode to the third floor. A secretary was waiting in his home office, and Otto fired off the day's dictation while basking in the light. In the afternoon, it was the Zander machines, doctor's visits, a meal with the family. Otto even created a *Golfzimmer,* installing a putting green in one of the countless basement rooms, to practice his stroke. He lived, worked, and convalesced in the building, the palace his ally in healing, reciprocating the care that he had lavished on it.

Spring was always a hopeful time for Otto, and, by that season in 1934, he felt much better. He had gone months without a truly debilitating episode. The attacks, whatever they were—heart, stomach, nerves, or all of the above—had faded. Otto was well enough to resume working in the bank and then to pick up his travels. Once again, the letters to Martha started flowing from all over the Continent. Otto visited Viky in Britain, reporting back:

> He already looks like an Englishman. His clothes: grey, dirty flannel pants with the yellow coat of his sports suit, underneath, a sweater, no hat, no coat, like all other boys. You would love it. Add coalblack hands and nails, because yesterday he repaired the muffler of one of the boys' cars in the college. Que faire? [What to do?] The riding lesson is really very nice and the teacher is excellent, but I couldn't forbid the jumping, because all 11 boys who have lessons with him are learning to jump. Que faire? Slowly you will come to respect me!

Viky was preparing to finish public school and to apprentice in a bank. No scholar, he hadn't taken his university entrance exams. But there was time for that. The younger children also seemed happier. The three girls would never be completely at home in the palace, but they had at least made some cozy spots their own: the library alcove, with its blue sofa; a little indoor balcony overlooking the second floor. They felt happy in these niches, doing their homework in their corner of the library or putting on shows on the balcony, staging *Romeo and Juliet* and dramas of their own invention. They had inherited their father's love of costumes, and the three of them liked to dress up as sailors or Chinese nobles and playact. The palace had made room for them.

Otto had warmed the house, too, by infusing it with some of the family's ancestral Jewish culture. There were Jewish books in the library: a Hebrew-German Bible, Graetz's *History of the Jews,* the monumental *Encyclopaedia Judaica.* He acquired a rare medieval rabbi's chair, which he displayed among his treasures. Otto arranged Hebrew lessons for the girls, administered by a Prague rabbi. The cleric must have been startled when he smelled *treyf* (nonkosher food) cooking; the only day that it was never served was Yom Kippur. But to the girls it was normal to have a pork roast at a Passover dinner or on Rosh Hashanah eve. They were Jewish but not very observant, even celebrating Christmas. Otto placed a huge copper kettle in the center of the Wintergarden ballroom, filling it with a hundred red poinsettias—at that time a rarity in Prague. A tree would have been too goyish for Otto, carefully balancing all his identities as a model for his offspring.

Pokorný and his wife helped the children feel more settled as well. The couple moved into the little two-bedroom gatekeeper's house just inside the entrance to the compound, where Mrs. Pokorný operated the switchboard for the palace. She was as jovial and round as her husband was lean and austere, greeting the kids warmly when they traipsed through the gate after school and offering them *koláč* (cake) or other treats. Her omnipresent husband was less demonstrative, but the children came to feel that he was fond of them—always watching to make sure all was well. The childless Pokornýs expended their affection on the girls, and it afforded the youngsters some measure of the security that Otto had felt as a youth from the generations of Petscheks that had constantly surrounded him. The Pokornýs won the three girls' hearts when they agreed to board a dog for them—the only condition under which Otto, after much pleading, would allow one. They got a dark brown dachshund, named him Asperin von Sternberg, or Aspie, and his presence ensured that the girls were regular visitors to the Pokornýs' dwelling.

By 1934, the bank's health, together with Otto's, had improved. He had steered it through the worst of the crisis, even if he sometimes had to do so while lying flat on his back. It helped that there was an uptick in the Czechoslovak economy, imports and exports both increasing in 1934.

⌣

THAT spring, Martha and her sister were planning a trip to the Alps, and Otto decided to join them to celebrate his recovery. In June they would visit Austria and their beloved Italy, where they had honeymooned twenty-one years before—a full generation ago. Martha was a bit anxious. Did Otto feel well enough? Of course he did. He had been traveling for work, hadn't he? He would be fine. He would take it easy, recuperate, while Martha explored with her sister.

When the day of the trip arrived, the bags were packed, and the chauffeur was waiting out on Winterova Street, at the bottom of the long gravel drive. Otto and Martha said goodbye to the three girls. He had barred Eva, the eldest, from the opera for poor Latin marks. She had spilled some ink on her homework and been marked down. She loved music and was dejected that she would miss three whole performances that her younger sisters were free to attend. Otto saw that she was upset about her punishment and rescinded it—the very last thing he did before departing on the trip.

The Italian Alps were the same as ever. There was little trace of Mussolini and the Fascists here. Italy's love of life took priority over the political winds of the moment. Otto looked out at the mountain peaks. They knew nothing of the Depression, of Hitler, Stalin, and Mussolini. They took no notice of striking coal miners, fluctuating exports, or racial hate. They simply endured.

Otto overindulged a bit at dinner that night. Martha warned him not to, but he insisted. In the early morning hours he was jolted awake by the familiar stabbing pain in his torso. Martha called the hotel doctor. He consulted remotely with Otto's physicians, administered the opium solution, and stayed by Otto's bedside as it took effect and the magnate drifted off to sleep.

By the next day the spell had passed, leaving Otto drained, his skin clammy and gray and his hands trembling. Of all the things he loved about Italy, medicine was not one. He decided to make for home.

They boarded the train but made it only as far as Vienna before the pain returned, more violent than before. Otto was rushed off the train, taken to the General Hospital, and met by Martha's cousin, the *Privat-dozent* Dr. Popper. Otto looked out the car window at Vienna under martial law. Soldiers and police were everywhere, the city tense, on guard. Inspired by Hitler, Austrian Nazis had tried to seize power. Chancellor Engelbert Dollfuss had cracked down on them. He had arrested thousands. The Hitlerians had responded with a campaign of street fighting, of shootings and bombings. Dozens of innocents had been injured in the latest Nazi outrage, in which grenades had been thrown into an Austrian sporting event. Beautiful Vienna was on edge. It was beyond anything Otto had seen, even when he had come here during the worst moments of the Great War.

At the hospital, Otto tried to calm Martha. Hadn't he always pulled through before? Stop worrying, *Dumme,* he told her. He would be fine; he would soon be home. The steadfast Pokorný rushed from Prague on the first available train. He must have been startled by his employer's condition, although Pokorný always maintained the same neutral expression. Otto interrogated Pokorný on how things were at the palace. He gave the majordomo precise instructions that all was to be made ready for his return.

But Otto would never make that trip. On the evening of June 29, 1934, as he was lying in his hospital bed, another attack came. There was an explosion of pain. Otto cried out. His face contorted. He gripped Martha's hand. He dug down to fight through. But he had no reserves left. Shortly before ten p.m., his heart stopped beating. In Prague, the servants closed the draperies and turned down the lights. Otto's palace, in mourning, darkened.

In August, a letter arrived for Otto from the city. Martha, disconsolate, all in black, unfolded the heavy, official stock and ran her eye down the page. Prague wished to inform JUDr. Petschek that a serious irregularity in the approvals for the palace had been discovered. An inspection had revealed an unauthorized deviation from the plans. "[N]o stairs to the basement from the north were made, the stairs are on the other side than the plans show." Moreover, documentation concerning the inspection had been lost, complicating matters. But JUDr. Petschek need not worry: Prague had determined that "the deviations were made technically correctly." The city approved them retroactively.

Otto's masterpiece was finished at last.

4

The Final Child

Sobrance, Czechoslovakia; May 1938

Sobrance, Main Street, 1930s.

"T HE Petscheks are gone!"
Fourteen-year-old Frieda Grünfeld took a moment to process her father's news. Was he joking? But Rabbi Zalman Leib Grünfeld's brown eyes were serious, with none of their usual twinkle, and his mouth was set into a line in his long black and gray beard.

Frieda was petite, just over five feet tall, with a dazzling smile. Unable to afford store-bought dresses, she wore clothes that her sisters made. The youngest of eight, she was doted on by her siblings and parents, who showered her with enough love that she forgot just how poor they were. In their small town of Sobrance, Czechoslovakia, most of the Jews were of modest means.

She had hurried home from school to welcome her father back from Prague, sprinting past the small shopkeepers along Hlavná ulica (Main

Street): Jacubovic, the tailor, his half-moon glasses perched on his high forehead; Salomon, the shoemaker, his leather apron cinched tight around his narrow waist; Grundberger, the butcher, with his large forearms. In a small shtetl—Jewish community—of just a few hundred families, they were all like relatives to her. Someone called out in Yiddish, "*Friduska, vi zent ir flisendik?*" ("Little Frieda, where are you running?"). "*Mein tateh iz kumendik heim!*" ("My father is coming home today!") she shouted back over her shoulder.

She had thought that she would be the one with big news: she was one of the very top students in her middle-school class—she, a *girl*. It proved the claim of her hero, the late Tomáš Garrigue Masaryk: girls were equal to boys. (He had gone so far as to take his wife's name, adding it before his own.) Now her teacher wanted her to go on to gymnasium—the first in her family who would do so.

Frieda had imagined her entire future unfolding so clearly, as if she were stepping out onto a balcony and seeing the palace of her dreams rise before her. She would work hard and excel in high school, then go to Charles University in Prague for a medical degree. When she graduated, she would return to Sobrance to work with Dr. Herskovic, a neighbor and the town's most respected professional. She imagined them making their rounds in his elegant little horse-drawn buggy, each with their own black doctor's bag.

Although excited, she had been a little apprehensive about telling her father. Theirs was an ultra-Orthodox family, Chassidic, her father the descendant of generations of rabbis, scribes, and mystics. The ultra-Orthodox were not enthusiastic about girls' education. The leaders of the movement, the Chassidic *rebbes*, felt that it led to assimilation.

Still, Frieda had been sure that she could persuade her kindly *tateh*, her dad. As the baby of the family, she often got her way. Her father had supported her school career up until now, even helped her with her studies. He taught her Jewish texts on Saturday afternoons. She knew how much he loved her; she was a late surprise and a much-cherished one. She thought—no, she *knew*—that she could persuade him to let her continue. *Pravda Vítězí* (Truth Prevails) was Masaryk's slogan, and the truth was that she *deserved* to get an education.

As Frieda had run to see her father, she brushed away considerations of the recent troubles in Europe that had been making him anxious. She had known only Czechoslovak strength and peace her whole short life. She believed in her country, second only to her faith in the divine.

Frieda had spotted her father on their porch, occupying the rocking chair, which had sat empty all week. He was already at work, several of the town's women lined up to see him, carrying freshly slaughtered chickens. They needed to know whether the birds were kosher. Zalman Leib was not only a rabbi but also a one-stop shop for all things Jewish: a *schochet* (ritual slaughterer), a *mohel* (circumciser), a *chazzan* (cantor), and a *sofer* (scribe). The inspection of the poultry was a familiar pre-Sabbath ritual.

There was barely enough room on the porch for her father and a single guest. Frieda had waited her turn to ascend the stairs, impatiently shifting from one foot to the other, hoping that he would notice her. The Grünfeld home was a modest structure, long and narrow. The family had added on to the rear, squeezing out every bit of space from the lot as the children kept arriving, so the house was now wedged right against the stream. It was a far cry from the Jewish villas of Prague, and the grandest of them all, the Petschek mansion.

But to the people of Sobrance, Reb Zalman Leib's little dwelling on Komárovská Street was magnificent. *Hamevin yavin,* as they said in their Hebrew: The knowing ones know. Not because of its physical presence but because of its *ruchneus,* its spiritual contents. Those included perhaps the largest Jewish library in the shtetl. It was packed with books, shelves lining every spare inch of wall space: giant volumes of Talmud and other large works of *halacha* (Jewish law); tiny Bibles and prayer books that you could slip into a pocket for travel; and every size in between. Zalman Leib had whole worlds in his library, pages of ancient rabbis in oriental robes and turbans debating metaphysics and ethics, fantastic legends of demons and saints, legal judgments addressing all human disputes imaginable (and many not), songs, poems, astronomical and astrological formulae—all these pages informing and fortifying him as he rocked on the porch. The ladies waiting used him as a portal to those millennia of learning, an entire vast civilization distilled into his inspection of the entrails of a chicken.

Frieda's father had made the twelve-hour journey home by train and bus from Prague, about as far away from Sobrance as you could get without leaving Czechoslovakia. He looked tired, absentmindedly stroking his long beard, inspecting the birds on a low table. Finally, the last customer left and he looked down from his perch. He saw Frieda and smiled at his baby. Her Yiddish name was Frimud (the religious one). Her birth had seemed miraculous to her parents, so they had dedicated her arrival to their faith.

Frieda had dropped into the guest chair before anyone else showed up. "*Tateh,* I have big news!"

He had looked at her, appraising her face, as if weighing a decision, then leaned in and whispered, "Me, too."

What news could he have? Her own announcement forgotten in a flash of curiosity, she had whispered back, expectantly, "Tell me." Zalman Leib opened his knee-length black caftan and reached for an inside pocket. He took out some folded papers and showed them to her: APPLICATION FOR UNITED STATES VISA.

"What? America?"

Her father had raised one of his long fingers, calloused from his ritual work of slaughtering, circumcising, and scribing, and placed it on his lips, shushing her.

"But why, *Tateh*?" she had asked.

Her own announcement forgotten, she listened to his narrative. Everywhere he had gone on his trip, people were saying that the Nazis could invade at any time. That would be dangerous for the Jews. To get to and from Sobrance, Zalman Leib had passed though the majority-German areas of Czechoslovakia. There had been open hostility toward him from the Czech Germans, with his Jewish garb and long beard: muttered comments on the street; glares on the train.

But it was during his stop in Prague that Zalman Leib had learned the most shocking news of all. And he now relayed it to Frieda—the Petscheks had picked up and left.

Apparently the entire extended Petschek family had fled, dozens of them, leaving their homes vacant, abandoning the country. They were perhaps the First Family of Czechoslovak Jewry, an object of fascination in the little house on Komárovská. Frieda and her sisters in particular were enthralled by them. They studied a newspaper photograph of the handsome heir, Viktor, when the media covered his marriage. They were shocked that he had married a non-Jew—a British heiress. She did look beautiful in the paper, though. The children had listened, wide-eyed, to the tales that their father brought back from his Prague visits: how the Petscheks had a whole department in their bank just for *tzedakah,* charity, and how the Czechoslovak government came to them for advice and loans. Frieda admired the way that they combined their Jewish identity with secular success.

Now the Petscheks had left the rest of them behind.

"Gone? How can that be?" Frieda asked.

"Wrong question, Friduska." Her father always told her that asking the right questions was more important than the answers. "The question is, Should we go, too? Is God trying to tell us something? Maybe *we* should consider a move," he said.

Frieda leaned in, ready to learn more, but stopped as she heard footsteps approaching. Another poultry-bearing customer for the rabbi. "Frieda," her father said, standing up, "*Shabbos* is coming"—the Sabbath. "Go inside and help your mother." Dazed, she stood and walked toward the front door. Her head was spinning. Leave Sobrance? Depart Czechoslovakia? Go to America? By the time she came back to her senses, the door had closed behind her. *Wait,* she wanted to call out, *I have a surprise, too!* But she had missed the opportunity; he was now occupied.

⌣

IT was hectic inside the little house—the weekly pre-Sabbath rush. Frieda's mother, Chaya, was in the center of the house, overseeing preparations for the holy day. She was even shorter than Frieda, just five feet tall, with a kerchief over her head covering every strand of hair, and she was *tichtig* and *richtig*: practical and righteous. Though Zalman Leib was an ultra-Orthodox rabbi, Chaya was even more devout, a book of Psalms and prayers tucked into her apron as she cooked. Whenever she had a spare moment, she took out the little volume and recited the contents, enunciating every word in a precise whisper. She was famously soft-hearted; when people from the shtetl were in trouble, they came to her for advice, a pot of food, a folded blue or pink banknote. Indeed, two of the ladies had come directly from their consultation with Zalman Leib to sneak in a quick complaint about their husbands, and they stood around her, murmuring in low voices, plucking their chickens. As quiet

as her husband was voluble, Chaya listened, occasionally nodding or saying a word as she chopped onions and stirred a giant steaming cauldron
of soup with a long wooden ladle. Frieda was more like her father, but
she tenderly loved her taciturn mother. She darted between the ladies
and gave Chaya a quick kiss on the cheek. Chaya absentmindedly smiled
at her daughter and resumed listening and cooking. If Frieda was hoping for an opportunity to share her big news with her mother—with
anyone—it would have to wait.

Frieda sighed and set down her books. The remainder of the afternoon was a mad rush to get ready. She tied on an apron and went to work
peeling a mound of potatoes that would be used for traditional Sabbath
foods, including the lunch entrée, *cholent,* a beef stew. Frieda loaded up
a large iron pot with meat, potatoes, barley, and water. Then her mother
sent her on various errands, delivering food parcels to families with new-
borns or illnesses. Chaya gave away Zalman Leib's meager income as fast
as he could earn it. The fact that the family barely had enough for themselves didn't matter to Chaya. Others needed it even more.

After the last of her chores, Frieda ran back home, just in time to grab
the *cholent* pot and speed-walk it to the main street's bakery. Gutmann
Basci (Uncle Gutmann) slid it into his big oven, next to the pots of the
other Jewish families. The *cholent* would cook overnight, and Frieda
would reclaim it tomorrow at noon, after attending synagogue, for the
family's hot lunch. She returned home as the sun sank toward the horizon, and she jumped into her Sabbath dress, another product of her sisters' sewing baskets, a bit threadbare but laundered to a gleaming white.
She barely made it into the common room—where the eating, cooking,
and living was done—for the lighting of the Sabbath candles.

It always amazed Frieda—the contrast between the frenetic preparations and the sense of calm that descended the moment the Sabbath
candles were kindled. Miraculously, everything got done every week.
Her mother stood before the *lachter* (silver candelabra), lit the candles,
and, covering her eyes, chanted the blessing that launched the Sabbath.
Three generations of women were illuminated, their faces glowing in
the flames: Chaya, then Frieda and two of her sisters—Faigie and Berta—
and finally Faigie's daughter, Yehudis, just four years old, barely able to
reach the candles.

While they waited for her father and brothers to come home from synagogue, Frieda set the table, working with Faigie, the firstborn of the family. Smart and tough, she had her own dressmaking shop. She had scandalized the town by divorcing her husband because they were unhappy—unheard of for an Orthodox woman of the day. Despite (or because of) that, she maintained a thriving trade in her little store. She had moved back in with her parents for the sake of Yehudis, so that the child would have a proper home to grow up in.

Frieda could finally tell someone her news. "Faigie, I am going to go to gymnasium! My teacher wants to come and talk to our parents. He says Czechoslovakia needs students like me; I owe it to the country to go. Thanks to Masaryk, women can do anything now! He gave women the vote. He believes women are equal—Jews, too. I am going to prove it—and be a doctor."

Her sister let Frieda go on. Faigie was perhaps the most independent Jewish woman in Sobrance and needed no lecture on the rights of women. She knew all too well what it meant for a woman to assert herself and the price it exacted. But she let Frieda gush. When Frieda finally stopped to take a breath, Faigie told her how proud she was. And she *was* proud—ten years older, she had taught Frieda her letters, helped her read her first words, reared her as she was now rearing Yehudis.

But Faigie also gently raised a problem with Frieda's big plans: "Our parents are going to make a match for you to get married at eighteen; they will not want you go to university and study medicine. That's not the Chassidic way." Faigie, too, had been a top student who had wanted to continue to gymnasium. Zalman Leib and Chaya had absolutely forbidden it, marrying her off instead. Faigie paused, and her younger sister knew what she was thinking. If only they had let Faigie go to school, she would have avoided her marriage—and her divorce.

"But if you didn't marry Aryeh, then there would be no Yehudis," Frieda blurted out, and Faigie laughed.

"True, it was all worth it."

"Faigie, you'll help me persuade them, won't you? That was a long time ago. Things have changed; they will see it differently now."

"I will try," her sister assured her.

Soon the men were bustling through the door. The family went right to the table and launched into the rituals that preceded Sabbath dinner.

Her father blessed each of the children, Frieda last, placing his hands over her head and reciting the prayer: "May God make you like Sarah, Rebecca, Rachel, and Leah," he whispered into her hair, "may he bless you and safeguard you." He led the entire family in a rendition of the song "Shalom Aleichem" ("Peace Be unto You"). Then he turned to Chaya and serenaded her in his finest cantorial tenor with Proverbs 31, "Eishes Chayal" ("The Woman of Valor"). The children joined in the lilting melody, Zalman Leib's powerful voice leading them, Chaya blushing as she did every week at the extravagant praise:

> *A wife of noble character who can find?*
> *She is worth far more than rubies . . .*
>
> *She selects wool and flax*
> *and works them with eager hands . . .*
>
> *She considers a field and buys it;*
> *out of her earnings she plants a vineyard . . .*
>
> *She opens her arms to the poor*
> *And extends her hands to the needy.*

In its entirety, twenty-one verses, it was the official job description of the Jewish wife—just singing the words was exhausting. But Chaya had earned the weekly serenade. Once, inspired by the secular novels she read, Frieda asked her mother if she and Zalman Leib were in love. Love? Her mother looked puzzled. That had nothing to do with it—they both loved the Lord; that was the only love that mattered. But Frieda intended to have a different kind of marriage, to love both her husband and God. She fantasized about marrying a handsome doctor. Religious, of course, but modern and clean shaven.

The initial songs and blessings were only the beginning of the rituals that framed their Sabbath evening meal. Usually Frieda enjoyed them: her father's ethereal voice as he chanted the *kiddush,* the long blessing over the wine; the washing of the hands using beautiful silver vessels; the blessing over the bread; the family singing song after song as the food was served. But tonight was different, as she impatiently waited to share her news.

She couldn't, however, just sit there on the edge of her seat. As the youngest, she was expected to help serve the meal. She was at the stove, ladling soup into bowls, when she heard a break in the music. She raced back to the table, the broth slopping over the dishes. But it was too late. By the time she flopped back down, someone had asked her father how his trip had gone.

He told them about what he had seen: the looming fear of a German invasion, the ugly looks from Czech Germans. And he shared all that he knew of the Petschek departure.

"*Nu,*" Zalman Leib asked, "maybe we should go, too? Is the cloud of glory lifting?" This was a reference to God's pillar of smoke that had preceded the Hebrews' wanderings in the desert. "Maybe *we* should consider a move? Friedeleh," he said, giving her a wink, "where do you think we should go? Maybe America?" He withdrew the visa application that he'd shown her earlier in the evening from the inner pocket of his long coat.

His children all tried at once to get a look at the papers. He handed them to Faigie, who passed them around the table. He had trained them to ask questions, to challenge, and that's what they did: *Was he serious? Was the Czech situation really that bad? Why America? How would we get there? When would we leave?* Chaya, quiet as usual, listened with worry creasing her normally placid face.

Zalman Leib, proud of his brood's probing inquiries, explained. "Something *nisht gut* [not good] is coming." He didn't like the way it felt, a black cloud moving rapidly from the distance. He brought to current events his knowledge of the Jews of Egypt, Babylon, Persia, Rome, Palestine during the Crusades. All were regions where the Jews had once been secure, and then, the *mabul* (flood). Was it going to recur, another convulsion of hate targeting the Jews? They should get out. America would be safe—that was where the Petscheks were supposedly headed, although no one seemed to know for sure.

As the table talked it through, it suddenly struck Frieda that she didn't want to go. She was a Czechoslovak. She had imbibed a strong draft of nationalism in her schooling, which coincided with the golden age of the new country. As a result, she was an enthusiastic proponent of

Masaryk's idealism, his vision for their nation, its limitless possibilities. She was not going to cut and run *now,* just when her country needed her. Hitler was in a whole other country. The Czechs were strong and could defend themselves. Besides, she had her future all planned out, here, not in some far-off land where she would be a stranger.

She couldn't take it any longer. She stepped into a fragmentary pause in the conversation and loudly proclaimed, "I don't want to go to America." Faigie gave her a warning look, but Frieda rushed ahead. "I want to stay here and go to gymnasium." They all stopped and looked at her. *Gymnasium? What are you talking about? What does that have to do with America?* Her sister tried to shush her, but Frieda could not pull back now. "My schoolmaster is recommending me for prep school; he is coming to the house. Czechoslovakia needs students like me; I owe it to the country to go," she blurted out.

Half the table started arguing about Frieda's proposition. The other half simply dismissed it (her siblings Berta and Boruch rolled their eyes). But Chaya had reached her limit. She finally spoke: *"Iz nisht Shabbos gereden. Tateh, iz de zman fir bentschn."* ("This is not Sabbath talk. Father, it's time to say the grace after meals.") Zalman Leib, relieved not to have to deal with Frieda's unexpected outburst, readily agreed. With effort, no one's more strenuous than Frieda's, the children contained themselves. It was required by the commandment *Kibud av va' em.* (Honor your father and mother.) The last round of prayers was chanted, and the dinner broke up.

Frieda went to bed in her tiny room at the back of the house, next to her parents' bedchamber. Through the thin walls, she heard her father and mother talking. Her mother's voice was entirely inaudible. Frieda knew that she was speaking only because of the long pauses in her father's speech. His tone grew louder and sharper between the pauses, peppered with the word *America.* She strained to stay awake and to pick up any stray scrap of information. But she drifted off, lulled by the murmuring on the other side of the wall.

⌒

By the time Frieda was shaken awake by Faigie the next morning, sun was pouring in. Everyone was already at synagogue for the Sabbath morning service, and her sister was hustling Frieda and Yehudis to follow. Frieda tried to raise her school plans again to get Faigie's take, but there was no time. "I told you not to bring it up in the first place," her sister admonished. "Why don't you listen? I said I would help you, and I will."

"But the teacher is coming *soon!*"

"Just leave it," Faigie countered. "We will discuss it later. But whatever you do, don't bring it up again with Mama and *Tateh,* not until I have had a chance to soften them up."

Frieda sped over to the house of worship, already late at ten a.m. She raced through the long, complex prayer service, barely catching up by the time the rest of the congregation reached the end. While her family headed home, she ran to the baker for the *cholent* pot. She waited her turn with the other youngest children of Jewish families until he fished out the Grünfeld vessel with his long baker's paddle. She walked home with the pot clutched in oven mitts, striding as briskly as she could with the heavy object, the rich aroma trailing her. By the time she arrived, the family was already at the table, joined by Sabbath guests from the village.

The family discussed other subjects with the visitors, carefully avoiding any mention of America or of gymnasium. There were songs, discussion of the Torah reading, and small talk. The family was on edge, but the guests didn't seem to notice. Frieda didn't remember the house being this full of tension since Faigie had announced that she intended to separate from her husband. Frieda was itching to get out of there and *spatzier* (stroll) leisurely with her schoolmates. But lunch went on and on, the guests oblivious, relaxing, praising the delicious *cholent.* By the time her father led them all—finally—in the grace after meals, the afternoon was well advanced. She tried to slip away, but her father called out to her. He required all his children to learn a few pages of the Talmud after Sabbath lunch. When she finally managed to break free, her friends had been walking around for hours and were already returning to synagogue for the afternoon and evening prayers.

Frieda didn't feel fully caught up to the day until nightfall, when she was back at home for the ceremony ending the Sabbath. All the lights were extinguished and the family gathered in a circle. The only illumination was the special *havdala* candle, which Frieda helped Yehudis hold as her father sang the last cycle of blessings concluding the holy day. When the Sabbath ended, they returned to the table, the center of their universe. Not only were the meals prepared and eaten there, but homework was completed, trousseaus were sewn upon it. Chaya had even delivered all her children on it, with the help of the shtetl's midwife.

The brothers sat down and opened large folios of the Talmud, their father helping them prepare for their yeshiva classes in the week ahead. The women sewed, knitted, or did needlepoint, led by Chaya and Faigie. They talked as they worked, and it was not long before the America debate broke out again. They had had a chance to consider the question, and the siblings formed two camps. Frieda's sister Berta and brother Boruch were open to the plan. Berta was the sibling closest in age to Frieda, who tagged along after her slightly older sister, always wanting to be included. Plump and pretty, Berta enjoyed life. She was smart but not as bookish as the younger sister whom she shooed away. She dismissed Frieda's reluctance; she could go to school just as well in the United States. The genial Boruch, with his round glasses and ready smile, agreed. They hadn't yet planted Czech roots so were receptive to America.

The older siblings, Faigie and Beinish, were opposed. As a Zionist, Faigie felt that if they were to go anywhere, it should be to Palestine. That was anathema to Zalman Leib—there would be no going back to the Holy Land until the Messiah came, and meanwhile its secular, socialistic kibbutz society was a horror to him. Faigie also didn't want to leave their two married sisters, Ella and Gittel (who lived in other cities), behind, which they would have to do, at least at first. Beinish, the slight, bespectacled eldest son, agreed and also urged that they consider Frieda's feelings. He was kind and gentle, with a soft spot for his baby sister.

The conversation caromed back and forth. They debated the strength or weakness of Czechoslovakia, hemmed in on the north, south, and west by Germany. They argued about the logistics, and mentioned those from Sobrance who had left before. As for the cost, they had been salting away funds at a bank in Switzerland in case of emergency, Zalman Leib smuggling the cash out on his travels. What would they do once they were in the new land? He would do just what he did in the shtetl, Zalman Leib responded. Even in America, they needed rabbis and scribes. There were two thousand slots for Czechoslovak migrants to the United States. Why shouldn't they be among them?

"No," said a quiet voice, halting all discussion. Chaya, not looking up from her knitting, her hands moving and the needles clicking, continued. "No, we are not going to America." Zalman Leib, paused, frozen, as the children gaped. They had never seen their mother defy their father.

"Chayaleh," he sputtered, "why not?"

"In America, even the cobblestones are *treyf*," she answered. She had seen what had happened to those who went to the United States. America was not a religious country; the Jews there were completely immodest. She had observed how those who had left for America behaved when they came back to Sobrance to see their families. They had departed properly, wearing beards, earlocks, and long coats. They returned clean shaven or, in the case of the ladies, wearing modern fashion, completely indistinguishable from the Gentiles. She would not risk that with her own children and grandchildren. *Chas v'sholom* (God forbid) that their next generations would be goyim. She was adamant: absolutely not.

Zalman Leib pushed back. "Plenty of people stay religious in America." They would set the example. Their family had always stayed on the path of religion. They would not stray, no matter where they lived. Chaya did not have her husband's eloquence, his mastery of argument honed through decades of Talmud study. But she didn't need it. She had her conviction that they would lose their Jewishness in America and that life was not worth living without it. Jews had always endured. The Lord had protected them through everything. They would survive the rest.

By the time they pushed their chairs back from the table after midnight, exhausted, one thing was clear. They were going nowhere. Zalman Leib had been stymied by his wife. He left the table frowning, but Frieda went to bed happy. Her gymnasium dreams were revived. As she snuggled into bed, she listened for voices on the other side of the wall but heard nothing.

⌣⟶

FRIEDA woke up the next morning to the clanging of pots and pans in the kitchen: the sounds of cleaning from the Sabbath and of preparing for the week ahead. She found the usual whirl of activity in the crowded house. Her sisters and her mother were bustling about, and her father and brothers were just coming back from the morning synagogue service. It was the first of the three daily services that shaped the rabbi's waking hours, a time for prayer but also for a bit of gossip with his friends and a *l'chaim,* a quick toast with the local plum brandy. Frieda was relieved to find her father's habitual good cheer restored. Her mother was busy preparing breakfast, placid once again.

"Are we still not going to America?" Frieda whispered to her brother Beinish as they sat down at the table. "Still not," he said, smiling.

Now that they were staying, Frieda had high hopes for her petition to go to prep school. It was a beautiful day, the sun was out, and, after all, if her father were willing to move to America, why wouldn't he let her travel the short distance to a gymnasium? For all his antique Chassidic garb and love of tradition, he had a modern streak. He read the newspapers and was proud of her good marks. His gaze was curious and alive to the wider world.

But would he be making the decision about her school, or would Chaya? After last night, Frieda was no longer sure who really called the shots. Those muffled conversations that she heard every night through the walls, those murmured lullabies that helped her drift off to sleep— had Chaya been giving Zalman Leib instructions all along? She studied her parents. But everything seemed once more as it usually was.

True to her word, Faigie, along with Beinish, went to work on their parents. Faigie sidled up to her father for a conversation as he was pulling books off the shelves to start work. She forcefully made the arguments for allowing gymnasium. Frieda was a good student; why let that go to waste? She was religious, and there was no reason to think that that would change. She would have a good income with a university degree. Zalman listened, nodding here, raising an eyebrow there. Frieda tried to read his face, glancing over out of the corner of her eye. He seemed to the ever-hopeful teen as if he were open to it. He told Faigie that he would think it over, before returning to his books.

Meanwhile, Beinish sought out Chaya and joined her in peeling carrots and potatoes at the sink. Unlike the pointed advocacy that Faigie deployed, Beinish took a softer approach. He stood next to Chaya, whispering all the reasons that Frieda should be allowed to continue her education. The only way that Frieda could tell that the two of them were talking was the incline of Beinish's head. Eventually the pile of vegetables was done and so was the conversation, Chaya wiping her hands on her apron and slipping away.

Frieda waited.

⌐

THE day of the schoolmaster's visit arrived. The educator had promised to come in the afternoon. All morning Frieda watched the clock's black hands slowly crawl around its white face. Lunch was an agony. She fidgeted, pushed her food around on her plate, then bolted for the porch with a book to wait for the teacher's arrival. Two p.m. passed, then three.

In the late afternoon, she saw her teacher coming up the street: tall and dignified, wearing a bow tie and a gray cap, his stride long. Frieda ran inside, called out, "My teacher is here," and dashed back to greet him.

Her father joined her just as the visitor was ascending the porch steps. Zalman Leib welcomed him and offered the guest chair. Frieda slipped back inside and stood next to her mother, Faigie, and Beinish.

The educator spoke, propelled by urgency. In times like these, the Czechoslovak state needed its best young people to step forward, be educated, and eventually take on leadership roles. Men and women alike would have to work to maintain Masaryk's dream. Who better than his brilliant young pupil Frieda to lead the way? She was an unusual talent, and she should attend gymnasium and then university. Anything else would be a terrible waste for her and for the country that they were trying to build.

After the schoolmaster finished, Zalman Leib weighed his reply. Frieda silently prayed, *Please, God; let the answer be yes.* Her father knew what it was to have an advanced education. He himself had received one, albeit in the Jewish world, attending not one but two yeshivas. He understood the life of the mind as well as anyone.

But, with a sigh, he told the teacher that he was sorry. He could not assent. Nobody in the family had ever gone to gymnasium. He had sent his daughter to school to secure basic knowledge. But he planned to arrange a marriage for her as he had already done for his three oldest daughters. In the meantime, she would help her mother in the house, work with her sister in her dress shop, and take care of little Yehudis. "My wife and I have discussed it, and we have made up our minds. We respect your tradition; Frieda had many years with you—I ask you to respect ours."

The teacher tried to argue. "Anything is possible for her, Rabbi. Don't let her talent go to waste. If you are concerned about Judaism, let her take the bus to Munkács, go to the Jewish gymnasium there." That was the wrong tack. Zalman Leib's face darkened. That gymnasium taught Hebrew, the holy tongue, for use in everyday conversation. It celebrated secular Judaism. It was Zionist! He was opposed to all that.

"Impossible," Zalman Leib said. Whatever hesitation he might have had, now his mind was made up. The rabbi stood and thanked his guest for coming and for all he had done for his daughter. The teacher was deflated. He hung his head as he took his leave.

Frieda rushed onto the porch. "*Tateh,* why?" she asked, tears welling in her eyes.

"Frieda, let me ask you: If you go to gymnasium, what will you do next?"

"University."

"And then what?"

"Become a doctor."

"And whom will you marry, Frieda?"

"Another doctor? A Jewish one," she added hastily.

"And do you think you two doctors married to each other will maintain *yiddishkeit,* will stay Jewish? No—you will both live as goyim. And if you don't, your children will, or your grandchildren. That, your mother and I will not allow. Never," he said firmly, with a note of sadness.

Angry and hurt, Frieda lashed back. "You were willing to go to America, the *trefeneh medina* [unkosher land], but you won't even let me go to school? I'm Czechoslovak, and I want to be a part of this country."

Confusion pinched Zalman Leib's face. "What are you talking about? We are not Czechs or Slovaks or Czechoslovaks. *Mir zenen Yiden, nur Yiden.*" ("We are Jews—just Jews.")

He tried to reach out, but she tore away and ran down the steps as her father rose out of his chair and called out her name. Chaya, Beinish, and Faigie stood in the doorway and watched her go.

Frieda ran down the block, sobbing. Out of view of the porch, she slowed to a walk. She looked down and saw that she was still clutching her book in her hand. She continued on to the end of the street, where the shtetl also ended, so she followed the river. She should throw herself in, she thought; *that* would teach them. But only drama, not self-destruction, was in her nature.

As the afternoon faded, she turned and slowly made her way back along the riverbank, but now behind the row of houses. She watched the water flow, saw the occasional fish darting through it. She envied their freedom. She would show her parents—she would *never* get married and she would find a way to get her education. Frieda stopped behind her house and walked up the steep bank to the back wall. She slid down until she was sitting on the grass, then opened her book, distraught, and began to read, sinking deep into the text to numb her pain. Once immersed, she dimly heard her family calling for her as the sun sank in the sky. Their voices barely penetrated the heavy curtain of her sadness.

Faigie's calls came closer. She turned the corner, saw her sister, and shouted into the house, "I found her! She is out back." She sat on the cool grass next to Frieda, stroked her hair, and told her she understood.

"Frieda, listen to me. You can keep reading and learning on your own. I will do it with you in the shop. And you don't have to get married if you don't want to. You can say no to the matches. Wait for the right husband, as long as it takes. *Keynmol farlozn,*" she added. "Never give up."

She slipped her hand into Frieda's, stood, and pulled her sister to her feet.

Part II

Rudolf Toussaint, 1941.

5

An Artist of War

Prague; Saturday, May 21, 1938; 6:00 p.m.

The black diplomatic Mercedes pulled away from the German legation in Prague's hilly Malá Strana neighborhood. Behind the chauffeur, in the backseat of the car, was a German officer: forty-seven years old and square-jawed. His dark blond hair was slicked back from his forehead, and he was wearing the dove-gray uniform of a Wehrmacht colonel. He was habitually calm and sat with ramrod-straight posture.

The chauffeur conveyed his passenger downhill through the narrow lanes of the venerable neighborhood, traversing roads where medieval cow paths had once woven, now cobblestoned and lined with ranks of baroque mansions. Leaving Malá Strana, they ascended again, climbing the winding road up the side of Castle Hill in the waning light of the day. At the crest, the vehicle passed into Bubeneč's flat, tree-lined streets, with their elegant villas and grand mansions, many owned by the famous Petschek clan.

At the moment, the neighborhood was experiencing a flurry of unusual activity. Limousines were waiting and people hurrying about at the residences belonging to some fifty members of the extended Petschek family. A car idled outside a compound, across which bowed a curved mansion: Otto's palace. Martha had rushed back in from a family meeting and told her three startled daughters to each pack one suitcase immediately. They were fleeing the country tonight, headed for Hungary first and then parts unknown, until they found someplace safe.

A careful observer riding through Bubeneč could not have missed the tense goings-on outside his car window—and the man in the backseat of the Mercedes was a *very* careful observer. He had trained as an artist—a lifetime ago, now—and that had taught him to really look at things. That watchfulness had evolved into wariness—including about the leader and regime that he served.

Colonel Rudolf Toussaint was the German military attaché in Prague. His Wehrmacht and the Czechoslovak military were hurtling toward conflict. A clash could trigger another war that could engulf the entire Continent. From across the border, the Wehrmacht was poised to attack the Czechs. Or were the Czech forces—who were giving every sign of full mobilization—ready to come crashing into *them*? It was the May Crisis.

To try to defuse it, Toussaint was hurrying to the Czech military headquarters, roughly halfway between Otto's palace and Prague Castle. Toussaint hated war with the particular loathing of one who had long been on intimate terms with it. He had survived some of history's ugliest confrontations during the Great War, distinguishing himself at the Battle of the Somme and many others on the bloody French-German line. He had seen a generation of friends and colleagues maimed and slaughtered in the fire, smoke, and chaos of combat.

Now Toussaint worried that the May Crisis would turn into another war. And after decades observing soldiers up close, Toussaint knew that the Czechs were not to be underestimated if that happened. They had been some of the toughest combatants of the last war, fighting their way out from far behind enemy lines in Russia, slicing through the nascent Bolshevik army. Today's Czech military had well-trained troops—more than a million highly prepared regular and reserve fighters—fleets of tanks and planes, a first-rate intelligence service, and a formidable leader in Masaryk's successor Beneš, experienced and wily, with the ear of the West and a skillfully woven protective web of mutual defense treaties. He and his countrymen were highly motivated to defend their nation. If the Czechs were backed by their allies in France and Great Britain, the Germans might well be crushed.

Toussaint hoped to spare himself and another generation of Germans that bitter experience. So he planned to appeal directly to the Czech high command, giving them his word of honor as a fellow officer that Germany was not about to strike. He knew the challenge that awaited him. Among other things, his commander-in-chief, Hitler, who contacted him frequently for updates, had a serious credibility problem after invading Austria a few months before.

Toussaint's car came to a halt before the huge Czech military head-quarters building. Like the Petschek residence, it also curved, in its case around the large traffic circle in front of it. But that arc was the only similarity between the five stories of grim gray concrete and Otto's masterpiece a few blocks away.

Toussaint stepped out of his Mercedes, snapped off a salute to the Czechoslovak guards standing in front of the building, and entered the headquarters. As much as any man in Europe at that precise moment, he had the power to stave off war. He resolved to try.

TOUSSAINT was born May 2, 1891, in Egglkofen, Germany, to a family that had long ago emigrated from France. As a youth, he showed promise as a painter and after graduating from gymnasium wanted to go to art school. But his father, who had served in the German army, had different ideas. He wanted young Rudolf to be a military man. That left him in the position of junior officer for all four bloody years of the Great War.

Toussaint had tried to transfer to the army's cartographic division after the hostilities ended. Making maps was preferable to killing, and it would also let him pursue his first love: drawing. But his transfer application was rejected, his samples apparently too artistic for the topographers.

Instead he served in a series of staff jobs in the War Ministry, where he waited out the turbulent years of the postwar era, when inflation was rampant and the succession of Weimar governments shaky. At least he had a salary to support his wife, Lilly. She was a former actress, doe-eyed and lithe-framed. She and Toussaint made a handsome couple, dancing in Berlin's nightclubs or sunbathing on the shores of Lake Constance. They became a trio when their only son, Rolf, was born in 1921.

In 1936, Toussaint was serving as an intelligence officer when he was offered the Prague attaché job, advising the German legation and officials back home. He jumped at the opportunity. He could retain his rank and utilize his expertise while also engaging in diplomacy, building bridges instead of blowing them up. Toussaint must have known that there would be challenges. The Czechs eyed Germany with suspicion and had anchored the security of their young nation in treaties and other relationships with Germany's adversaries: France, Great Britain, and even the Soviets. But he seems to have assumed that he could handle anything that was thrown at him.

There was another advantage to the Prague posting: it would put some distance between Toussaint and the Nazis. For years, he had warily watched their rise and turned aside their overtures. Like others who had come up through the ranks of the conservative Wehrmacht, he was loyal to the German army, not to the new party enforcing radical ideas and deploying paramilitary units. The Nazis had also tried approaching Lilly, apparently hoping she would embrace National Socialism and persuade her husband to do the same. But she was averse to politics and even more so to the National Socialists. Her brother had gotten tangled up with the Nazi Party and died mysteriously thereafter; whether it was by his own hand or theirs was murky, but she wanted no part of them.

The Nazis did have some success in seducing the Toussaints' son, Rolf. Fifteen years old in 1936, he was indoctrinated with the Hitlerian ideology that was omnipresent in his schools, youth programs, and summer camps. He announced to his startled parents that when he was old enough he planned to fight for the Waffen-SS, the military arm of Hitler's paramilitary force. Toussaint refused to allow it. He told a sullen Rolf that he could join the Wehrmacht if he wished when he came of age at eighteen. But the SS? Never.

The Czechs had no idea that Toussaint harbored his own reservations about the Nazis, and his life in Prague got off to a rocky start. The first sign of the bumpy road ahead came when the German legation notified their hosts about the arrival of the new military attaché at the end of 1936. Instead of the customary welcome, Toussaint was met with frosty silence. Czech officialdom looked warily at their much larger neighbor and their own sizable German minority.

Despite their initial refusal to acknowledge him, Toussaint set out to convince the Czechs of his goodwill. In his first months on the job, he attended receptions and built one-on-one relationships. He told people of how he had personally met with the father of the country, Masaryk, on an earlier visit. When the government organized a hunting trip and invited every attaché except Toussaint, his fellow attachés advocated on his behalf until the Czechs relented.

Toussaint had trouble with the Czech press, too. In February 1937, a Prague newspaper ran an insulting piece stringing together a series of half-truths and outright lies about his career. The following October, Toussaint was stunned to read an article implicating him in an attempt to kidnap a German right-wing dissident who was living in Prague. The paper reported a plot against Otto Strasser, an ex-Nazi turned Hitler opponent. Strasser was purportedly to be snatched using Toussaint's car, by his chauffeur.

Toussaint insisted to the head of his legation that he was innocent but that his driver (who had supposedly recruited Sudeten Germans willing to carry out the job) was entirely capable of such a crime. Toussaint suspected that an ardent Nazi who had departed from the legation staff was behind the scheme. Toussaint and his boss immediately went to the Czech police, expressed their willingness to cooperate, and supported a fast and effective resolution. The police interviewed the plotters, and the true story eventually came out, but a stain remained on Toussaint's reputation.

In November 1937, Toussaint was given the opportunity to escape these irritants. He was offered a posting to Bucharest, Romania, another beautiful city and one where tensions with Germany were less pronounced. But he demurred. The Czechs' suspicions of him notwithstanding, he had fallen in love with Prague. He worked out a compromise with Berlin: he would retain Prague as his home base and cover Bucharest remotely, persuading them that the "situation was too complex for a new attaché to handle"—a prescient observation indeed.

⁓

As 1938 dawned, it was clear that there was a gulf between Germany's private and public statements to the Czechs. Privately, Berlin instructed Toussaint and everyone else at the legation to communicate that Germany had no ill intentions. Toussaint complied, hoping that it was true, while trying to continue improving relations with his (rightly) suspicious Czech interlocutors. Yet, publicly, Hitler was increasingly aggressive. On February 20, in an international broadcast, he complained vehemently that ten million Germans in Czechoslovakia and Austria were being tormented by their host countries. He threatened that, like England and other great powers, Germany would protect its people abroad.

But the speech was mere prologue to the shock that awaited the Czechs at 5:30 a.m. on March 12, when Germany, after alternately bullying and negotiating with the Austrian government, entered Austria at the supposed invitation of its leaders. It was the *Anschluss*—the annexation. Hitler had achieved what he had sought ever since the Austrian Nazi uprising of 1934—the one percolating outside Otto's hospital window—had failed. Now the Czechs were in a vise, with German power on their northern and southern borders. In Prague, Minister Ernst Eisenlohr (the head of the German legation) assured Beneš that Hitler would respect Czechoslovakia as a sovereign state. In Berlin, Hermann Göring, the air force chief, gave the Czech envoy his *Ehrenwort* (word of honor) to the same effect.

Still, Czechoslovakia was jittery—giving Toussaint the opportunity to be a peacemaker. On March 16, 1938, he received an urgent message: Come at once to the Czech General Staff Headquarters. There, a visibly alarmed group of senior officers told him that "according to information available to the Czech General Staff, [German] military preparations were taking place in Bavaria and Saxony which were causing anxiety to Czechoslovakia." Toussaint knew that the reports were false. He would have been aware of any imminent invasion through his many close Wehrmacht relationships. He replied, truthfully, that he "knew nothing of such preparations and that there was no cause at all for anxiety in Czechoslovakia." They cross-examined him, told him that they would further investigate his claims, and dismissed him.

Toussaint won another small measure of credibility when his assertion was proven correct. This was what he had been working for: to prevent conflict instead of wage it. It was a small victory, but the trust accrued would be useful—and sooner than he thought.

THE focus of Czech anxiety soon moved from the German side of the border to their own. Starting on April 23, 1938, the Sudetendeutsche Partei (Sudeten German Party, SdP) held its annual congress in Carlsbad, the famous spa town in northwestern Czechoslovakia. The SdP's demand: power for the ethnic German minority of Czechoslovakia and autonomy for the area of that state where its members were a majority, the Sudetenland region abutting Germany.

The party was led by Konrad Henlein and Karl Hermann Frank.

Henlein, a stout gym teacher and World War I veteran, was a recent convert to Nazism and displayed all the zeal of an acolyte. Henlein's deputy, Frank, would loom large in Toussaint's career. Tall and thin, he wore a perpetually sour expression on his gaunt face. Like many Nazis, he had failed at the traditional military. Although he was Henlein's number two, Frank was more adept at organizing and more ruthless at party discipline. With Frank and Henlein at their head, the Czech Sudeten Germans thronged the streets of the northern towns, crying, *"Ein Volk, ein Reich, ein Führer!"* ("One people, one empire, one leader!") That fervent ethnic German nationalism was heavily flavored by the anti-Semitism that Hitler espoused.

Then came the May Crisis. On May 19, reports started circulating through Prague that the German army was assembling near the northern border. The Czechs were already on edge. Backed by intelligence reports, they believed the German troop movements signaled an imminent invasion. On the twentieth, Beneš, Defense Minister František Machník, and Commanding General Ludvík Krejčí ordered emergency measures. Overnight, placards were pasted up all over Prague, proclaiming that the military was being mobilized. Several hundred thousand Czech reservists and specialists began streaming into the Sudetenland with mechanized infantry, guns, mortars, and other arms.

Perhaps Toussaint, who remained an ardent amateur painter, was standing before a canvas, brush in hand, when news of Czech military stirrings first reached him early that Saturday morning. Why the sudden activity? The attaché network would have alerted him if there were regular maneuvers scheduled. At around 9:30 a.m., he called his contact at the Czech General Staff and was assured that this was just an exercise. But when Toussaint headed to the legation, traded notes with his colleagues, and talked to the other attachés, it became increasingly apparent that it was not; it smelled as if it could be something more serious.

Toussaint reached out to the General Staff liaison once more at around noon and received a different story: the Czechs were taking measures "for the restoration of law and order in the frontier region." Toussaint telegraphed back to Berlin that the call-up was "provisionally concerned with internal politics." But as he puzzled through the size and scale of the military measures the Czechs were taking, something didn't feel right—troops appeared to be mobilizing for battle, and in huge numbers. Seventy thousand of the best reservists were marching into the Sudetenland, as were another 114,000 specialists. In total, nearly two hundred thousand troops were called up, and the Czech army swelled to a force of almost four hundred thousand. Could the Czechs be preparing a blow against Hitler?

Toussaint decided to find out from the highest authority available to him: the head of the Czech General Staff, Krejčí. At six p.m., he was driven to the military headquarters in Vítězné náměstí (Victory Square), adjacent to Bubeneč, to meet with the general.

⌒

TOUSSAINT soon found himself standing before Krejčí. The name meant "tailor" in Czech, and the man could have passed for one: short, balding, and pug-nosed, with thinning black hair combed over his high forehead, and a sizable paunch. In fact he was shrewd and professional—a soldier who had been personally chosen by Masaryk to harden the Czech forces and had subsequently built a formidable military. He was also known for his brutal honesty.

Toussaint described everything he had learned about the technical military measures that the Czechs were taking. He told Krejčí that he could not view them as training exercises; they were mobilization measures. In his report to Berlin, he had given the Czechs the benefit of the doubt, willing to chalk all this activity up to pacifying the Sudeten Germans. But he no longer believed that and told the Czech general as much.

True to form, Krejčí was straightforward. This was no mere exercise, nor an internal political move; it was to protect the borders from German attack and was justified by reports of the movement of German troops toward the borders. Krejčí looked Toussaint in the eye and declared that he had "irrefutable proof that in Saxony a concentration of from eight to ten [German] divisions had taken place." Toussaint vehemently denied any such movement—giving his word as an officer. The two went back and forth. Finally, Krejčí agreed to reverse the mobilization, at least in part, if what Toussaint swore was true.

As Toussaint returned to the legation to confer with his colleagues and cable Berlin, similar interventions were going on all over Europe: in Berlin, Paris, and London. The Germans and Czechs were claiming no hostile intent, while the French and British were assuming the worst and attempting to get both sides to back down. No one knew for sure what was going on. Toussaint and Minister Eisenlohr telegrammed their information to Berlin and worked late into the night. At 10:50 p.m., they cabled for permission to begin burning their files, in case conflict was imminent. Throughout the night and the next day, Toussaint and his colleagues anxiously waited. Meanwhile, reports arrived of flashes of violence, including the Czechs shooting two Sudeten Germans—Nikolas Boehm and Georg Hoffman—who had refused to stop at a border crossing. But no burn order came. By the end of the day on Sunday, it seemed that tensions were easing.

If Toussaint heaved a sigh of relief, it was a hesitant one. Although both sides had taken a step back from the brink, the situation in the Sudetenland was still extremely fraught. The Czech army and police were on high alert, and it felt as if Prague were under martial law. The Sudeten Germans remained keyed up by Hitler and Henlein's rhetoric and by the presence of the Czech army and police. The Red Defense was a threat, too. These Communist militiamen, whose disdain for the "bourgeois" Czechoslovak government was exceeded only by their hate of Hitler, were also ready to jump into any fray—they hoped that this was the beginning of the revolution. The forces of Czech democracy, the armed Communists, and the Fascist-leaning German minority were a combustible mixture. Then Hitler personally tossed a lit match into the middle of things: his military attaché in Prague.

⌒

TOUSSAINT and Hitler were acquainted by 1938. Perhaps they first met at the annual gathering of the military attachés from all over the world in Berlin, which the Führer periodically attended. To Hitler, the Wehrmacht was the establishment, and Toussaint certainly looked the part. Hitler had studied his appearance closely, referring to him as "the brown-eyed" officer. As tensions rose in 1938, Hitler reached out directly to Toussaint in Prague, soliciting his on-the-ground observations. We can safely surmise that when the Führer called, Toussaint kept his reservations about the Nazi Party to himself.

On Monday, May 23, in the middle of the May Crisis, Toussaint received a perplexing order from the bureaucrats in Berlin. He was to represent the Führer at the funeral of the two German sympathizers who had just been killed. The ceremony would be held in the Sudetenland. And, worse still, it would be in Cheb, one of the area's hottest flashpoints. The town, adjacent to the northern border with Germany, was overwhelmingly ethnically German. In Cheb (or Eger, as its German-speaking majority called it), separatism, militarism, and anti-Semitism had seeped into the town like the black tar of an oil spill.

It was madness to send the most senior German military officer in the country into perhaps the most unstable spot in all of Europe—all the world—that week. Most in the border region were on edge, and many were armed. All it would take was one hothead on either side to set off a conflagration. The slightest miscalculation by a Czech soldier or policeman, let alone a Sudeten Nazi, could trigger it.

Toussaint and his colleagues protested his attending the funeral. The legation urged Berlin to reconsider. But word came back that the objections had been overridden by the highest authority in Germany: the Führer himself. Hitler felt the eyes of the Sudetenland, and of the world, upon him. He wanted someone whom he knew personally to represent him—someone who looked the part. Toussaint would be Hitler's emissary at the funeral. He was ordered to hand carry two wreaths from the Führer and to lay them at the graves of the fallen men.

There could be no further argument and no question of disobedience. So Toussaint made the three-hour trip from Prague to the border for the Wednesday-morning ceremony.

TOUSSAINT was soon in Cheb's cemetery, immaculate in his gray Wehrmacht uniform. In front of him were the graves of Nikolas Boehm and Georg Hoffman, the two Sudeten Germans who had been shot while riding together on a motorcycle during the clash with Czechoslovak troops at the nearby border. Exactly what had happened and who was to blame was unclear—but not to the tens of thousands of German residents of the region who stood behind Toussaint. The crowd was sure the two men were innocent; they were martyrs to the cause of Hitler. The dictator's popularity was far higher here than in his own country.

The silent throng of thousands had raised their arms and hands aloft, locking them in the rigid diagonal Nazi salute. Standing on Toussaint's left was Henlein, and next to him, Frank—the Sudeten leaders. Both were holding their arms stiff and straight, mirroring the mob. Toussaint maintained a military salute, the side of his hand at his brow.

The atmosphere was tense. Hitler was not above using provocateurs to incite violence. Toussaint was a prime target for a Communist or other agitator as well. The crosshairs of a sniper's rifle could be aimed at his back that very moment. The air was charged as he stepped forward. He placed first one wreath, then the other, on the graves, adjusting the ribbons, displaying Hitler's name clearly. He stepped back and snapped off a sharp salute.

He returned to his place next to Frank and Henlein. No shot was fired. The Czech police and soldiers had given the occasion a wide berth, melting away during the memorial. As for the Führer, it seemed that he would save any provocation for another day. Soon the crowd dissipated, and Toussaint was ushered away in his chauffeured staff car. The high-water point of the May Crisis had passed.

Toussaint must have been relieved that trouble had been avoided. As the green of the countryside undulated gently outside his car window on his return to Prague, he could loosen his tunic and bask in a private kind of glory. He had helped prevent war through diplomatic skill. The Czechs, too, were grimly satisfied that they had held off Hitler.

Neither Toussaint nor the Czechs had any idea of the dangerous consequences of defusing the May Crisis. Hitler felt humiliated. He didn't care whether the Germans were outnumbered, whether the Allies would back the Czechs, whether the Wehrmacht was ready. On May 30, three German service chiefs received Hitler's Plan Green for the invasion of Czechoslovakia. The version that predated the May Crisis had read, "It is not my intention to smash Czechoslovakia in the near future." But the new one declared, in unequivocal terms, "It is my unalterable decision to smash Czechoslovakia by military action in the near future . . . October 1, 1938, at the latest."

THE summer of 1938 was blazing, bringing a blanket of heat so stifling that it seemed to muffle overt hostilities. In a June report to Berlin, Toussaint wrote, "The situation here is relaxing in that the Sudeten Germans have become more cautious under the pressure of the military, [and] on the other hand, the government is anxious to avoid an incident." But although conditions did not worsen, neither, to Toussaint's disappointment, did they improve. Toussaint believed a negotiated settlement was the solution. He was a loyal German, and he was sympathetic to the complaints of the Sudetens. But what he did not want was a war, which risked disaster for his countrymen and everyone concerned.

By August, the situation was deteriorating once more. Toussaint cabled his superiors: "Negotiations between the government and Sudetens are hopelessly deadlocked." That was no accident; Henlein and Frank had instructions from Hitler to only feign negotiations. Henlein secretly described the essence of their orders: "We must always demand so much that we can never be satisfied." The harder the Czechs labored to find a solution, the more the Sudeten Germans resisted one.

At the end of the summer, Toussaint feared that, without a negotiated settlement, there would be conflict. The Czechs had demonstrated their willingness to fight. Who won would depend on who struck first and on whether the British, French, and Soviets would actually aid the Czechs. The British obligation was solely moral, but the French were bound by a long-standing treaty and the Soviets by a newer one that President Beneš had secured (an expedient that would have caused Otto to shudder but was now desperately needed). In August, Toussaint wrote to his superior, General Alfred Jodl, that those three major powers' embassies had said that they would assist the Czechs at any cost. But "as to how these states will actually behave at the crucial moment, he cannot predict."

As September dawned, envoys from each of the three countries secretly suggested to President Beneš that they were not prepared to fight. With horror, Beneš and the Czechs saw their support evaporate. The French, whose treaty commitment was the cornerstone of Beneš's elaborate twenty-year project to secure democracy, wobbled. They intimated their tepid intentions, though they scrupulously did not disclose them publicly, and especially not to Germany. Great Britain's obligation was solely to France if it was attacked; the British had no direct treaty with Czechoslovakia and were highly resistant to going to war for the benefit of that small, faraway nation. And the Soviet obligation was looking contingent as well. Beneš's whole treaty structure was falling apart, leaving the Czechs with no hope of holding off Germany. In a desperate bid to please his allies, Beneš made increasingly generous offers to the

Sudeten Germans, culminating on September 5 in a meeting at Prague Castle, where he gave their leaders a paper and pen and told them to write down what they wanted—he would sign it, no matter their demands.

Confused, the Sudeten negotiators played for time. It was difficult to turn down a blank check. But Henlein was under orders from Hitler not to parley. The Führer's ego had been wounded by the May Crisis, and he wanted to make a point by destroying the Czechs. Henlein contrived a clash with Czech police, using it as an excuse to break off negotiations.

IN the midst of the deterioration, General Jodl called Toussaint to Berlin. What he had to share was too sensitive for anything but a face-to-face conversation. Jodl confided that Hitler intended to wage war against the Czechs. Jodl wanted a candid assessment from Toussaint. *Will the Czechs fight back? Will the Allies join?* Toussaint told Jodl that he "judge[d] the Czech situation to be favorable." That is, the Germans could beat the Czechs alone. Then he pivoted to talking Jodl out of trying. The "general situation," he cautioned, was "serious." If the Allies intervened, Germany would be at risk of a larger war, one it could well lose. And the Wehrmacht did not seem ready for one; Toussaint was "shocked about the slack mood and aversion to fight among the officers (with a few praiseworthy exceptions)." Perhaps fearing that he had given away his own ambivalence, Toussaint added that of course *he* was determined.

Once back at the legation, Toussaint confided his true feelings to a colleague, First Counselor Andor Hencke. The short, prematurely gray Hencke was an amiable career diplomat. Toussaint considered him a friend and vice versa. But Toussaint's indiscretion was reckless; Hencke was also a member of the National Socialist German Workers' Party (NSDAP). Nevertheless, Toussaint trusted him. He informed Hencke that there would be war by the end of September or the beginning of October. Toussaint bitterly criticized the Führer himself: "Hitler has established a nice, big Wehrmacht and now wants to play with his soldiers for the first time."

To Toussaint, it was no game. He and his legation colleagues would be at risk from all sides. The Luftwaffe would surely bomb Prague Castle. The legation was right next to and just below it; it would not escape collateral damage. Even if the staff survived the bombing, they would be enemy nationals in hostile territory. Hencke and Toussaint quietly supervised the construction of a bomb shelter beneath the legation. They took the German air force attaché, Friedrich Möricke, into their confidence about the coming attack as well. All their lives were now at risk.

⌣

TOUSSAINT's dismay was deepened by Hitler's speech at the annual Nazi rally in Nuremberg that September. Screaming and raving, Hitler openly referenced his humiliation during the Czechoslovak partial mobilization of the May Crisis as grounds for military involvement. He bellowed that the Prague government had deliberately tried to wipe out the Sudeten Germans "like helpless wild-fowl for every expression of their national sentiment." Toussaint felt "completely broken" after the speech. Now Germany faced a real risk of defeat and further devastation—the First World War and its aftermath all over again.

Hitler's speech had a very different effect on the Sudeten Germans. The Führer's rantings were taken by Henlein, Frank, and their followers as an invitation to open rebellion. Violent riots broke out immediately. The next day, Toussaint informed Berlin that the Czechs were rushing troops to the border region in response to the escalating demands of the Sudeten leadership. On September 15, Henlein raised the stakes even higher, proclaiming, "We want to return to the Reich." He proposed that Czechoslovakia cede all territory with a majority-German population to Hitler within forty-eight hours. In response, the Czechs dissolved the SdP and declared a state of emergency.

The legation was flooded with irate phone calls and hate mail, all promising retaliation against the diplomats for Hitler's and Henlein's behavior. Anti-Hitler and anti-Sudeten protests raged through Prague, with thousands massing outside the legation, spilling down the narrow streets. Czech police and military assumed stations outside the site but were vastly outnumbered by the crowds. Toussaint, the senior military official on the premises, was charged with protecting the building. He formulated a defense plan. If the mob broke through, he, Möricke, and a few others would hold them off with tear gas while the rest of the staff escaped by climbing ladders and dropping over the walls into the adjacent gardens of the Swedish and British legations. The Swedish envoy said that he would welcome them. The British envoy was less enthusiastic but promised that he would not bar escapees.

While Toussaint and his colleagues were contemplating ways of defending themselves, they learned that Henlein and Frank had responded to the crisis, too: by bolting across the border to Germany. Contempt for that decision was evident in the cable Toussaint sent (with Hencke) to Berlin: "Spreading of the news that Sudeten German Party leaders had fled has had a crushing effect in the German area. Czechoslovak Government at present really master of situation."

As Toussaint attended to the defense of the legation and looked out the window at the thousands of protesters, he was more determined than ever to secure some kind of negotiated resolution. He just needed an opening. Events far away were about to provide one.

⌣⟶

THE British prime minister, Neville Chamberlain, was a tall, mustachioed businessman and Conservative Party stalwart. He had risen through the political ranks from his days as mayor of Birmingham. Like Toussaint, he was one of the Great War survivors, part of a generation that would do almost anything to prevent a return to violence on that scale. Their reaction to Hitler's Nuremberg speech was the same: horror. But, unlike Toussaint, Chamberlain was not confined to quarters. On September 14, Chamberlain made an overture to Hitler: he would come to Germany to negotiate a resolution. The dictator accepted; he was not yet ready to openly display his insistence on war.

Toussaint and his fellow German diplomats in Prague got no advance details about the preparation for the first meeting between Chamberlain and Hitler, which took place on September 15 at the Berghof near Berchtesgaden. Nor did they receive dispatches from their headquarters about what went on during the meeting. Like citizens across the world, Toussaint had to gather his intelligence by scrutinizing media reports: listening intently to the radio and poring over newspaper coverage. After the Berchtesgaden conference ended, Toussaint and his colleagues in Prague took a break from standing guard at the windows and digging their air-raid shelter to peruse the scanty official communiqué. Then they went next door to the British legation and, careful not to reveal how little they knew, gleaned what additional details they could. It seemed that Chamberlain would attempt to broker a compromise of some kind between Hitler and Beneš.

Toussaint and his colleagues were dubious, and all the more so when they learned that Germany had refused to provide the British with notes from the meeting. So it came as a surprise to Toussaint when, on September 21, the Czechs accepted a British-French proposal to cede significant portions of the Sudetenland to Germany to avoid war. Beneš had acceded under duress after initially rejecting the terms. Chamberlain had warned him that if he did not accept, the Allies would not defend him. Beneš's self-defense project relied on his allies, but that gave them enormous leverage over him as well.

The next day, the Prague demonstrations resumed but with new force, fueled by outrage at the British and French pressure on the Czechs. The Watchers of Prague felt that their city was under threat, and now they took to its streets not to admire but to protect them. When they came up the narrow medieval lanes of Malá Strana, it was no longer just the German legation that was their target—they also took their pickets and chants to the British and French embassies. Chamberlain and the French prime minister, Édouard Daladier, would return to Germany for a second meeting to try to close the deal, and the Praguers were enraged. They marched on the castle and protested Beneš and the Czechoslovak government for assenting.

On September 22, Chamberlain arrived in Bad Godesberg to resume discussions with Hitler. At 10:35 that morning, Toussaint was on guard, tear gas and firearm at hand, stealing glances out the legation windows. A secretary approached; General Jodl was on the phone for him. It was the first call that the legation had received from Germany in days; communication had dried up precisely when they needed it most.

Toussaint got on the line.

Jodl, sounding concerned, asked Toussaint how he was getting along. Was he all right?

Toussaint, facing the daily threat of assault by the Czechs from the ground and his own forces from the air, could not resist a touch of sarcasm. "Thanks, excellently," he replied.

The dark humor did not seem to register. Jodl hurriedly explained the reason for his call. As Hitler and Chamberlain were preparing to meet, German intelligence had intercepted a message from Prague that a mob was about to, or had, stormed the legation and killed Minister Eisenlohr. Göring, the head of the air force, was preparing to bombard Prague on the Führer's command.

Although Jodl did not say it in so many words, Hitler would have liked nothing better. Hitler regretted the assurances that he had given in his previous meeting with Chamberlain and had startled the prime minister by telling him that the previous deal was now off the table—much more was needed. The Sudetenland would no longer satisfy him; he now required additional terrain. And a guarantee of a reasonable timeline for the evacuation of Czech inhabitants was off the table. Hitler was clearly looking for any excuse to abandon the peace talks. He was champing at the bit to "play with his soldiers for the first time," as Toussaint had intuited after meeting with Jodl earlier that month.

Toussaint defused the situation. He replied that Minister Eisenlohr was not even *in* Prague. Hencke, operating as chargé d'affaires in the envoy's absence, was in good health, thanks to the police who were holding the legation gates. The protesters had moved up the street to the castle and were now focused on Beneš. Jodl was clearly disappointed by this news and made no effort to hide it. He hung up and went to inform Göring that the rumor was incorrect.

Toussaint sought out Hencke to debrief him after the call. Both were incredulous that false reports had been passed to the Führer's headquarters—but even more agitating was Jodl's evident regret that no legation personnel had been killed.

That day and the next, Toussaint and his colleagues kept up a steady stream of cables to Germany. As with his call with Jodl, Toussaint's candid reporting proved critical to keeping peace talks alive. His and Hencke's warning that the Czechs were mobilizing for war arrived on the twenty-third, as a recalcitrant Hitler seemed ready to break off his parley with Chamberlain. When the news of the Czechs' readiness to fight arrived, the room fell into "dead silence." Hitler was stunned. The information was intended by Toussaint and Hencke to serve as a warning of the danger posed by the Czech military, and it had a sobering effect on the Führer. He backed down, assuming a more placatory stance with Chamberlain. While the talks continued, Hitler repeated his pledge not to strike first, and he eased off on a number of sticking points in the negotiations.

Twice in as many days, Toussaint had helped avert war. By the time Chamberlain departed Bad Godesberg on the following morning, the negotiators had felt their way through to a possible compromise. Hitler assured the British prime minister that the Sudetenland was his last demand, and he agreed to allow two more days for the evacuation of the territory, extending his ultimate deadline to October 1. Chamberlain, burned by Hitler's previous flip-flop, announced he would communicate the terms to the Czechs, though he would make no guarantees that they would accept.

⌒

TOUSSAINT hoped for peace but readied for war. On the night of September 23, as the Hitler-Chamberlain talks drew to a close, the staff of the German legation gathered. With Czech mobilization, the police and army had sealed off the building. Both the German and the Czech armies were ready for battle, and word came of French and British preparations as well. At 11:30 p.m., Toussaint and Hencke gave orders to burn all files. A bonfire was lit in the garden behind the legation and fed with reams of cables, memos, and letters, fragments of paper flying through the air. Thick volumes of documents were hacked to pieces with hatchets before being tossed into the flames.

It was almost dawn before all the documents were gone. Toussaint personally destroyed the military files; they would be among the most valuable if the legation were seized by Czechs, whether by the government or a mob. As the sun rose over a tense Prague, a sweat- and soot-streaked Toussaint said to the equally exhausted Hencke, "If peace breaks out, my men and I will be lost—we've burned it all down to the last administrative file. . . . We have only pencils and erasers left."

In the following days, Toussaint again made use of those pencils to help prevent an accidental war. He cautioned against German provocations, writing to Berlin that "[a]ll attachés said the incidents at the border, such as the attacks against customs houses and the propaganda, damage Germany's prestige" and were making the British "extraordinarily hostile towards the Germans."

Then came the waiting. Toussaint knew it well from his First World War years sitting in trenches. He learned through his Wehrmacht network the date and time of the German strike and told Hencke: September 28 at two p.m. The legation staff were free to come and go during that tense week, but for security reasons they largely stayed cooped up together during the day. With few exceptions, most spent nights there, too. If there was a surprise, their hastily dug bomb shelter would be better than nothing. They sat together without regard for rank, Toussaint brushing shoulders with the most junior civil servants. Berlin gave them no guidance, so they again relied on radio and newspapers and slipped out to visit their foreign diplomatic colleagues and trade rumors. They tried to pump the British head of mission—their next-door neighbor— for information about the status of Chamberlain's offer. The diplomat, though known for his dislike of the Czechs and their president, made no secret of his disgust at the Germans' unwillingness to compromise.

On the twenty-fifth, Beneš angrily rejected Hitler's new terms. The Czechs were not bluffing about preferring war to humiliation. The Czechs and the Germans took up positions on either side of the border. The British and the French mobilized as well. On the twenty-sixth, Hitler gave a shrieking speech attacking Beneš:

> It's not a question of Czechoslovakia, the problem is Mr. Benes! . . . In 1918, under the slogan of the "self-determination of peoples," Central Europe was torn to bits and shuffled around by a few mad so-called "statesmen" . . . Czechoslovakia owes its very existence to this procedure! . . . The Czech state was born in a lie and the father of this lie was Benes . . . *He* convinced the framers at Versailles . . . The whole development of the country since 1918 is proof of one thing only: Mr. Benes was determined to exterminate German identity . . . I have put forward an offer to Mr. Benes . . . The decision is his now: peace or war!

Hitler was so carried away in his revisionism that he even slandered the long-dead U.S. president Woodrow Wilson, the "itinerant professor" who peddled the "poison of democratic jabber." And the new decibel levels he reached caused some formerly neutral and even admiring observers to believe he was losing his sanity.

By now it was unofficially known throughout the legation that hostilities would commence on the twenty-eighth and even that they would begin at 2 p.m.; it was hard to keep a secret in such close quarters. Legation employees made the most of September 27, believing it would be the last day of peace for some time. It was unusually beautiful for that late in the month, and the staff took turns stepping out of the legation and savoring sun-dappled Golden Prague. Hencke got a haircut and paid his bill to the barber and to his tailor, who clasped hands with the diplomat in farewell.

That night, Toussaint and Hencke sent their final warning that the Czechs would not be pushovers: "Calm in Prague. Last mobilization measures carried out . . . Press and radio strengthen the Czech people in their belief that France, Great Britain, and Russia have already given a binding promise of military help . . . [T]otal call-up is 1,000,000; field army 800,000." On this calculus, the Czechs and the French alone outmanned the Germans by more than two to one.

The apprehension evident in the note was by no means confined to Toussaint and Hencke. The ranks of the career Wehrmacht from which Toussaint came had long opposed conflict with Czechoslovakia in favor of a negotiated resolution; they feared and even predicted defeat at the hands of the motivated and substantial Czech forces backed by France, Britain, and perhaps others. Some were prepared to do something about it. Senior Wehrmacht officers, including many with whom Toussaint had served, were discussing a coup. If the British and the French stood up to Hitler, they would find willing partners within his own officer corps, at least some of whom were ready to depose the Führer if the West led the way.

The would-be defectors were not motivated by any love of Czechoslovak democracy; they resented Hitler's military adventurism. It was their lives at stake, and the lives of their soldiers and their sons. And war, should it come, could even serve as an opportunity to wrest control from the Nazi Party and restore sanity to German policy.

In Berlin, Hitler had a restless night. He feared being outnumbered; he was worried about losing. He knew that even fellow Fascists such as Göring and Mussolini were hesitant. Most troubling, the German people seemed unenthusiastic—the day after his big speech attacking Beneš, he had appeared on his balcony at the chancellery to watch a parade of Wehrmacht troops headed for the Czech border. Few members of the public came, and those who did were tepid. He was later heard to mutter, "There is no way I can wage war with this people."

⌒

THE next morning broke clear and sunny; another beautiful fall day in Prague. The city was eerily tranquil, but its peace was a symptom of war: the city's military-age population was largely at the border, waiting for the German attack. It felt like a Sunday or a holiday, only quieter. There was little work to do with Hitler's deadline approaching—so Toussaint and Hencke decided to go out for an early lunch. They strolled to a famous old Prague restaurant that was a short walk from the legation. As they ate and drank, Toussaint was relaxed, while Hencke was on edge.

After lunch, the two friends walked back past the palaces and churches lining the narrow medieval streets. At two p.m. sharp, they found themselves in front of the British legation. They stopped and stared at the sky, blue and cloudless. They expected to see German planes appear for reconnaissance, or perhaps the feared bombing runs, but only songbirds were flying overhead. The men returned to their legation. One hour passed, then a second, then a third. But nothing happened.

At five p.m., Hencke, needing something to do, departed for the Foreign Ministry to arrange the terms for Czech handling of legation staff and their abandoned building in the event of war. The Czechs were befuddled and asked him what he was doing there. Didn't he know that Chamberlain was heading to Germany for a third visit? Back at the legation, Toussaint received a radio message from Berlin. Hitler had invited Chamberlain, Italy's Mussolini, and France's Daladier to confer: the Munich Conference. The message was terse and straightforward, with no room for interpretation or predictions. Nevertheless, after Hencke rushed back and compared notes with Toussaint, the chargé d'affaires was relieved. If Hitler had invited the other leaders to meet and they had accepted, it was hard to believe that the parties to the conflict would come to blows tonight.

Suddenly, official channels fell silent. There were no further communications from Berlin. All their information came from the media, with dribs and drabs from Toussaint's attaché network. It was scanty; whatever negotiations were going on were not being shared. They waited, together with the world, as the four powers debated the fate of the Czechs.

It's hard to know what Toussaint was thinking then. But perhaps he allowed himself to hope. Maybe all his efforts over the course of the year, averting crises and moderating conflict in March, May, and September, *had* made a difference.

⌒

IN the middle of the night on September 30, Hencke was awakened by an urgent call. It was from Berlin. The Foreign Ministry dictated the text of the Munich Agreement to him. Hencke's job was to formally transmit it in writing to the Czechs, who had been excluded from the negotiations. A six a.m. appointment at the Foreign Ministry was set, then moved to six thirty to allow adequate time to prepare the document informing Beneš and his colleagues that their nation was being dismembered. The legation twittered to life in the still-dark night, as multiple secretaries typed up Hencke's notes and Toussaint and his attaché team arranged transportation.

Toussaint had been hoping for peace. He had worked hard for it. But the details of the Munich Agreement must have startled him. This went beyond what the Czechs, British, and French had initially agreed to less than two weeks ago. Not only was Hitler getting all the German-majority border towns, he was also receiving many *Czech*-majority municipalities: 11,000 square miles in all, with almost a million Czechs under his sway. The Czechs were losing most of their industry: chemicals, glass, textiles, iron, and steel, not to mention the vast seams of brown coal that Otto Petschek had once controlled.

Jodl had told Toussaint that the Führer intended to disable the Czechs. He had done so, with the active assistance of their closest allies. Even the United States had gotten into the act, Franklin Roosevelt writing the identical letter urging settlement to both Beneš and Hitler, as if they were morally equivalent. To Beneš, it was "the final blow" before the arrival of the Munich Agreement itself.

The West didn't know it, but it had abandoned another potential ally: the group of Wehrmacht officers who had planned the coup against Hitler. Dejected, they set aside their plans. The Führer's hand was strengthened now. War was coming.

⌒

ON March 15, 1939, Hitler approached Toussaint in the receiving room at Prague Castle. It had been five months and two weeks since the Munich Agreement. Despite his promises that if the Sudeten issue was resolved he would seek no more land, Hitler had gobbled up what remained of Czechoslovakia in its weakened, post-Munich state. Beneš had abdicated and fled to exile in London, and Hitler had browbeaten his successor, Emil Hácha, an elderly, frail judge, into submission. The day before meeting with Toussaint, Hitler called Hácha to Berlin and, on threat of invasion, forced him to sign a document dismembering the country that had been created just twenty years before. Slovak independence under local Fascist rule was granted, and the remaining Czech lands would become the Protektorat Böhmen and Mähren (Protectorate of Bohemia and Moravia). Britain and France, realizing what they were up against, withdrew their ambassadors. As Toussaint had feared in 1938, the countdown to European war had begun.

Hitler had followed his army into the Czech lands and was greeting German legation members in a magnificent salon at the castle. He worked his way down the receiving line perfunctorily. He arrived at Toussaint. Before him alone, the Führer stopped and lingered to speak. Hitler trained his eye on the slightly taller Toussaint, who was wearing Wehrmacht dress grays, as he had done when attending that dangerous funeral in Cheb as this man's envoy. Hitler too was in military uniform, a simple brown one that he had designed for himself. The two men each wore Germany's medal for outstanding bravery: the Iron Cross, First Class, earned by both in battle in World War I.

The Führer had just captured Prague Castle without a shot being fired. Hitler was smiling, taking his time chatting with Toussaint. It was a moment of triumph for the Führer, and Toussaint had helped him secure it. If Hitler had known what Toussaint had thought, felt, and said through it all, how Toussaint had fought his efforts to trigger a war, or his sentiments about the Nazis, the Führer might not have been quite so cordial. If Toussaint experienced any unease, he did not show it. Finally, Hitler moved on down the line, much more brusque with the others in the room.

Toussaint soon received another sign of the Führer's trust: the Oberkommando der Wehrmacht (Wehrmacht High Command, known as the OKW) in Berlin informed him that he would be moving east, setting up shop full-time as attaché in Belgrade. Toussaint must have wondered, after his Prague experience, how long it would be before he was welcoming Hitler to take possession of Yugoslavia.

⌒

As Toussaint wound down his service in Prague, the permanent bureaucracy of German occupation moved in. They arrived by the thousands, military and civilian. The Watchers of Prague looked away or openly wept for their city—its buildings physically intact but its whimsy lost, its eccentric spirit broken. The representatives of the Reich watched Prague, too, with wolves' eyes. They needed buildings to work and live in, and they made lists of what they desired, shopping from the inventory of what was left behind by the Jewish families who had fled the country.

The Petscheks' four-story bank building downtown, with its heavy Medici ornamentation, was chosen by the Geheime Staatspolizei (Secret State Police): the Gestapo. The fortress-like structure would be its new headquarters in Prague. Its basement vaults—small windowless rooms with iron doors that locked from the outside—would be put to use as holding cells and become the most feared place in the city.

And Otto's palace, his expression of three hundred years of Enlightenment and progress? It was chosen to serve as the seat of the incoming Wehrmacht commander, General Erich Friderici. He would receive the gardens, the house, and its contents: the red Bohemian glassware and the ormolu French clocks, the matching Genoan bombe chests and the pair of gilded Renaissance thrones. The Germans were good at appraisal. In inventorying all the many Petschek residences, they assigned the highest value—by far—to the microcosm of Europe that Otto had created on his compound in Bubeneč. The Wehrmacht general would even inherit a trained house staff, led by a butler who lived in the little gatehouse and knew everything about how to keep the property running.

One night before the Germans took occupancy of the palace, Mr. Pokorný entered the mansion. He glided through the curved hallways, a silent ghost. In his hand he carried a thick canvas sack. It was like the ones Otto had used to wrap the roots of the trees that he imported, now deeply anchored in his garden.

Pokorný moved along the arcing spine of the palace, into and out of the rooms, and filled the bag with Otto's silver and other valuable items.

He picked only the choicest pieces, leaving enough behind that what was missing would not be obvious.

When the sack was full, he sealed it and slipped into the backyard. He found a dark corner of the estate, where he dug a pit deep enough to contain the large bundle and buried it underground, shoveling the earth back over it. Then he returned to his gatehouse, in the darkness, ready to protect the palace as best as he could.

6

THE MOST DANGEROUS MAN IN THE REICH

Rudolf Toussaint (right) looks at Reinhard Heydrich (left).

T OUSSAINT'S BEHAVIOR AFTER LEAVING PRAGUE MIGHT EASILY have landed him in a concentration camp—or an unmarked grave. Instead, he ended up as the master of the Petschek house.

He had moved on to his new Belgrade assignment in 1939 and watched from that perch as Hitler took aim at Poland, using the same strategies that had won him Czechoslovakia: constantly escalating demands for territory; promises to negotiate if his terms were met in advance; and professions of peace coupled with staged border provocations. The Germans finally invaded on September 1. Wiser after Munich, Poland's allies Britain and France declared war on September 3.

Toussaint had been able to speak frankly to Hencke in Prague despite his Nazi associations. In Belgrade, he looked for another confidant to share his views of Hitler's rapacity and the folly of war. He thought that he had found one in his deputy, Arthur Laumann, the air force attaché.

Laumann must have seemed trustworthy. He was, like Toussaint, a heavily decorated World War I veteran and a bearer of the Iron Cross.

But Laumann was no Hencke. Although he had been pushed out of the air force after World War I, he'd wormed his way back through one of the Nazi Party's volunteer paramilitary brigades. He'd been appointed an *SA-Standartenführer* and was eventually reassigned to the new German air force overseen by Hitler's corpulent crony Hermann Göring. Laumann evidently resented Toussaint for his role as chief attaché and coveted that post for himself.

Laumann started secretly filing reports on his boss, methodically documenting Toussaint's heresies. He sent them to Berlin throughout the fall, perhaps hoping that higher authorities would remove Toussaint and put Laumann in charge. But months passed and, to Laumann's frustration, nothing happened. Distracted by the Polish campaign and the evolving hostilities with Britain and France, Berlin was apparently too busy to attend to the growing stack of reports about a Belgrade attaché's "reactionary" views.

Then matters came to a head. On November 8, 1939, a time bomb exploded near the podium in Munich during a Nazi rally. Hitler and his top aides were spared by mere minutes, having unexpectedly left early. Eight people were killed and sixty-two others wounded by the powerful blast. The next day, with the culprit still at large, Toussaint, Laumann, and other officers of the Belgrade legation gathered for a meeting.

The Nazi press representative, Dr. Gruber, claimed that the bombing was a Jewish-British conspiracy, parroting Berlin's party line. Toussaint lashed back in front of the legation's senior staff. "I cannot agree with the opinion of Dr. Gruber that the plot could be traced to a Jewish-English initiative," he asserted. "It is rather clear that the plot comes from our own circles. Goebbels and Himmler need to prove that they are really capable of keeping the inner order. Propaganda is not enough. There is no doubt that the opposition in the party stands behind this."

The room was shocked into silence. Had Toussaint really just said that Nazis *themselves* were behind the bomb? Questioned the competence of Joseph Goebbels and Heinrich Himmler? Exonerated the British and, worst of all, the Jews?

Laumann couldn't believe his luck. Now, surely, Berlin would act. He rushed off a report.

Within days, Toussaint received orders to return to Berlin immediately and appear before the head of army intelligence to answer charges that he was anti-Nazi. He must have felt dread as he packed his bag. Dissenter disappearances were becoming more common, including in the German diplomatic corps—the Nazis had already murdered at least one embassy attaché for opposing them. Toussaint left Belgrade not knowing if he would ever return.

⌒

IN Berlin, General Kurt von Tippelskirch cross-examined Toussaint. The thirty-nine-year-old head of army intelligence with the prematurely gray hair had advanced quickly into the senior ranks of the Wehrmacht based on his keen intellect. His shrewd readings of data—and people— had been an important part of the Reich's military successes.

Toussaint could not very well deny what happened. There were too many witnesses. So he claimed that he was drunk, that his words were taken out of context, and that he did not mean them. Toussaint was not in the habit of drinking on the job, and von Tippelskirch surely knew that.

Von Tippelskirch passed his findings on to the army's chief of staff, Franz Halder. Sporting buzz-cut hair and pince-nez glasses, General Halder was, like Toussaint, very Old Army—a longtime Wehrmacht loyalist. He had been a leader of the secret coup that would have been triggered if the West had stood up to Hitler at Munich, aborting it in tears when Britain and France caved. He had no intention of losing a good officer to this rumormongering. Toussaint's transgression was minor compared to what Halder himself was secretly mulling: assassinating the Führer. At the time, he carried a small gun in his pocket, should he suddenly decide to do the deed himself.

Halder determined that the case against Toussaint would go no further in the Wehrmacht disciplinary system. Toussaint was fortunate that it was still 1939 and that he was only being investigated by the military bureaucracy to which he belonged—rather than by the parallel SS apparatus. Still, the allegations had come through a Luftwaffe informant. The head of that branch—Hitler's deputy, Hermann Göring— needed to be satisfied as well.

Halder arranged a meeting between Toussaint and Göring at air force headquarters. Göring had been a World War I flyer but was now too fat to squeeze into a cockpit. His office, too, was oversized. It was spread out like an airplane hangar and had all the charm of one—a stage for a grand, global drama in which he considered his billing second only to that of his beloved Führer. Göring's corpulence, his elaborate outfits, and his boyish enthusiasm for the toys of war led some to underestimate his viciousness. But he could pivot in a moment from genial flamboyant to icy killer.

Göring tore into Toussaint: "Don't say so much bullshit when you are drunk!" Göring's bulk trembled as he screamed. Fortunately, Himmler and Goebbels—whom Toussaint had criticized—were Göring's rivals. Indeed, Göring himself had been known to savage them. He chose not to take revenge on Toussaint for doing the same.

With that, Toussaint was free to go. Halder concluded that he was the victim of mere "rumors in Belgrade." He told the head of the army, von Brauchitsch, that "the matter will not be followed up any further." Toussaint must have shocked Laumann by returning to Belgrade unscathed. Toussaint resumed his attaché duties. But he had not learned his lesson.

⌒

IN summer 1940, Hitler, once more over the objections of many of the German career military, attacked France. He breached the Maginot Line, routed the combined forces of the French and the British, and captured Paris. Von Tippelskirch, finding himself in more distinguished company than Toussaint, escorted the French leaders at Compiègne to sign their surrender with Hitler proudly looking on. The Führer soon added Belgium, the Netherlands, Luxembourg, and many more to his list of conquered territories.

Nor was he done with his conquests—or with Toussaint's role in them. As 1941 began, Hitler's ravenous gaze turned east to his ultimate objective. He was contemplating Operation Barbarossa, his takeover of the Soviet Union. He had a devil's deal with Stalin, a nonaggression pact, signed by their respective foreign ministers in Moscow in 1939 with help from a German diplomat assigned to the task: Toussaint's friend Hencke. But Hitler had no intention of honoring that piece of paper for very much longer.

Before his main course, Hitler decided on an appetizer: Yugoslavia. Toussaint once again found himself serving the Führer as a possible human sacrifice. He was ordered to remain in Belgrade in the run-up to the German bombing after almost everyone else in the legation was evacuated. He didn't like it any better this time than he had in Prague, recklessly writing to an Old Army colleague, "I struggle internally against the idea that in this case too the possibility of a diplomatic solution won't be considered, and instead it should again fall on the soldier to force a resolution." If the letter had fallen into the wrong hands, it could have made trouble for Toussaint. Germany no longer brooked even the mildest criticism of Hitler. Fortunately, Toussaint's correspondent does not appear to have leaked.

He had other problems soon enough. The bombing, raining down all around the legation, devastated Belgrade. Toussaint could easily have been killed by a single errant projectile from a Nazi aircraft and buried deep beneath the rubble. But his battle luck from the Great War was still intact, and he survived unscathed. That left him the most senior German on the Yugoslav side of the line. He helped accept the surrender of the city on April 10.

Hitler used it as a stepping-stone for his push to Moscow that summer. Toussaint watched Hitler's advance with anxiety: Rolf was among the young officers helping lead the troops east. Toussaint's son had made good on his desire to fight, joining the Wehrmacht in 1939 at age eighteen. As a father, Toussaint was afraid as the Germans pushed east, but, as a professional soldier, he must have been impressed. Hitler rapidly conquered the Baltics, Belorussia, and Ukraine in a stunning show of force: about four million soldiers and six hundred thousand motorized vehicles penetrated a front almost two thousand miles long.

By October 1941, the Germans were just a few miles outside of Moscow. An ebullient Hitler made a round of promotions, including elevating Toussaint's rank. He would from now on call Toussaint the "brown-eyed general." With this new rank came a new assignment—effective October 1, Toussaint would be Wehrmachtbevollmächtigter (Wehrmacht plenipotentiary) in Prague—and a new home: Otto Petschek's palace.

TOUSSAINT returned that fall to the Golden City in his new capacity. He again saw Prague Castle, with red roofs sliding downhill from that seat of Czech kings like an army spreading out across the municipal basin. Their progression was punctuated by steeples, belfries, and turrets, and by the Vltava River, which flowed through the middle of the city, crisscrossed by ancient bridges connecting Malá Strana to the Old Town. Ruins may have been smoldering across Europe, but the City of a Hundred Spires had not lost a single one to bombing.

One of the buildings that made Prague the envy of Europe was Toussaint's own to enjoy. From the palace's Wintergarden ballroom, he could survey the expansive grounds. The trees were losing their leaves, their long bare arms scratching across the sky. The landscape was like a painting, the Platonic ideal of autumn, framed by the room's hammered gold windowpanes. The ballroom's vivid colors outshone the scene, though: the crimson-and-yellow medallion set into the marble floor, the green and pink of the china dogs set into the curving walls. But the brightest hue shone above the room's three chandeliers: the glint of elaborate ormolu-and-porcelain bouquets, each containing the ceramic plumage of a large Meissen bird.

The palace and the city that harbored it were an oasis in a continent on fire. To the east, German forces were pushing into the Soviet Union. To the west, the air war was relentless: Germany still flying sorties over Britain, the dogged British bombing Germany back. But here in the Petschek compound, the only incendiaries were the logs burning in the library fireplace. Their light shone on the Goethe, Schiller, and Wagner lining the shelves in neat rows.

Lilly arrived from Munich, Toussaint glad to be sharing a house with his beautiful wife again. She and Toussaint bundled up and sunbathed out on the patio, their Scottish-terrier puppy sitting in Lilly's lap or tearing around the vast lawn. Their son, Rolf, visited on leave from the Russian front, and the family was reunited. Rolf had seen great carnage as he fought in the east over the summer of 1941 and had suffered two serious injuries himself. He had been bayoneted through one arm and shot in the leg. The wounds did not dampen Rolf's enthusiasm for the fight. His superiors noted his "great zeal and energy" and "positive attitude towards national socialism," finding him "very, very promising." Toussaint was alarmed by his son's enduring sympathies for Hitlerism and forbade him from associating with the Nazi Party, just as he had stopped him from joining the Waffen-SS during his adolescence. Still, Toussaint

Rudolf and Lilly Toussaint on the palace lawn, circa 1941.

was proud of his only son's service and relished their time together. They dueled at chess, the warm glow of Otto's chandeliers casting shadows on the board.

Pokorný and the staff came to accept, and even to like, their new proprietor—as much as they could an occupier. He had elegant manners and treated the locals who worked for him with great politeness. Toussaint observed that the palace was operating smoothly under Pokorný and allowed the tall, grave Czech a completely free hand to run things. More than that, Toussaint seemed to appreciate the spirit of the palace. The butler and his colleagues must have been surprised the first time they saw the general indulging in his hobby of painting, and shocked to observe that he was quite good at it. That aestheticism gave Toussaint a sensitivity to the palace and the precious objects that filled it.

Toussaint certainly compared favorably with the two generals who had lived there before him. They had treated the palace cruelly. Silver, china, and glass had been carted off. Martha's closets were stripped bare to outfit wives or girlfriends: "[O]ut came the minks and beavers, the wonderful sable and ermine, the great Paris toilettes and capes, dozens of white glace gloves, heaps of silk dresses, underwear and negligées, linen of the trousseau embroidered in monasteries"—two decades of lavish gifts from Otto carried away in a single morning as Pokorný and the staff peered down from the second floor, careful not to be observed.

The Germans had meticulously inventoried what was left behind after their raids. Furniture and other articles were numbered, labeled, and rubber-stamped with the *Reichsadler,* the Nazi regime's symbol: a stylized eagle, its head turned to the left, its wings spread, grasping in its talons a wreath encircling a swastika. It was affixed to the underside of rare antiques and kitchen stools alike. Among the objects that were so branded was an antique table from France with an ornate cherrywood top, scalloped edges, and thin, curving legs ornamented with brass. It would eventually end up in the oval rotunda that served as a reception room for the palace, the swastika and serial number permanently residing on its underside, waiting to be discovered by future generations.

Toussaint seems to have neither stolen nor inventoried. He relied on Pokorný, indulging him in his dedication to preserving the house exactly as Otto had left it. The butler maintained the pulley system for the retracting wall and the other internal mechanisms, the mysteries of which only he understood. He personally washed windows, shined Otto's gold-alloy fixtures, and stripped and rewaxed the wooden floors. He saw that the books on the library shelves were dusted and the furniture polished and cared for—and was quietly fanatical about keeping each item precisely where Otto had placed it. He resisted any alteration, believing that Otto's taste was the ultimate standard.

The keenly observant Toussaint must have noticed that Otto's Jewish books remained in the library: an Old Testament Bible, with Hebrew and German on facing pages; Graetz's *History of the Jews;* the ten large volumes all in a row of the *Encyclopaedia Judaica,* published in Berlin; a complete set of Heine; and many more. Toussaint did not throw out the tomes, nor did he dispose of other Jewish artifacts in the palace, such as the medieval rabbi's chair. He could have gotten in trouble if the wrong dinner guest had noticed them. But he kept them anyway.

Pokorný could have done worse than Toussaint—much worse, as demonstrated by an article that appeared in the Czech press not long after the general moved in. It took a considerably different approach to Otto and his creation:

> The Jew Petschek considered himself a prince . . . His own palace was rebuilt three times before finally meeting the wishes and demands of the Jew. It has huge marble halls, tall doors, marble staircases, wall-tiling with colored stones, whose designs were mainly Zionist stars. It was supposed to amaze visitors and guests. But the arrangement of these halls and rooms was so foolish that one needs a map to get around the palace . . . And what were the circumstances of the workers in the brown coal mines who were earning money for the Jews here, which they then squandered? . . . [T]he Petschek family has abandoned the proud villa . . . Petschek legs will never enter the beautiful country of Bohemia and Moravia, nor [the] palace.

Pokorný hoped that the Petscheks were safe, wherever they were, and he protected their home and all in it as if they would return at any minute. He would have been even more anxious had he known the intentions of the Nazi regime for the family. As part of contingency planning for war with Great Britain, the SS, in the spring of 1940, compiled a list of targeted civilians and had it typeset, printed, and bound in a convenient pocket-sized edition. The "Gestapo Arrest List for England" consisted of 2,820 souls to be immediately hunted down and detained should the Germans occupy the island nation. Among the names listed: Victor, Eva, Rita, and Ina Petschek, all denoted "Jude."

⌣◞

TOUSSAINT's promotion brought with it a social obligation that he could not decline. That October, Hitler invited Toussaint to dine at Wolfsschanze—the Wolf's Lair—Hitler's top secret, elaborately protected complex of bunkers in the forests of eastern Prussia, near the Polish border. Toussaint flew north in a Luftwaffe plane to meet the man who was, confounding his own generals' expectations, scything through Europe. Hitler was nearing the height of his power, and the final assault on Moscow had begun: Operation Typhoon.

Hitler welcomed Toussaint at two p.m. on October 6 in his private dining room. A picture window overlooking the forest was behind the Führer, a map of Operation Typhoon on the wall next to him. Toussaint was directed to the place of honor across from Hitler. The two men— both painters—exchanged some art-related small talk. Soon Hitler settled into an extended monologue—his typical manner at these lunches. It was clear that his guests were there to serve as an audience. Toussaint, although new, quickly ascertained the exercise and listened intently as the courses came and went. Hitler allowed his guests to eat while he went on and on, though the meat-loving Toussaint may have found the fare dubious: Hitler was a dedicated vegetarian.

Hitler began with an overview of the Czech political situation for Toussaint's benefit. Hitler's hated opponent, President Beneš, sat in London, brewing trouble from afar. Beneš's elderly replacement, Emil Hácha, was pliable enough; Hitler almost pitied him, he was so easy to manipulate. But others had been caught taking orders from Beneš, including the now-jailed Czech prime minister. Hitler believed that Beneš was still driving the country in absentia, the Czechs were not knuckling under, and the economy was plagued by sabotage.

Hitler described to Toussaint what he had in mind for the new administration: a "ransom/hostage system." He proclaimed, "If one responsible for an act of sabotage is not immediately determined, then ten predetermined hostages from the same factory will be shot. In factories that achieve good work performance, and at the ones that have no acts of sabotage, the workers will receive higher food rations." Hitler then went off on a long tangent indulging in his obsession with food, declaring that "the Czech woman is famous for her cooking skills" and expounding his theory that "when a worker receives a larger food ration, then the wife of this employee will see to it that the work in this factory is satisfactory."

Toussaint looked down at the vegetables on his plate and said nothing. But it got worse, Hitler turning to the only people he hated even more than Beneš and the Czechs: the Jews. "All Jews in the Protectorate must be removed, and not to anywhere in the General Government, but rather straight on to the East. This is momentarily not feasible because of the need of the military for means of transportation for the Eastern campaign. All Jews from Berlin and Austria should disappear simultaneously with the Protectorate Jews. The Jews are the conduit everywhere through which news from the enemy spreads with lightning speed." He turned next to the Czechs: "After the war, I intend to transfer the racially undesirable elements in the Bohemian area to the East and settle them there . . . [I]f one scatters them in the Eastern territories, they would be very good overseers."

Whatever his thoughts were, Toussaint kept them to himself. It was one thing to rebut conspiracy theories about the Jews in a Belgrade conference room, quite another to say anything here. After lunch, he flew back to Prague. There could be no escaping the nature of the Protectorate enterprise he was joining.

TOUSSAINT's discomfort was only amplified by his new boss, who had been announced at the end of September: Reinhard Heydrich, the acting *Reichsprotektor*. Just thirty-seven, he was the top German official in the Czech lands and a model Aryan: blond, athletic, and coldly handsome, but for his very long nose and his blank eyes. A Hitler favorite, some even whispered that he would be the Führer's eventual successor. Heydrich had been drummed out of the navy because of his misbehavior toward a woman, but he had found his second chance in the Nazi Party. He made the most of it, distinguishing himself by planning and executing Hitler's purge of his Nazi competitors on June 30, 1934 (the same evening that Otto had died): the Night of the Long Knives. Heydrich was also a key organizer of the SS and had helped build it out from its humble origins of fewer than a thousand members into a force of more than two hundred thousand by 1941—a strong paramilitary apparatus that rivaled Toussaint's traditional military as a power center. In the process, Heydrich had risen to become Himmler's deputy, a role that he retained along with his Prague duties. It was a testament to how important the Protectorate was that Heydrich was dispatched there.

Like many others in the Old Army, Toussaint apparently had little sympathy for Heydrich. The distrust went both ways, not least because Toussaint was associated with Heydrich's longtime antagonists in the military. But that dislike was no protection against Toussaint being drawn into his web as the two of them settled into their new roles.

In October 1941, Heydrich secretly met with his cronies in Prague. The group decided to create a Jewish ghetto in the Protectorate, claiming that it would be a "temporary transit camp" for the "evacuation" of the Jews to "the eastern regions"—the same rhetoric that Toussaint had heard Hitler use in his secret bunker. Someone suggested the garrison town of Terezín. But the Wehrmacht was quartered in part of the town; would the new Wehrmacht head give it up? Heydrich said that he would discuss it personally with Toussaint. Then he seems to have thought better of it, perhaps fearing an embarrassing rebuff. Heydrich was extremely sensitive regarding his own honor, and some whiff of Toussaint's reputation must have made its way to him. Instead he ordered his SS subordinates to speak to the Wehrmachtbevollmächtigter.

Toussaint considered the request. He was not being asked to do anything untoward himself—just to move his men from Terezín. Any Czechs who were forced to relocate in the process would be paid. Still, he could have had no doubt by this point about what he was enabling. On October 15, 1941, he told Heydrich's aide Horst Böhme that if it was politically necessary he would clear the garrison. Perhaps there was a mild whiff of reluctance in that condition, but if so it was waved aside. Toussaint would have been a better man if he had justified Heydrich's fear of a rebuff, but the freshly minted general instead went along.

Heydrich seems to have been encouraged by Toussaint's assent. The corollary to moving the Jews out of the Czech lands and farther east was moving the Germans in, the first steps of realizing Hitler's plans to create German *Lebensraum*. In November, Heydrich's deputy invited Toussaint to talks about the creation of buffer zones around German military sites, to be populated exclusively by Germans. Heydrich's number two was none other than Karl Hermann Frank—the very same Sudeten German leader with whom Toussaint had worked in 1938. Frank was thin, his skin stretched tight over his flat face, his ears protruding like bat wings. The plans under discussion had originated with the OKW in Berlin. Toussaint would have some say in determining which property could be taken, and all further action would require coordinated agendas. The draft memorandum delicately balanced responsibilities between the *Reichsprotektor*, the Wehrmacht, and a land resettlement company based in Berlin. Yet it also flatly stated that the objective was "settling politically reliable and racially and biologically worthwhile German families in the areas surrounding military properties." Heydrich, and Berlin, expected Toussaint to sign it. Once more, as with Terezín, the new Wehrmachtbevollmächtigter complied.

⌒

As fall changed to winter in 1941, the scene viewed through the retracting wall in the Wintergarden shifted again. Toussaint and Lilly looked out at the park blanketed in snow, its bare trees rising up into the gray canopy of sky. The more muted daylight of the season leaked into the ballroom—softer, but enough that Toussaint could paint there without exposing himself to the elements. It was a benefit of Otto's design. The Wintergarden was always at its most surreal as the old year wound down and the new one arrived. Inside, the chandeliers, their ormolu flowers in permanent bloom, had the warmth of summer's memory; outside, the actual gardens were blanketed with white, like a sculpture draped in a sheet.

That winter, Toussaint's life in the palace was increasingly overshadowed by events outside its walls. By mid-December 1941, the United States had joined the war—Toussaint remembered all too well its role in tilting the balance in World War I. And he worried about Rolf on the eastern front. Winter had brought privation to the Germans in Russia, as it had to Napoleon's troops a century before. German losses mounted, and Toussaint heard increasing reports of his friends or their sons—or both—perishing there or on the western front. His old Prague colleague Friedrich Möricke was among the dead. With every new report, Toussaint's hair grew a little grayer.

As he settled into the job, Toussaint chafed at the methods of the SS, to the point that he was again indiscreet. He was "ordered to write a memorandum explaining why arms production at Prague had declined by 11 percent." He replied that "the main reason for the declining output of the Czechs . . . lies in the throttling of every healthy reason for industry and life among the population. . . . Their two main grievances are: 1) There is no redress against the despotic acts of the SS and 2) The population is allowed to keep only the smallest amount of money at their homes. Thus, a man cannot have the feeling that he is working for himself and his family."

The Czech people were getting restless under the SS abuse, causing

Toussaint to contend with another new worry: possible guerrilla activity. Multiple reports came in of parachutists dropped into Bohemia and Moravia. Toussaint negotiated a protocol with Heydrich and his deputy, Frank, for apprehending the commandos. Heydrich undertook a huge security sweep and arrested hundreds of Czechs. But he found no parachutists. With characteristic arrogance, he concluded that if he couldn't find them, they must not exist. Toussaint, for his part, wasn't so sure. He commanded his men to continue their search.

HEYDRICH was constantly coming and going from Prague. Toussaint likely thought nothing of it when the *Reichsprotektor* left yet again on January 19, 1942, if he even noticed. Heydrich hardly advertised the reason for his trip. He was headed to Berlin to chair the top secret Wannsee Conference the next day, launching a new phase in the ongoing effort to eliminate every Jew in German territory. Heydrich had invited senior representatives of the dozen government agencies whose responsibilities touched on "the Jewish question." They slipped into the villa one by one, their destination concealed from even their colleagues. Heydrich's SS subordinate Adolf Eichmann helped him run the meeting.

To his attentive audience, Heydrich was candid. The Nazis would annihilate the Jews by working them until they dropped and by processing them in factories of murder—death camps, to be set up across the territory that Germany controlled. Heydrich was aligning the intricate and far-flung Nazi state with Hitler's genocidal vision. The gray and bespectacled men around the conference table looked like paper pushers. They were actually mass murderers in training, quietly joining in one of the most horrendous crimes in human history. They were satisfied by the efficiency of the plan, and there was a spirited discussion of how to implement and improve it. The Final Solution had been set into motion.

LATER that spring, Toussaint and Lilly were invited by Heydrich to attend a concert that he had organized to honor his late father. Richard Bruno Heydrich had been a notable opera singer, a somewhat less celebrated composer, and the head of a music conservatory. His son had been named for Reinhard, the hero of Bruno's deservedly forgotten opera, *Amen*. As *Reichsprotektor,* Heydrich could remedy the world's failure to recognize his father's work. It would now get star treatment in the Wallenstein Palace on May 26, 1942. This was another invitation that the Toussaints could not decline. They filed in and took their front-row seats next to the Heydrichs. Socializing with the Nazis could not have been easy for Lilly, given her brother's fate.

Four musicians affiliated with Bruno's music school performed portions of *Amen*. There was, however, one number that they made sure to avoid: an aria titled "Reinhard's Crime." When the performance finished, there was strong applause, with one exception. Toussaint kept one hand by his side, the other holding his program as he studiously inspected it, head lowered.

Heydrich did not notice. His father's music was being played in halls usually reserved for Mozart and Beethoven. And, better than that, Heydrich had a delicious secret: tomorrow he would be traveling to see Hitler, possibly about expanding his new role as the master planner of the Final Solution. He was eagerly looking forward to the meeting.

THE next morning, Heydrich's chauffeur called for the *Reichsprotektor* at his villa at about ten a.m. They set off with Heydrich in the backseat of the green Mercedes convertible. He planned to stop at Prague Castle, then continue to the airport.

Two of the parachutists that Toussaint had warned Heydrich about were waiting for him at a hairpin curve at the bottom of the hill. Jozef Gabčík and Jan Kubiš were dressed in street clothes. Beneš, as president of the government in exile, had dispatched them from England to strike back at the occupation. The Slovak Gabčík was a fireplug of a man, short of stature but strongly built. He pretended to be waiting for a bus at the stop where Heydrich would turn onto the main road. Although it was a pleasant day, sunny and warm, he was wearing a raincoat, which concealed a machine gun. The Czech Kubiš, slender and handsome, with a strong jaw and cleft chin, was across the street, tucked into a recessed doorway, carrying two antitank grenades in his suitcase. Slightly up the hill stood a third parachutist, Josef Valčík. His weapon? A shaving mirror. He would use it to reflect a flash of sunlight, cueing the others as Heydrich approached.

For the most successful assassination attempt of World War II, the operation was a near-complete botch. When Heydrich's convertible came down the hill, Valčík signaled as planned. Then everything went wrong. As the vehicle approached the turn, Gabčík was the first to act. He withdrew the machine gun from his coat and attempted to fire on the car as it passed the bus stop. The gun jammed. Heydrich stared at him from the backseat, disbelieving—someone was trying to kill him; here, in the land he thought he had pacified. Gabčík's eyes didn't break from the *Reichsprotektor*'s gaze as he furiously tried to get the gun to work.

Heydrich's arrogance saved the operation. If he had fled, he would have remained untouched. Instead he ordered his driver to stop the car so that he could kill Gabčík, who was still standing in place, pulling the trigger in vain. The car braked with a squeal right at the corner, giving Kubiš the chance to step out of the doorway and throw a grenade into the now-stationary vehicle. But the explosive fell short, striking the rear wheel, blowing it up and sending shrapnel spraying everywhere, including into Kubiš's face.

Heydrich, his uniform stippled with shrapnel, stumbled out through the smoke of the explosion, pistol drawn. He headed toward Gabčík, who finally ran. The seemingly indestructible Heydrich chased him, then suddenly collapsed in agony. The shrapnel had penetrated his body, perforating his organs. Meanwhile, Kubiš, his face covered in blood, was pursued by Heydrich's driver, who had drawn his gun. Kubiš managed to mount his bicycle and pedal away before the driver, disoriented from the explosion, could stop him. The driver's gun jammed, too, victim to the spirit of malfunction that had descended over the makeshift battlefield that day. Valčík, his mirror tucked into his pocket, the least visible of the trio, strolled away.

Word soon reached Toussaint, and he ordered his men to go door-to-door, searching for the assassins and any clues about their identities or whereabouts. A bicycle and raincoat had been left behind at the scene. The jammed weapon was discarded at the spot where it had failed to work. Pieces of the grenade littered the street. All traffic to and from Prague ceased; every German in uniform was pressed into action.

On learning of the attack, Hitler ranted about killing ten thousand Czechs. Toussaint was relieved when his direct superior, General Friedrich Fromm, instructed that he should not allow his men to engage in reprisals against civilians. Toussaint believed that the Wehrmacht was different from the Nazis—independent and honorable. However morally untenable, that was the line he had drawn, one he believed marked him off from the worst evil of the regime he served.

⌒⟶

ON June 4, Heydrich died of an infection resulting from his wounds. Beneš had struck back at Hitler, and now the people of the Czech lands held their breath.

The next day, Toussaint was managing the search for the commandos when a call interrupted him. General Wilhelm Keitel, the minister of war, was on the phone. Keitel, thanks to his sharply angled head, thin mustache, and the monocle and paunch that he sported, looked like a sadistic grandfather. He was loathed in the Wehrmacht because of his toadying to Hitler; the other generals even called him "Lackeitel" (a conflation of lackey and his name).

What the Reich war minister said now reflected that reputation. The reprisals for Heydrich's death would be forthcoming in the name of Hitler. Toussaint and his Wehrmacht units were ordered to participate fully. Keitel stated that "the active intervention of the Armed Forces was necessary as a matter of German prestige."

Toussaint's conversations with Fromm had led him to believe that the question of civilian targeting had been put to rest. His men were professional soldiers, not war criminals. Keitel reminded him that the tension between the Wehrmacht and the SS was at a peak with the death of the latter's deputy chief. Keitel barked that passivity would exacerbate those tensions at a time when they could least afford it. Toussaint was ordered to facilitate a mixed Wehrmacht-SS battalion and do so immediately.

Toussaint phoned General Fromm to report the conversation. Doing so was insubordination of a dangerous kind. Toussaint had no way of knowing if the wires were being monitored by the SS or if Fromm would turn him in for defying a direct order from his and Fromm's superior. But Fromm welcomed the call. He was infuriated. The army's independence had to be preserved. Fromm instructed Toussaint to do nothing for the moment and await further orders. The two men quickly hung up: one or both of their phones might be tapped, and the penalty for insubordination in time of war was execution.

That night, Toussaint waited in the palace for Fromm's answer. Time seemed to slow there in the evenings: the long hallways, the cool stone walls, the rooms bathed in shadow, conferred a tranquillity that made the minutes float by at a different pace. This stillness was Otto's gift to all palace residents. It was a quiet that amplified one's thoughts, and Toussaint's must have been uncomfortable. What would he do if he was ordered to participate in atrocities? Would he have the courage to refuse? What would become of Lilly if he defied Hitler, of Rolf? Indeed, what would become of Toussaint himself?

It was a long twenty-four hours before news reached him: Keitel's order had been canceled. Keitel had fought it, but Fromm had stood his ground. There would be no mixed battalion. The Wehrmacht troops would continue to stand apart, at least for the moment.

⌒

TOUSSAINT traveled to Berlin for Heydrich's funeral on June 9 and spent most of the day with his friend General Friedrich Olbricht. Olbricht had also spurned the Nazi Party and was that rare German military officer who supported the Weimar Republic. He was known for his courage, including in following his own conscience, which had resulted in him spiriting away some of the targets of the Night of the Long Knives and defending a high-ranking officer accused of homosexuality. He had leaped in front of his division during the Polish invasion, loading soldiers in his staff car and speeding ahead to secure bridges.

As he greeted Toussaint among the throngs of military men gathered for the funeral, Olbricht looked more like a greengrocer than a war hero. He was of average height and meek appearance, with round glasses, a short chin, and a ready smile. But Olbricht outranked Toussaint and almost everyone else present, having been highly promoted for his bravery. The funeral had attracted the most powerful men in the Reich, all the way up to its very top. Hitler and Himmler were among the speakers paying tribute, and the service went on for many hours.

Olbricht was no more sentimental than Toussaint about Heydrich, and the two men slipped away from the burial, standing outside the walls of the cemetery, smoking and talking with other Old Army veterans. Afterward they met to discuss army affairs, including planning military exercises. With Heydrich gone, and the likes of Halder (who had spared him from discipline in 1941), Fromm, and Olbricht in Berlin, perhaps things would improve in the Czech lands. Of course, the commandos who killed Heydrich had to be caught first, but that would surely happen soon.

⌣⌐

TOUSSAINT was awakened in Berlin early on the morning of the tenth by a phone call from his distraught *Oberstleutnant* (chief of staff), Oskar Vorbrugg, back in Prague. He said that there were big things happening there: rumors of atrocities. He dared not say more over the phone. They both understood why. Vorbrugg begged Toussaint not to stay in Berlin any longer. He needed to come back to Prague at once.

Toussaint commandeered a flight and landed in Prague at ten a.m. Vorbrugg greeted him with a grim salute. "Sir," he told Toussaint, "some very wild rumors go around in the Staff about such atrocities perpetrated by the Gestapo that the staff officers are in quite high anxiety. One village was destroyed and there is significant excitement among the men as they do not have any detailed news. I myself could not learn any more detail."

Toussaint wanted to know the source of these outlandish claims. The officers brought these messages from the press, Vorbrugg insisted. Toussaint still could not believe it. By the time he got back to the palace to shower and change his uniform, the radio reports had gone global. A Prague station broadcast the news:

> As the inhabitants of the village Lidice near Kladno committed the harshest offence by supporting the assassins of SS Obergruppenführer Heydrich, the male adults have been shot; women have been transported to a concentration camp and children given proper re-education. The buildings of the village have been leveled to the ground and the name of the community has been deleted.

It was incredible—the Nazis were actually advertising what they had done. Toussaint moved through the day in shock, appalled as more details emerged. The leveling of Lidice was a warning against any resistance, but the murders inspired international revulsion—and made Toussaint sick, too. It defied not only the strictures of the Old Army but everything decent.

Calls came in to the palace asking whether his men were involved. No, no, no, Toussaint shouted into the phone, agitated. The Wehrmacht had nothing to do with this. He ordered Vorbrugg to convene the full staff, bringing all officers under his command together. He questioned them. No one here was involved in Lidice, they assured him. He condemned the attacks in language that even some of his own men felt was indiscreet. Toussaint told them that he would go to Frank and demand an explanation. In the meantime, they had to squash the rumors that they had any role in this horror show.

He found Frank, who was even paler than usual. The late Heydrich's deputy confirmed that the radio broadcast was accurate: Frank and his officers had killed the men, sent the women to the camps, carried off the children, and razed the place. They had information that Lidice was tied to the commandos, and the retaliation was a direct order from Hitler.

Toussaint asked Frank if he knew how Germany looked in the eyes of the world thanks to his actions. It was a trenchant question. The facts of the massacre had provided a propaganda windfall for the Allies. If Toussaint—a German general—was disgusted, how must the world feel? Frank retorted, "If you only knew what the Führer demanded from me. He wanted me to take violent action against 10,000 to 15,000 people."

Frank continued, "You should judge my behavior differently because I struggled against the Führer. There aren't too many people who have done that." Toussaint reminded Frank that there were limits, even in wartime. Frank had had enough. He curtly replied that any order of the Führer could not be criticized, and the discussion was over.

More bad news was on the horizon. Despite Toussaint's orders, and Fromm's, the Wehrmacht *was* involved in Lidice. The SS had commandeered troops of the army reserve who were on R&R in a remote Czech village. Those troops had guarded Lidice's perimeter during the massacre, and one soldier had even volunteered for the Lidice execution squad.

In addition, the SS had imported Wehrmacht explosives experts from a garrison across the border in Plauen, Germany. They had helped to demolish Lidice after the killing ended, ensuring that there was nothing left.

None of the troops were subject to Toussaint's command, but it didn't matter. There was now no moral boundary left between the Wehrmacht and the SS, between Hitler and Germany. They had bled into one another.

7

IS PRAGUE BURNING?

Prague; Friday, May 4, 1945

RUDOLF AND ROLF TOUSSAINT WERE PLAYING CHESS IN THE palace. Father and son bowed their heads in concentration over the board and made their moves. They shared the same hawk-nosed profile, Rolf a leaner, dark-haired version of his father. Rolf's style of play was slashing and bold, reflecting his propensity for risk. The younger man had survived more than fifty battlefields, outdoing his father's tally from the previous war. He seemed to have the family luck, narrowly escaping death over and over again. Most recently, while fighting in a trench, Rolf had been overrun by a tank. Trapped under crushed earth, he clawed his way out, gasping. That was the final straw for Toussaint, who summoned Rolf to Prague as an aide in the waning days of the war, undoubtedly hoping that he could watch over his reckless only child and spare him further trauma. (Toussaint had safely tucked away the third member of the family, Lilly, in rural Germany, far from the front.)

Toussaint was now a three-star general and the commander of military forces in Prague, helping to direct Germany's last stand as its power crumbled everywhere else. Toussaint's worst fears for his country had come to pass. Western Europe had been retaken by the British and Americans, and Berlin had fallen to the Soviets two days before; although fighting continued in pockets, the capital was lost. Hitler was dead, joining the tens of millions more that he was responsible for murdering. Large swaths of the Continent were smoldering, in ruins.

But the palace endured. The Wintergarden's porcelain birds, forever frozen midsong, shone inside the chandelier cages. The library still safeguarded the Petscheks' books. Pokorný hovered as ever, maintaining a high gloss on every surface. This house was one of the last spots in which one could, if only for a strained moment, imagine that prewar Europe still lived.

Any illusion of tranquillity was about to end. Two great armies were closing in on Prague. To the east, the Red Army's Fourth Ukrainian Front was rumbling toward the city, with the First and Third fronts marching to join them. To the west was General George Patton's Third Army. Almost half a million men strong, it was among the greatest fighting units that any nation had ever deployed. It had repeatedly crossed the Rhine for successful assaults, taking more than twenty important urban centers and capturing almost three hundred thousand Germans. The tall, imperious American general, wearing his steel helmet and pearl-handled revolvers, was famous for his speed, his giant force moving like a commando platoon, skimming the earth.

Toussaint studied the ranks of chessmen and mulled how to get Patton to take Prague before the Soviets did. The alternative—a Communist invasion—was too horrible to contemplate. Toussaint knew all too well the brutality of Soviet retribution. If Soviet marshal Ivan Konev beat Patton to the Czech capital, Toussaint would have no choice but to fight. Toussaint, his troops, Rolf, the city itself—everything was at risk of destruction.

But all was not yet lost. An audacious sequence of moves was available if the board was played just right, and Toussaint had agreed on them with Frank. First the Germans could dissolve the Protectorate. Then they could transfer power to the collaborationist Czech government within Prague. Finally, the Czechs—with Toussaint's help—could dispatch an emissary to invite General Patton's Third Army to take the metropolis. No blood need be shed. The city could be saved, and Toussaint and the Germans could surrender to the Americans with dignity.

As Toussaint played out the chess game with his son, he was waiting to learn whether the larger gambit had been authorized. Frank had gone to Germany to get permission from Hitler's successor, Admiral Karl Dönitz. For all his seniority, Toussaint still lived by the soldier's code: abide by the chain of command. Nonetheless, he was cautiously optimistic that he would get what he needed as he and Rolf finally pushed back their chairs and retired for the night.

⌒

EARLY on Saturday, May 5, Toussaint was notified that Frank was back. Frank's office in the Czernin Palace was a short drive away, and Toussaint was soon at his door. Frank, looking especially gaunt and drawn, had good news for a change: Dönitz had approved the plan.

By ten that morning, the two men were meeting with the collaborationist Czech prime minister, Richard Bienert. Stout and mustachioed, Bienert was a stickler for detail. Frank maintained a façade of autonomy for the complicit Czech government—and Bienert used every inch of the short rope he had.

Toussaint said little as the two men negotiated. This was politics, and he was just a soldier. He had confronted Frank in this same office following Lidice. Now Frank was backpedaling from power as furiously as he had once sought it, attempting to curry favor with the Americans. If the Red Army came to Prague, Toussaint could perhaps expect some minimal courtesy from the Soviets as a Wehrmacht representative and a general—not to be shot on sight, at least. Frank, a leading Nazi, was unlikely to be granted any mercy.

After an hour, as Bienert and Frank were agreeing on the details, the meeting was suddenly interrupted by the sound of shots being fired in the distance. An aide rushed in and announced that Czechs had seized the radio station; they were in a gunfight with German troops, who were storming the broadcast building. Civilians, Czech police, and Czech members of the Protectorate military were refusing to obey German commanders. Partisans had taken control of the Old Town Hall and arrested the pro-German mayor.

The meeting dispersed abruptly. The Prague Uprising had begun.

⌒

By Saturday night, Toussaint had a full-fledged revolt on his hands. Thousands of Czechs had armed themselves with War War I rifles, sticks, shovels, and anything else that could conceivably be used as a weapon. They were flooding the streets, overwhelming the Wehrmacht and SS garrisons. Most of the German troops had been stationed outside the city to counter the oncoming Soviets, never anticipating a civilian revolt.

But the Watchers of Prague were tired of being watched themselves. They were disgusted with what the Nazis had done to their city, transforming it into a Teutonic outpost with German street signs and swastika flags everywhere. They were fed up with being treated as second-class citizens: yelled at, searched, and arrested without justification or explanation. They were angry about the parents and children who had disappeared forever into the former Petschek bank or who were sent to the Terezín garrison that Toussaint had emptied of his men, now a concentration camp.

The Praguers' pent-up anger exploded, surprising their overlords. The rebels erected more than a thousand barricades across the city. Armed partisans had beaten back all German attempts to recapture the radio station and the town hall. They also held the train station, the phone exchange, the post office, and a host of other official buildings. Bienert had been seized and, under duress, had renounced the Germans. A new authority proclaimed itself over the seized airwaves: the Czechoslovak National Council (ČNR).

Toussaint's instinct was to fight the rebellion but also "to prevent the destruction of Prague and its inhabitants." He had issued plenty of severe commands during the course of the war and had long since lost any illusions about the nature of the regime that he served. But his reluctance to commit atrocities himself had in the years since Lidice led to grumbling among some of his colleagues in the German officer corps. They whispered that he was a *schlapper Kerl* (wimp).

His superior felt that way about Toussaint's response to the rebels. As high-ranking as Toussaint was, he still had to answer to Field Marshal Ferdinand Schörner, the commander in chief of the army. The bespectacled Schörner, whose small features in the middle of a large face gave him the look of an overgrown baby, was a ruthless killer and a favorite of Hitler. As the ultimate demonstration of that favor, Hitler had left Schörner in charge of the military in his last will and testament. His nickname was Bloody Ferdinand. He had earned it for his willingness to sacrifice large numbers of his own men in pursuit of victory—and to shoot malingering or insubordinate soldiers on the spot.

Beginning on Saturday and continuing through the weekend, Schörner pressed Toussaint to push back harder against the rebels and to "liquidate the uprising without hesitation." Toussaint had spent a lifetime following orders, even when he knew better. At the time of Lidice he had used the chain of command to evade them. Now there was no such recourse, and he capitulated, adding another moral failing to his ledger. He conveyed Bloody Ferdinand's instructions to his officers: "On the order of SS Feldmarschall Schörner, incipient disturbances are to be stifled at birth immediately with the most brutal violence. Measures taken hitherto and the energy shown are in no way sufficient."

But it is one thing to transmit a proclamation and another to act on it. Toussaint did not implement Schörner's demands fully. He dragged his feet all weekend, stalling for time. Bloody Ferdinand was vicious but not stupid. He was bitterly dissatisfied with Toussaint's lack of follow-through. The dispute between the two men escalated to the point that Schörner finally threatened to court-martial Toussaint if he didn't shut down the uprising in accordance with the field marshal's cruel instructions.

On Sunday night, with the rebellion still raging, Schörner dispatched five divisions toward Prague. They were due there by nightfall on Monday. If the unrest did not cease by then, he expected Toussaint to use them to level the city and everyone in it.

Had Patton dashed forward with his usual alacrity, Toussaint's dilemma would have been resolved. Dönitz's orders authorized surrender to the American general. And on Sunday Patton had taken Plzeň, leading everyone to conclude that he would arrive in Prague before Konev. But, inexplicably, most of Patton's army had not budged since then. Unbeknownst to Toussaint, Patton wanted to continue, but General Dwight D. Eisenhower had promised the Soviets that the Americans wouldn't cross a mutually agreed demarcation line, and Prague was on the wrong side of it.

Ike was exclusively focused on winning the war and didn't see any particular military advantage in taking Prague. Nor was there one. The upside was entirely political. The nation that liberated Prague would have an upper hand in the postwar posturing for influence over the restored Czechoslovak state. British prime minister Winston Churchill felt so strongly about seizing this opportunity that he appealed directly to President Harry Truman. But the president, newly elevated to replace FDR and still feeling his way, had so far declined to overrule his top general in the theater.

Toussaint was growing desperate. He dispatched one of his most trusted aides, Colonel Max Ziervogel, on a perilous mission through enemy lines to find Patton and determine what was causing the holdup. While Toussaint waited for Ziervogel's intel, Konev's Red Army was on the move, slow but steady. At this rate, they would arrive in Prague in a day or two.

Toussaint's aide interrupted him to inform him that the ČNR was on the phone for him. Toussaint and Frank had been parleying with the Czechs on and off all weekend. But the call wasn't a continuation of those negotiations. It was something else entirely.

The Czechs had captured Rolf.

Toussaint picked up the phone, his heart racing. An unfamiliar voice was on the other end.

"Is this General Toussaint?"

"Yes."

"Here is your son."

Rolf, his voice strained, reported that he had been captured. He had disguised himself as a Czech parliamentarian and driven out, he said, "with a white flag and a paramedic," to collect the injured and dead. "There, civilians fell upon me, and I would not have made it out alive if a Czech officer in an old Czech uniform had not grabbed me and put me into a car, and driven me to the Czech headquarters." Rolf had been slightly injured in the chaos.

The phone was wrested away from Rolf and the other voice came back on the line. "Mr. General, surrender the city or your son will be shot."

Toussaint had seen a great deal of death and suffering, but the threat to a child is unlike anything else. His son! What would he say to Lilly?

But if Toussaint abandoned his obligations now, what would that make of his war? Of his life? If he surrendered Prague unconditionally, with no guarantee of safe passage for Germans to the American lines, he would be putting the lives of all his men at risk.

Toussaint asked to speak to his son again.

"Rolf, you must understand that personal fate is not decisive here. I have to act in accordance with my responsibilities towards my soldiers."

The answer was no. Toussaint would not surrender the city.

The phone was torn from his son's hands; then the line went dead.

TOUSSAINT brushed Frank aside and personally took over negotiations with the ČNR. Since March, Toussaint had been in discussions with the Czechs, and now he took the German side of the bargaining in hand himself. He hoped that a negotiated settlement might save them all, Rolf included.

But it was no good—the Czechs would not settle for anything less than unconditional surrender. They wanted one last chance to recover their dignity, by winning their own freedom before the Soviets arrived. Toussaint was desperately searching for a way out of his bind, but was not prepared to accept those terms. They were directly contrary to his orders, and furthermore they would leave him and his men at the mercy of the Red Army, moving closer to the city with every passing hour.

Monday's negotiations failed. The murderous havoc of the day painted an ominous picture of what Tuesday would bring for Prague. The main threat to the city was the Waffen-SS. They were theoretically under Toussaint's jurisdiction but were really controlled by their leader, General Baron Carl Friedrich von Pückler-Burghauss. Pückler was a Nazi true believer, enthusiastic about suffocating the uprising and destroying Prague. *"Das ganze Nest muss brennen,"* he felt—"The entire nest must burn." For every shot that rang out from the barricades, Pückler's Waffen-SS had retaliated brutally and disproportionately. Pückler found pretexts to attack, like a vicious dog straining at the leash. The SS had shelled the barricades with artillery, then stormed them, killing hundreds of the poorly armed Czechs. They had massacred captured civilian fighters all over Prague. Now SS reinforcements were arriving. Between them and Schörner's five divisions, Tuesday promised to be a bloodbath.

At midnight an exhausted Toussaint sat in the palace trying to figure out his next move. The uprising was raging; surrender negotiators were at loggerheads. Schörner and the SS were coming unhinged. Patton's army remained stationary and fifty miles away on the other side of the river. The Soviet juggernaut was rolling ever closer, threatening the total destruction of a great city. And Rolf was still missing. Toussaint's face was pale and drawn, dark circles beneath his eyes.

Otto Petschek's compound was, at least for the moment, still cocooned from the devastation outside its walls. But the stillness of the warm spring night was punctured by occasional booms of Panzer shells, as the SS took aim at the Czech barricades. The rattle of machine-gun fire echoed along the curved halls of the palace, the *rat-tat-tat* at odds with the lonely knell of the ornate gilded French clocks as they struck midnight.

Just after the chimes quieted, Toussaint's reverie was broken. One of his men brought peculiar news: there was an American colonel right outside the palace, accompanied by a German officer.

We can imagine Toussaint's reaction: An American? And a German officer? *Now,* just after midnight? Perhaps Ziervogel had made it to Patton after all!

But no. It was Colonel Wilhelm Meyer-Detring, the chief of army military planning, from Berlin, with an American escort.

Toussaint ordered them brought to him at once.

⌣

MOMENTS later, surrounded by Toussaint's men, the American and the German were walking up the long driveway, gravel crunching. The house where they would deliver their message came ever closer, its cupids and cupolas barely outlined against the night sky in the light of the quarter moon. They were an unusual pair. Colonel Meyer-Detring was head of planning for the OKW staff. The German was in full Wehrmacht dress uniform, wearing the long military coat and the turned-up cap of his rank. He was a career soldier: cerebral, professional, and, like Toussaint, no Nazi. Toussaint knew and liked him.

Walking next to him, sporting the bowl-shaped steel battle helmet of the US Army, was Lieutenant Colonel Robert H. Pratt of Milwaukee. He was by profession an electrical engineer, one of the citizen-soldiers who had helped the Allies win the war. Among other accomplishments, he had helped plan the turning point of the war in western Europe: the surprise D-Day assault on Normandy.

Out of the millions of men on both sides of the conflict, these two had been selected by Eisenhower and Patton for this mission. They had been flown to Plzeň and given an armed guard of forty men, raced over roads pitted with bomb craters and mines, evaded Soviet patrols and Czech partisans, and managed to talk their way through the German barriers protecting the palace. They were accompanied into the compound by a few of their coterie, including their translator.

Once inside, the Americans were amazed by the contrast between the house and the battlefields and barricades through which they had passed. The master of the palace was almost as imposing as his residence when he received the officers. Toussaint's face was lined and his uniform creased, but his bearing had lost none of its dignity.

He greeted his guests formally but politely. They were all soldiers and shared the code of military courtesy. The fact that a German and an American officer had traveled here together only underlined the ancient rules of their martial brotherhood. The GIs were overwhelmed by the beauty of the place, but they also felt at home; American music played on a radio console. Toussaint offered them a choice of drinks: cognac, wine, or champagne. Surely Pokorný served them, as he customarily did visitors to the palace. It would be unlike him to be absent when the master of the house had guests. Pokorný would have poured, bowed, and reversed out of the room, silently wondering what conversations it would hold tonight.

The visitors were pressed for time. They told Toussaint that the Third Reich was about to end. Toussaint's former superior Jodl had signed surrender documents earlier that day on behalf of Dönitz. The surrender would take effect at midnight the following day.

The German requested that Toussaint negotiate an end to the fighting with the Czechs. But how could he do that? Toussaint was under strict orders from Schörner to fight the uprising, and the rebels would settle for nothing less than total capitulation. It was impossible to reconcile the two imperatives. Pratt and Meyer-Detring said that they were on a mission to find Schörner and persuade him, too. In the meantime, Toussaint should act based on his own authority.

Patton wasn't coming to Prague, they said. The Soviets would take the city.

Toussaint could obey orders, stay, and fight, or cut a deal with the Czechs and run. He had for years sought moral cover under the fig leaf of following orders. But Toussaint had had enough of death: Möricke, shot down over Britain; General Olbricht executed by firing squad for attempting to kill Hitler; Halder, stripped of his command and sent to Dachau; so many friends and colleagues purged by the Nazis or dead in battle. Rolf might soon be among their number.

Then there was the risk to Prague. It was perhaps the last major city of Europe unscarred by the fighting. To abandon her now would be like razing history; it would mean the destruction of the medieval monasteries constructed of rough-hewn white stone, each massive block a declaration of faith in eternity; of Charles Bridge, with its statuary saints beseeching God for miracles and martyrs for whom divine intervention never came; of sprawling Prague Castle, stitching together cathedrals, churches, and crypts, with its crown jewels and the royal bones of those who had worn them over centuries.

And there was danger to this palace, too. The residence of which he had become so fond would be among the first targets of the rebels if Toussaint followed Schörner's orders. The Czechs were just a few blocks away, on the other side of the barricades. If they didn't besiege it, the Soviets surely would.

So Toussaint agreed. He would try yet again to negotiate with the Czechs. He ordered his men to reach out to the ČNR and schedule another meeting. And he told his visitors where he thought they might find Schörner: near the Silesian border, hours outside of town. Armed with this information, the odd pair took their leave.

Around two a.m., Toussaint finally climbed the long staircase to the second floor for his last night's sleep in the palace. He didn't know when or where he would be able to lay his head to rest again. By this time tomorrow, he would be either leading his men away from Prague toward Patton or hunkering down to do battle against the Soviets. He ascended the Savonnerie carpet atop the steps—a block-long rug that continued across the entire span of the second floor, with a blue ground and a flowered border, custom woven for Otto Petschek in France. Toussaint would try to save the palace and everything else he cared about in Prague. Nothing was assured: neither his freedom, nor his life, nor the life of his son. It would all depend on the next day's negotiations.

⌒

AT ten the next morning, Tuesday, May 8, Toussaint and his aide Arthur von Briesen presented themselves by agreement with the ČNR at the Red Cross office in Malá Strana. It was right next to the German legation building, where Toussaint had worked in 1938. Another clear Prague day awaited, like the one seven years ago when he had stood on this same block and watched with Hencke for the bombers that never came.

A Red Cross official exited his office. He would travel with the two Germans and act as an intermediary, guaranteeing their safety. Soon three rumpled, tough-looking *barikádníci* (barricadists, a new word coined for the ragtag but fierce civilian fighters) drove up in a sedan. They had blindfolds for Toussaint and von Briesen, crafted from a swastika flag that they'd torn in half, folding each piece repeatedly. The rebels bound the two Germans' eyes tightly and led them into the car. It bumped along for fifteen minutes, stopping and starting in order to pass through a series of barricades, before lurching to a final halt.

Toussaint, his eyes still covered, was led inside a building and down a hall. As he was guided over a threshold, he stumbled. One of the *barikádníci* caught his arm. He entered a room and stood motionless as the *barikádníci* tore off his blindfold. Toussaint was momentarily stunned by the bright morning light pouring through a window. He staggered again, this time catching himself. Von Briesen's blindfold refused to budge, his escort tugging away as the German officer grimaced. Finally the guard untied the fabric, unfurling the torn Nazi banner.

Seated around a large table was the ČNR: its chairman, Dr. Albert Pražák; his military deputy, Captain Jaromír Nechanský; and two vice presidents—Josef Kotrlý, a lawyer and Social Democrat, and Josef Smrkovský, a Communist. With them were the heads of two military cells in Prague, General Karel Kutlvašr and Colonel František Bürger. One of the ČNR members remembered that Toussaint "stood with his Adjutant General Briesen in impeccable uniforms, both freshly shaved. This contrasted strikingly with our scruffy appearance. We had wrinkled clothes and we were unshaven." They were a microcosm of the state that Masaryk had created, Otto had supported, and Beneš had preserved: Czechoslovakia—tenacious and now confronting its oppressors.

Most of the talking was done by Toussaint and Kutlvašr, who faced each other across the table. Kutlvašr's rumpled First Republic khaki uniform hung loosely around his thin frame. He had aged from when Toussaint had last seen him: his hair had thinned, his mustache was now white, and the war had cost him some weight. But his ramrod posture was still that of the hero who had single-handedly disabled machine-gun nests—twice—during the First World War. He had patiently waited out the past six years, working undercover at the Finance Ministry as part of a military cell. He sported rows of gold medals across his chest and a general's insignia in the Czech red, blue, and white on his collar. The country's colors popped against the subdued brown of his uniform.

For all Kutlvašr's bitterness about the years of occupation, he was cordial with Toussaint, who reciprocated. It helped that Toussaint was generally regarded as the most decent man among the handful of Germans who ran Prague. But beneath their chivalry, salutes, and "Mr. General"s, Kutlvašr and Toussaint were tough negotiators.

Kutlvašr pressed Toussaint about the events of the past twenty-four hours: the increasing ferocity of the Germans' response, their failure to exercise restraint. Kutlvašr was clearly skeptical of Toussaint's sway over his own men—after dancing around the subject, he demanded, "Do you have enough authority to stop this fighting?"

Toussaint chose his words carefully: "I do not have the authorization of the commander, Feldmarschall Schörner, who in turn threatened to take me to court martial if I prevented the troops from combat . . . SS troops are under the command of Pückler . . . It is possible that an order given by me would not be heard by some units, or some units, such as the SS, also might not accept it. Although I am the territorial commander, the SS has reserved certain parameters for freedom of action."

The distant booms of artillery and tank fire intensified. A messenger brought a disturbing explanation: the SS were advancing on the Old Town Square, just a few blocks away. The negotiations continued, but more bad news followed: incendiary shells had struck the Old Town Hall. It was on fire. The rest of the building, including its clock tower, the symbol of the city, was threatened. Kutlvašr, exasperated, finally cut Toussaint off. "No more talking! In the interest of the Old Town of Prague, it is necessary that the ceasefire be issued."

Toussaint hesitated. He was being asked to violate an order from his direct superior. In more than three decades in the military, from his days as a cadet before the Great War until now, and as one of the highest-ranking German generals left in command, Toussaint had never done that. Even when Keitel had instructed him to commit atrocities, he had appealed to Fromm rather than disobey outright. Following orders was the most fundamental principle of his code, its first commandment, the bedrock on which the whole system rested.

But where had that gotten him? Obedience had bound Toussaint to Hitler and the Nazis. It had implicated him in their terrible crimes. It had stained his honor. But maybe he could scrub off some of the taint.

"I am willing, if this order is on the basis of reciprocity." Toussaint insisted that the Czechs permit "withdrawal of the German troops that are in Prague," sending them to Patton. Innocents who could not leave, Toussaint said, "will go into care of the International Red Cross. . . . Women and children who can be taken with the departing troops will be taken with them. All this is done by me on my own decision. It is possible that I will be called to account, however I will do it because I am convinced that the fight as it is led here in Prague, is not in line with the purpose of the war and that it is unnecessary bloodshed, destructive of my values, and without any benefit. The implementation of my order, however, is possible only in case I receive full assistance from the Czechoslovak state authorities."

Smrkovský pounced on this. They were all suspicious, but the Communist most of all. "What kind of assistance?" he demanded.

Toussaint replied, "I mean that all fire will be stopped by you too, and the departure of the Germans, civilians and military, will not be impeded."

Kutlvašr, still skeptical, asked, "How do you imagine this will happen?" The SS assault was growing closer by the moment, and Kutlvašr's point was unmistakable: Could Toussaint really control Pückler?

Toussaint replied, "I will use all means to stop the firing immediately, once a mutual agreement is reached here. Should individual SS units disobey this order, I am willing to take steps, on my own responsibility, to force the units to obey by using troops under my own command."

Now they had pushed Toussaint to his limits. What more did they want of him? He had offered to fight the SS if necessary. He had been telling the ČNR for three days that he could not surrender outright. This was the best that he could do. He warned them that if they did not accept it, they would share the responsibility for the destruction of Prague and its people: "In case an agreement is not reached, I will not have any control over the situation. It is completely against my concept of war that in this period life and ancient cultural monuments should be destroyed." His implication hung in the air: Were the Czechs willing to say the same?

Kutlvašr reacted angrily to Toussaint's suggestion that the rebels were in any way responsible for putting Prague at risk. "We were not attacking, we just fought back," the Czech insisted.

That was more than Toussaint could take—as a general and a father. "No. The violence spread from the Czech side. My son, who had gone into town . . . disappeared without a trace. He was not wounded by the Germans, but in the wild shooting of civilians."

A hush fell over the room. All eyes turned to Smrkovský. The Communist had wanted to execute Rolf when Toussaint did not surrender the city over the phone. He replied, defensively, "[Your] son was found wounded on a street and the next day, when he was revived, he said that he was injured by a shot from a German tank." He ended weakly, conceding, "It is true that the situation was unclear when it happened."

Kutlvašr and Toussaint looked again at each other. Toussaint asked that his son be freed as part of the package. It was a fair trade, and they both knew it. Did the Czechs want it or not? Kutlvašr nodded—they did. At his signal, one of the fighters exited and returned with a haggard and unshaven Rolf. A bandage was wrapped around his head, blood staining the gauze. But he was alive.

Rolf was ushered back out of the room; he would be released if a final agreement was reached. Toussaint and Kutlvašr agreed to a break from negotiating to do two things. The first was to visit the radio station, where they would jointly broadcast the news of a temporary cease-fire. The second proposition was much harder: Toussaint had to find Pückler and make him honor it.

⌒

TOUSSAINT and von Briesen climbed over the barricades and rendez-voused with the SS general around noon. Pig-faced, bald, with a small jaw, Pückler was proud of the dueling scar that disfigured his face—the mark was one of distinction among a certain class of Germans. He had represented the Nazis in the Reichstag and as an officer in the SA before transferring to the SS in 1939. He had also published three books about hunting and war; his account of the terrible years of 1939–41 was titled *Gesehen, Gedacht und Gelacht* (*Seen, Thought and Laughed*).

Now Pückler was not laughing. He was frustrated by Toussaint's restraint, by the slow progress of SS reinforcements fighting their way through to Prague, and by communications difficulties. For three days, Pückler had been peppering Toussaint with aggressive plans for the defense of Prague. Now that Pückler had the commander there in person, he offered up his latest brainstorm: blow up the dam outside Prague, flood the city, and drown the rebels. And for good measure, he would also explode the historic Charles Bridge.

Toussaint cut him off. He told him that he had achieved a deal to save them all, German military personnel and civilians alike, from the Soviets. Pückler's face darkened. His brain, steeped for decades in Nazi ideology, was pickled by hate. Toussaint would be safe with the Americans, but Pückler was a Nazi. Now the *schlapper Kerl* was going to make him surrender?

Pückler would not go along. What about their orders from Schörner? If Toussaint did this, Pückler would arrest *him* for treason.

Toussaint drew his gun and pointed it at Pückler. The Nazis had plagued him for years. They were responsible for the death of his brother-in-law. They had made his wife miserable. They had almost seduced his only son. They had drawn the Wehrmacht into the Lidice massacre. They had led Germany to ruin and disgraced the German military. They had murdered Olbricht, put Halder in a concentration camp, and done evil to countless others. Toussaint stared at Pückler, with eyes as dark as the hole in the barrel of his pistol.

Pückler stared back. Von Briesen's hand was on his own gun. But Pückler was not ready to die, at least not at the point of Toussaint's weapon. He begrudgingly told Toussaint that he would honor the cease-fire.

Toussaint and von Briesen climbed back over the barricade. Von Briesen made the rounds to other troops to report the news of the radio announcement. Blindfolded once more, Toussaint was returned by the *barikádníci* to finish negotiations.

⌒

WHEN the parleying with the ČNR resumed that afternoon, a guard escorted Rolf back in. Kutlvašr, perhaps thinking that his son's presence would sway Toussaint, made one last demand for surrender without conditions: "Ten hours are left, and you will have to capitulate. I understand that it's a difficult fate, but these are the hard facts. We ask you to sign an unconditional surrender. . . . The situation of Germans is very difficult and they would commit great offense [by continuing to fight]. We obviously agree with the proposal to protect women and children under the Red Cross."

They were back to where they had started. Son or no son, Toussaint refused. That would put all of them in the hands of the Soviets, who were about a half day away by now. He looked at Rolf, at the armed guard next to him. He knew that if his offer was rejected, they might never see each other again. The answer was still no.

But Toussaint made a counteroffer. Kutlvašr could call it a surrender if he wanted, but "the departure from Prague of all German forces must be part of the conditions." The canny Kutlvašr seized on Toussaint's concession.

"What happens with weapons?" he asked. "Where are the weapons laid down?"

From there, things moved quickly. A little before four p.m., Toussaint was able to offer final terms: "Heavy weapons will remain in place; German troops leave Prague with light weapons to the northwest." He insisted on protecting his men to the last and on resisting the Soviets to the extent that he could: "[T]he weapons will be handed over in Czechoslovakia so that they come into the hands of the Czechs and not another army; the ČNR shall take measures to ensure the departure of German troops will not be disturbed on their way." And he remained true to his concerns for avoiding atrocities, finishing his offer by promising that "the German side will be just as forcefully ordered not to put civilians in danger."

Kutlvašr agreed; the deal was done. While it was being typed up for signature, Rolf was allowed to join his father. Toussaint embraced his son and wept. Then the two stood by the window, talking quietly.

For Toussaint, the conflict was over. He was on the losing side again, a war and an end more awful than the last time. But at least Rolf was alive, and safe.

The surrender document was brought in. Toussaint inspected it, made some changes, and dashed off a signature in his oversized scrawl.

"Who am I now?" Toussaint asked, melancholy. "A general without an army! All I can do is go home and sit in the ditch and look up at the blue sky."

Then he offered the very last of his candid assessments of the conflict—the final one in a long series that had put him at so much risk over the past seven years.

The Germans had lost the war, Toussaint told his astonished Czech listeners, "but we deserved it."

8

"If You're Going Through Hell, Keep Going"

Outside of Bockholt, Germany; May 2, 1945

Frieda, standing (slightly bent, center) with other survivors, Germany, 1945.

THE NAZI AMMUNITION TRAIN HURTLED THROUGH THE LUSH landscape of northern Germany, bisecting the shadows of trees and slicing out again into the afternoon sun. A fat curl of black exhaust trailed through the clear air. The straining engine was pulling six or so cars behind it, although they were not filled with their usual load. Instead of bullets, torpedoes, and shells, the train carried the people who manufactured them: about three hundred Czechoslovak and Hungarian Jewish women, slave laborers from an arms plant in Lübberstedt, Germany.

Frieda sat toward the end of the train, her back against the warm metal and wood wall of the boxcar. Light filtered in through slits and gaps, dimly illuminating the dozens of women crammed into the car. The air was dense with sweat and other human smells, mingling with the lingering aroma of gunpowder. Most of the women were propped against the car's sides, the rest sprawled on the rough wooden floor-boards. There were a few older women on board, but most were, like Frieda, in their early twenties. All swayed and bounced with the pitch of the train, speeding north.

It had been twelve days since their SS captors had ordered them onto the train, saying that they were going to Denmark to be exchanged for German prisoners of war. They were dazed with hunger and thirst, kept on short rations the whole trip. Frieda had once loved to travel by rail—spending long stretches on trains for the summer trips she had taken with her family. Her father and her brothers would sit together, quietly studying the Talmud or saying their prayers. She would cluster around her mother with her sisters, sewing, reading, or eating hard-boiled eggs and homemade bread out of a wicker picnic basket.

Frieda no longer knew where any of them were, or whether they were even alive. They had been torn from her at Auschwitz in May 1944, with one exception: her sister Berta, who now dozed next to Frieda in the ammunition compartment, her head resting on Frieda's shoulder. By a stroke of good fortune, the two had ended up in the same barracks in the sprawling Auschwitz complex and then, three months later, had been transferred together to the ammunition works in Germany. Once zaftig, Berta had loved to eat and to socialize—a bon vivant compared to her studious little sister. But after a year of captivity, Berta was emaciated, weighing less than ninety pounds. She too had become quiet, worn out by illness.

Frieda stared ahead in the ammunition car; she still believed that the rest of her family was alive. It kept her going: the vision of returning to Sobrance; of walking up the steps, entering her house; of finding her parents, her brothers, her sisters, and her favorite niece, Yehudis, waiting for her. Surely she and Berta were not the only ones from their family who had managed to hang on. She was determined to survive, to get back home, where the other survivors would be waiting.

She was nearly through the worst. A friendly guard—not SS, but an older, disabled Wehrmacht man—had whispered to her that the British were approaching, that war would soon be over. When she peered between the slats of the speeding train car, she saw a stream of Germans—soldiers and civilians; men, women, and children—carrying suitcases and bundles, fleeing the advancing Allied forces. She could read defeat in the faces of the train's SS guards, too. Their posture was a little less erect, their uniforms slightly unstudied. Even their guns didn't look as carefully polished.

She remembered Faigie's words to her: *Keynmol farlozn.* (*Never give up.*) And so she kept going.

⌇

FRIEDA was one of the first to notice the sound. She wasn't sure what it was. It began as a vibration, barely audible above the noise of the moving train. She nudged her sister awake, asked her if she heard it. Berta shrugged and closed her eyes again.

But Frieda kept listening. This was how she had survived (along with *hashgaha pratis*—divine protection—and a little bit of luck). It was the drone of planes, distant but audible enough to catch her ear. Then the noise mounted, the low growl of aircraft engines. It grew louder until it roused the other women. Suddenly the racket was punctuated by the full-throated roar of gunfire, wave after wave of staccato thunder directly above them.

The women screamed and threw their hands over their ears. A few clutched at each other, while some shrank against the wall or floor. Frieda threw her arms around her sister. The train stopped, shuddering, the brakes squealing as the women pitched forward. The guards were shouting as they threw the train doors open and ordered the people off the train. *Raus, schnell, schnell!—Move, quick, quick!*—they barked. The women jumped down, hundreds of them pouring out of a chain of freight cars and into the fields.

As Frieda let herself down and helped her wobbly sister do the same, she saw five or six aircraft streaking off to the north in a V formation, like a line of geese. *The Allies,* she thought.

There was no time to stare after the planes as their guards hustled the women into the fields, expecting the aircraft to wheel and turn. Frieda got about twenty feet from the train and lay flat on her belly next to her sister. She waited for the planes to return, her face pressed into the sweet scent of the grass. It made her think of home.

After a few minutes, there was no sign that the planes were coming back. Frieda raised her head. The SS stood talking to one another, assessing the damage. Frieda and the other women rose, moving uncertainly about the field; their wandering reflected how much discipline had broken down in the past few weeks. But no one strayed far.

The SS guards, though distracted by the damage to the train, were surveying the sky for the planes' return. Frieda spotted a copse of trees not far away. She estimated the distance between the field and the trees, measuring each step over the grass. It couldn't be more than twenty feet. She could crawl on her hands and knees, or even slide on her belly. Just a few feet from freedom.

But she was exhausted, with no food or water, in an unfamiliar part of the world—one still under Nazi control. And then there was Berta, who was in even worse shape. Frieda always took care of her older sister as Berta took care of her. When a scratch on Berta's leg had become infected at Auschwitz, she had pleaded with Frieda to let her go to the camp's infirmary. But Frieda was adamant—no one ever came back from there. Instead, Frieda shared her meager bread ration, took on Berta's work. Frieda couldn't leave her now.

She looked over at the train. Remarkably, its cars and the people they carried were not much worse for wear after the attack. She dusted the blades of grass from her dress and arranged her clothes as best as she could. Even in captivity, she tried to take pride in her appearance—that was something that couldn't be taken from her. She had washed herself in the cold water whenever she could, pinching her cheeks for color. Berta had found some old fabric and made kerchiefs to cover their hair, which was growing back in patches after their heads had been shaved at Auschwitz. Frieda adjusted hers into place now.

While the SS spoke among themselves, a few of the Germans came over and guarded the women. Frieda's friend was among them, the older injured Wehrmacht man. He told her that it was the British who had strafed them. The Allies were getting closer. It would not be long now until liberation. Frieda just hoped they could survive their saviors' efforts.

But the planes did not seem to be coming back, and the Germans ordered everyone back into the freight cars. The women reflexively did as they were told, helping one another climb back up.

Once inside, Frieda and Berta sat down, taking a spot in the middle of their car to give others their turn at the support of the car's walls. The women had been rotating positions for the whole trip. After many months of surviving side by side in the ammunition factory (some of them had even been together since Auschwitz), they had learned to share. The doors were closed, and the train resumed its journey, gradually picking up steam through the fields.

They had gone only a few miles when Frieda heard the distant buzzing again. She instantly recognized it this time: another wave of British fighter planes approaching, the low drone of engines.

"They're coming back!" Frieda cried out. Screams filled the car and the women banged on its slatted sides, calling out to the Germans to stop the train. The growl of the aircraft engines grew louder, building into a roar that drowned out the women's pounding and shouting. Frieda knew what was coming next. She grabbed hold of her sister, trying to make them both as small as possible, willing herself to be the tiniest target.

The firing began. Frieda heard the bullets striking the moving train but had no time to process what was happening. Total chaos erupted. Now the explosions were all around her, raining down from above, the women shrieking in terror and in pain as the bullets pierced the roof and ricocheted through the car, the wood splintering, sparks flying, smoke and dust stinging their eyes. The train lurched to a stop, and the Nazis fled the cars, yelling and firing back at the planes.

Suddenly there was a deafening blast. It rocked the train so violently that Frieda thought it would tip over. The doors of her car were thrown open, and everyone in it jumped down and ran. Some of the women were covered in blood; others waved white fabric—shawls, rags, scarves— anything to show the pilots that they were civilians. Frieda and Berta climbed down hand in hand and threw themselves facedown in a pasture, covering their heads as the planes buzzed above them.

Then it was over. The attack had lasted a couple of minutes, but in Frieda's dazed state, time seemed to have stopped. She lifted up her head, her ears ringing, and stood to watch the line of planes fade away. She patted herself and touched her sister. They were unhurt, among the lucky. Injured women lay all around them, bleeding profusely. Some were marked by gaping shrapnel wounds or had lost their limbs. Others were dead. One of the cars was on fire, black smoke flooding the clean pastoral air.

Frieda thought, fleetingly, of freedom, of using the chaos as a cover, but dismissed the idea. The injured and dead were her friends. She and Berta did their best to help, comforting the wounded and tearing fabric from clothing to make bandages. There was little to do for the more seriously hurt, so Frieda had to be content with holding a hand or caressing a brow. There was some morphine on the train. After treating themselves, the Germans gave the sedative to the women in the greatest pain, to Frieda's surprise—another sign that the end of the war was near. She looked for the friendly older Wehrmacht guard and saw him helping administer first aid.

Frieda could see the line of holes where bullets had strafed the car. They had just missed her and Berta. The empty space where they had been sitting was flanked by dead women. If she had moved only a few feet, she would have been among them. She scanned the sky warily, lest the bombers reappear, listening for that first hum—the warning of death approaching by air. Friends or no friends, she would grab Berta by the hand and break for the forest if the planes returned.

The SS must have called for help, because eventually emergency personnel arrived, making repeated trips. They carried away dozens of seriously wounded survivors of the attack. Out of the hundreds on the scene, Frieda guessed one of every five was dead or maimed. Many others had lesser wounds. All had survived the Nazis only to be hurt or killed by the Allies.

The SS conferred with one another, arguing sotto voce. Frieda watched, seated next to her sister in the clearing, as several officers approached the crowd of women spread out before them. They shouted orders. "Up. Back onto the train. We are continuing. Back on the train. *Raus!*" The SS was going to complete its mission. But Frieda and the hundreds of other women did not budge. The seated ones did not stand. The standing ones did not step forward. They had endured seven years at the hands of the Nazis and their collaborators, forced out of their jobs and then their homes; survived the horror of the ghettoes, then concentration camps. They had been torn from their families and friends; seen the people they loved the most murdered. Just minutes ago, they had lost fifty more to death or grievous injury. They had had enough.

The Nazis repeated the command, their words hanging in the late-afternoon air. It smelled of war: gunpowder, burned wood, diesel, blood. The immobile women, their faces turned up, were emaciated, gaunt; their clothing a motley collection of discards; their garments, faces, and hands now streaked with soot from the attacks. But they were defiant, steely eyed.

A murmur rippled softly through the crowd. "No." Then someone called it out, louder. "*No.*" It blossomed into a chorus of defiance, and Frieda joined in the music. The women were united. They would not get up. And they would not return to the train. They did not want to die, not now, with the end of the war so near.

One of the senior SS officers came over to the crowd. He was one of the more well-groomed despite all that had transpired that day. Not a hair out of place under his peaked cap—the *Parteiadler,* the Nazi eagle clutching a swastika, which was centered just below its sharp peak, rising up like the point of a spear. His gray-green tunic was neatly buttoned, the silver buttons on his pockets and chest glinting. He was, Frieda reflected, not as bad as the Auschwitz SS. The Lübberstedt SS had been charged with keeping them alive, if only barely. But when it came to the Nazis, evil was relative: they were all heinous men.

In Auschwitz, Frieda thought, they would have been killed on the spot for so much as picking up a stray potato peel. But now the SS were moving more cautiously. The Allies controlled the skies—how long before they were on the ground, too? The Nazi knew that he would be held accountable, and soon. Frieda could see it in his calculating gaze.

"We are taking you to Denmark," he said. "It is just a few hours away; we will turn you over to the Red Cross there." They had heard this before, their captors' claim that the women were to be exchanged for German prisoners of war. They listened, sullen, afraid, but did not budge. Even if it were true, what good was hypothetical freedom if certain death preceded it?

The rest of the SS guards had encircled the women, moving closer. Suddenly they started clubbing the prisoners with their rifle butts, swinging the weapons wildly, trying to force them back onto the train. Others grabbed the women by the arms, trying to drag them to the cars. It was a melee. The SS shouted and yelled, and the captives screamed and resisted, dodging the soldiers. A few feigned fainting; some actually fainted. The prisoners who were chased onto the trains then clambered back off when the SS turned to round up more women. Others fell to the ground and lay flat.

Frieda, toward the front, was several rows deep into the crowd and protected from the worst of it. She hunched over, fearing a blow, and braced herself for worse, listening for the ringing of gunfire. She raised her head and saw the SS men struggling with their prisoners. There were not enough SS to cope with them; the women had the Germans outnumbered. The Wehrmacht soldiers joined the SS and waded in, making halfhearted efforts to haul the women forward. Frieda's Wehrmacht friend passed by and grabbed her arms, pretending to try to lift her. He whispered to her that the war was over; she didn't have to obey. Then he gave up and moved on. She realized that he was just as afraid of getting on that train as she was. Now she was helping save the life of a German—by resisting, the women all were.

Then the ranking SS man, surveying the fracas with his gloved hands on his hips, gave in. "Fine," he called out, "we will proceed on foot." He turned on his heel and walked back to the train. The Germans stepped back, confused. The women had won.

Frieda stood up, smoothed her dress, patted her hair into place, gave her cheeks a pinch, and prepared to march with the rest of the prisoners. The women were too drained to pause to take pride in what they had just accomplished.

The next day, their German guards began melting away until none were left at all. The day after that, Frieda and her friends were greeted by the cheerful smiles of a platoon of British soldiers. Under her breath, she whispered the *gomel* prayer, said when escaping great peril: "Blessed art Thou, Lord our God, King of the Universe, Who bestows good things upon the unworthy, and has bestowed upon me every goodness."

She was free.

⌒

THE British were well equipped to fight Nazis but had little idea what to do with 250 Czechoslovak and Hungarian Jewish female refugees. So the soldiers commandeered a nearby U-boat training base on the Bay of Lübeck and installed Frieda and her friends there. It was yet another camp, and the conditions were spartan. But the women began to recover nonetheless. After some initial food shortages, they had enough to eat. It wasn't exactly home cooking, but it was sufficient, and they rapidly gained weight. There were beds and blankets, no five a.m. roll call. Showers, too, sometimes even with hot water. Frieda was given a bar of soap, which she cherished as if it were a brick of gold.

The base was located in a beautiful part of Germany, and the verdant landscape helped them heal as well. Lübeck had once been a holiday destination and was dotted with lakes and walking paths, flowers blooming as if the war had never existed. Frieda began blossoming again, too. She was even able to put her *goldene hent,* her golden sewing hands, to work. She found a bolt of gingham, likely meant for draperies or tablecloths. Using the dressmaking skills that she learned from her eldest sister, Faigie, she sewed clothes for herself, her sister Berta, and their friends.

Some of the women were content just to recuperate, to gather their strength before venturing out into the world; some were quite ill and had no other choice. But not Frieda. She was burning to get back to Czechoslovakia, to Sobrance, to the little house on Komárovská Street. If anyone else from her family was alive, that's where they would go. She badgered the British, the aid workers, and everybody else to try to get a message through to the mayor of the town or to their non-Jewish neighbors that she and Berta were alive, that they would be home soon.

But no one could guarantee that the messages had been received, and no messages came back. Frieda was tormented by the thought that her parents, her siblings, her nieces and nephews might be there, waiting for her. How she had longed to escape that house, to go to gymnasium, to be a doctor. Now all she wanted was to be back there with all the Grünfelds, sitting at the kitchen table where they prepared and ate meals, where they read and studied, where she had been born; the lamps glowing, her father studying the Talmud, and her mother listening while she sewed.

Frieda and her sister were in no mood to linger in Germany. Even the warm German breeze was complicit. Now that the Nazis had been defeated, there were less sinister forces in her way: her lack of transit papers, train tickets, food, or money for her trip. But what were such trifles to a woman who had survived the ghetto, Auschwitz, Lübberstedt, and the death train? She agitated for the management of the refugee camp to help her get back.

By early August, Frieda was heading for the train station. Berta was already gone; a slot had opened up to travel through Budapest, and she had seized the chance. They agreed to rendezvous in Sobrance. Berta would get there as soon as she could.

On the platform, Frieda hesitated before boarding. Another train. She swallowed and forced her foot up off the concrete platform and onto the first of the steps. The rest of her followed, and before long the locomotive was pulling out. Germany, or what was left of it, disappeared mile by mile through her window. The scars of war were everywhere—and Frieda's view was a never-ending tableau of bombed cities, unplowed fields, burned-out tanks and other vehicles, German refugees on the march, prison camps full of German soldiers. Frieda didn't know how the Germans could ever rebuild—and after what they had done to her, that gave her more pleasure than she would have cared to admit.

How delicious it was to see the Czechoslovak flag flying at the border crossing, to be welcomed back home by the Czechoslovak border guards. To hear her impossibly complicated mother tongue spoken once more! Western Czechoslovakia had been spared the worst of the war; the country looked just the same to her. Where there had been damage, her countrymen and -women were rebuilding. At station stops, the Czechs welcomed the returning refugees with food and drink, sometimes in traditional Czech costumes. Frieda was offered slivovitz, the traditional plum brandy, which she declined, and *čaj a koláč,* tea and pastries, which she gratefully accepted. Farther to the east, as the train chugged on, she was given a *mun* cake, one stuffed with poppy seeds. Hundreds of the tiny black orbs, poor man's caviar, coated her tongue; Frieda closed her eyes, tasting the sweet memories of her mother's baking.

Everywhere Frieda saw pictures of her hero, Tomáš Masaryk, and his disciple, Edvard Beneš. The student had, she felt, equaled the master. She spent some of her limited resources on newspapers and magazines, to read and savor Beneš's triumph. He had kept Czechoslovakia alive—even if only as an idea—from his exile in London. As at Versailles at the end of World War I, Beneš had again adroitly maneuvered, ending the war honorably. Now the ordinary Czechoslovaks, such as Frieda, had their country back. And Beneš had returned to Prague Castle.

But as she traveled deeper into her homeland, Frieda's anxieties mounted. Soviet soldiers were everywhere. Posters of Stalin and of the Czech Communist leader, Gottwald, adorned windows and walls. Many Czechs seemed newly sympathetic to the far left, wearing red ribbons or other Communist badges, talking excitedly about their politics. She was alarmed, both as an acolyte of Masaryk and as her father's daughter. The ultra-Orthodox Zalman Leib was a sworn enemy of the antireligious Bolsheviks. How outraged he had been when a youthful relative had renounced Judaism and joined the Communist Party. Frieda had laughed with Faigie about their father's uncharacteristic overreaction. But now she felt uneasy at the distinctly pro-Soviet environment that greeted her.

There was something else. Frieda saw ethnic Germans waiting on train platforms and walking on foot, marching west. She watched the elderly, clutching bundles and suitcases or pushing their belongings in carts and wheelbarrows. Mothers cradled babies in their arms or held sad, dirty children by the hand. For all her hatred of Germany, the sight of the deportees left her queasy. What had the infants done? She thought too of the disabled Wehrmacht man who had been so kind to her and of her own deportation not so long ago. It troubled her that some of the exiles looked Jewish. No, she decided, *that* would be too much. Czechoslovakia would never do that.

As she moved farther into the country, she became even more unsettled. The warm reception had chilled. Not everyone was unkind, but it was impossible to ignore the sidelong glances and turned shoulders. A few people muttered that "more Jews are coming back than left." She was reminded that some Slovaks had been glad to break away from Czechoslovakia in 1939, that they had supported the Fascist regime of Father Jozef Tiso (now jailed for collaborating with Hitler).

She had heard it remarked that the Jews were the only true Czechoslovaks. She had taken it as a compliment—that the Jews had embraced the new state combining the Czech lands and Slovakia. Now she realized that it wasn't necessarily intended as praise—that some in Slovakia resented being forced together with the Czechs, as well as the Jewish enthusiasm for that. Still, she had hung on to her optimism through the concentration camps, and she wasn't about to let some sullen faces shake that. She would prove them wrong by helping rebuild her country, by making it better than ever.

⌇

THREE days after leaving the refugee camp, Frieda finally embarked on the last leg of her journey—a three-hour bus trip from the nearest train station to her hometown. She dozed off and woke with a start as the bus pulled to a stop. "Sobrance," the driver called out. Groggy, she peered through the smudged, dirty window. She could make out Hlavná ulica. She was home! Still half-asleep, she hefted her suitcase down from the overhead rack and stepped off the bus and onto the sidewalk.

The short main street had been devastated. There were gaping holes in some storefront walls. Windows had been blown out of others. The post office had burned entirely, black soot coating its exterior. She looked for any trace of her friend Grundberger, the butcher, who used to call out to her as she ran home. But his shop was boarded up, the sign gone. Nor was there any sign of Salomon the shoemaker or Jacubovic the tailor. There was no one she knew. She stopped a Czechoslovak soldier, a stranger. What happened? she asked. He told her that the front had come through here, the Soviets and the Axis clashing.

"Boom," he said, both sardonic and sympathetic, before continuing on his way.

Frieda wished that Berta were there waiting for her. But she shrugged that pang of sadness off. They hadn't agreed on an exact day or time; how could they? Maybe Berta was at the house, she thought, and her pulse quickened. Perhaps some of the others were already back, waiting with her: their brothers and sisters, nieces and nephews; even their parents! She knew it was too much to wish for. But she was a dreamer: her mantra was that tomorrow would be better than today. Besides, if *she* was alive, anyone could be.

Fortified, Frieda took her suitcase in her hand and hurried down the street, trying to ignore the damage around her. As she approached Komárovská, she remembered how she had sprinted down this same sidewalk to see her father in 1938. *Tateh*, she wanted to tell him, *you were right. We should have run away to America while we could.*

She turned the corner and continued down Komárovská, waiting for the house to come into view. As she got closer, she could see something where the dwelling should be. It didn't look right: too small; misshapen. She could view too much of the river and too much of the sky. It didn't make sense. She took a few more steps down the empty street and squinted, trying to get a better look. Suddenly she stopped. Her heart plummeted. The suitcase fell from her hand. Where her house had stood was a ruin: broken, burned walls; voids where had once been windows; no roof. She closed her eyes, shook her head, and tried to reorient herself. Maybe she had somehow gotten turned around? But when she opened her eyes again, there was the river, the road, and the school. Her vision blurred, her eyes burned, and Frieda realized that she was crying.

Part III

Ambassador Laurence Steinhardt on Charles Bridge, Prague.

9

—

"He Who Is Master of Bohemia Is Master of Europe"

The Palace; July 1945

O<small>TTO</small> P<small>ETSCHEK'S</small> <small>PALACE WAS IN DANGER, AND</small> L<small>AURENCE</small> Steinhardt was determined to rescue it.

The newly arrived US ambassador to Czechoslovakia had decades of practice in saving the day. His crisis-resolution skills had made him a sought-after Manhattan lawyer, representing everyone from Vaslav Nijinsky to the archduchess Maria Theresa. Those triage abilities had suited him well to the exigencies of a presidential campaign when he helped FDR win the White House in 1932. And they had led him to thrive as a diplomatic troubleshooter whom the president had dispatched to hot spots all over the world, from Moscow to Ankara. Now he had been sent to Prague to help democracy recover and to push back on Soviet influence. It was his fifth chief-of-mission job, at just fifty-two years of age.

The palace hadn't *looked* as if it were in distress when Laurence first laid eyes on it. It was under the control of the Czech military, and he was calling on its occupants in his capacity as America's new envoy. His limousine rolled up the driveway of the old Petschek home, bumping slightly over the rough gravel. He was immediately taken with what he saw. Turrets and domes, cherubs floating on the corners like hummingbirds—one exquisite form after another—and then the full force of the design: wings, bays, and gambrels, stretching on and on.

The car came to a stop at the front entrance, flanked by giant classical columns that evoked the ancient sources of the Czechoslovak democracy that his country had just expended so much blood to help restore. Laurence was ushered into the oval receiving room, the intricate black, green, and red geometry of the marble floor below the white dome vaulting overhead. On either side were interior courtyards with fountains burbling, bronze sculptures of putti playing with swans, Greek myths frozen into statuary. Beyond this room were others, ending in a gold-framed bank of windows and an enormous park at the heart of the compound. As a veteran diplomat, Laurence had been in a lot of palaces, from Stockholm to Lima, Istanbul to St. Petersburg. But he had seldom seen anything like this.

Laurence wanted to learn more about this extraordinary building, and his questions were answered by the palace's caretaker: Adolf Pokorný. He and his wife were still occupying the gatehouse, watching over the palace, and now serving the Czech officers and other VIPs, such as the new American ambassador, who filtered through. (Some even stayed overnight because of Prague's hotel shortage.) Tall, balding, and austere, his livery as impeccable as ever, the older man described to Laurence his original employer and the home's history.

Pokorný informed Laurence of its latest chapter: the Soviets had seized the building when they liberated Prague. They had done more damage in a few days than had been sustained throughout six years of war. They had somersaulted a piano down the grand staircase, leaving scars on the stone where it exploded at the bottom of the landing. The lawn stretching out beyond the retracting wall sparkled as if covered with diamonds. The glint was thousands of shards of glass, from bottles broken in shooting competitions by the Soviets.

The Czech military had eventually managed to evict the Soviets from the palace. Stalin's men now occupied the larger but much less precious premises built by Otto's brother Fritz, a few blocks away. (The Soviets had helped themselves to a second Petschek house in the neighborhood as well, erected by another relation.) Czech soldiers took over Otto's compound, but predations by Stalin's forces continued. Just a few days before, Pokorný said, "some Russian officers had driven up to the house with trucks and taken all of the silver, all of the linen and some of the porcelain." The rest of its treasures remained, but for how long?

As the ambassador looked at the shattered stonework and the glass fragments on the lawn, he must have felt a surge of outrage. He had fought to protect the vulnerable throughout his legal career, representing victims of crime and working for a Jewish homeland in Palestine. He had done the same as a wartime ambassador, battling Stalin, aiding refugees, and rescuing downed Allied pilots. He had even built up a collection of old Russian icons while serving in Moscow—offering a home, despite his Hebraic origins, to the little religious paintings cast off during the Communist regime. As a Jew himself (and proud of it, despite being highly assimilated), he identified with those in danger.

Now the palace was calling out for protection. An idea hit him. Why couldn't he try to live there himself, taking it under US custody, flying the American flag over the compound? He would be doing the Petscheks, its absentee owners, a favor. And moving into the palace would solve another problem: Laurence's own living situation. His current apartments downtown were in a crumbling Renaissance building, a jumble of residential and office space with an illogical labyrinthine layout. But the palace—it took the best ideas from millennia of European architecture and made them livable. Laurence could accomplish a great deal with this dazzling site as ground zero for America's battle to win the sympathies of the Czechoslovaks.

He just needed a plan to secure it. His mental gears began to rotate.

LAURENCE returned to the US embassy. It was nestled in the narrow streets of the Malá Strana quarter of Prague, which poured down Castle Hill all the way to the left bank of the Vltava River. Known as the Schönborn for its longtime prior owners before the United States purchased it in the 1920s, the embassy dated back to the seventeenth century. Now the base of the US government in Prague, it looked good on the outside. Two massive wooden entry doors swung open to reveal a large cobblestoned courtyard, guarded by a pair of eight-foot statues of mythological warriors swaddled in stone lion skins and wielding marble clubs. Three wings enclosed the courtyard. Directly ahead as one entered, a tiered garden ascended a hill, topped by a two-story white summer pavilion, a *glorietta*.

But the interior of the building was stitched together from five medieval homes and a malt house, with rooms added over centuries of incoherent redesigns. The design ensured that everyone who visited or lived there would get lost, short journeys becoming protracted wanderings, ending up back where one started or in the basement staring at the crumbling ancient foundations. It might be described as Kafkaesque, and with merit: Otto's former law classmate had rented a room there before it was an embassy. The then-boardinghouse's poor heating likely affected Kafka's health—the tuberculosis that would kill him first manifested there—and the Schönborn's surreal spirit infused his writing.

The United States had closed up the property and left in 1939, and, after six years of vacancy, the interior was dirty and decrepit. Amenities such as toilets, electricity, and heat had been retrofitted and were subject to regular malfunctions. Laurence joked to a friend that he was "camping out in this covered stadium which, with the exception of a few rooms, is without central heating, 17th century plumbing, and it often seems every time the lights go out to have been wired during Thomas Edison's experiments." The Schönborn, though grand, was run-down and badly in need of repair—perhaps a suitable metaphor for postwar Europe, but not a very livable one. Otto's rational, symmetrical, well-constructed palace offered a much more attractive vision of the Western liberalism that Laurence was in Prague to advance.

The Schönborn's flaws were magnified because Laurence's days in the building were such long ones. He was often the first of the Americans at his desk and the last one out. Embassy staffing had not yet caught up with the postwar rush of administrative work, including handling the flow of requests to locate missing Jewish relatives of American citizens.

Laurence's other main preoccupation was how to help save Czechoslovakia from the Soviets. The country was divided into two zones. In the north, which Patton had liberated, several divisions of the US Army were now stationed. About thirty thousand GIs patrolled the German border and distributed food and other supplies to civilians, while keeping a wary eye on tense relations between ethnic Czechs and their German-speaking neighbors who had supported the Nazi invaders. The other expanse of the country, outside the American zone, was swarming with a quarter of a million Soviet troops.

It wasn't just the occupying forces through which Stalin and the Communists maximized their sway. Communist leaders, directed by

Moscow, were disproportionately represented in the provisional government that Beneš had cobbled together. And other slots were occupied by ostensible democrats whom Stalin had lured into his fold.

But perhaps Laurence's heaviest lift was the Czech people themselves. As Stalin (and Patton) had foreseen, they welcomed their liberators, and in Prague, as in most of the country, those liberators were Soviet. That was a daunting obstacle for Laurence. By holding Patton back, Eisenhower had handicapped the restoration of freedom in Czechoslovakia. Laurence was among those who had wanted the opposite. He "had hoped that the Third Army would be instructed to enter Prague—which it could readily enough have done." Indeed, his State colleagues had "crawled to the White House on hands and knees" to secure that outcome, without success. FDR had died in office in April, and it was, apparently, too much to ask that the newly elevated President Truman countermand Ike—and Stalin. Laurence fretted that Americans didn't fully appreciate the Soviet threat and might even still think of the Soviet Union as an ally: the courageous fighting partners who had closed the eastern half of the vise on Hitler, led by rustic Uncle Joe.

Laurence knew Stalin personally and harbored no such illusions. He had seen the Soviets' capacity for murder up close, and they killed humans as casually as they had smashed the Petschek piano and vandalized Otto's gardens. Franklin Roosevelt had dispatched Laurence to Moscow as ambassador in the first days of the 1939 Nazi-Soviet alliance. FDR wanted his "hoss-trader," as he called Laurence, to keep an eye on Hitler's unlikely Communist bedfellow. Laurence warned Roosevelt and the State Department that Stalin and his circle were not to be trusted, that all the mustachioed tyrant understood was force. The Soviets got wind of and hated Laurence for that. They attributed it in part to his ethnicity and religion, dismissing him as "a wealthy, bourgeoisie [*sic*] Jew who was permeated with the foul smell of Zionism." For his part, Stalin detested Laurence so much that he ignored the ambassador's warnings that Hitler was isolating him from other nations. Laurence had deduced that Germany was planning to invade the Soviet Union by piecing together a mosaic of clues; the last puzzle piece fell into place when he saw a German diplomat sending his beloved boxer back home by train. Only impending war could have parted the Prussian aristocrat and his dog.

When the Nazis did invade and a shocked Stalin was forced to oppose

Hitler, he was none too eager to be reminded of his mistakes. One of his demands to his new ally Roosevelt was that Laurence be replaced—and it was quickly met by the American president. Laurence told people that FDR needed him in Ankara to block the Turks from swinging to the German side (as they had in World War I). Laurence also said that the Moscow job had become principally a logistical one, of moving war materiel to the Soviet state. There was truth to that, but it was a painful demotion nonetheless. Though Laurence thrived in Ankara, he harbored a grudge against Stalin.

Now, in Prague, Laurence had the chance to exact his revenge—and for a good cause. He laid out his plans in a letter to the State Department in late summer, writing that Prague was the one capital in Eastern Europe "where we have a fighting chance to recover lost ground and to stop the westward tide of communism." If they held off the Soviet advance, Laurence thought, the Americans could in just a year or two also improve things in Warsaw, Vienna, Budapest, and Bucharest. "I am now more convinced than ever that Czechoslovakia will be the first country in Europe to make a real recovery and that it can play an important role in aiding the surrounding countries to recover," he wrote.

Laurence's old adversary Stalin was equally determined to advance Soviet influence in Czechoslovakia, and he appealed to Slavic nationalism to do it. Earlier in 1945 he had told Beneš and a Czechoslovak delegation: "In the First World War, as well as the Second World War, the Slavic peoples suffered most . . . That is why we, the new Slavophile-Leninists, are so insistent on calling for the union of the Slavic peoples." He proclaimed the innocence of his pan-Slavic intentions. "There is talk that we want to impose the Soviet system on the Slav peoples," he told his audience. "This is empty talk. In friendship with the Slavic countries, we want genuine democratic governments."

Laurence was ready to fight Stalin, and to "recover lost ground." He just needed a good excuse to do it. While he looked for one, he returned his attention to securing Otto's palace.

⌒

LAURENCE was not one for half measures. He went straight to the top to discuss the palace: Beneš himself. The ambassador made the short drive uphill through the winding streets to Prague Castle. After bouncing along the cobblestoned streets for ten minutes in his tan Packard limousine, Laurence emerged from a narrow lane into Hradčanské náměstí, Castle Square. Three sides were bordered by fairy-tale-like homes, stores, and office buildings covered with sgraffito: a layer of white plaster laid over a black ground, then strategically scraped away, leaving behind elaborate designs such as swirls, curlicues, trompe l'oeil stone blocks, and bearded wise men.

On the east side of the square loomed the castle, considered the largest in the world. It consisted of disparate buildings erected over many centuries, connected by stretches of statuary-topped walls—all knitted into a single enormous rectangular perimeter that dominated the hilltop and the city.

Laurence drove up to the main gate, which was flanked on both sides by black-and-white-striped sentry boxes. Members of the Castle Guard stood at attention in front of each box, rigid but alert, holding rifles with bayonets affixed. They looked tough, but they were dwarfed in ferocity and size by what was above them. On the castle wall were two eighteen-foot statues of warriors, each standing over a vanquished foe. Known as the Fighting Giants, they were sculpted by Ignác Platzer for the Habsburg monarchs, to impress and intimidate visitors to the castle throughout the ages.

President Beneš was, at first glance, less imposing. Slight, with a thin mustache and receding hairline, the courtly Beneš looked mild. But appearances were deceiving. He had been balancing the great powers against one another since World War I. He had helped birth his country, and when the Nazis took it from him, he had played his hand shrewdly from his wartime headquarters in London. As the head of the Czechoslovak government in exile, he had persuaded the embarrassed Allies to revoke the Munich Agreement, remotely engineered the assassination of Heydrich, and served as part of the coalition that had vanquished Hitler. The Platzer statues were an apt symbol of his current situation vis-à-vis that onetime foe.

Beneš greeted Laurence warmly. The Czech leader never forgot that Woodrow Wilson had supported the founding of the country in 1918. And if Roosevelt had failed him in '38, he had more than made up for it thereafter in helping win the war and restore Beneš and the Czechoslovak state. Beneš only hoped that Truman would be as strong a leader.

After discussing other matters, Laurence brought up the issue of Otto's compound. He wanted to rent it. The Schönborn was badly in need of repair, essentially uninhabitable. There was only one house in all of Prague that he felt would suffice. The Soviets had two other large Petschek houses—surely it was only fair that the United States be permitted to rent the third.

The president considered Laurence's request. Beneš knew the property, of course. He had walked through the echoing receiving room, strolled down the quiet, curving hallways, strode past the questing heroes and meandering yeomen stitched into the tapestries. He had dined there with Otto, that archetype of the First Republic, the King of Coal. The optimistic banker had once helped make the Czechoslovak economy the envy of Europe. Would Beneš allow a symbol of that heyday to pass again into foreign hands?

But Beneš had long ago learned to suppress sentimentality. He liked but also needed the United States, and that meant that he needed Laurence. The American ambassador promised to be an important friend to the Czechs, and here was a chance to make a deposit in the American favor bank. Beneš believed that it was "a matter of political wisdom" to reward Laurence and cultivate his future favor. And Beneš prized political wisdom. It had, after all, returned him to a castle of his own.

So Beneš told Laurence that he would do his best. Laurence was pleased with Beneš's willingness. He believed that the president could help him protect the palace if he wanted to, and it seemed that he did. Laurence had not squandered the lessons of his many ambassadorial postings. He could feel justifiably satisfied as he returned to his Packard, exited between the behemoth warriors overlooking the castle gate, and headed back to the Schönborn.

Still, as a longtime State Department hand, Laurence knew that his intervention with Beneš was only the first step. He would also need Foggy Bottom's assent and that of the rightful owner of the house. Laurence knew that there was an heir, Viktor Petschek, who now resided in the United States. He decided to reach out to him.

Laurence wrote to his friend Francis Williamson, the assistant chief of the Central European Affairs Division at State, asking him to find and convince Otto's son:

I would not wish to occupy one of his houses without his full knowledge and consent . . . I hope therefore . . . that I can enlist your persuasive qualities in an endeavor to convince Mr. Petschek that he should not object to my leasing one of his houses from the Czech Government. Any chance that he may have of ever getting it back in good condition with the furnishings intact or getting adequate compensation for it from the Czech Government would in my opinion be enhanced by my residing there.

Laurence also asked Williamson to figure out to whom to talk for permission from Main State to rent. Williamson agreed to put things in motion. Laurence eagerly awaited a reply.

LAURENCE was spoiling for the fight to "recover lost ground" from the Soviets, and he soon picked one. He could not rewrite history so that Patton liberated Prague; he could not evict the Communists from the Czech cabinet, nor could he banish the crypto-Communists. But he *could* help oust the Soviet soldiers who roamed Czechoslovakia, stopping pedestrians and demanding wallets and watches, menacing women and girls, raiding stores and homes as they had done Otto's, and otherwise pillaging the land.

The worst episodes were not unlike the conduct of the SS that Toussaint had complained about. The Soviets had even taken Laurence's deputy, Alfred Klieforth, prisoner when he stumbled upon a group of them occupying a building; they held him at gunpoint for hours, and Klieforth had not fully recovered from the scare. Soviet soldiers had stolen a car from another member of Laurence's staff, also while brandishing a gun. And these victims were American diplomats; the reign of terror over ordinary Czechs was far worse.

So Laurence seized on a strategy to end it: he would broker the withdrawal of American troops in exchange for the removal of Soviet ones. Laurence knew from his conversations with US military leaders, including his close friend General Ernest Harmon, the head of the American divisions in the country, that the US troops were going to have to leave sooner than the Czech public realized. The boys wanted to go home, and their families were even more anxious to have them. Laurence concluded that it was crucial to oust the Soviet forces at the same time. The huge concentration of unruly Soviet soldiers frightened the Czechs. With the first postwar elections coming up early in 1946, voters would be influenced by fear, unable to make a free choice under Soviet arms.

Laurence immediately had to confront a complication: the public drumbeat that the United States must go, unconditionally. Anti-American cries were heard in Prague from left-wing government officials, some press outlets, and even ordinary citizens. Laurence suspected that this had been ginned up on orders from Moscow. There was no way that the majority of Czechs could actually want the Americans gone. But too much was at stake to go on instinct alone. To confirm his hunch, he scheduled a meal on August 24 with Foreign Minister Masaryk.

The names Masaryk and Beneš were still paired in running Czechoslovakia, as they had been throughout the young country's history. But now it was the great man's son, Jan, who occupied Beneš's old office at the Czernin Palace and Beneš who filled Jan's father's seat at Prague Castle. The balding, clean-shaven, portly Jan had his father's intelligence and fundamental decency, but the resemblance ended there. The earnest elder Masaryk's motto was *Pravda Vítězí* (Truth Prevails), and he had lived by it—from his rebuttal of the Jewish blood libel to his ardent feminism, far ahead of his time. Jan, by contrast, was sarcastic. His motto was "*Pravda vítězí, ale dá to fušku.*" ("Truth prevails, but it's a chore.") But when it came to America, Jan's ties were even deeper than his father's: his mother was American, as was his fiancée, and he had served as the Czechoslovak ambassador in Washington.

Johnny, as Masaryk's American friends called him, tended not to take things too seriously, and that included the public demands that US troops depart. He told Laurence as the two dined that he and Beneš— and indeed most other members of the interim government—wanted the United States to keep its troops in place until the Soviets were also ready to withdraw. Laurence took Masaryk's word for it. They likely sealed the deal by pulling out their pipes (both were tobacco devotees) and puffing away together. Later, Laurence telegrammed Washington that his conversation with Masaryk left him satisfied that the Czech government wouldn't want US forces gone unless and until Soviet forces exited.

Laurence was optimistic that his strategy of engineering a simultaneous troop withdrawal could work, helping ensure free elections. He did not imagine that he was about to be blindsided by his own team.

⌣⌒⟩

LAURENCE's request to Viky for permission to occupy the palace passed in a series of telegrams and phone calls from Prague to Washington to New York. In August 1945, it finally made its way to Otto's son in the United States. He was now a thirty-one-year-old man who had spent World War II in the US Army. Just back from eighteen months in Europe, he had put his German to good use in army intelligence, including interrogating captured Nazi soldiers. He was the oldest of his immediate family still living. Exile from Prague had proved too much for his mother, Martha. She died less than a year after emigrating, collapsing at her daughters' feet in a Toronto boardinghouse while awaiting admission to the United States. Viky had managed to help get his sisters from Canada to the United States, and all three were safely in America.

The travails of his family, the war, and the passage of time had beaten the frivolity out of Viky. He had tried his hand at business in the Czech lands and then in America before enlisting. He lacked his father's skill, however, and his uncles had not entrusted him with a leadership role. (Otto's youngest and equally strong-willed brother, Hans, ended up in charge of the family business.) So Viky struck out on his own, trying everything from magazine publishing to importing bicycle parts—again without notable success.

Viky had also been tasked with the recovery of Otto's fortune. His mother and his uncles had been smarter than most. Under pressure from the Nazis (including Göring himself) to sell their holdings to preferred buyers, they had negotiated the best deals possible under duress. Although they had received just pennies on the dollar for their holdings, even that small fraction of their fortune enabled Viky and his sisters to live in relative comfort. Now Viky was figuring out how to reclaim or get paid in full for what was rightfully his: the coal mines, the factories, the bank, and, of course, his father's palace.

What Viky learned from Laurence was chilling. Williamson had conveyed the contents of Laurence's original message: "What the Soviets have done to the two Petschek houses that they occupy is just nobody's business. I have been in both of them on official calls and they are a mess, with soldiers tramping all over the place, removing and damaging everything in sight." Those were his uncles' houses! And as for the third house that the Soviets had invaded after the war—his own childhood home—Viky learned that they had raided it, removing silver, linen, and porcelain. But much else remained, including the furniture, and the palace itself was not yet irreparably damaged.

The situation would have horrified Otto: Armed Soviet Bolsheviks pilfering his things and occupying two of the other houses that had belonged to the family? The threat of commissars returning and sitting in Otto's dining room on one of his Louis XV chairs, eating off his Meissen china, ascending the staircase to spend some time in his green-tiled bathroom, followed by a long nap on the built-in bed in the master suite, snoring so violently that the tiny flowers carved into the wood shook? Viky's relationship with his father was a complex one, and he had no love for the palace, but this scenario was a nightmare nonetheless.

So he accepted Laurence's offer, and on August 28 sent a formal authorization back via an official in the family office in New York City: "On behalf of Mr. Viktor Petschek I hereby state that the above premises of Mr. Petschek may be occupied by the Ambassador . . . and that neither Mr. Viktor Petschek, nor I, nor any one on his behalf will make any claim of any nature or description for rent or for any payments for use and occupation of the said premises against the said United States Ambassador, the Government of the United States or the Government of Czechoslovakia."

LAURENCE's own State Department was less enthusiastic. Williamson wrote to Laurence that he had met with one of the longtime bureaucrats at the Buildings Office to ask that the United States rent the palace for Laurence.

The man listened, face sour. Finally he spoke: "The answer is 100% no." The embassy was habitable, he said, so Laurence should live there. The official told Williamson that he himself had visited Prague, and he produced a custodian's report of the embassy—dated 1939, before the war.

Williamson "blew up." Obviously the embassy had deteriorated, and Laurence needed to rent somewhere else while it was being restored, but the man was adamant.

"I will tell the Ambassador to write directly to the Secretary of State," Williamson replied.

The official retorted, "My office is full of complaint letters from Ambassadors written to the Secretary of State."

Williamson was a loyal friend, so he pushed back again. Eventually "the conversation was carried on in a more reasonable atmosphere," he informed Laurence.

Still, it was clear to the ambassador that State Department authorization to sign the lease would not be arriving anytime soon. It was not Laurence's first clash with Foggy Bottom, and they could drag things out forever. No matter. Laurence intended to occupy the palace, with or without permission from Washington, D.C.

ON August 31, Laurence got far worse news. The commander of the US troops, his friend General Ernest Harmon, told the ambassador in strictest confidence that two of his three US divisions guarding Czechoslovakia were being sent home by September 10 and would not be replaced. The third division was to be withdrawn by the first of November, at the order of Supreme HQ, headed by none other than Eisenhower. Ike was likely just responding to all those American families and their congressmen who were saying that the war was over and they wanted their boys back home. But he was displaying the same neglect of political consequences that had led him to allow the Soviets to liberate Prague, tilting the Czechs to the Soviet side in the first place. This latest decision threatened to make that damage permanent.

But this time, Laurence was on the ground to contest it. He launched a full-out assault, starting by bluntly telling the secretary of state, "The sudden withdrawal of all American forces from Czechoslovakia at this time while the Russians continue to maintain large forces in the country in violation of their promise to withdraw would constitute an abrupt reversal of our policy," and would be seen by Beneš and the Czechs as "an abandonment by the US of Czechoslovakia to further Russian influence."

To press the fight, Laurence consulted with perhaps the wisest man at the State Department, the number two in command, Dean Acheson. Both Laurence and Acheson were Ivy Leaguers and New Dealers turned diplomats. Unlike some at State, the Harvard Law–trained Acheson was comfortable with Jewish lawyers becoming American envoys. The two settled upon an idea: because their own government seemed indifferent to the virtues of simultaneous US and Soviet withdrawal, why not ask Beneš to take the initiative? The Czechoslovak president was well situated to advance the idea to the Soviets that they and the Americans withdraw at the same time. If Stalin concurred, the US Army could be persuaded to wait a little longer. Acheson asked Laurence to determine whether the Czechs would go along with this ploy.

On September 14, Laurence again made the trip up Castle Hill to see the Czech leader. Now, as he passed between Platzer's two Fighting Giants standing over their conquered opponents, they represented the ultimate threats that the Czechs faced if his plan failed. Laurence knew what Stalin's proposed "union of the Slavic peoples" would mean. The secret police sharply rapping on doors at midnight. The tortured confessions in basement cells. The show trials and the Gulags that came after that. In Beneš's office, Laurence explained his proposal for simultaneous troop withdrawal and put the question to the president: Would he make that request of Stalin?

It was one thing to help Laurence find a new home, but presenting a veiled ultimatum to the most feared man in Europe? That was not how Beneš had survived all these decades in international politics. He replied by asking if he could speak freely with Laurence in strictest confidence. Beneš explained that he was already quietly doing what he could to push back on the Soviet occupation. He had just dispatched his top general to a Soviet counterpart to complain about the soldiers and their depredations. Beneš described to Laurence a string of clashes between the Czech and Soviet soldiers, even "many murders" of Czech civilians by Soviet troops. Beneš thought that his general had made progress—so he was sending the man to Moscow "to ask for the immediate fulfillment of Stalin's promise to reduce Soviet forces in Czechoslovakia."

However, Beneš said that he was not prepared to go as far as Laurence's request. The Czech explained that any "attempt by him to obtain approval of the Cabinet to a request of US and Soviet Governments to effect simultaneous withdrawal . . . might precipitate dissension within his Government." The government was full of Communists, and they wanted the Soviet troops to stay. But Beneš had an idea. What if the *United States* proposed that Stalin withdraw, offering to do so simultaneously with the Soviets? True, it would be a bluff, because the United States had no intention of staying regardless. But Beneš could certainly promote it to his government and even support it in conversation with Stalin.

Beneš, wily as ever, had hit upon an approach that just might work—one of the intricate diplomatic minuets at which he was so practiced. Laurence thanked the president and returned to the embassy to report to D.C. His cable urged the adoption of the Beneš plan, because it was "the best prospect of achieving simultaneous withdrawal." And Laurence also stressed that the United States should keep two divisions in Czechoslovakia, at least "until the possibility of bringing about simultaneous withdrawal has been thoroughly explored." An order for troop reduction was already in place—set to take full effect in less than a week—and Laurence urged that it be reversed.

He waited for word back from Washington no less anxiously than a death-row prisoner anticipating a pardon. At the end of September, a response arrived: the military brass would postpone the withdrawal while they decided whether or not to be a part of Laurence's proposed stratagem. It rubbed them the wrong way to have their men serve as pawns in Laurence's chess match with Stalin, but at least they would consider it.

Laurence thought that he knew how to close the deal. Eisenhower had helped create his problems in Prague. Now Laurence would lure the general to the Golden City to solve them.

⌒

As for the palace, Laurence decided to take matters into his own hands. If the State Department refused to rent the palace for him, he would just do it himself. The D.C. bureaucracy couldn't stop him if he wanted to personally obtain a rental property; on such matters, unlike troop withdrawals, an ambassador had virtually unlimited authority.

The Czech Ministry of Defense was the custodian of the property, and that September Laurence negotiated a lease with the officials there who were tasked with executing Beneš's wishes. The Communists among them wrinkled their noses at turning over the palace to an arch-capitalist. (They might have been surprised to learn that Laurence's own government had misgivings, too.) But the president's wishes carried the day, and the ministry signed a one-year lease for Otto's palace and compound in September. Rent was set at 150,000 Czech crowns per year.

Now the property was under Laurence's protection—but not, he soon discovered, ready for his occupancy. Laurence had to enlist the Czechoslovak government's help to evict squatters in the two houses on the other side of the gardens; one of the illicit occupants was the local representative of the International Red Cross. Next Laurence turned his attention to repairing the palace, rushing to beat the winter as Otto had done year after year during the construction. There were almost twenty leaks in the roof and innumerable other urgent fixes needed.

Laurence replanted the grounds, tending to a new ring of flowers and greenery surrounding the palace. He wrote to the Netherlands and New York for thousands of bulbs for the garden: crocuses, jacinths, narcissus, tulips. He hoped to use the huge indoor pool, which had not been filled since Otto closed it more than a decade before, but the water pipes were hopelessly clogged. Laurence put plumbers to work, and soon they were digging up the lawn to locate the blockage. It was a familiar scene to the Watchers of Prague, the flaneurs once more strolling the perimeter, remembering Otto's many building complications.

In October, after weeks of work, Laurence finally moved in. For all the losses and wear, the opulence of the home and its contents was still breathtaking. Much had survived, down to the collection of miniature paintings dotting the palace, resting on small easels atop ornate inlaid tables: Saint Jerome kneeling next to a lion, a self-possessed royal infanta, a child in a Dutch cap, praying.

Mr. Pokorný, remarkably, had endured as well. He had preserved it all and entrusted it to a new proprietor—a sympathetic one, at that. His plea to Laurence in July—if it was one—had worked.

The impassive butler seldom let his feelings show. But they were reflected in a story that is still shared among the Watchers of Prague. When Laurence took occupancy, according to the legend, Pokorný dug up the valuables that he had buried in the backyard before the Germans occupied the premises and presented them to Laurence for display in the palace. The story may or may not be true—unlike the interment of the bag, the reports about its exhumation that survive are uncertain—but the existence of gratitude and trust that the story conveys surely is.

Laurence ran the US flag high above the compound on an exceptionally tall pole to announce that he had moved in. Just let the Soviets try to raid the palace now.

⌒

On October 11, Laurence welcomed General Eisenhower to Prague. The ambassador met the supreme commander of the Allies at the airport, ushered him into his own car, and used their time together to advocate for his troop withdrawal solution. Eisenhower, the Kansas farm boy who was now a five-star general, was a shrewd analyst, though he liked to hide it behind his folksy manner. As Laurence badgered him (albeit diplomatically), Ike listened. He was polite but noncommittal as Laurence escorted him from one Czech official to the next.

Adoring crowds lined the streets for a glimpse of the soldier who had led the effort to deliver Europe from the Nazis. (Little did they imagine that he shared responsibility for allowing the Soviets to seize most of the country.) Laurence made sure to include a stop at the Petschek palace for Eisenhower. The general was accustomed to finery—but surely even he was impressed by Otto's masterpiece. Laurence wasn't just showing off his new home; the palace, with its recapitulation of centuries of European culture, was also a reminder of why Prague was worth saving.

The day culminated in a lunch with Beneš at Prague Castle. The Czech president warmly greeted the Americans and pinned medals on Eisenhower and his entourage. That flattery and all the day's attentions seem to have worked: Eisenhower ordered his staff to reexamine the withdrawal of American troops.

With just one visit, the palace had paid for itself.

⌒

Almost as an afterthought, Laurence sent the lease that he had signed to Viky, "so he will know just what it is that he has approved." The ambassador undoubtedly thought that Otto's heir would be pleased at how neatly the transaction had been done. But when Laurence's letter and the lease made it to Viky that October in New York, he was livid. He may have hated the palace, had no intention of living there, and endured a rocky relationship with its creator. But he was still its rightful owner and his father's son. Why was the lease with the Czechoslovak government and not with him? He had extended temporary rights only to Laurence—he had given no such authority to the Czechs.

By what legal authority did Czechoslovakia claim dominion over his property?

And why was the ambassador paying the Czechs 150,000 crowns per year? Viky had intended the occupancy to be rent-free, not to fatten the coffers of the state. If anyone should be collecting rent, it should be he.

Viky had volunteered for the US Army. He served almost two years overseas, putting his life at risk for America. He was decorated with four campaign stars and honorably discharged. He was now a US citizen. He was not going to be treated this way.

He pulled out his pen and began to write.

⌁

LAURENCE'S initiative with Eisenhower got off to a promising start when the general's staff visited the ambassador to follow up. They understood the need for simultaneous withdrawal and seemed receptive. The usual flow of paper to and from Laurence and D.C. ensued. The capital never seemed to fear Stalin's hand moving the pieces at the other side of the board quite as Laurence did. The need to avoid removing American troops when the Soviets remained was so obvious, however, that Laurence allowed himself to hope.

But in the end, Czechoslovokia's Eisenhower jinx proved too powerful to overcome. During deliberations at US Army headquarters in Frankfurt, Ike's well-intentioned staff made a comment about perhaps leaving troops in place over the winter. That caused the D.C. brass to convulse. They dreaded the prospect of explaining the decision to the parents and spouses who would not have their sons or husbands home for Christmas—or, more to the point, the congressional representatives of those families.

The visit had bought Laurence a little more time to maneuver, but not even much of that. After a stream of dueling cables, an absolute final deadline was set for American withdrawal, deal or no deal: December 1. At the end of October, the secretary of state sent a memo to President Truman (perhaps the one American official even more plainspoken than

Ike). The memo asked Truman to write to Stalin and propose simultaneous withdrawal no later than the end of November.

The gambit was not without risk for Truman: if Stalin refused and the US troops left anyway, America would look weak. Just months before, in May, as a newcomer to the Oval Office, Truman had refused to intervene in Prague's fate. Now the president had found his footing, and his innate decency did not allow him to make that mistake a second time. On November 2, he penned a note directly to Stalin:

> As you know, ever since the time when the late President Wilson intimately associated himself with the liberation of [Czechoslovakia] from Habsburg rule, my country has followed with deep and sympathetic interest the struggle of the [Czech] people for national independence and economic security . . .
>
> The continued presence of Allied troops . . . is proving to be a great drain on [Czech] economic resources and is delaying the normal recovery and rehabilitation of this Allied state which remained longer under Nazi domination than any other member of the United Nations. I therefore desire to withdraw the American forces from [Czech] territory by Dec 1, 1945 . . . I should therefore like to propose to you that the Red army be withdrawn simultaneously with our forces.
>
> I hope that you can give consideration to my proposal and that, in withdrawing our forces simultaneously, we can announce to the world our intention of removing any obstacle which delays the recovery of the [Czech] state.

Now matters were in the hands of Laurence's nemesis. All the ambassador could do was wait anxiously for an answer from Stalin in the comfort of the palace. At least, he believed, he had secured that property.

10

Lush Life

O N November 8, Stalin's answer arrived.

The day was cold and the sky a pale gray. The soaring branches of the eight great trees ringing the lawn of the palace gardens were largely bare now. Inside the house, Laurence stepped down the baronial staircase. He was polished: his tie tightly knotted, his black brogues shined to a high gloss as he passed below the enormous Flemish tapestry of Jason on bent knee before Neptune. Laurence was planning a visit to the castle to see Beneš later that day.

At the embassy, Laurence checked the overnight cables, flipping through the decoded blue papers to see if there was any word back on Truman's offer to Stalin. He had been waiting for days, and there was still no news. Why was it taking so long? What game was Stalin up to? Would Laurence's strategy succeed, or would Stalin call his bluff?

Soon he was in his car, making the familiar, bumpy trek through the narrow cobblestoned passageways of Malá Strana up the winding incline to their pinnacle: Prague Castle. After just four months, the American envoy had become such a frequent visitor that he could almost stand between the Platzer Fighting Giants at the gate, close his eyes, and find his way blind through the broad courtyards and narrow avenues of the keep.

Laurence entered President Beneš's office, prepared to make excuses for the lack of information on their troop-withdrawal strategy. But that day Beneš had a surprise for his American friend. Ludvik Svoboda, the pro-Soviet Czech defense minister, had just left the castle. He had broken dramatic news to Beneš. Moscow had ordered the Soviet commanders "to begin the withdrawal of . . . forces from Czechoslovakia immediately and to complete the same within three weeks."

It must have taken an instant to register before it hit the unsuspecting Laurence. The strategy had worked. The Soviet troops were leaving. It was a sweet moment for the ambassador, his first major policy success in Prague.

True, it was a strange way for him to find out about it. Stalin had likely sequenced his answer so that the Soviets could be the first to notify the Czechs, taking credit and squeezing every drop of advantage out of the situation. But what did it matter? Elections would take place the following year without the presence of the Soviet troops.

It was not merely a diplomatic triumph. It was a win for democracy— and a big one. Beneš, at least, knew who was responsible. He beamed at the American ambassador, "expressed his keen satisfaction with the message sent by President Truman to Stalin and requested . . . [Laurence] transmit his thanks to the President."

Formal confirmation arrived the next day. Washington telegrammed the reply that President Truman had at last gotten from Stalin:

I have received your message concerning the withdrawal of the American and Soviet armies from Czechoslovakia. Unfortunately, it was delayed in reaching me in view of the irregularity of air mail from Moscow to Sochi in connection with the variable weather. Your proposal concerning the withdrawal of the armies during November can only be welcomed particularly since it fully accords with the Soviet plans for demobilization and withdrawal of armies. Consequently, it may be considered that the withdrawal of the Soviet and American armies from Czechoslovakia will be completed by the first of December.

The supposed basis for the delay was dubious. Laurence knew well from his own experiences there that no one in the Soviet Union dared slow anything headed for the dictator, for fear of their lives. It didn't matter. The Soviets were leaving, and Laurence was too delighted to mind the subterfuge.

HIS good mood was punctured when Viky's letter arrived later that month. Otto's heir applied only the thinnest veneer of politeness to his anger, using a tone that would have been familiar to his father's correspondents:

> I was, of course, very much astonished to see that the lease was not concluded by somebody representing me but by the Czechoslovak State . . . I was also surprised that the lease provides for an annual rental of 150,000 Czech crowns . . . [as I had] the intention of not having any annual rental charged to our government . . . I should appreciate it very much if you could . . . have the great kindness to inform me how the Czechoslovak State represented by the Ministry of National Defense has purported to acquire title to my property.

The insinuation was unmistakable: Laurence's occupancy of the palace was tainted, even illegitimate.

Perhaps Laurence should have considered all that Viky had lost, or asked how *he* would have reacted under these circumstances, or even reopened negotiations with the Czechs.

Instead, Laurence was infuriated. He had saved the property, was spending his own money to do so, and expected some gratitude. Besides, he had already moved in, giving up his apartment in the embassy. Housing in Prague was scarce, and he had no place else to live.

Viky's letter put Laurence in a moral bind—and a legal one. His goal had been to protect the palace. Now he was at risk of being accused of collaborating with the Communist-laden Czech government to expropriate the property of a Holocaust refugee.

Laurence wasn't ready to respond to the tricky problems that Viky's letter posed. So he didn't write back immediately. Instead, he did nothing—for one day, then for a second and a third.

In the frenzy of Laurence's work—addressing the logistics of the troop withdrawal, figuring out how the embassy would cope without the soldiers assigned to tasks there, engaging with the Czechs about a thousand other follow-on details—it was all too easy for him to put off grappling with the hard questions in Viky's letter. There was always something urgent that needed his immediate attention.

⌇

AMONG those distractions was a new friend: Countess Cecilia Sternberg. Although she was thirty-seven, she remained girlish, with a cheeky
grin and wavy blond hair. From her father she had inherited ancient
German lineage and debts; on her maternal side, new titles and money.
Her mother, Lilly Whitehead Hoyos, was a dazzling beauty descended
from the English entrepreneur who invented the modern torpedo. The
young Cecilia had her mother's looks and the explosiveness of her great-
grandfather's munitions. The lovely, wild girl was shipped off at twenty
to live with her grandmother in Vienna. She sought to tame Cecilia and
arrange a suitable husband for the free-spirited young woman. Instead,
Cecilia soon became a fixture at parties across the city, dancing the
Charleston with the highest kick in the Austrian capital.

Her husband, Leopold, Count of Sternberg, was twelve years older
than Cecilia and a known playboy when he first admired her dance
moves, that slim foot flashing in the air over her head. He was one of
Vienna's *Gloriosen* (glorious ones), equally at home with the *erste Gesell-
schaft* (elite of the emperor's court) and in the nightclubs of the city. The
freethinking Leopold prized Cecilia's untamed nature. It amused him
to think of providing her with a gilded cage—but with its door ajar. Their
marriage was a happy and open one. They both had paramours but never
let that interfere with their domestic harmony.

Laurence's relationship with the countess began unpropitiously. She
and the count invited him to a shoot at their country house, Častolovice.
But the night before, Laurence stayed up late working (likely on the all-
consuming troop-withdrawal issue) and overslept the next morning. By
the time he woke, jumped into his clothes, and raced the ninety miles
from Prague to the Sternbergs' estate, he was more than two hours late.

At noon, Laurence roared up to Častolovice in an American sports
car, "long, low and bright," parked, and dashed through the main gate on
foot. Častolovice was a thirteenth-century fortress with a large interior
courtyard where Laurence's host, hostess, and the hunting party were
awaiting his arrival.

Count Leopold seemed composed as Laurence approached, but
Countess Cecilia was fuming, her high brow furrowed. Guests were
expected to be strictly punctual. "The head forester, the gamekeep-

ers, loaders, and a hundred beaters had all been kept waiting," she later wrote. A couple dozen aristocrats milled around as well, also visibly annoyed. All were decked out in brown or forest-green hunting attire made from thick, water-repellent fabric and sported matching felt hats adorned with silver insignia and medals.

They were the leading members of what was left in Czechoslovakia of the Austro-Hungarian aristocracy. The Sternbergs and their friends had avoided collaborating with the Nazi occupation. Cecilia and Leopold had been punished with confiscation of their estates, and others of their circle had suffered far worse, including deportation to concentration camps, torture, and execution. Those who had survived had their property returned. They were Laurence's natural allies in his campaign to fight Communism—and would have been glad to see him if he were not two hours late. The ambassador's Jewish heritage also did not recommend him to everyone in attendance.

To make things worse, as the American envoy got closer, Cecilia saw that he was "oddly attired." He had "a broad, shiny, very new-looking cartridge belt strapped tightly round his waist, and a largish felt hat on his head."

"Here comes the Wild West," whispered a friend to the countess as Laurence finally reached them and bid them a cheerful good morning, seemingly unaware of the seriousness of his faux pas. The count, bemused as ever and accustomed (unlike some in the group) to socializing with Jews from his years in café society, introduced Laurence around. Perhaps he found the contrast between the irate aristocrats and the oblivious ambassador funny.

But when Laurence asked the countess if he could take a bath, Cecilia couldn't hold back any longer. "We've been waiting for two hours, Your Excellency," she told him in none too gentle a tone. His offense finally registered. Laurence apologized, explaining, "I'm sorry, I had a late night and overslept." But in trying to make amends, he only dug his hole deeper. He pulled a small package out of his bag. "This is for you," he said, smiling, handing it to Cecilia. Expecting a traditional housewarming gift, the countess unwrapped it and found a dozen nylons and a bottle of Chanel No. 5. It was "the typical GI gift to his girl," she thought—hardly the usual present for the noble hostess of a hunting party.

Unable to bathe, Laurence settled for a quick trip to the bathroom, but it was not fast enough to prevent the group from acidly discussing his failings. While he was gone, they tore him to pieces. "Diplomatic customs seem to have changed," said one aristocrat. "In my day ambassadors were always punctual," muttered another.

The countess, her pique fading now that she had vented it, and always a bit of a contrarian, found herself defending him. "How can he know our routine?" she asked. "Or even how to shoot?" someone fired back. Cecilia's sister-in-law tried to smooth things over, noting, "He's very handsome . . . Spanish-looking."

But even this was assaulted by the irritated nobles. "Spanish! Jewish, you mean," hissed one of the other guests, Princess Marika. Cecilia's uncle Franzi replied, matter-of-factly, "Sephardic." Franzi was the dean of the group and was trying to be a peacemaker.

When Laurence reappeared, they finally made their way to the shooting grounds in a nearby deer park. As they set up, Uncle Franzi was apprehensive. The hunters were each given spots around a lake. Franzi and Cecilia were positioned next to Laurence. The older man whispered to the countess, "We may be in great danger from the ambassador" if he was clumsy with his aim. "I've been peppered before, but you don't want to get it full in your pretty face. Stand close behind me."

Cecilia found that she was more worried about Laurence further embarrassing himself than she was about being injured. Would this Jewish diplomat be able to even fire his gun? "The head forester blew a single note on his horn, then came the great soaring of ducks rising from the water and volley after volley of shots. To my amazement I saw Steinhardt . . . accurately and neatly bring down one bird after another."

If she was surprised, Uncle Franzi and the rest were downright astonished. "Well, I'll be damned," exclaimed Uncle Franzi. "Good shooting!" he called over to Laurence. Cecilia exhaled with relief. She caught her husband's eye and saw that he was also glad that their guest had been spared embarrassment. More than that, Laurence had transformed himself in the eyes of the hunting party. She felt that it was "stupid arrogance," but "Steinhardt, having proved himself their equal at a gentleman's sport, would impress them far more by this than by the fact that he was the representative of the most powerful nation in the world."

She smiled warmly at Laurence and he reciprocated, grinning back.

Cecilia felt a spark flare between them. "The ambassador didn't do too badly, did he?" she asked her uncle.

"Remarkably well for a little Jew," Franzi answered.

The slur made her shudder, especially coming from Franzi. He was normally broad-minded, had supported the resistance to the Nazis, and had himself survived a stint in a concentration camp for his efforts. She wheeled on him.

"Why," she asked crossly, "shouldn't a Jew shoot as well as a Christian?"

"Because of their ancestry. They were never killers—we are," her uncle mildly replied.

⌒

AT lunch, Cecilia sat Laurence in the place of honor, at her right. The American had felled the third most ducks of the group; his tardiness, his Buffalo Bill ammo belt, his Hebraic origins—all were forgotten in light of the success of his shooting. Even Cecilia, although she knew better than to judge a person by such irrelevancies, found her attraction to Laurence deepened by his prowess with a rifle.

The anti-Semitic Princess Marika, however, continued to eye him unpleasantly, as if a spoiled dish of food had been placed before her. When Laurence piled his plate with pork, Marika slid a platter of cold pheasant in his direction. "Would Your Excellency not prefer this?" she loudly asked.

"Thank you, later perhaps. This ham is delicious, as good as our Virginia ham."

"But it's pork; I thought perhaps because of your religion . . ."

A hush fell over the party. The princess had intended to put him in his place. But Laurence had dealt with anti-Semitism his whole life: from the Waspy New York legal establishment to elements within the State Department's notorious bureaucracy to the Kremlin's open hostility. He made short work of his adversary.

"Oh that! I'm not very Orthodox, I'm afraid. Our biblical ancestors had very good reason to forbid the eating of pork, because of the danger of trichinosis, but by now it's tested in every country and quite safe." His voice was clear and firm.

"Neatly countered," Cecilia's cousin whispered to her. "What a bitch!"

Later, when the kills were displayed and a ritual horn blown as the hunting party doffed their caps, Cecilia took Laurence aside. "Aren't such . . . absurd ceremonies rather difficult for an American to understand, in this day and age?"

"Not at all—our Indians and those of South America have much the same customs. The spirits of the animals killed have to be appeased lest they never return to the hunting ground. Come, I'll drive you home. It's a brand new car they've sent me—let's see how fast she can go."

Cecilia slipped in beside him. "How lightly and almost casually his hands rested on the wheel, yet how certain his control of the powerful car," she recalled later.

"I think you and I are going to be great friends," Laurence said.

"Not at a hundred miles an hour," she said, her eye on the speedometer.

He slowed down. "I didn't want to frighten you," he said. "It's just that I'm rather impatient by nature. Once I know my way and where I want to go, I like to get there fast. Do you understand?"

She felt the same way, and she let him know it. Their affair had begun.

ON November 20, Laurence was in Plzeň, site of the American military headquarters, for the farewell ceremony to the American troops. He was seated on the dais next to Masaryk. The two colleagues—Masaryk, with his American antecedents, and Laurence, with his European ones—were the picture of diplomacy, both elegantly hatted and gloved, their breath puffing before them. They watched the American troops parade by the thousands, joined by their commander, General Harmon, whose tip to his friend Laurence had made this moment of triumph possible.

The waves of soldiers passing by were orderly, yet very American: relaxed and loose-limbed. The cadence was chanted by the cheerful troops, the beat in swing time, bringing to mind Glenn Miller, Benny Goodman, and Frank Sinatra. What a contrast to the rigid, severe strutting of the Nazis whom they had defeated and displaced. Thousands of Czechs had shown up to see their heroes off, to thank the departing GIs. The streets were crowded with them; they filled windows and terraces and were even perched on ledges and hanging from lampposts.

Laurence watched with pride, but he couldn't ignore the specter of what might have been. If Eisenhower had just listened, letting Patton liberate Prague, this ecstatic affection for Americans wouldn't be on display only in Plzeň; it would also be alive in the capital. Instead it was the Soviets who had captured that political advantage.

But diplomacy had its limits, and Laurence had done what he could: he'd come up with a plan to contain the damage, fought for it in his government, and ultimately pulled the levers to get Stalin to agree. How different this parade would feel if the Soviets were staying back. For today at least, Laurence was visibly pleased. His pride only grew when Foreign Minister Masaryk delivered his remarks:

> General Harmon, Mr. Ambassador, officers and soldiers of the American Army! I'm going to say a few words in English. I'm not going to be long—it's too cold for long speeches. During the last war, Woodrow Wilson, your great president, took a very definite stance about the settlement of the war and the establishment of peace . . . Woodrow Wilson helped to discover Czechoslovakia . . .
>
> You young Americans rediscovered Czechoslovakia a few months ago. You came at the moment of the greatest emergency the lovely land of Bohemia has ever experienced. You helped to free us and you stayed while we were catching our breath after seven years of hell . . .
>
> Now you are about to leave us and I am here to say thank you and God bless you! . . . Soon you will be passing that symbolic lady, the Statue of Liberty. Will you please tell her for us that we too believe in liberty, that we refuse to live without liberty . . . We shall not give it up. God bless America and you her sons, who fought so well to save the world. You did a swell job.

As the painfully cold winter set in, Laurence continued to defer answering Viky's letter. He had another distraction, and a welcome one: his family. Laurence's wife, Dulcie, and their twenty-year-old daughter, Dulcie Ann, had rejoined him. He had installed them snugly in the palace, seemingly one of the few properly heated structures in the entire city, thanks to Otto's flair for modern engineering. Laurence must have been repelled by the thought of taking any action that might dislodge his family.

The three breakfasted together in the intimate family dining room at the south end of the second floor. This was where Otto had once struck the beat of operas on the oval table, challenging the children to guess the aria. He had designed the room to seat his family of six. Otto's love for rich color and pattern was still evident in the fireplace of veined marble, the zebra-wood bureaus against the paneled walls, and a nineteenth-century Persian madder rug atop the parquet floor. He would have felt right at home had he come strolling through the door, the room unchanged but for the Steinhardt family photos and knick-knacks on the mantel.

Laurence's wife, Dulcie, was small and beautiful, with symmetrical features and perfectly smooth skin. She wore fur at all times, suffering from a neurological condition that left her chilly even on the hottest summer days. They had been married since 1923, and they had once loved each other, Laurence's warmth and humor balancing out Dulcie's reserve and sophistication. But they had gradually drifted apart. Now each looked elsewhere for companionship. Laurence (contrary to type for a man of his generation) turned a blind eye to her affairs more readily than Dulcie—who had a jealous streak—did to his. The situation did not lend itself to marital harmony, and their rows had become louder and more frequent over the years, with even the occasional talk of divorce.

Yet they remained married, above all to avoid injuring the third person at the breakfast table, contentedly sipping her coffee and eating her buttered toast: their daughter, Dulcie Ann. She was lovely and shyer than her mother, though she shared her fair skin and round face. One could see her resemblance to her father in her curious, almond-shaped eyes. Dulcie Ann adored both her parents and took no sides in their grievances. She was her mother's primary confidante, dissecting world events and exchanging embassy gossip with her in the second-floor sitting room of the palace, once Martha's boudoir, beneath the inset paintings of the Four Graces. And Dulcie Ann was her father's partner in his more clandestine diplomatic adventures. In Moscow and Ankara, she had discreetly shuttled sensitive papers from her dad to Jewish families or to other diplomats (including the compassionate papal nuncio to Turkey, Angelo Roncalli, later to become Pope John XXIII). When an extracurricular mission could not be trusted to anyone outside the family, Dulcie Ann would accompany her father into the countryside after dark to pick up an envelope, a package, or even a person, holding Laurence's revolver ready in her lap, just in case. She was a dead shot. Neither parent seemed concerned about the risk to Dulcie Ann. Indeed, Dulcie herself was not averse to occasionally pitching in on these excursions, despite her medical condition.

After breakfast, Laurence headed off to the embassy. Many days, Dulcie Ann left with him, winding down Castle Hill in their Packard, known for its slightly wobbly steering. With the diplomatic mission still understaffed and the piles of paper—which included ever longer and more painful lists of Jewish Americans' missing relatives—mounting, Dulcie Ann had volunteered to help with the filing. And, with her mother frequently ailing, Dulcie Ann often spent a substantial part of the day managing her father's official social life and accompanying him in the evenings to events.

On one of those occasions, Dulcie Ann demonstrated her fearlessness. She was attending a diplomatic dinner with her father at another one of the Petschek houses: that of Otto's brother Fritz. The Soviets who had occupied it after leaving Otto's premises had handed it over to their country's ambassador, Valerian Zorin, for his use. It was even larger than Otto's home but boxy and cold, ostentatious without personality.

As Dulcie Ann entered the banquet hall and took her seat at the long table, she was surprised to see, framing her round dinner plate, Otto Petschek's silverware. The entire table was set with it, gleaming knives, forks, and spoons arrayed upon the white tablecloth like soldiers guarding the china, the utensils emblazoned with a stylized baroque letter *P*. It was the palace silver that the Soviet soldiers had seized in their raid.

Dulcie Ann could be every bit as bold as her father, and she decided to confront Zorin. He was an intimidating figure, tough and crafty enough to weather Stalin's periodic purges of senior officials. After serving as a liaison to the Czechs during the war, Zorin had been assigned to maintain Moscow's influence in Prague. He was Laurence's opponent in the battle for the country—and thus, according to the principle of daughterly loyalty, Dulcie Ann's as well.

She waited for the right moment. When there was a lull in conversation, she turned to the Soviet ambassador and demurely informed him that he was using Otto Petschek's silver. It had been stolen from their home by Soviet troops. She was soft-spoken but steely.

The ambassador denied it. But Dulcie Ann could tell from the monograms. They looked down at the stylized *P*—it was unmistakably Otto's mark. Dulcie Ann had caught Zorin out, and they both knew it.

A few days later, a large, heavy crate from the Soviets was delivered to the palace. The lid was pried off to reveal the Petschek family silver. The heavy utensils were nestled in the container, each adorned with a single tiny, ornate, twisting capital *P.* Laurence was delighted. His daughter had scored another small victory against the Soviets and a significant restoration of property for the palace he had come to cherish as if it were his own.

⌒

THE presence of Laurence's family did not slow his relationship with Cecilia. She reciprocated his ardor. "He was still in the prime of life when we met—a handsome, vivacious man, radiating energy and optimism," she recalled later. She was unabashed about sex, leavening that frankness with her sense of humor. With a wicked twinkle, she called Laurence "Your Excellency." They both laughed at her silliness, though he never really objected to being reminded of his position.

They discussed everything: politics, the arts, society, and other people—especially aristocrats. She became an important source for him in his diplomacy, one of his confidantes who had known Prague not only before and after the war but during it. Her and Leopold's apartment had served as a clandestine meeting place for resisters, and she could tell Laurence who was who. She had been brave in other ways as well. When the Nazi persecutions began, she would go to the Jewish ghetto near the Old New Synagogue. There she saw Jews queuing for trains, "gathered together like cattle, branded with the yellow star." Despite the danger posed by the German sentries, she did what she could to help the terrified people, pressing "a little money stealthily into their hands" and whispering prayers on their behalf in the adjacent Old Jewish Cemetery among its helter-skelter ancient tombstones.

Over time, even Laurence's and Cecilia's spouses grew close. The two couples were at the head of their respective social orders in Prague, the aristocratic and the diplomatic. As a result, the four of them were constantly thrown together at cocktail gatherings, formal white-tie balls, and even weekend house parties. Dulcie and Leopold were soon carrying on an open flirtation of their own. The rich and socially prominent Dulcie was used to people falling all over themselves to please her, but

Cecilia observed that Leopold "could not have cared less if she had been the Empress of China." Dulcie knew that Leopold liked her for who she was, and that meant a great deal. "He teased her out of moods and tempers, laughed at her airs and graces, shocked her with ribald jokes, and hugged and kissed her most disrespectfully whenever they met."

Dulcie returned Leopold's attentions, though as far as Cecilia knew the relationship never went beyond flirtation (not that the open-minded countess would have objected). Cecilia was also fond of Dulcie—up to a point. Dulcie hoped for "heart-to-heart woman's talk," the kinds of confidences that Cecilia shared with no one. The war, with all those covert, desperate conversations at their home, had taught Cecilia to beware of making disclosures, especially about herself.

Most uncomfortably for the countess, Dulcie tried to probe the relationship between Laurence and Cecilia. She would ask thorny, embarrassing questions: "Do tell me, was there a little romance between you and Laurence before I came to Prague? I wouldn't blame you in the least. After all you didn't know me then—and he is very attractive to women." Cecilia's mind raced in those moments. She didn't want to lie, but she couldn't bring herself to tell the truth, either. So she took a more direct tack. "Romance? What do you mean, Dulcie? Do you mean sex?" Cecilia's ploy worked; Dulcie reversed course: "I didn't mean anything as crude as that."

Others were curious as well. Communists had muscled their way into key Czech security positions, including in the Státní bezpečnost (StB), the state security police. The StB and its informants were everywhere in Prague, collecting information in scraps and in bushels—an ugly new auxiliary corps among the Watchers of Prague. That surveillance was often reinforced by a second set of peering eyes: Stalin's spies, the KGB officers whose presence swelled the ranks of the Soviet embassy, filtering out into every part of the capital.

If Laurence and Cecilia's affair had been exposed, they could have faced blackmail or scandal. Cecilia could afford to dismiss that, having disregarded public opinion since her days as a Vienna debutante flapper. But Laurence was another matter. He was one of America's leading diplomats and responsible for protecting the sole remaining democracy in central and eastern Europe.

Yet he too seems to have shrugged off the danger. Sometimes the best place to hide was in plain sight, he had learned. And that was how he carried on his affair with Cecilia: openly. If the two of them made no show of subterfuge and were regularly seen in a foursome with their spouses, how could anyone claim their behavior to be out of the ordinary? So Laurence sailed ahead, intoxicated with the beauty around him—Cecilia, the palace, and Prague.

VIKY's letter was ignored into December and might have stayed that way indefinitely. But Viky enlisted powerful allies, and they forced Laurence's hand: the Dulles brothers, John Foster and Allen, two of the most feared lawyers in New York. The grandchildren of one secretary of state and the nephews of a second, they had served every American president since Wilson. Both men were fierce opponents of Communism, which Foster once described as "Godless terrorism." The two would go on to serve as secretary of state and Central Intelligence Agency director, respectively, during the height of the Cold War, ruthlessly prosecuting it.

The Dulleses' emissary to Laurence, chosen from among their firm's cadre of ex-spies and anti-Bolsheviks, was their protégé Bernard Yarrow. Born in the Ukraine as Bernard Yarrowshevitz, he emigrated to the United States in 1922, anglicizing his name. Like Laurence, he was of Jewish ancestry, a Columbia Law grad, and with a Prague connection, having spent the war years as a liaison between the US Office of Strategic Services (the precursor to the CIA) and exile governments in London, including the Czechoslovak one.

Yarrow arrived in Prague in early December 1945 and was welcomed by the ambassador. The visitor explained that he was there to begin the process of reclaiming all the Petschek interests, including the full and vast network of mines, factories, banks, and residences spanning the Czech lands (and beyond). Viky wanted full restitution from the Czech government and others now asserting ownership. Yarrow does not seem to have expressly mentioned the palace or Viky's letter about it. He didn't have to. There could be no mistaking his point.

Whatever Laurence may have been feeling, he was experienced in the ways of both New York lawyers and international diplomacy. He countered Yarrow's thrust with a parry of his own. He fully supported Viky's interests—so much so that he was already doing everything he could to protect them. He genially explained to Yarrow that "the country is still living through the last stages of the 'revolution' . . . [so] the time is not propitious to press for the immediate settlement of the claims." Viky needed to practice some patience and to trust Laurence. If he did, the ambassador was prepared to get the Czechs to solve "these problems on the basis of compensation in American dollars."

Laurence meant it, too—he really was committed to protecting everything owned by Viky and other Americans, the palace included. His decision to expend his own cash to rent the place was proof. But he was annoyed that Viky didn't see it that way; Laurence would not be bullied by him, the Dulleses, Yarrow, or anyone else. On December 17, Laurence finally sent a reply to Viky's letter via messenger, coldly answering his long-pending questions:

> Your property was taken over by the State pursuant to a Presidential Decree and assigned by the State to the Ministry of National Defense . . . the legal situation is extremely conflicting because of the many Presidential Decrees which have been issued . . . such things as were in the house when [the United States] took it over are safe and probably will continue to be so, as long as [the United States] occupies the premises. . . . All in all . . . it [is] very fortunate that your house has been occupied as an Embassy or otherwise if reports here are correct the premises would doubtless have been taken over by occupying armies and the contents lost.

He had come some distance from the man who, just a few months before, had sought Viky's permission before he would even consider moving into the Petschek compound. Laurence had taken possession of the palace, but the reverse was becoming true as well.

⌒

WHATEVER emotions Viky and Laurence, remotely dueling across the Atlantic Ocean, may have felt, Bernie Yarrow approached the situation with an intelligence officer's detachment. He remained in Prague for almost all of December to conduct his own independent due diligence and determine whether to accept Laurence's offer or, perhaps, evict him from Viky's property. The swashbuckling ambassador was of interest to the American press, and it would have taken only one leak to a Walter Winchell to generate some heat. The Dulleses were certainly not above such ploys.

For his part, Laurence maintained perfectly cordial relations with Yarrow. He even invited the visitor, far from home, to spend Christmas Eve as Laurence's guest at the palace. Like Otto, Laurence and Yarrow celebrated the holiday in spite of their Jewish roots.

On December 26, 1945, Yarrow wrote to Foster Dulles to convey the results of his investigation. He had talked to President Beneš; the prime minister; the ministers of finance, industry, and foreign trade; and others. Yarrow's recommendation: Take Laurence up on his offer. Indeed, they had no other choice: "I was informed by the various Ministers that . . . to all intents and purposes, Ambassador Steinhardt will in fact be counsel for all American interests." The road to restitution for the palace and all Viky's property passed through Laurence.

That was that. Laurence was free to remain in Otto's creation. If Viky felt any twinge, we do not know it. The ambassador was magnanimous, sending a message through Yarrow. How much did Viky and his family members want Laurence to ask for the palace—and everything else? Yarrow wrote to Foster Dulles: "The Ambassador suggested that you . . . give him an idea of what amount in dollars would be a good settlement of all the claims of our clients. Also, he would like to have another estimate as to what a fair settlement would be, and finally a minimum in dollars which our clients would be willing to accept."

There was one hitch, Laurence candidly told Yarrow. The exact price would depend on the Czech elections and their aftermath. But as he saw Yarrow off, the ambassador felt confident that democracy would prevail, due to his success in ousting the Soviet troops. Careful lawyer that he was, Laurence prepared his own memo of his meeting with Yarrow. In it, Laurence wrote that "the Communists will be lucky to poll 20 per cent of the total vote," losing two and maybe three seats in the cabinet. Waiting until after the election would likely produce a more favorable outcome for Viky. "The Petscheks occupied a position in Czechoslovakia somewhat similar to that of J.P. Morgan in the United States . . . To obtain a fair hearing for the claims of families as wealthy as the Petscheks . . . I should prefer a somewhat calmer atmosphere which I am hopeful will prevail in the spring."

11

SMALL SALVATIONS

Spring 1946

Laurence, Dulcie (center), and Dulcie Ann (left) in the palace.

THE PALACE GARDENS FLOURISHED UNDER LAURENCE'S CARE. Where not long before, shards of broken glass had glittered, the lawn was now perfectly manicured. The quarter-mile gravel track framing it was raked smooth, while the surrounding plantings blazed with the colors of the thousands of flowers that Laurence had acquired from around the world.

The Watchers of Prague spied this beauty through gaps in the fence; among them were more Communists than ever before. Leftists looking at the palace saw an ostentatious tribute to wealth in the style of Versailles and the Bourbon throne. These proletarians found things in common between the Jewish mine owner who had built the palace, the German occupier who had seized it, and the American imperialist who now occupied it.

Czechoslovak democrats were also among the Watchers, though. They considered the palace a monument to the prosperity of the First Republic and one of its greatest entrepreneurs, restored by America, the ally that had twice rescued Europe and the Czech lands from Germanic domination. They gazed with respect and even reverence at the Stars and Stripes flying high overhead on the especially tall flagpole that Laurence had installed.

But the political leanings of many who came to ogle were somewhere in the middle. To them, Otto Petschek's masterpiece was one of the wonders of Prague, and they didn't worry too much about what it represented. How that middle voted would decide the upcoming elections and set the postwar course of the country and perhaps the region. In 1946, the Continent was teetering between Communism and democracy. To the east, Stalin had seized influence through takeovers by puppets in Hungary, Poland, Romania, Bulgaria, Albania, and other lands. To the west, democratic regimes remained in place but feared electoral or more violent takeovers by the far left in the postwar chaos and privation. Germany and Austria were still occupied, split between the Western powers and the Soviets. Europe was hanging in the balance, and Czechoslovakia could well be the tipping point.

Laurence was sure the majority of its voters would embrace democracy. He wrote to his friend Williamson back in D.C., "Unquestionably there is a strong Communist influence in the Government but it appears to be weakening from day to day and I am reasonably certain that by the fall of this year any danger of Communism as such in Czechoslovakia will have passed."

He dismissed the electoral aspirations of the Communist leader, Klement Gottwald—the same fiery champion of the miners who had railed against Otto decades before, eliciting gales of laughter from his disdainful fellows in the Czechoslovak Parliament. Gottwald's goal of an outright far-left majority seemed absurd to Laurence. Two weeks before the May 26 elections, the ambassador predicted a sweeping win for the moderates, fortified by his belief that "the influence of western civilization and culture here is in my opinion too strong for Communism to overcome it." Mindful of his commitment to Yarrow, Laurence reassured him that he would "initiate further action for the settlement" of the Petschek claims in June, following the balloting, when the Communist hand would be weakened.

ON election day, Laurence attended the tally of the votes at the Ministry of the Interior, just beyond the Bubeneč neighborhood, a short drive from the palace. The bureau oversaw Czech police and prisons, and the premises emitted a whiff of that penal quality: three severe modern wings jutted out, punctuated by small square windows. Its warden was the gruff Communist interior minister, Václav Nosek. He had been installed there by Gottwald, and the two had bonded over their hatred of Otto and his ilk. Nosek was a former coal miner who had made his name organizing protests and strikes against mine owners. He had helped lead the big Most mine strike in 1932 that had hit the Petschek properties hard. Now he was on hand to offer a taciturn welcome to Laurence and the other election observers, including diplomats and dozens of journalists.

The initial numbers for the democrats were far short of what Laurence had expected. Was it an anomaly? As the night wore on and the tallies trickled and then poured in, it became clear that Laurence's predictions were off, and badly so. From Cheb to Brno, Prague to Bratislava, Karlovy Vary to Sobrance, the Communists were polling better than expected virtually everywhere across the country. Finally, Nosek, his stolid face barely concealing his satisfaction, showed Laurence the final tally. The Communists would have the most seats of any party in the national legislature.

Since entering presidential politics in 1932, Laurence's defining electoral experiences had been FDR's four victories. Now he found out just how cruel an election night could be. Forcing himself to keep the shock from his face, Laurence ran an eye down the columns of Nosek's figures. It was a disaster. All his hard work, all the effort that he had put into ejecting the Soviet soldiers, had been for naught. It was not only a catastrophe—it was a public one. The journalists swarmed him, their usually controlled access to the ambassador thrown open. But whatever he felt inside, Laurence pulled himself together in front of the reporters. An embassy aide was impressed: "They would come at him and he would begin with an oblique answer which was just five degrees off-line, not direct, and maybe add a little more comment, going farther, farther, farther from the subject. Five minutes later, he was still going strong, talking about something entirely different. He got away from the subject beautifully."

Later that night, back at the Petschek palace, likely over a strong drink, Laurence considered the wreckage. He had predicted that the assembly "would be controlled by the Moderates with 171 votes out of 300 as against the Radicals . . . with 129 votes." The actual count: just 147 for the pro-Western parties versus 153 for the pro-Moscow ones. That 24-seat difference between his estimate and the actual number swung the incoming parliament from the hoped-for Western tilt to a Soviet one.

The palace attracted optimists, though, and Laurence was one. His cable to Washington from the Schönborn the next morning put the best face he could on events. They looked better in the light of day. Although the Communists had received a large number of votes, they still did not have an absolute majority in the assembly; it was only thanks to a coalition with the Socialists (known as the "Social Democrats") that they controlled most of the seats in the national legislature. "[I]n spite of the unexpectedly large vote the Party received . . . [t]here is little doubt that the Government . . . in which all of the parties are represented will continue, and while there will be changes in personalities . . . there is little probability of any material change in the character of . . . its policies," Laurence wrote.

As the results sank in, he went even further in embracing the outcome. By June Laurence was praising the Communists, who were about to become his partners in negotiating his hoped-for palace deal, and much more. He cabled to D.C.: "I find no disposition among the Communist leaders to gloat over their gains or to minimize the extent of the anti-Communist vote. They seem sobered by their responsibility." There would be a new Communist prime minister, but Laurence wrote that he regarded him as a man "of common sense and native shrewdness willing to learn, a thorough Czechoslovak patriot unlikely to embark on further extremist ventures": Klement Gottwald.

⌣

GOTTWALD and his colleagues agreed that conversations about compensation for Americans' property to which Czechoslovakia asserted claims—such as the palace—would start a month after the new government had been inaugurated. Laurence wrote John Foster Dulles that this was a good sign but repeated his warning about the impact of the election: "I have every reason to expect an uphill struggle." But Laurence was used to that from his litigation days and knew how to counter it: "drive a hard bargain." He reoriented US policy to Czechoslovakia around restitution, threatening to limit US support for the country unless the Czechs paid a reasonable amount for properties that rightfully belonged to Viky and others like him who were now American nationals.

The negotiations proved as steep a hill as Laurence had imagined. No sooner did Foreign Minister Masaryk schedule the first negotiating session than he was unexpectedly called to Moscow, initiating a long delay. By the time the two sides finally sat down, Laurence thought that the Czechs parleyed with "smug self-satisfaction."

That same tenor of Czech resistance was equally evident in Laurence's escalating battles over maintenance of the palace. His lease called for the Czech government to make repairs to the home, and these became absolutely necessary. The roof began to spring more leaks. The sewage pipes backed up. Panes of glass fell out of the greenhouses in the rain. It had been more than two decades since Otto had broken ground on the palace, including the years of hard living during the war. The grande dame was showing signs of time's toll, like the first lines on the face of a famous beauty.

Laurence's point of contact under the lease, Colonel Kučera, initially agreed to arrange the repairs. Kučera was the career soldier who had evicted the Soviets from the palace, taking it under the ministry's wing before leasing it to Laurence. But his minister, an ardent Communist supporter, blew up at the colonel when it came time to actually fund the repairs. Were they supposed to take resources away from their still-recovering forces to pay for new windowpanes for a capitalist? Kučera received orders transferring him out of Prague and then out of the country altogether.

Laurence, his repeated entreaties to Kučera unanswered, finally wrote to the ministry. He pleaded with them to honor the lease and help him keep the palace from harm:

> [T]he important consideration is that this entire property is one of the most valuable in the city of Prague ... it seems tragic to incur further damage within the next few months which will amount to millions of crowns by the failure to undertake the necessary repairs immediately so as to keep them before the cold weather starts.

The staff at the Ministry of Defense met in August 1946 to decide how to deal with Otto's palace and the persistent American who occupied it. Postelection, the considerations that Beneš had urged upon them in 1945 no longer seemed quite as salient. They decided to wash their hands of this annoying tenant and terminate the lease. The purported grounds were that "the palace originally served as a hotel for foreigners in order to serve visiting military dignitaries. The past year has demonstrated that the hotel for foreigners was needed after all. It was a mistake that the palace was unavailable to serve this purpose, and caused unnecessary expense."

It was a fabricated excuse—the flow of dignitaries had in fact slowed dramatically. Regardless, Laurence had to go. But, perhaps sniffing a hint in their long silence, he was too fast for them. Before the ministry's slow-moving bureaucracy could generate a letter of termination, he sent off a September note to inform the officials that—whatever their failings—he was renewing the lease for another year. Notwithstanding his complaints, he had become thoroughly besotted with the palace, and he had committed to Viky, Yarrow, and the Dulleses to protect it. Having gone to such great lengths to move in, he had no intention of leaving.

Now it was the ministry's turn to up the stakes. They were a military institution, not a real-estate one. They decided to rid themselves of the palace, and Laurence, altogether. He was notified that the ministry had no authority to accept his renewal of the lease; the building had been transferred to the City of Prague. A city official, Dr. Janeček, then called on Laurence and explained that the city was just a temporary holder. They did not yet have legal authority to accept the rent, either.

Who could extend the lease, then? Laurence asked.

No one, Janeček replied.

Perhaps he and those who had sent him thought that this would be sufficient to flummox the American. But clearly Janeček didn't know many New Yorkers. Laurence calmly replied that he had the right under the original lease to remain and intended to do so. And there was one more thing, Laurence continued: How about those repairs? Did Janeček really want a property that "could not be replaced for tens of millions of crowns" to be destroyed when "the repairs to preserve and protect the property would only cost . . . 200,000 or 300,000 crowns"? Janeček, the tables turned, suddenly found himself being grilled by an adept cross-examiner—and one who was none too pleased about the Czechoslovaks' failure to care for a precious heirloom. By the time Janeček finally escaped, he had conceded that Laurence could arrange the repairs.

But Janeček, too, eventually went mute. He ignored Laurence's increasingly irate letters about the city's failure to honor its obligations and the effect it was having:

> It has been my practice all of my life to pay my bills promptly. You have brought me into disrepute by allowing some of my bills to run unpaid for months while I was endeavoring to extract a routine approval from you . . . In the meantime other repairs have become necessary and I have been humiliated by having firms in Prague decline to undertake this work because the old bills remain[ed] unpaid.

The palace was once again weighing upon its master's credit. Laurence finally went ahead and paid the bills himself, keeping a running tally and deducting them from his rent.

A cascade of other vexations came with being the protector of Otto's compound. A neighbor insisted that he had acquired the legal right for his cars to occupy Laurence's garage and demanded that Laurence help him obtain a new American vehicle as compensation for vacating it. A Czech woman rumored to have been a Nazi collaborator asserted that her furniture had ended up in the palace and threatened legal action to reclaim it. Under an obscure statute, the director of the National Museum claimed title to the palace's art masterpieces. And on and on it went, each claim triggering a campaign of dueling letters, calls, and fruitless meetings.

It appears that the palace was even a rare point of disagreement between Laurence and Cecilia. Whereas the ambassador found the palace "beautiful and extremely comfortable," Cecilia disparaged "its opulence and extreme gaudiness," even quoting a quip comparing it to "an expensive brothel." She felt no jealousy toward Dulcie or other women, but her envy apparently flared in response to her lover's deepening infatuation with his house.

THE conflicts over the palace began affecting Laurence's work. He wrote to one correspondent that the clashes were "interfering with [his] proper duties in Prague which are the maintenance of good relations between Czechoslovakia and the United States."

But he never seems to have considered just abandoning the palace. With the Left in power, his home would be at more risk of abuse than ever. Like its creator, Laurence had sunk too much of his own time and money into the place to walk away. The palace would not let him go; "this little mother has claws," as Kafka wrote of Prague. He began to worry about what would happen after he finished his posting. Even if he was successful in cutting the deal for Viky, that would leave the palace in the hands of the Communist-dominated government. It had amply shown its disregard for his magnificent dwelling. Nor can Laurence have relished the thought of what that outcome would do to the loyal Pokorný, who cared for the palace with all the tenderness of a parent toward a beloved child.

As 1946 dwindled and Laurence nestled into the embrace of the palace for the long, cold months of the northern winter, he struggled with all of this until he found a solution. As part of the contemplated global deal with Viky, Czechoslovakia would acquire the property—what if the United States then bought it from the Czechs? Laurence thought he could pull it off without actually having to appropriate any additional US funds. There were outstanding American government loans to the Czechs that could in theory be forgiven in exchange for Otto's compound—money that, moreover, was otherwise unlikely to be repaid.

But that could work only if the larger deal to compensate Viky went through. As 1946 became 1947, Laurence cajoled with new urgency the special Czech envoy who had been appointed to handle property claims, Dr. Miloslav Niederle. They understood each other: Niederle was, like Laurence, a World War I veteran, a lawyer, and a diplomat. He was unflustered by the ambassador's energetic attack, having grown accustomed to turmoil in a professional life that had mirrored the vertiginous ups and downs of the Czechoslovak state. Besides, Niederle was personally sympathetic to the Petscheks. The problem was that he reported to the cabinet, and many of its far-left members remembered Otto and his family none too kindly.

In early 1947, Niederle came to Laurence with news. The Czechs were ready to make some payments to foreign claimants. Niederle would soon reach an agreement with the Swiss to that effect. And the government, though Communist led, was willing to do the same with Americans. But there was a hitch. The government would not extend that courtesy to those naturalized as Americans after September 1938—the measure was clearly designed to exclude the Petscheks.

Laurence was unyielding. He held out for Viky. He had given his word, and, besides, if Viky did not get his deal, how could Laurence's plan for the palace be executed? Laurence told Niederle that either all Americans would be restituted, or none would.

In April, Yarrow visited Prague, joining the negotiations. He wrote to Foster Dulles that there were "great obstacles" to an agreement because of the Communist hatred of the Petscheks but that Laurence was doing a superb job to bridge the gaps: "The influence and persuasion which Mr. Steinhardt has been able to bring to bear among high governmental officials of all parties has been of the greatest assistance, without which the prospects of any positive results would have remained highly doubtful." Whatever their distaste for the Petscheks, the Czechs—even the Communists—were by and large personally fond of the indefatigable American ambassador.

On May 31, 1947, there was a breakthrough. Yarrow cabled Dulles that Laurence had achieved an agreement with Niederle on a total pay-

ment to Viky for all his claims of $8 million.* Although it was still sub-
ject to Czech cabinet approval, it was a breakthrough. Having acquired
the palace, the Czechs agreed to transfer it to the United States for the
forgiveness of the old debt that the United States likely would never have
collected anyhow. Laurence was exultant.

⌒

JUST days later—as if to reward the Czechs—Secretary of State George
Marshall offered Europe massive financial aid to rebuild after the devastation of the war: the Marshall Plan. Laurence had some reservations.
The Marshall Plan ran contrary to his "drive a hard bargain" philosophy
in his dealings with the Czechs. He feared that infusions of aid would
undo his preliminary deal for Viky as well as other progress. The ambassador eventually came around to support the secretary's initiative,
though he wondered if the Soviets would actually allow Czechoslovakia to participate. He had seen firsthand the hostility to America of the
Czech Communists and their Soviet masters.

Laurence was pleased when Masaryk immediately accepted a July 4
invitation to participate in the Paris Conference that would kick off plan
negotiations. But later that night, Laurence learned that his initial caution had been merited. Stalin had commanded Masaryk, Gottwald, and
several other government officials to fly to Moscow posthaste to meet
the Soviet overlord.

The Czechs appeared before Stalin and his foreign minister,
Vyacheslav Molotov, on July 9. Within hours, Laurence had in his hands,
thanks to a covert source, Gottwald and Masaryk's telegram to the cabinet in Prague. The Slavic nationalism that Stalin had used to embrace
the Czechs in 1945 had now become a weapon. The cable read,

Both Stalin and Molotov did not conceal the fact that they were surprised at the decision of the Czechoslovak Government in accepting the invitation to Paris . . . [T]he Soviet Union would regard our

---

* Roughly $90 million in today's currency, per the Bureau of Labor Statistics' con-
sumer price index (CPI) inflation calculator: https://data.bls.gov/cgi-bin/cpicalc.pl?
cost1=8%2C000%2C000&year1=194705&year2=201706.

participation as a break in the front of the Slav states . . . according to Stalin, we should withdraw our acceptance to participate and he thinks we could justify this action by pointing to the fact that the non-participation of the other Slav nations and the other eastern European states has created a new situation under which our participation could easily be aimed against the friendship with the Soviet Union and our other Allies.

As Laurence scanned the telegram, the Czech cabinet was already meeting. They were struggling with what to do. So was Laurence. He might have swung into open intervention—speaking out in the press, lobbying the government, rallying Marshall and Truman to intervene. But that would make him and the United States look just as heavy-handed as Stalin. Besides, Laurence had far fewer levers at his disposal than the Soviets did. Having withheld US support until the Czechs addressed Viky's and other Americans' claims, he had little else beyond the Marshall Plan itself to work with.

So he stayed his hand. He was influenced by his faith that Beneš would make the most of Stalin's blatant intervention. "[H]e is now in a position to make it clear to the Czech public that Czechoslovakia's foreign policy is being dictated from Moscow," Laurence wrote. Surely the people would recoil from this assault on their independence. He believed in Beneš's commitment to democracy and his ability to influence moderate parties—to convince the Czech public that their country had been obliged by the Soviet Union to act contrary to its own interests.

But, to Laurence's disappointment, neither Beneš nor moderates in the government stepped forward publicly to fight for the Marshall Plan. The Czech government's announcement late at night on the tenth parroted Stalin's sentiments and, in many places, his exact words: "All Slavic states and other states in central and eastern Europe, had rejected participation in the conference . . . Under these circumstances Czechoslovakia's participation would be interpreted as an act directed against our friendship with the Soviet Union and our other Allies. Therefore the Government unanimously decided not to participate in this conference."

Beneš, Laurence later learned, had been felled by a mild stroke and was temporarily incapacitated. The other moderates and pro-Western advocates in the government had no such excuse. Yet they too were mute. They meekly went along with Stalin's diktat.

It was a devastating blow to Laurence. He had been sent to Prague to save the country for democracy. After his initial success, the gravitational pull of Communism had asserted itself with increasing intensity, drawing Czechoslovakia toward Stalin's orbit. Laurence was desperate to find a way to help the country resist the pull and was vexed that Washington did not seem to share his sense of urgency. Although it hardly signified in the larger scheme of things, he was also disappointed by the frustration of his efforts to help Viky and to preserve the palace. The tense political environment made it unlikely that the cabinet would consider his laboriously negotiated deal anytime soon. He broke the news to John Foster Dulles in a letter: "[T]he political situation here has deteriorated since Czechoslovakia's withdrawal from the Marshall Plan to a point at which it was quite clear that it would not be possible to obtain ratification or even informal approval from the Cabinet of any agreement involving the settlement of an American claim."

All, however, was not lost. Elections were scheduled for May 1948. As in 1946, Laurence looked to them for salvation in the larger battle for Czech freedom, as well as in the smaller obligations that he had undertaken:

> The election campaign here has already begun two or three months ahead of time with unusual ferocity . . . the Communists will either gain absolute control of the country between now and May—the date fixed for the general election—or they will not. If they gain absolute control, any signed formal agreement entered into at this time would not only be repudiated but would be publicly attacked as a nefarious Wall Street attempt by the American imperialistic war-mongers to devour Czechoslovakia. If they fail to gain absolute control of the country and the moderates win the election, there should be relatively little difficulty in consummating a satisfactory settlement.

Laurence held out hope for that result, above all for the country's sake, but also for Viky's, and that of the palace. And as one more winter came, his third in Otto's compound, Laurence's confidence grew. He reported to Washington that the Communists were weakening. The democratic forces were strengthening their position. Laurence once again predicted that the pro-Western candidates would achieve substantial gains, as he had in the run-up to the 1946 elections.

The Soviets had secretly arrived at the same conclusion. Their belief in the Czech Communists was fading. The Kremlin was coming to doubt that the party would triumph at the polls. The Soviet ambassador returned to Moscow and complained that "with Anglo-Saxon support, the 'reactionary elements' intensified their effort, displayed hostility against both communists and the USSR, and praised the virtues of Western democracy."

It looked like Laurence might succeed in his mission after all—but Stalin was not about to allow him that satisfaction.

THE Communists' definitive grab for power came in February 1948, as Laurence was returning to Prague from a US trip for medical treatment. When he was forty-eight hours away, a crisis erupted in the cabinet. Its two equally divided wings, the twelve Western-leaning democrats and the twelve Eastern-tilting Communists and Socialists, had their most serious clash yet. The democrats, quietly smarting over the Marshall Plan withdrawal, had since been subjected to outrage after outrage: lies and slander in the Communist press; creeping Communist control of the intelligence apparatus and of the secret police and spying; a Communist bomb plot against pro-Western officials.

Then Interior Minister Nosek fired eight non-Communist police officials and replaced them with his followers. At the cabinet meeting on Febraury 17th, the democrats demanded that the firings be rescinded. Gottwald refused to discuss it on the grounds that Nosek was absent—an absence that had in fact been ordered by the Communist Party for just that purpose. The dispute grew heated, with shouting and table pounding, voices and tempers rising, and representatives of the two wings actually coming to blows before the meeting broke up in chaos. It was the last meeting that that cabinet ever had.

Laurence rushed back, touching down at the Prague airport on the nineteenth; the tang of airplane fuel hung in the frozen winter air. His embassy staff had alarming news. Laurence's old adversary, Ambassador Zorin, was back in town, too. Now the deputy foreign minister of the Soviet Union, he had landed shortly before Laurence. The ostensible reason for his presence was to supervise a Soviet grain shipment to Prague. In truth, the moment of crisis had come, and Stalin wanted ground control.

Laurence's staff briefed him. Both camps in the cabinet were furiously maneuvering. The democrats refused to work with the Communists unless the fired police were reappointed and their Communist replacements removed. The Communists urged the dismissal of the democrats as "reactionary agents."

All courted the aging, frail Beneš, trying to get the upper hand. In a parliamentary system, the president, even one weakened by illness and long service, still had great power at a moment such as this. He could, from his grand chambers in Prague Castle, pressure the Communists to rescind the police appointments and work with their opponents. If Gottwald no longer commanded a majority in parliament, Beneš could allow someone else—the Socialists or Western-oriented democrats, for example—to form a government. Or he could overtly choose a side, using his stature to condemn the Communists and call for snap elections. A note from Masaryk welcomed Laurence back and summarized matters succinctly: "[T]he situation is messed up and not clear—*vederemo*" (that is, "we shall see").

As the first master of the palace had done long ago, Laurence put his faith in Beneš to save democracy. On February 21, he cabled Washington that Beneš was very much against accepting the resignations and that he planned to persuade Gottwald to reappoint the dismissed police officials: "Should the [Socialists] fail to bring about a compromise in an area which is steadily narrowing, the alternatives will be for the Communists to carry out their plan to take over the government or for Benes to exercise his constitutional authorities in the hope of forcing Communists to modify their program."

But while Laurence and the country waited for Beneš, the Communists, with Zorin looking over their shoulders, moved swiftly. Laurence reported developments to Secretary Marshall in urgent cables. Gottwald held a massive rally in Old Town Square and, in his nationally broadcast speech, made it clear that the Communists were ready to use force. He ostentatiously armed police with rifles and deployed hundreds of "action committees"—gangs of thugs—to support them. The leftists occupied government offices, telling non-Communist workers to stay home. The police and others also entered the offices of opposition parties and threatened their leaders with trumped-up charges of attempting to overthrow the government. The authorities even sealed the borders, suspending passports and all travel.

On the morning of the twenty-third, Laurence summoned one of his longtime aides, Walter Birge, to his office. Laurence prized Birge, who had been with him since Ankara, as a like-minded adventurer and rule breaker. Making his way there, Birge had noted, "There were far fewer pedestrians than usual; moreover, I had been aware that Factory Militia detachments, armed with carbines, were patrolling with the regular police." The Factory, or People's, Militia was a paramilitary force of toughs recruited from workplaces, and they were an intimidating supplement to the regular forces. Even in the Schönborn, the heart of American power and protection, "the embassy receptionist . . . looked frightened." She asked Birge what was happening, but he didn't know, either.

When Birge presented himself before Laurence, the ambassador's expression was "positively grim and his eyes, flinty." He asked Birge, "Are you ready to drive to the German border?" When Birge assented, Laurence directed him to smuggle one of the democratic leaders and his wife out of the country. Warrants had been issued for their arrest, and they needed to leave.

Birge rushed to meet his charges at a designated rendezvous. They would be the first of a stream of Czechs whom Laurence and his embassy colleagues would help escape.

THERE was one passenger on his underground railroad whom Laurence had to book personally: Cecilia. He made the short trip from the Schönborn to the Sternbergs' apartment a few blocks away. As Laurence wended his way through the darkening streets, he felt the chill that had fallen over Prague. It was one that the Watchers of the city had not felt since the Nazi era. They were in hiding; the streets were largely empty. Those few people whom Laurence did pass looked down and moved hurriedly on.

To Cecilia, Laurence "seemed to have aged" since she had seen him last, before his US trip; she noted that "his face, always golden brown as if tanned by some ancestral sun, looked grey and worn, and his dark eyes lacked their usual sparkle." He immediately sensed her pain and terror. Leopold was there, too, and Laurence spoke frankly. He told them that they had to leave.

"There's not a hope left for people of your kind in this country," he explained. Leopold protested, telling Laurence that people in Prague still liked him and would protect him, including those within the ranks of the Communist Party.

"You'd be crazy to stay," Laurence interrupted. "Save your lives at least. Everything else is lost. I fear for your safety." His audience was frightened but not persuaded, so he continued. "I can't be responsible for letting you stay—your pro-Western sympathies are too well known. Once the Russians take over, as of course they eventually will"—here Laurence stopped, placed the edge of his index finger on his neck, and drew it across, miming a slit throat.

"But where should we go?" Cecilia pleaded.

"To America, of course, where else?" Laurence answered. He relayed that this contingency plan had been hatched long before, and he had even debated with the British ambassador whether the United Kingdom might be a better destination for the Sternbergs in the event of a Communist takeover.

Cecilia looked at Laurence with amazement and gratitude. But Leopold was angry. "So you always knew," he said. "Why didn't you tell us?"

"There was still hope. Why rock a boat before it sinks?"

Laurence urged them to go to America. "It's a great country and anyone with any sense can still make a living in it. It may not be easy to get you your entry permits, but I think I can manage it and I'll look after you once you are there.

"The main problem now is to get you out of here. You need a cure," he told Leopold. "I've been informed they only allow travel by now in cases of bad health. Vichy in France would do wonders for your leg. Send in your passports immediately, and whatever other documents they ask for. Say you desperately need a cure and that you are too ill to travel without your wife; naturally she cannot leave her child. It may just work."

At that, Cecilia later recalled, Laurence "stood up laughing, made us a little bow like a conjuror who has successfully pulled a rabbit out of his hat, then, reassuring us once more that he would see to everything, he left."

On February 24, Laurence's hopes for his host country quickened when Beneš declared that he would soon speak by radio, that he was dealing with the situation, and that people should remain calm and keep working. But the day passed with no speech, only with intensifying Communist repression. On the twenty-fifth, Laurence learned the devastating news that Beneš had folded. He had accepted a new Communist-led cabinet purged of all pro-Western elements. This was the worst of all possible outcomes; the president had not only failed to beat back the coup but also given it the appearance of democratic legitimacy.

Laurence rushed to Masaryk to try to understand what had gone wrong. His friend was distraught, his usual veneer of sophistication stripped away by the crisis. He told a shocked Laurence that he was questioning Beneš's competence. The president "had been subjected to such pressure and to such physical strain that he was surprised that he had survived the past week." But why hadn't Beneš at least resigned, to show the coup for what it was? Masaryk said that Beneš had considered it but feared that chaos would erupt if he did so. Instead, he would accept the new government and then resign. Masaryk said that Beneš was "a broken man." He expected that Beneš would not live much longer.

But what about the radio broadcast? Had the Communists blocked it? Masaryk replied, "There was no evidence that Beneš would have been denied the use of radio but that his physical condition, particularly his difficulty in articulating, had made it impossible for him to speak." Stunned, Laurence asked Masaryk why he himself did not resign. His friend started to cry as he attempted to excuse his participation in a regime now completely in the hands of the Communists. Perhaps it was better to be on the inside, fighting, than to surrender. Like Laurence, he too provided a covert escape service and claimed to have already saved approximately 250 people. Masaryk hoped that he would be able to cushion the blow of Communist brutality for a time, ferrying refugees across the border.

Laurence cabled all this information to D.C. and awaited instructions from Marshall. This was the last possible moment to go all out and fight, as Stalin and Zorin had done—the final chance for Marshall, Truman, and the West to resist. But they had been outmaneuvered. They had counted on Beneš until it was too late. Now they were helpless, short of armed conflict. Truman had the atomic bomb, and Stalin, at least for now, did not. The president was certainly not going to threaten to use that weapon over Czechoslovakia, nor was he going to make any moves involving US troops. The American people were exhausted from the last war. They were not ready again to sacrifice their children, in the haunting words of Chamberlain from a decade before, "because of a quarrel in a far-away country between people of whom we know nothing."

In the end, Marshall even declined Laurence's request to issue a strongly worded personal statement, reasoning that it would do no good. Nor did the State Department take Laurence's recommendation that America punish the Communists economically by suspending all US freight shipments into Czechoslovakia. State wouldn't even allow him to tarnish the Soviets by revealing that Patton had wanted to liberate Prague in 1945 but had been held back at their demand. A request to declassify the documents that proved this was mired in D.C. red tape that was never completely cut. Marshall, when asked by journalists why the US Army had not continued to Prague, said that he could not remember.

Just a decade after Munich, Czechoslovakia was once more lost to totalitarianism. The Iron Curtain had fallen "with a loud thud."

⌒

THE last days of February and March 1948 went by in an aggravated blur for Laurence. A stream of cables poured out of his office, interpreting each new day's Communist outrages for Washington: anti-American propaganda, a flood of arrests, and accelerating property confiscations. Laurence and his colleagues rivaled Masaryk in helping their best contacts and other desperate souls flee the country, following in Cecilia and Leopold's footsteps. Anxious Americans flooded him with inquiries about their relations or their property. Too many: Laurence again worked around the clock—pushed by the lives now at risk.

In early March, Masaryk came to the palace for lunch. He brought Dulcie his usual armload of red roses. The Steinhardts fed him his favorite food—lobster—in the wood-paneled dining room, the Watteau-esque troubadours silently serenading the diners as Pokorný oversaw the service. The gathering was surprisingly cheerful, perhaps buoyed by Otto's handiwork all around them. The arc of history was visible in the curve of the long hallways bathed in light and the artifacts that they contained, the products of centuries of European culture. The palace expressed the reassuring belief that the slow forward march of progress would continue, no matter the horrors transpiring immediately outside the compound walls any particular day, week, or year. Johnny Masaryk appeared relaxed, his typical "delightful, witty" self. Many believe that he and Laurence had a private word about the next traveler on the American escape route: Masaryk himself. The foreign minister was secretly contemplating his own plans to flee the country. After lunch, the two clasped hands and parted.

They never met again. Within a week, Masaryk was dead on the cobblestones of the courtyard of Czernin Palace. His body was twisted and broken by the impact of a fall from his bathroom window, three floors above. The official account put out by the Communists claimed that he was despondent and had committed suicide. The Watchers of Prague believed that they knew better. Rumors abounded that Masaryk was planning to escape. The Czechs, who loved him as they had his father, were certain that he had been murdered, probably by Soviet agents who knew he was about to bolt. A sick sense of humor had apparently informed the method of the assassination: defenestration was a centuries-old Prague style of execution.

A grieving Laurence, having seen Masaryk's tears, could understand the suicide theory. He knew that Masaryk was the subject of "the bitter criticism of some of his most intimate friends," deeply affecting him. So Laurence added to his already overwhelming daily burden the responsibility "to run down every clue or rumor as best we can . . . that Masaryk was murdered." He knew that Masaryk wasn't self-destructive by nature and that the Kremlin hated him—"perhaps more because of his jocular contempt for the Soviets." Masaryk was shrewd, too, and though there was speculation that he had left behind a politically inconvenient suicide note that had been destroyed, Laurence thought that that made no sense. His friend would certainly have made copies of that letter, perhaps even leaving one with Laurence himself. "If it was murder," Laurence wrote, "I believe that sooner or later we will get a lead or a clue that will solve the puzzle—even though we may never be able to prove assassination."

At Masaryk's memorial service, Gottwald painted recent events in distinctly Slavic nationalist tones. "The February storm clarified the horizons of our foreign policy . . . It is the end of the idea that the republic politically sits abroad on two chairs [West and East]. Let it be said to all sides that Czechoslovakia is and remains a faithful and reliable member of a Slavic family." Another Communist leader later hammered the point home: "Slavs have come together recently and realized their common destiny by virtue of their affinity and shared aspirations . . . Slavic reciprocity, which in the past was just a spark of hope for the oppressed, has become today the expression of the true brotherhood and unity of all those who wish to cooperate in the construction of world peace."

It was not long before Beneš joined Masaryk in death, a destroyed man. The line of democracy so trusted by Otto, the names of Masaryk and Beneš, sundered by Hitler with the reluctant help of Rudolf Toussaint, was now definitively broken. Even before Beneš died, he had been unceremoniously shoved aside to make room for a new Communist president: Gottwald.

Laurence wrote about how distraught he was: "[T]he past three weeks have in many respects been the most heartbreaking that I have had to endure in all of my diplomatic service." He had to witness his friends being "arrested or hunted like animals," with no real recourse. "The only difference between the pattern here and elsewhere," he wrote, "has been the rapidity with which all semblance of democracy and personal freedom has been stamped out." The Communists had shown their true, Stalinist face: "What has taken place in Czechoslovakia is merely conclusive proof that it is not possible to compromise with Communism and live in the same house with it. Like fire, it ultimately consumes everything it touches."

⌒

LAURENCE distracted himself with intense activity. Every day, wave after wave of urgent business crashed up on his desk, as on the shoreline after a shipwreck. Every new letter, memo, or phone message was a potential life-or-death matter. One concerned General Toussaint, whom Laurence recognized as his predecessor, a former inhabitant of Otto's home. The Vatican was asking whether Laurence knew where the general was. It seemed that the Americans had turned him over to the Czechs for trial before the coup. There had, however, been no such proceedings, and now, with the Communists in charge, could Laurence get him back?

Laurence didn't have time to respond to every request, and this one did not even concern an American, much less one of the many pro-Western Czechs that he was laboring (and mostly failing) to save. Toussaint had been a German combatant and an occupier of Prague. But the brotherhood of the palace carried some weight, even where such a man was concerned. Perhaps Pokorný put in a good word for his former master. Whatever his reasoning, Laurence wrote to the Prague government, then wrote to them again—and again. He pestered them for the "return to the United States Military Authorities of the former German General, Rudolf Von [*sic*] Toussaint."

Laurence must have known that it was unlikely to work. Nor did it; the Czechs had no intention of returning a German prisoner. Yet it did help shame the Czechs into actually trying Toussaint, even if it was a show trial rather than the due process that the West had afforded at Nuremberg. The German was found guilty, including for Lidice; those few Wehrmacht men hauled in by the SS from elsewhere were as damning as he had feared. But unlike some, Toussaint was spared execution. Instead he received a life sentence—a silent admission that he had been less cruel than others.

That assessment was reaffirmed in prison. One by one, the new Communist government purged Toussaint's partners in the May 1945 parley that had saved Prague from destruction. As they arrived in jail, they befriended the man who had worked with them to preserve the city and its people. The Watchers of Prague claim that Toussaint was playing chess with General Kutlvašr when the Communist negotiator, Josef Smrkovský, was led into the cell. "What are you doing here?" Toussaint is said to have asked, without looking up from the board. "I thought your side won."

The Watchers also say that after Toussaint was eventually released years later, he came back to Prague and walked the perimeter of the palace, looking into the garden through the bars of the fence.

⌐⁀

LAURENCE'S failure to buy the palace for America, permanently safeguarding it, gnawed at him. It meant that, once he left, it would be turned back over to Communists. Some Czech or Soviet commissar would be using his thousand-stream shower. And onward assignment was imminent; ambassadors customarily served for three years, and his anniversary was rapidly approaching. He would be posted someplace else, taking up his position there before the end of the year. He had to do something before it was too late. As improbable as success seemed, Laurence decided that he would try to renew negotiations for the United States to acquire the compound.

Despite the hostility between the newly Communist Czechoslovakia and the United States, Laurence remained on good terms with Masaryk's replacement, Vladimír Clementis. The new foreign minister was a Communist, yet a good-natured one, an intellectual who had spent the war years in London as a broadcaster. Laurence was even closer to his deputy, Arnošt Heidrich, a jovial, obese functionary with a decided, though now cautiously hidden, pro-Western tilt. He quite liked the American envoy.

Laurence resumed negotiations for the house with them, picking up where he had left off in 1947. He reported back to Washington on April 7, 1948, that his first approach "was more successful than I had hoped for. It remains to be seen whether the little 'Politbureau' [the government inner circle] . . . will permit the Czech Communist officials . . . to go through with the transaction."

As the spring sun shone on the palace, its white façade glowing, the negotiations moved forward at a surprisingly brisk pace. Whatever problems the Communists had with the United States, many of them liked Laurence personally. And by allowing the Czechs to credit the palace sale against their debt to the United States, Laurence was making an attractive offer. There was no disputing the underlying lend-lease and other loan agreements. They were valid and binding under international law. The United States still held the wartime gold reserve of the Czechs, and if they wanted it back, the Czechs would have to satisfy their debts.

In May, the Czechoslovak government bowed to those realities. The Politburo would after all honor the deal for the palace that Laurence had secured in 1947. In the two months that followed, the Communists fully reaffirmed the prior agreement on price and terms, exchanged diplomatic notes confirming their accord, and even passed a law authorizing the sale to be made, subject to entry of a final agreement with the United States.

On July 19, Laurence signed the contract with the Czechs. He had done it: the palace had been made over to America. Otto's compound was the centerpiece of the transaction, but various other, lesser properties were transferred as well, including a building in Bratislava that would serve as a consulate. It was a triumph of negotiation under the most adverse of circumstances—one last flourish by Laurence before he departed Czechoslovakia for his next posting. The price was not cheap—$1.57 million.* But it was a bargain, particularly because no money would actually change hands; the difficult-to-collect Czech debt would merely be forgiven by the United States. He was paying for the house in "wooden money," Laurence said, laughing, to Dulcie Ann.

The world took note. *Life* magazine sent a team to do an elaborate story and photo spread on Laurence and the palace, noting, "The ambassador's residence is by far the most magnificent—and expensive—in Prague." Otto would have been delighted, his decade of effort receiving its due at last thanks to *Life*'s global readership. The magazine offered page after page of lush images to prove its point: a portrait of Laurence with his wife and daughter in front of the formal staircase, the furs Dulcie wore year-round draped about her shoulders; a panoramic shot of the basement bathing chamber in all its glory, its scagliola columns and walls so meticulously faked by Otto on full display; photos of the oval entrance hall, dining room, library, *Herrenzimmer*, and on and on. The journalists even peeped into Otto's most intimate gift to Martha, her bathroom, with its gold-alloy fixtures; striated marble floors, walls, and pillars; and elevated tub.

The photographs were a touch of real-estate pornography for subscribers still dealing with postwar privation in Dubuque, Decatur, and Des Moines. But for readers who looked closely, there was plenty of genuine passion as well. Pokorný can be seen in one shot squeegeeing the

---

* Worth approximately $16.3 million today (Bureau of Labor Statistics, CPI Inflation Calculator).

basement swimming pool. His impassive face betrays a hint of relief and perhaps even satisfaction. It was shared by others; *Life* quoted one of the Watchers of Prague, who asked to remain anonymous for self-protection in the Communist state: "I like to be able to come and breathe the air in here every day."

There was only one problem. Preoccupied with his efforts to save the property and his preparations to leave Prague, Laurence apparently neglected to obtain Viky's consent to the sale—or even inform him about the negotiations. Viky was shocked to learn about the transaction from a media reference. Nor, it seems, was he much mollified when he read that "the Czech State promises adequate compensation to the owners provided the property is not subject to confiscation otherwise." Not otherwise subject to confiscation? That was hardly an ironclad guarantee. He ordered his lawyers, the Dulles brothers and Yarrow, to block the sale.

Laurence rushed to the United States and met with Yarrow at the State Department in July to resolve the impasse. Laurence explained that he still intended to get the larger bargain restoring all of Viky's property; this was just the first step. Yarrow was dubious about that, to say the least, and direct about the palace: Viky would not approve this acquisition "unless the Department considered that the acquisition of the property was of paramount diplomatic or strategic interest or of utmost importance in the interest of prestige."

The conditions were a conundrum for the ambassador. Laurence couldn't honestly say that prestige demanded the purchase, nor could he with a straight face claim that the property met the "paramount interest" criterion, as much as he loved it. A number of State Department colleagues were in attendance at the meeting as well, and they would never let him go that far. The department had resisted his interest in the palace from the get-go.

But, having come this far, Laurence had no intention of throwing the palace upon the mercy of the Czechs, even at the request of its rightful owner. So Laurence pressed Yarrow on Viky's logic: What sense did abandoning the house to the Communists make? Viky was not going to live there. He was much better off with a fixed price being set, for when he eventually received restitution. The Americans held all the cards in that regard: they still had the Czech gold reserve, after all. Yarrow, unemotional as ever, saw the point. But he was at the end of his negotiating authority. He called Allen Dulles back in New York. Laurence got on the phone with them, too.

It turned out that Viky had given Dulles the power to authorize the sale. Perhaps Viky did not trust himself to be part of the conversation. His feelings about the palace and the man who built it were too complicated—unpredictable even to him. Viky had no intention of ever going back there to live, and he evidently trusted his lawyer to decide what was in his long-term interests.

Dulles heard Laurence out. The ambassador's arguments were good ones. Dulles was a famously unsentimental, and even ruthless, calculator; in the CIA posts that he would shortly take up, he would prove ready to unblinkingly authorize coups, invasions, and even assassinations. Relatively speaking, severing a son's tie to his father's legacy was small beer. Laurence's proposal would be to Viky's eventual financial benefit. In the end, Dulles assented.

It was done; the palace would enter the permanent protection of the United States. Whatever else had happened on his watch, Laurence had accomplished that—and one thing more: he made sure to provide for Pokorný as well. He implored the State Department to keep the Czech on staff permanently: "Adolf has an intense sense of personal loyalty to the property which he regards almost as his child, I urgently recommend to the Embassy and to my successor that his employment be continued indefinitely." Bowing to the wishes of the envoy, Washington agreed. The butler would remain in charge of Otto's creation, and he and Mrs. Pokorný would continue to reside in the little gatehouse, on what was now American soil.

⌒

SIX weeks later, as Laurence prepared to leave Prague for good, he did so with one last act of salvation: Operation Flying Fiancée. This time, it was Walter Birge who came to ask the ambassador for a dangerous favor. One of their best embassy contacts had escaped the Communist regime. But they had promised to get the man's fiancée, Mila, out as well. The ambassador was soon flying away for the last time—could they contrive a way to smuggle the woman out on his plane? Laurence deliberated, wearing his sternest expression. Finally he nodded.

"If you can get [the] girl on my plane safely and undetected, I'll go along."

Birge and the ambassador, in consultation with a colleague, devised a plan. Whenever a chief of mission departed, Laurence's friend, the portly deputy foreign ministry official Dr. Heidrich, hosted a champagne reception in the airport terminal. On this occasion, Mila and the embassy's four female secretaries would carry bunches of flowers for Dulcie to the reception. The five young women would walk as a group with Dulcie to the plane, then leave the bouquets on board. But only four of them would exit the aircraft. Mila would stay behind, slip into a washroom in the back of the cabin, and remain there, door locked, until the plane was in the air.

Mr. and Mrs. Pokorný with Aspie in front of the palace.

On departure day, things started out smoothly. Birge picked Mila up and brought her to the airport. It was full of people and loud with their chatter. The petite Dulcie was encircled and practically hidden by the four embassy secretaries and their large floral bouquets. Birge brought Mila over, and she was immediately absorbed into the group of flower-bearing accomplices.

Birge mingled, then casually moved to the nearest exit—the one that opened onto the tarmac and the ambassador's plane. The door was locked. Two sturdy men wearing leather coats were standing on the other side of it, staring back at him. They were likely from the StB, the secret police. That was a problem; when the portal was opened and the party attempted to move to the plane, the men would be on their guard for anything unusual. Perhaps they would even demand identification or stop anyone other than the passengers from leaving the terminal.

No sooner had Birge realized this than a colleague rushed over to him and whispered, "Did you know that according to the flight schedule on the flight board in the main hall, the ambassador's flight has not been cleared?"

Birge found Laurence and quietly updated him on the multiple complications. Laurence became angry. Birge observed, "Like a panther approaching its intended prey he rapidly covered the short distance to the airport office."

"Are you in charge here?" Laurence demanded, confronting an officer on the scene, Captain Novák.

When the startled man replied in the affirmative, Laurence—seething, cutting each word sharply—said, "Mr. Birge tells me that my flight to Frankfurt has not been cleared. What is the explanation, Captain?"

The frightened captain stuttered an incoherent excuse.

"Get me General Boček on your phone," Laurence demanded. Boček was the chief of staff of the Czechoslovak armed forces. The captain's hand shook as he placed the call.

Laurence snatched the receiver out of the man's grasp and said, "Is that you, General Boček? Ambassador Steinhardt here."

Laurence was quiet as he listened.

"Thank you for your good wishes, General. Now, would you kindly explain why my flight to Frankfurt has not yet been cleared for take-off? I assume that a flight such as this on the occasion of my departing from Prague for my new diplomatic post comes under your jurisdiction."

Whatever answer Boček gave was unsatisfactory.

"That is no explanation, General, and is an insult, not only to me, but to the United States." Laurence continued, "Now, let me tell you something, General. If my flight is not given immediate clearance, do you know what I am going to do? I am going to call the US Air Force base at Rhein-Main and I am going to ask the officer in command of that base to send a flight of fighter-bombers over here to bomb the hell out of your Ruzyn [*sic*] airport. And do not labor under the illusion that my request will not be acted upon!"

Another ten seconds of silence.

Laurence passed the receiver back to Novák, calmly saying, "General Boček wants to speak with you, Captain."

The Czech listened, nodded, then hung up the phone. "Mr. Ambassador," he said, "the technicalities which have delayed your flight clearance have been overcome. Your flight to Frankfurt is now cleared."

There remained the problem of the locked door, and the StB agents. Laurence and Birge huddled. They decided to make use of a second door for luggage at the other end of the small terminal. It was wide open, but Birge saw that it was guarded by a gigantic, gun-toting soldier whose "legs were like oak trees and his neck, that of a heavyweight prize fighter." But the man did not look very fast, and, unlike the alert StB agents, he was not expecting trouble. Laurence returned to Dulcie and her flower-bearing entourage, Mila among them, and began briskly shepherding them toward the second exit. The whole party moved with them, dozens of dignitaries led by the rotund Dr. Heidrich. Birge loitered at the sliding door, a few feet from its huge, unsuspecting guardian.

Then Birge heard the buzz of conversation, and Dulcie "came into view at the far end of the customs area, surrounded by the moving garden" of the five women carrying flowers, "and—most important—there, waddling beside them was Dr. Arnost Heidrich, all three hundred pounds of him," representing Czech officialdom.

Birge looked at the huge guard to gauge what his response to the approaching crowd would be. As Birge did so, in a sudden burst of inspiration, he swore and cursed the man in English, upbraiding him in words sure to not be understood by the sentinel. Confused, the armed giant was startled into immobility, and the gaggle had poured around him and through the open portal before he could react.

Birge and about fifty other people got to the plane less than half a minute after exiting the terminal. The pair of StB agents were still positioned in front of the other, locked door. Another, more alert guard was rushing across the tarmac to the plane, and the two stationed at the passenger exit began moving to do the same. But Dulcie and the five flower girls were already climbing the steps to the aircraft.

Laurence followed them, then stopped in the middle of the stairs to block any pursuers while Mila entered her hiding place. He made a show of the moment, waving and talking to the crowd assembled below him. By now Mila had entered the washroom and locked the door behind her. Behind Laurence, in the plane's doorway, the crowd could see Dulcie, her arms folded across her chest—small but fierce.

Laurence turned to enter the plane, and the StB colonel in charge of security for the airport materialized. He stated that he wished to inspect the aircraft before takeoff. "A normal procedure," the colonel said, "and for the ambassador's protection."

With a sarcastic smirk, Laurence invited the colonel onto the plane, hamming it up for the crowd. "He seems to think I have a stowaway on board!" Laurence declared. One or two of the onlookers chuckled; most were too tense to laugh.

The colonel climbed the stairs and entered the plane, passing Dulcie, her arms still crossed. Behind her was the bathroom door, shielded by flowers. The colonel looked to the right and to the left. All he saw was the visibly displeased Dulcie, a more relaxed-looking Dulcie Ann, and an entire florist shop's worth of blossoms.

The colonel gave a nod, turned, and started walking down the stairs. "Are you quite satisfied?" Steinhardt called out sardonically as the crowd stared at the show. The colonel turned around and snapped off a salute.

The door of the plane was slammed shut, and the craft immediately taxied down the runway, turbines growling and propellers turning. Moments later, Laurence, Dulcie, their daughter, and their hidden passenger were in the air, heading for Germany.

It was a battle won by Laurence. There had been other successes, too, including saving the palace and Cecilia. But the war was lost.

12

"NEVER, NEVER, NEVER GIVE IN"

Karlovy Vary, Czechoslovakia; March 1948

Frieda Grünfeld in Karlovy Vary, 1948.

THE MAN WAS BEHAVING ODDLY.

Frieda stood before him, wearing a new polka-dot dress that she had sewn just for today, with skirt pleats sharp enough to cut glass. She was holding her white patent-leather pocketbook in both hands in front of her. Her platform shoes added a couple inches of height to her five-foot frame, and she gained a few more by standing up very straight.

The man was seated behind a desk piled high with papers. The brown walls of his office were in need of a fresh coat of paint, and the stacks of old bills and files gave the place a musty-paper smell. But to Frieda, the promise of this building made it no less glorious than the spa town's luxurious Grandhotel Pupp, a five-story yellow-and-white extravagance and the site of café splurges and nights spent dancing.

Today was her first day of work. The man had hired her from dozens of applicants as his new secretary, receptionist, and file clerk—three jobs for one person. She would be truly independent for the first time in her twenty-five years.

Free.

She had clawed her way there from nothing over the past two and a half years, starting out with just her small suitcase, her wits, and the sewing skills that she had learned at her kitchen table and at Faigie's shop in Sobrance. Frieda moved from place to place, living with friends and relations, doing piecework and alterations—chasing any work that she could get to survive and to put away a few *koruna*. In her spare time, she embarked on an aggressive self-improvement plan: reading, taking secretarial courses, ridding her Czech of her eastern accent. She toted a little pile of books around with her: *Gone With the Wind*, a poetry collection, H. G. Wells's *Outline of History*. She had a plan: save some money, go to school, get a degree, and become a physician. But it all started with finding a well-paying job.

Her sister Berta and others in their Orthodox Jewish milieu were dubious. The real occupation for which she was qualified, they kept telling her, was marriage and a family—to give the names of her murdered parents to a new generation, as Jewish custom required. Berta had married a widower with an eight-year-old son (a sweet boy despite the horrors that he had seen—he had lost his mother and siblings to the Nazis). Soon he had two younger brothers named for the dead. Berta seemed happy, the bustle of three children distracting her from the terrifying memories.

But Frieda had rejected every attempted fix-up. Fewer Jewish men than women had survived the war, and she felt no spark with any of the suitors. Regardless, she was hungry for knowledge and independence. She wanted an education and a career; a life of her own. Hadn't her hero, *Tatíček* (Grandfather) Masaryk, said, "Let women be placed on a level with men culturally, legally and politically," even adding his wife's name to his own to emphasize the point? Those ideas inspired her. And now she had a real job. But why was her new boss acting so peculiarly?

Finally, he spoke. "I am very sorry," he said. "But it's the . . . situation."

"What situation?" she asked.

"The . . . er . . . political situation," he replied.

What did that have to do with her? she thought. She had followed the events in Prague, distracted as she was preparing for her new job—sewing dresses and memorizing her secretarial handbook. She read about the democrats walking out of the government. The Socialists' waffling, Gottwald's bullying, and Beneš's final acceptance of the new cabinet. But she and her Karlovy Vary friends had minimized the crisis. They joked that the mild Czech national character did not lend itself to tyranny. "Švejk is no Stalin," they said, referring to the national icon, a (fictional) reluctant Czech soldier in the Austro-Hungarian army. In Karlovy Vary, visitors and residents still strolled the long Greco-Roman colonnade on the main street and took the cure as people had done for centuries. They filled their porcelain cups from the evenly spaced brass faucets along the shaded walk, each tap offering a slightly different temperature and mineral composition, and sipped the famous waters. Prague, only two hours away, felt much farther than that.

"I don't understand," she said.

The man explained: "I just don't see how I can take on someone new. Everything is so uncertain. I don't even know what will become of *me*."

Her heart sank, but only for a beat. She asked, as politely as possible, whether they could just try it for a week. She knew that if she could get her foot in the door, he would see how valuable she was. This job was her lifeline. She offered to defer her wages; to take a pay cut. She tried to explain why he would need a good secretary now more than ever.

It was no use. The harder she pressed the more passive he became. He grew sadder with every argument. But he was immovable. When it was clear that he would not budge, she made one final entreaty, then left.

When she got back to her room, she buried her face in her pillow and sobbed. She was furious with the Communists—they had spoiled everything. But she made sure to cry quietly; she now worried who might be listening.

FRIEDA forced herself to smile at her fellow passengers and sit up very straight on the long trip back east to her sister's apartment in Košice, trying her best to avoid wrinkling her tweed travel suit (the heavy brown fabric had been damn hard to sew). She was returning with no job, no money, and no prospects—only a heavy satchel full of new clothes and old books. She steeled herself for a barrage of criticism.

But Berta and her husband, Shausher, hardly noticed Frieda's arrival, distractedly telling her that she could sleep on a sofa in the crowded apartment. The two younger children were playing on the floor, the third and eldest was doing his homework. Even though the domestic scene appeared normal, the air was tense.

Berta whispered to Frieda as she helped prepare the evening meal. There were signs that Shausher would lose his small clothing factory in the government's wave of expropriations. But maybe it was just as well. They were religious Jews—they had no future in a Communist land. The leftists hated religion of any kind, and the Jewish Communists tended to be no exception. "Jews can be the worst anti-Semites," Berta hissed. She had three children she was responsible for, putting her in a state of high alarm.

Later, after dinner, the adults lingered over tea and Berta's homemade pastries. The sisters were joined by the only other resident of the Sobrance house who had returned from the camps: their brother Boruch. He was gregarious and easygoing. Like his sisters, he was more durable than he looked: he had been shipped from Auschwitz to Dachau and had endured them both as others around him fell in piles. Whatever nightmares that he had, he hid behind his grin. He viewed his baby sister's independent streak, and much else, with benign tolerance, smiling when he saw her.

Frieda saw that the others had already made up their minds about what to do. They were planning to get out of the country. Berta's husband, Shausher (who had also pulled up a chair), was sure that his factory was going to be confiscated. And everyone knew what befell observant Jews under Communism. They had survived one totalitarian regime and were not inclined to take a chance on a second. They had to leave Czechoslovakia and just assumed that Frieda would go with them.

She resisted the thought of having to start again somewhere new. This was her country. And she wasn't ready to flush away two and a half years of work rebuilding her life, just like that. The religious considerations weighed less with her. She was the least observant of those around the table, her prewar devotion having been eroded by the terrible things that she had seen. She was not as far gone as her more secular Prague and Karlovy Vary friends, who had shrugged off her losing her job, urging her to stay and find another one. "Don't worry, Frieduska," they had said. "The Communists won't ban dancing." Some of them also made the point that the Communist redistribution of wealth was not such a bad thing. Why should the rich have so much, and the rest of them so little? But most of her peers seemed content to just tune out politics.

Frieda, as casually as she could, asked whether the family should consider staying. The other three turned to her incredulously. Even the normally imperturbable Boruch looked shocked. After what they had been through? They had all lost parents and siblings; her brother-in-law's first wife and two of his children had also been murdered. Only through extraordinary exertions had he saved his son and himself. Taking that risk again with another group of totalitarians was out of the question.

"What if someone comes back—how will they find us?" Frieda asked. "What if Beinish is still alive?"

They had not seen or heard from their oldest brother since 1941, when he was snatched off the Sobrance streets by the Nazis' Hungarian allies for a military work brigade, or *munka tábor*. If Faigie had inherited their father's disposition, Beinish had captured their mother's: extremely religious and extremely kind. Frieda had fasted for his safe return every Monday and Thursday (the weekdays when the Torah was read in the morning synagogue service, the traditional days for fasts of hope) from 1941 to 1944, when she was deported. After the war, they had still hoped. But it had been three years since the war had ended, and almost eight since they had last seen Beinish. The attrition rates had been horrible for the *munka tábor*—as bad as the camps. Hope was now gone.

"Frimud," her brother Boruch said gently, putting his hand on hers. "It's 1948. Please."

Frieda felt her rage against the Communists rise again. But, as her methodical father's daughter, she was able to concede the force of her family's arguments. She gave in and agreed to leave with them.

They spent the next few days talking through every possible destination, from Palestine to Canada to Venezuela. But the Czechoslovak authorities were not so eager to let people out. And, seemingly, every Jew whom they knew in Košice wanted to leave. When it became clear that nobody was going anywhere soon and she tired of sleeping on the couch, Frieda went back to stay with her friends in Karlovy Vary.

She had her own idea about where the family might go, and she wanted to investigate it herself. It was her father's idea, from ten years before: the United States.

⌣⸜

FRIEDA could see the American flag protruding from the embassy as she made her way up Tržiště Street from Karmelitská. She had taken the bus into Prague from Karlovy Vary and was staying with friends in the Jewish Quarter. Some had an old-boy network. Hers was an "old-girl" one: the women she knew from the camps. A spare bed was usually available, and, if not, they sorted out another solution.

When she had arrived in Prague, Frieda had started with the American Information Center downtown, run by the United States. It was thronged, Czechs standing outside, reading the materials posted in the windows, and inside, poring over American books and magazines. As soon as she inquired about visas, they directed her to the embassy.

She had heard rumors that the Americans were allowing Czechoslovaks to immigrate. Everyone knew about the quotas, of course, and how hard it was to get in. But word was that now they were setting up a special preference for Czechs. The details were hazy, but, Frieda thought, why not try?

Some in Czechoslovakia were bitter about the United States. They said that Wilson's promises of 1918 were empty. That had been proven by 1938. Then the Americans hadn't bothered to liberate Prague in 1945, leaving rescue to the Soviets. They had abandoned the country again in 1948. They couldn't even save Jan Masaryk, and he was half-American.

Frieda harbored no such grudges. She was looking to the future. She allowed herself to daydream about life in America. She would perfect her English. She had read that they had whole colleges just for women. She would win a scholarship and get her degree, become a doctor—a dermatologist, she had decided, combining medicine and her love of beauty. She knew that it couldn't all be like what she saw in films or read in books, but even when she applied a substantial discount, it still seemed good to her. She redoubled her efforts to improve her English, reading *Gone With the Wind,* page by painful page.

The street leading to the embassy was narrow and cobblestoned, the sidewalks barely wide enough for a single pedestrian to pass. She had dressed in her best again, in the polka-dot frock. As she approached, her heart beat faster.

The embassy was being watched by the Communist authorities.

There were uniformed policemen across from the building, and the street was littered with others who, she was sure, had eyes on the place. A pair of big men in black leather coats loitered. More men lurked in door-ways or in large, official-looking parked cars. Who did they think they were fooling? Maybe that was the point, though—to be so conspicuous that they scared visitors away from the American embassy.

Frieda had seen worse. Not just the Nazis, but also the Hungarian officers who had patrolled Sobrance and loaded her onto a cattle car; the planes that had strafed the death train in 1945; the Soviets prowling her country. At least these were Czechs and their guns holstered. They didn't seem to be stopping pedestrians, who were passing in and out of the embassy. She took a deep breath and, her pulse racing, entered.

She soon found herself talking to an actual American diplomat. He was younger than she expected, polite but neutral as he explained the immigration program to her. She would need an immigrant visa. There was a waiting list just to apply. Then he went through the requirements for the visa itself. The list of documents alone made her head spin: birth certificates, testimonies, Czech government records. They would also need Americans to vouch for them, to provide affidavits.

But the financial requirements were the worst of all. They would need to be financially self-sufficient. Her family didn't have that kind of money; despite her fancy dress, she personally didn't have *any* money.

"But what about the special quota?" she finally asked. "For refugees from Czechoslovakia."

"Sorry," he replied, "you don't qualify. You are *in* Czechoslovakia. That only applies to people who already got out."

She was confused. Why would they need a visa if they'd already gotten out?

He explained that it was for people who were stuck someplace else.

"But what about the people who are stuck *here*?" she replied.

He said that they were subject to the regular quota and asked whether she wanted him to sign her up for the waiting list or not.

Even if the family pooled what they had, it would not be enough. She told him that she would have to talk it over with the others.

She left, so dejected and demoralized that she didn't even check to see whose eyes were watching her as she trudged out of the embassy.

THERE was a sharp rap on the door of the apartment where Frieda was staying. She froze. It was insistent, intrusive—the knock of a stranger.

She opened the door to a messenger in a green cap and a matching suit, holding a telegram. She couldn't recall ever getting a telegram—it must be bad news. "The children!" she thought, a flash across her mind.

Hands shaking, she fumbled to open the envelope. The message from her family was terse: BEINISH ALIVE. COME AT ONCE. Beinish. Alive? After all these years? It was surreal, as surprising as if Faigie or Yehudis had come back from *olam haba* (the world to come).

As she hurriedly packed, checked travel schedules, and made her way to the station, she knew that she should be happy, but all that she felt was shock. She thought that she had experienced every possible human feeling, but this was new. Maybe she had had too many surprises and could no longer react to them. People whom she thought she could count on had turned their backs. Those whom she hated had helped save her life. Seemingly strong *shtarkers* wilted. Scrawny wisps turned out to be invulnerable. And people returned from the dead.

It was a miracle that Beinish was alive. But as her father had taught her in one of their Sabbath study sessions, the Lord preferred not to have to work miracles. Unleashing the Ten Plagues or parting the Red Sea upset the natural order of things, which he had taken such pains to establish.

Frieda met Boruch and Berta in Košice. They explained that Beinish had written to the mayor of Sobrance and was returning there from Russia. He provided the date that he would arrive. If any of his family members were still alive, Beinish asked, please tell them that he was coming home.

Frieda wondered whether they would even recognize him. But when his bus finally arrived on Hlavná ulica, there was no mistaking Beinish, who walked down the steps carrying a little satchel. He was as slight as ever, with thin arms and a face framed by huge glasses; her big brother. His kind smile, his radiant modesty, his small stature—all reminded her of Chaya. Suddenly she was sobbing. Everyone was crying—Boruch, Berta, and Frieda crowded around Beinish, hugging and kissing him.

His eyes, large behind the thick lenses, sought theirs. Where was everyone else? he seemed to ask. They shook their heads.

A few of the other surviving Jews of Sobrance were there to greet him as well. They approached, asking about their brothers, sons, or husbands, those seized with him in 1941. Had Beinish seen them? Were they alive? Now it was his turn to shake his head. He was the only survivor.

Someone asked, "How did you live?" The question hung in the air. Everyone held their breath, waiting for his answer as though he were a *chacham*—a sage—for enduring the unimaginable. Most had made it through a year or so of captivity. They knew others who had survived for two years or, in rare cases, even three. Beinish was gentle, slightly built, barely five feet tall, and so soft-spoken. Yet he had survived for *eight* years. How?

Beinish opened his satchel up, and he took out a little sack holding his tefillin—his phylacteries, the boxes that observant Jews don when they say their morning prayers—two small black lacquered cubes, each about an inch square. Sealed inside each were tiny rolled parchments with a few verses of Torah, and outside, leather straps to affix one box to the forehead and the other to the left bicep, next to one's heart. He held up the little bag containing his tefillin and said, *"Ich hob g'leigt tefillin yeden tog, un d'iberiker is nisht gevein in miner hint."* ("I put on my tefillin every morning, and the rest was out of my hands.")

Later, back at the apartment in Košice, Beinish told his siblings everything that had happened since he had been grabbed by the Hungarian occupiers of Sobrance off the street: his miserable treatment in the *munka tábor,* supporting a Hungarian Army division and being captured by the Soviets at the Don River in 1943. What it was like in the

Soviet POW camps—the freezing winters and the sweltering summers. How his friends from home had died, one by one. He had buried them himself, said kaddish for each until no one was left and he wondered who would say the memorial prayer for him. Then he was told that he was being repatriated, once Czechoslovakia became a fraternal Communist state.

He told them in an urgent whisper that they had to get out, now—before it was too late.

No one argued with him.

THE only viable exit option for Frieda and the family was Israel. Its statehood newly declared in May 1948, Israel would gladly take every single one of them. The raison d'être of the fledgling Jewish state was that it would accept any Jews, from anywhere—as long as they could get there. That was the problem. First the family would have to escape from Czechoslovakia, its borders sealed and its authorities generally hostile to emigration. Then they would have to make their way across Europe and the Mediterranean Sea with little children in tow. All of that to take refuge in a war zone: five Arab states had attacked Israel immediately after independence was declared, and hostilities had not entirely ceased.

But it could be done, Frieda thought. Czechoslovakia had followed Stalin in recognizing Israel. The Soviet bloc had high hopes for the new state: many of the Israeli leaders were Socialists, and their signature institution, the kibbutz, largely dispensed with private property. One of the kibbutzniks had been summoned from his fields to serve as the first Israeli ambassador to Prague. Frieda was delighted. An official representative of the Jewish state presenting his credentials at Prague Castle? It was as much of a miracle as Beinish's return. They had been waiting only eight years for their brother—the Jews had been waiting two millennia for a state. She wished that her Faigie, that ardent Zionist, were here to see it—though her father, that equally fervent anti-Zionist, would have been dismayed. She could hear him saying, "The man is a Socialist, is completely *frei* [nonreligious], and so is the country!"

But to Frieda, a Jewish state was a Jewish state—thank God there was one to which to flee. Frieda loved the idea of Israel, but, unlike Faigie, she had no burning desire actually to live there. She researched whether they had medical schools and was disappointed at the rudimentary opportunities. Still, she was a realist: they had to get out, and Israel was the best option.

In July, the new Israeli ambassador in Prague announced that Israel was sending planes to fly in 250 Czechoslovak immigrants per month. He suggested that much larger numbers would be allowed to depart shortly. The family formally registered with the Israeli consul. They had company: there were soon twenty thousand visa applications from Czechoslovak Jews pending with the beleaguered envoy and his skeleton staff.

Frieda made one last trip to Karlovy Vary that September to attend a wedding and to say farewell to her friends. The white city lining the valley seemed relaxed. She basked in the sun with people she knew there; walked the colonnade, sipping each of the different spa waters to remember them; and hiked up to the observation tower on Doubská Mountain overlooking the town. Many Jews here in the western part of the country were more assimilated, and it seemed that fewer had signed up for the flights to Israel there than in the east. She was surprised to learn that some of her acquaintances had even joined the Communist Party. They didn't really believe that *narishkeit* (nonsense) of course. They were doing it to get along. Friduska, they urged, you could go to college, to medical school, here. It is not too late to change your mind.

Any second-guessing was shut down by an episode at the wedding that had brought her to town. The reception had two long tables: one was kosher, and another was *treyf,* for those who did not care. It was not really *treyf,* of course—no pork or shellfish. Rather, the beef and chicken served had not been ritually slaughtered and so were not religiously acceptable. In Košice, Frieda would never have dared to eat at the *treyf* table. Someone might have seen her, and it would have created problems with her strictly observant family. But with her friends in the west she was more relaxed, and she joined them at the other table.

As she was laughing and having a good time with the others, a gaunt figure strode up to her. It was one of her father's friends from the yeshiva, a schoolmate from long ago. Few of that generation had survived. The man had not recovered to health—his cheeks were sunken, his back bent into a curve. Where had he come from?

He looked at her sternly, his eyes burning beneath the brim of his fedora. Not caring what she or her friends thought, or that he was at a festive occasion and might chill the atmosphere, he pointed a long finger at her. He declaimed, *"Zalman Leib's tochter est fin der chazzerisher tish?"* ("Zalman's Leib's daughter is eating from the nonkosher table?") Frieda flushed red as her friends fell silent.

She got up and went to the kosher table, humiliated. Once the shame faded, she accepted the reminder and was even grateful for it. She had wandered too far from the house in Sobrance. She never again tasted nonkosher meat and no longer considered making a life in Czechoslovakia.

⸺

DESPITE the Israeli ambassador's bold prediction, the Czechoslovak government continued to allow only a few hundred people a month to leave in autumn 1948. Communist officials held up passports and exit permits. They interposed a constantly changing and escalating series of fees. Bribes were demanded. The few lucky Jews who managed to leap every bureaucratic hurdle said very quiet goodbyes to the rest of the community. Those hoping to join them were careful not to antagonize the Communists.

Frieda was back in Košice, sleeping on a bed in the corner of her sister and brother-in-law's home, living out of her suitcase, and helping out in the family's garment-manufacturing business. When there was nothing for her to do there (fabric was scarce under Communist rule), she took whatever classes she could find: English, the new universal language; accounting, to learn the math that she would eventually need for her advanced education; Hebrew, to make her way around her destination.

That fall the arrests of Zionist leaders began, the news blowing through the crowded apartment on Štúrova Street with the first icy winds of the season. Some of the most prominent Jews across Slovakia were taken into custody, one by one, on trumped-up charges, starting in September 1948. The authorities put different pretexts forward in each case, but for Frieda there was no mistaking the pattern. She had seen it before.

Even more frightening for her family was the police crackdown on the black market. Their small garment operation was keeping all of them alive, barely. But they couldn't make clothing without fabric, and wholesalers and other above-ground sources had none to sell—one of many shortages that were being felt under the new regime. The only way to get material was surreptitiously. That was illegal, and the authorities were vigorously prosecuting offenders.

Frieda had observed the workings of the black market for as long as she could remember. Her father had supplemented his income that way; she had observed how he concealed the contraband—gold, jewelry, dollars—when she traveled with him. She took her turn now at the illicit transactions. She was terrified that she would be caught. But there was no other way to afford food and other necessities—not to mention securing the resources that they would need to pay the fees and bribes required to exit.

In December, when the days were short and dark, the cold crushing, and the family starting to lose hope, there was a burst of sunny news: the Israeli ambassador had reached a formal agreement with the Czech Communists. Twenty thousand Jews would be allowed to emigrate within the next four months.

The family started preparing in earnest. Frieda, well-spoken and pretty, was often the one who made the rounds of the bureaucracy: the Czechoslovak government offices, the Jewish relief organizations, and the Israeli immigration authorities. The family filled out countless forms (the American demands for documents didn't seem so daunting in comparison). They paid taxes, duties, and passport fees, drawing down their already scant nest egg. They inventoried their possessions for Czech personal export permits, listing everything from furniture and appliances to individually numbered pairs of socks. Nothing of value was permitted to be removed from Czechoslovakia, so Berta's stepson, Monu, was put to work making everything look worn: scraping the sides of the toaster with a piece of sandpaper and scratching table legs with a sharp implement. They joked that even the rolls of toilet paper would have to be marked "used." The family's cutting sense of humor had carried them through a great deal, and they were not going to abandon it now.

The lists were returned to them, with many of the items denied for export. Why couldn't they take a lamp, or a kosher pot, or a kitchen chair? Frieda could not fathom why she could transport some of her books but others were blacked out on the list. There was no logic to it and no arguing with the government. What they couldn't take, they sold to Czechoslovaks staying behind, for a fraction of the value. They were systematically stripped of their assets. Whatever last residual openness Frieda had toward socialism was forever boiled away.

The travel papers came through for an April departure from Bratislava—but only for Berta, her husband, and their three youngsters. The Czech officials assured the family that all was in order, that the April deadline for the program would be extended, and that everyone's papers would be processed—eventually. Frieda didn't believe a single thing they said. She had planned too many reunions that had never happened and said too many temporary farewells that turned out to be final. But the opportunity to get the children out safely could not be passed up. In April, they said their goodbyes, Frieda hugging her sister tightly and kissing each of the kids. "See you in Israel, *im yirtz HaShem* [if God wills it]," Frieda said. Who knew if he would will it? Once so confident in her faith, she no longer understood what he did and didn't will. Then the five were gone. The once-overcrowded apartment suddenly felt very empty.

Boruch and his wife, Rachel, were the next to leave. They were approved for a May departure. The visa program had been extended as promised. "Just because it happened doesn't mean they weren't lying," Frieda told them. There were more hugs and kisses, then they were gone, too.

Now Frieda and Beinish were left to look out for each other. Meals were a quiet affair, just the two of them around the table. In the near-empty apartment, preparing to leave her home, Frieda felt keenly the absence of the other Grünfelds: her mother and father, her sisters, her nieces and nephews—all the family members who had once been so numerous in this part of the world, her circle now reduced to just her and her brother. Frieda looked at Beinish, mild and gentle, and marveled again that he had survived. But then she caught her own reflection and wondered the same.

Frieda and Beinish's departure still was not scheduled. The visa program was approaching its current, and already repeatedly extended, end date of May 15. The Jewish community was thinning out. And the Czechoslovak hostility to the Jews who remained was increasing. There were more arrests, and more attacks on Israel as a bourgeois country bearing "the yoke of capitalist exploitation." A year after independence, the hoped-for Israeli gravitation to the Soviet bloc had not materialized. Frieda and Beinish had a small margin of error but not an infinite one. Suppose they were trapped?

Beinish refused to worry. "It's *b'ydei shamayim* [in the hands of heaven]," he said. Frieda wished that she still had such pure faith. He was the one who deserved her Yiddish name, Frimud Zissel, "devout sweet one."

Then word came: their papers had been issued. They would embark for Romania on July 12 and from there sail to Haifa. Beinish smiled at the news and went about his day, attending synagogue, praying, studying the *sforim* (the sacred texts). His petition to God to return him to the Holy Land, uttered as part of the daily worship all his life, was about to be granted.

Frieda thought that she would be relieved but instead was restless. She paced the apartment, afraid to go out. The Communist terror was mounting, seizures of people and property common—it had moved well beyond the Jews, though they remained a particular target. There were openly anti-Semitic slurs in the press now, ones that brought back the worst memories of the war years. *Zionist* had become a code word for *Jew,* permitting all manner of invective. There were even whispers that Jews in the Communist ranks were starting to come under suspicion— that they too were all of a sudden seeking to emigrate. She feared for her Karlovy Vary friends. She couldn't shake the feeling that she was leaving her dead behind as well—severing a tie to her parents, sisters, nieces, and nephews.

After anxious waiting, it was suddenly July 12. The export inspector showed up, looked through her and Beinish's shipping crate, compared it to the approved list, and sealed and franked it. She took a last look around the flat, now stripped completely bare, and gazed out the window at the Czechoslovak streets. She thought back to the happy times in this land: reading books by the river, the evenings with her whole family, helping her mother with the sewing, studying with her father, visiting her sisters, and playing with their children; how enthralled she had been by the lessons of her schoolteachers, when she had truly believed in the idea of Czechoslovakia, in Masaryk, and in his promise of liberty. She had even had a taste of it, for that brief moment in Karlovy Vary, when everything had seemed possible.

But she had also been spat into hell from here and was being forced out again. All of Czechoslovakia's glory went hand in hand with horror, she thought, as she and Beinish put out the lights and closed the apartment door.

She would go to Israel, but she wouldn't settle there. She wanted total freedom.

There was one nation above all that promised that.

She was determined to end up there.

Part IV

Shirley in the palace in 1989.

13

Nothing Crushes Freedom Like a Tank

The Palace; Tuesday, August 20, 1968; about 1:30 p.m.

THE BLACK LIMOUSINE PASSED THROUGH THE GAP IN THE PINK wall that separated Communist Czechoslovakia from official US soil. The iron bars of the gate swung closed behind the car as it crunched up the gravel driveway of Otto's palace. Seated in the backseat, behind a local driver with a pronounced Adam's apple, was a forty-year-old American woman. Petite, slightly plump, she wore a sober navy dress with a broad white collar, attired for the official business that she had come to conduct: persuading the Czechoslovak government to join the International Federation of Multiple Sclerosis Societies.

She was the most famous multiple sclerosis activist on the planet. She began acting in films at the age of three, was an international star by the time she was five, was awarded an Oscar at six, and was the world's number-one box-office attraction by age seven. Now an adult, she was still just over five feet tall, and her dancer's legs with their sharply defined calves dangled off the backseat of the automobile, barely reaching the floor. She wore her hair in a brunette bouffant instead of the fifty-six perfect blond ringlets that had once been her trademark. But her round, pretty face, framed in the window of the car, was unlined. It was instantly recognizable, with its famous dimples, as the same one that once "could melt an audience at the downtown Bijou or bathe it in warm pleasure": Shirley Temple Black.

Outside Shirley's car window was the miniature world that Otto Petschek had created, still intact. She had visited some extraordinary estates in her life—including Hearst Castle where her friend William Randolph Hearst had often hosted her—but there was nothing like this back home. To her left was a curved guardhouse with an oval porthole, like something out of *The Wizard of Oz*. Next to that was what looked like an ancient wall with Roman arches, a simulacrum of a ruin—a folly, hiding rows of greenhouses, the sun bouncing off their panes. Then she caught a glimpse of an enormous English park bathed in midday light, its trees and lawn dazzlingly green in the late-summer heat; and finally, as they ascended the driveway, the palace itself. Its pinstriped stone façade unfurled before her, one wing after another jutting out in turn, each with a flourish of columns, porticos, and pediments.

Sights such as this were part of the reason that she had volunteered to make this trip—that and the fact that Czech Communism was finally thawing. She was intrigued by First Party Secretary Alexander Dubček and his liberalizing reforms, including the abolition of censorship: the Prague Spring. Noncommunist minorities were being heard in decision-making processes. Relations with Western organizations such as hers were being revived. Later that afternoon, she would be meeting Dubček himself—one of the most talked-about new leaders in the world.

She exited the vehicle and entered the palace. It was too much to take in all at once: the echoing domed ceiling of the oval receiving room; the multihued marble floor; the tapestry chairs with their royal crests; the inlaid tabletops, their surfaces made of dozens of shades of wood, an artist's palette of flowers, birds, and butterflies.

US ambassador Jacob Beam and his wife greeted Shirley, together with a cluster of embassy staff and their wives. Beam was tall and patrician, with chiseled features above his bow tie; smart and decent but tough. He had enjoyed a front-row seat for the twentieth-century struggle between democracy, Fascism, and Communism: monitoring Otto's beloved League of Nations in Geneva; serving in Berlin during the rise of Nazi Germany; observing Churchill in London during the war; stationed in Moscow when Stalin died; and then continuing across the Communist world, an officer on the front lines of the Cold War. Even so, it was not every day that he got to welcome Shirley Temple to his premises.

Shirley took no offense at the appraising stares from him or anyone else, instead smiling and shaking hands. She had been watched for as long as she could remember. But beneath her polite smile as she strolled to the luncheon table with the ambassador, she was restless. It was her nature, and had been ever since she was cast in *Baby Burlesks,* her first one-reel, in 1931 at age three. She needed an outlet for her boundless energy. As much as any other reason—advancing MS research, seeing Prague, or meeting Dubček—it was that urgent necessity that had caused her hand to shoot in the air when the federation asked for a volunteer for this trip.

As the ambassador escorted her into the dining room, the painted troubadours strummed their mandolins in the lunettes above. Their eternally reclining mistresses listened as intently as they had since Otto installed them there four decades before. The passage of time was evident only in the *craquelure,* the fine cracks that had formed and deepened in the paintings, lining the faces. Shirley and the ambassador ate and amiably chatted. They were no more aware than the daubed musicians and their ladies that within hours they would be trapped in a Soviet-bloc invasion.

HOWEVER serene the palace may have seemed on that August afternoon in 1968, the world outside it was in turmoil. In the United States, antiwar and civil-rights protests had peaked. American streets were crowded with marchers, chants, banners—and tear gas and police batons. Martin Luther King Jr. had been murdered in Memphis and Bobby Kennedy assassinated in LA. The country seemed to be falling apart. That turmoil echoed around the world, with protests from Paris to Philadelphia, Rio to Rome. And it had even penetrated the Iron Curtain, to Prague. Until recently, Czechoslovakia's leadership had been encased in the Communist stasis that had descended after Laurence Steinhardt's departure—it was a hard-line, authoritarian, one-party police state. To be sure, there had been a rebound from the lowest points, such as the anti-Semitic show trials of Jewish Communist leaders in 1952. But even as Communist nations like Yugoslavia and Romania had demonstrated independence from Moscow and others had rebelled, with protests or revolutions put down in East Germany, Poland, and Hungary, Czechoslovakia had stayed an obedient Russian client throughout the '50s. When the 1960s arrived, Stalin-era hard-liners had remained atop the party and continued to control the government in Czechoslovakia, their grip on power seemingly forged of the same impenetrable metal as the curtain that separated East and West.

Then change started brewing as the decade unfolded. Some of the first signs appeared in the arts. A series of Czech films slyly undermined the regime. Taking that cue, members of an official Communist writers' conference startled everyone by openly demanding freedom of speech. Some politicians pushed harder for liberalization as well, and none more than Alexander Dubček, whom Shirley was so looking forward to meeting.

Dubček had undergone a transition not unlike that of his country. The child of a hard-core Slovak Communist who had moved the family to the "workers' paradise" of the Soviet Union, Dubček lived there through his adolescence, imbibing his father's ideology and that of their hosts. Dubček was just eighteen when he returned and joined the Communist Party in Czechoslovakia, fighting Rudolf Toussaint's Wehrmacht and their collaborationist Slovak allies as a partisan in World War II and then loyally aiding the 1948 Communist takeover. In the years that followed, Dubček rose through the ranks of the party, annoying his elders with his stubborn independent streak, his admiration for the maverick Communism of neighboring leaders such as Tito in Yugoslavia and Nicolae Ceauşescu in Romania, and his increasingly urgent advocacy for liberalization from the inside. Despite repeated attempts to demote or sideline him, he always popped back up. When the spirit of change began to accelerate in 1967, Dubček sympathized with those pushing for more rapid evolution both within and outside the party. He wanted to reform Communism, not replace it, and he rallied internal support from a younger generation of like-minded comrades.

Dubček took over as first secretary of the party in January 1968. That spring, he famously called for "Socialism with a Human Face": liberalization of the economy, speech, the press, and the arts. "The apex of hope went high through March, April, May," liberalization taking hold and spreading. A long-pent-up explosion of popular energy was released. People started small businesses. Creative theater, film, and fiction flourished, overtly criticizing Communism and the history of the past twenty years. Most of all, the people who had been fearfully shuffling through the streets—the Prague Watchers—started raising their eyes again.

Even Otto's house was involved in the renaissance. Official Czech television ran a documentary on the Petscheks and their Bubeneč homes, including the most glorious of them all: the palace. The broadcast spoke freely about the US connection to the property, surprising the Cold Warriors at the embassy. "[T]he television reporter simply pointed out . . . 'Here's the American ambassador living in this Petschek house,'" an embassy staffer recalled. "And they didn't say 'boo' about the exploiters being in one. . . . [I]f somebody who didn't know Communism had seen that, he would have said, 'Well, it's like what you see on television.' But you didn't see that on television in Communist countries." Once reviled, the palace was now acknowledged as part of Czech history, current American ownership and all.

Sadly, the man perhaps most responsible for its preservation was no longer alive to see it. Adolf Pokorný had served seven more ambassadors after Laurence, caring for the palace as if it were his own. He had continued investing his energy and love in polishing the silver candelabras and flatware, maintaining the mechanisms of the retracting wall and Otto's other idiosyncratic wonders, and guarding from pilfering hands the precious objects that his first master had collected.

Pokorný had worked his usual long day on Sunday, January 29, 1967, then took the short stroll down the driveway to get a few hours' sleep in the gatehouse. When he did not show up the next morning, the staff knew that there could be only one explanation. Viky came from the States to pay the family's condolences to the grieving Mrs. Pokorný, herself aging and ill, and to arrange for her care. Viky's feelings about the palace were ambivalent (and undoubtedly aggravated by the fact that the Czechs still had not paid him his due from the sale that Laurence had engineered—the matter was now in litigation against them). But how could he not be grateful to the majordomo who had cared for his father and all of them, made it possible for his sisters to have a dog, helped them and his mother pack their valises and escape in 1938, and safely sailed his father's creation through the crashing waves of democracy, Fascism, and Communism?

Pokorný would have been pleased—in his usual, barely perceptible way—to see the signs of liberalization blossoming everywhere in 1968 like the roses, hyacinths, and tulips in the palace garden. And he would surely have been curious about the American movie star who visited the palace on her pilgrimage to see Czech freedom blooming.

SHIRLEY returned to room 21 of the Alcron Hotel at the end of her first Tuesday in Prague, around ten p.m. She flopped onto her bed, exhausted but happy. She had accomplished her mission; the Czechoslovaks had agreed to join the MS federation. The minister of health had been delighted with her proposal, approving the terms on the spot. Shirley had been greeted with equal warmth by experts in neurology and biology at Otto's alma mater, Charles University. She was "charmed out of [her] boots by these friendly, intelligent people," who had gathered to meet her on the venerable premises of the university founded in 1348.

Her only disappointment was the fate of her meeting with the star of the show: Dubček. While Shirley was engaged in discussions at the university, a secretary had brought her a message: "Your meeting with Mr. Dubcek in 15 minutes is canceled—he is all tied up." The party leader had offered to see her the following day, but she had to decline. She had been away from her children, husband, and elderly parents for a week. Much as she wanted to meet Dubček, it was time to go home.

Shirley forced herself back up off the bed. Compared to the lavish surroundings of the Petschek palace, her room was spartan, her sole window looking out on "a bleak stone wall across a light well." The hotel itself was an art-deco landmark, its lobby featuring multihued striated marble; streamlined, low-slung furniture; and a smooth, golden statue of the goddess Diana, naked, her arms flung wide, palms to the sky. But the better rooms had already been taken; the hotel was packed with geologists in town for a convention, reporters covering the liberalization, and other foreigners. She did not complain; she seldom did.

Shirley's last event of the day, a press conference, had lasted for five hours, "as those things do in this part of the world." She had missed dinner, so she went digging through her suitcase for her emergency backup: Droste chocolate pastilles, carefully packed in her luggage by her children.

The day had been lengthy but highly productive. Bed, she thought, "seemed very good indeed." But before going to sleep, Shirley turned on the radio. She had grown up through the dawning of radio's golden age and liked to sleep with a station on—even when she couldn't understand a word of the broadcast. She turned the dial to Czechoslovak Radio. As she was dozing off, the report ended and she heard something that she could recognize: the plaintive tones of the Czechoslovak national anthem, "Kde domov můj" ("Where Is My Home?"). She missed hers, containing her children; her husband, Charlie; and her parents, half a world away in California.

She was glad to be heading back there in the morning, although she wondered if she was doing the right thing in turning down Dubček's offer of an alternative meeting time. As she was about to learn, "it was an appointment neither of us could have kept."

⌣⟶

SHIRLEY had barely nodded off when the phone rang, startling her awake. It was the hotel operator. A messenger had just arrived from the airport. The operator explained that he was insisting on seeing her immediately.

It seemed like a particularly odd request, but she was used to people behaving strangely around her. Her celebrity threw them off-kilter, sometimes extremely so. A few years before, one deranged fan had shown up at her home on Clay Drive carrying a gun; Shirley had shooed her family away by waving her hand behind her back and, while they called the police, calmly placated the disheveled man until the officers arrived.

The messenger got on the phone. He was speaking mostly Czech, but she could make out "airport" and "you must come down to lobby." Shirley politely but firmly thanked him and asked him to leave his message with the hotel staff. "Whatever it was," she told herself, "it would keep until morning."

She lay back down. She heard the infant of an American journalist cry softly once or twice in the room next door. Eventually all was still, and she fell asleep once more.

At some point in the night, she awoke again, this time to "the shriek of a low-flying jet plane." Shirley saw that the room was "still in darkness . . . There were some distant shouts in the street and a rattle of gunfire. Next door, the baby cried, and a typewriter was clicking away. Then things quieted down." Still drowsy, Shirley wondered at all the activity. But, she told herself, "Children often cry at night, some planes fly low, and newsmen often work late. If Czech militia choose to conduct noisy exercises at night, it's their business." She rolled over and returned to sleep.

The next thing Shirley knew, it was daybreak, and she was jerked awake by the loud thumping of someone pounding on the door. The person cried, "Awake, madame! We are invaded! The Russians have seized the airport! Tanks and troops are entering Prague! Oh, madame, it is a terrible thing!"

Shirley ducked into the hallway. It was empty. She had not had a proper meal since her lunch at the Petschek palace the day before; her only sustenance in the past sixteen hours had been those small chocolates. She saw that some room service diners had left hard rolls uneaten on the trays outside their doors, and she furtively took several. Shirley rushed back to her room and turned on the radio.

With no street view and the radio broadcast unintelligible, Shirley decided to leave the confines of her room to learn what was happening. She bit into the rolls as she dressed, stepping into a pair of yellow boots and covering her unwashed hair with a white beret. Then Shirley exited room 21 and headed upstairs to the roof.

Crouching behind the parapet like Priscilla, the child soldier in her movie *Wee Willie Winkie,* Shirley looked down at the street. The military might of the Soviet Union streamed down Štěpánská toward the expanse of Wenceslas Square at the end of the block, like a tributary flowing into the ocean. "Great green tanks, grimy and oily from the long night race from the border, thundered along . . . guns depressed toward the gathering crowds . . . Grim-faced crews were up in the turrets," wearing helmets with long earflaps extending down to their chins to help muffle the noise of the war machines. As they rumbled over the cobblestones, the soldiers occasionally fired "short bursts from automatic weapons at autos parked along the street and over the heads of the spectators," causing Shirley to flinch.

The scale of the invasion was overwhelming. "Personnel carriers rolled down the street, crammed with soldiers. They were in full kit, green-gray uniforms with red markings, black jackboots, unsmiling. . . . MiG-21 jets shrieked [overhead] in low rooftop passes," recognizable from the dark triangles of the wings below the dart-like fuselages. Balalaikas, they were called, after the Russian guitars with pyramid-shaped bodies—though their high-pitched screams were hardly music to Shirley's ears.

Czechs stood in clusters on the street, milling about despite the periodic gunfire. They were the Watchers of Prague, staring in "disbelief and confusion." The observers were predominantly students but were accompanied by furrow-browed parents as well as pensioners, their faces wrinkled and lined, their eyes looking back in time. A new horror to add to their trove of observations was unfolding before them: the liberators of 1945 had become akin to the invaders of 1939. "Then a small knot [of people] surged out in the path of one tank, which had paused. A Russian soldier waved his gun," but the people did not budge. The Czechs began to argue with him and his comrades, perched upon the turret and roof of the tank. Finally, "his commander, a hulking man, shouted, 'Vypyryod!' *Forward*!" Shirley feared that the people would be mowed down. But as the tank moved ahead, the crowd parted.

"A block away, at the corner of Wenceslaus [*sic*] Square, a mob of several thousand people pressed around a stationary tank. An old man tried to stuff a hank of heavy rope into the tank tread. Suddenly two more tanks rounded the corner and opened up with machine guns," once again over the heads of the crowd—but now closer.

Shirley backed away. She had seen all that she needed to—too much, in fact—so she slipped back indoors.

SHIRLEY headed downstairs, emerging into the dim art-deco lobby, her shadow long from the artificial light cast by the crystal chandeliers. The lobby, though safer, was almost as chaotic as the street. "While tanks continued to roam along in front of the Alcron Hotel, the reception room was overflowing with several hundred guests, all exchanging speculations on what would happen to us. Dutch, Austrian, English, American, Greek, German, all of us were leveled by the common denominator of our plight." The waiters served breakfast, their eyes red rimmed and teary, and the maids robotically moved through the halls to clean the rooms, crying.

Bits and pieces of information came through from the radio and the television in the hotel. The day started with the local stations still in the hands of Prague Spring supporters. The broadcasters explained that the Soviet bloc had invaded the country: primarily Russians in Prague, joined elsewhere by Poles, Bulgarians, and Hungarians. Dubček was in party headquarters with the other reformist Czechoslovak leaders, surrounded by Soviet tanks. The American embassy warned its citizens to remain in place, wherever they were.

There was one TV set in what the hotel called its dry bar, a gathering spot where no alcohol was served. "Chambermaids, busboys, and guests were all crushed in together, all glued to the announcers, in this case a grim man and a sad-eyed woman." Prague television, to Shirley's professional eye, had "seemed a lively and entertaining channel of the new Czech free speech." But now the female announcer came on. Another guest translated: "She could not stay on the air; keep a calm stance everyone; support Dubcek." The presenter began to cry as the first notes of the national anthem began. There it was again, "Kde domov můj." If last night it had suffused Shirley with longing, now it plunged her into sadness. It crossed her mind that she had no idea when she would see *her* home again. Who knew what would happen to her, to any of them? The television image faded out.

Shirley and the others in the hotel crowded around the radio, which was still broadcasting. But for how much longer? The announcers had earlier reported, "Military units are approaching the radio building. They are slowly approaching along Vynohradska [*sic*] Street and they are only a few score meters from the center of our radio building." The building was just a five-minute walk from the Alcron, so as Shirley monitored the radio bulletins with one ear, the other listened for shooting.

But then something unexpected happened. The speaker crackled: "Crowds of citizens are gathering around armored transports with Soviet soldiers outside the building of Czechoslovak Radio." As the Russian troops continued to mass outside the barricade, Praguers who spoke their language—of which there were many, especially among the younger generation—began talking to the soldiers, trying to reason with them. The Czechs told the troops that they were welcome—as long as they were not there as occupiers. The broadcast continued, "All Soviet soldiers are repeating in the same way: They have come here to liberate us from West Germans, that they have come to liberate us as in 1945." What Germans? the group asked. Where were they?

The Russians shrugged sheepishly as the people blocked them, and not just with their bodies. Some youths had barricaded the radio station with cars, buses, and a streetcar. Had Shirley stepped outside, she would not only have heard the Russian response, she would have seen it. She was around the corner from the standoff. "Russian tanks by the scores rushed into downtown Prague, and troops flooded in by the thousands. Czech crowds grew, swelled, surged, and broke before a phalanx of soldiers, who marched stiffly along to clear the streets, firing above their heads or sending point-blank bursts into the crowds."

Through it all, the radio was still transmitting, describing the imminent battle. Shirley was struck by "one overriding impression . . . through all these initial hours of the crump, crump, crump of automatic weapons, the crashing of tank treads across the cobblestones, the rumble of troop carriers, and the heave and surge of the street crowds. It is the air of defiant and undaunted spirit of resistance one senses among the people. The Russians seem to have grasped a nettle."

Finally, as Shirley and the others listened anxiously, the Russians made their move. Two tanks attempted to break through the barricade. But the students had done a good job with their makeshift barrier: the tanks got stuck. As their engines idled, a single Czech crept up to the hulking vehicles and punctured holes in the canisters of extra gas affixed to the back of each tank. Then he tossed a match into the fuel that had spilled into the street, and suddenly the cobblestones were on fire.

The announcers reported that a tank too had ignited, flames shooting high into the air. The crew piled down its side into the arms of their comrades. More of the heavily armored vehicles appeared on the scene, some firing wildly. Five tanks caught fire, their flames spreading to two trucks carrying tank ammunition. "Soviet troops were trying to put the fire out with clothes offered by civilians." Tank shells were firing off in all directions, one landing on a bus on a side street, which burned vigorously before exploding; its gas tank had been freshly topped to the brim. Two apartment houses ignited as well.

In the distance, Shirley could hear the gunfire, the explosions of the shells, the screams of the people. "Nine ambulances wailed by our hotel toward the square," but the Russians wouldn't let them through. Then they started firing again. "People fled before the shooting and threw themselves to the ground. After the shooting, they again returned to the Soviet armored cars and spoke to the soldiers."

The Russians at last allowed the ambulances to pass. Miraculously, the radio remained on the air. For the moment, the people of the city had won. It was a triumph for the Watchers of Prague, joining with and becoming fighters to protect their beloved city as they had when they rose up against Toussaint and the Germans in 1945. But, as in that year, their stand came at a high cost. "Twenty badly wounded persons were taken to Vinohr[a]dy hospital in Prague mostly suffering from bullet wounds" and legs that had been crushed by the tanks.

In the Alcron lobby, there was pandemonium in the wake of the battle as people struggled to determine what had transpired. A long-haired young girl wearing a peace-symbol medallion approached Shirley: "What's going on?" she asked. "What's happening?"

Shirley explained, "Czechoslovakia is occupied by the Russians, and we are in the trap too."

"No kidding," the young woman said. "There are twenty-five of us in a youth hostel down the street, and we don't know anything." The girl was just a little older than Shirley's own daughter.

"Well, look here," Shirley said, "go back to the hostel. Stick with your tour director."

"He's gone," the girl replied. "We haven't seen him since last night. What do we do?"

That was the question that they were all asking themselves. Shirley didn't know the answer, but she did her best to talk it through. Soon a crowd had formed around them—not just hotel guests, but a stream of Americans from all over town. Word had apparently spread among tourists trapped in Prague that Shirley Temple was there. Absurdly, as chaos ensued on the streets, a line of autograph seekers soon formed in the hotel. Shirley obliged despite the unusual circumstances. The German writer Heinrich Böll happened to be staying at the hotel and was struck by the surreal scene. But Shirley realized that she could be useful, her celebrity calming people and distracting them. "Sparkle, Shirley, sparkle," her mother used to say to her, right before she went on camera. However terrified she may have felt, she had long ago learned the art of masking it, and at this moment she could use that gift for good.

By the middle of the day, it had been almost twenty-four hours since Shirley had eaten her last full meal in the serene air of Otto's palace. She was suddenly ravenous—invasion or no invasion. The hotel dining room was open for lunch, and she went in. "A large cardboard sign had been erected behind the buffet, with 'Dubcek' written twice, first in Czech and underneath in Russian [Cyrillic]. Outside, the machine-gun fire continued."

The waiter stood very straight, but his eyes gave him away. He looked as if he had been crying "as he presented a platter of meats and fresh vegetables arranged like the crown jewels. 'The veal is very good today, madame,' he said." His tears began to flow again from eyes as pink and raw as the cuts of meat on his tray.

From the nearby square came the jolt of machine guns. "A heavyset man who had forgotten to shave pressed his transistor radio to his ear. 'Poor Radio Prague. They say tanks are firing into the building. When they play the national anthem, it will mean the Russians have entered the studio.'" The improbability of Shirley's circumstances struck her. She and the other guests were "eavesdroppers on history."

As she cupped her warm coffee mug in her hands, in rushed a tourist from the Netherlands, bringing news from outside. Scores of Czechs had gathered in Wenceslas Square. They carried posters of Dubček and taunted the Soviet soldiers, and then someone had fired into the crowd. "One boy had ripped off his shirt and, drenching it in the blood of a fallen comrade, waved it overhead, shouting, 'Free Czechoslovakia!'"

Shirley returned to the lobby, where "the talk got around to telephoning out or in—both were problems." The room phones were only for local calls. Long distance was handled in the five public booths in the lobby, but those phones were not working. The hotel switchboard couldn't offer any relief. Shirley watched the hotel operators "performing heroically, but outgoing calls seemed impossible, and incoming calls were jammed up."

It was early morning in California, and Shirley's family would be waking up to news of the invasion. She badly wanted to call home, feeling sure that her husband, Charlie, would be attempting to reach her. Not that he would be unduly worried: a World War II combat vet, he was not easy to rattle. And he trusted her as he would a comrade in arms. So strong was his confidence in her quick-wittedness and instinct for self-preservation that he had let her wave him off and deal with that crazed armed man at their front door on Clay Drive while he called the police. Still, he would want to talk to her, to know she was safe, as would the rest of her family.

She spotted a bulky brown house phone on a glass-topped table near the hotel's main entry. It was totally dead. "If you look through the glass table," she was told, "you may note that the phone has a cord but no place to plug into." It was Communism in a nutshell.

Just as she was beginning to feel desperate, a communications channel opened up. Calls started coming in from representatives of American news media, asking for her. Reporters on the ground in Prague had filed their first stories, noting her presence right in the heart of the war zone. Soon journalists from coast to coast in the States were trying to reach her. She took call after call, doing her best to describe the situation: the invasion, the barricade, the Czech casualties. She asked each reporter to be sure to say that she was fine, because her parents were "old and tend to worry." She passed along Charlie's contact information, too, and the names of the people with her in the hotel, asking the journalists to let their families know that the other guests were okay also and that they were all trying to find a way out.

As she juggled the media, Shirley also greeted a stream of her new Czechoslovak friends. An impressively large number of the Praguers whom she had met on the previous days of her trip threaded their way through the Soviet occupation forces to the Alcron. They came to inquire about her safety and to ask her about her plans, of which she had none. One woman whom she knew from the discussions regarding the International Federation of Multiple Sclerosis Societies approached quickly and drew her aside. "Things are deteriorating," she informed Shirley. "The American Embassy cannot help you. We can get you out safely. It is all arranged. You must come immediately."

Shirley weighed what to do, aware that the woman's plea was as genuine as it was grave. Could she defy the embassy, which had insisted that she remain where she was? Leaving would require navigating through many miles of countryside to cross the border to safety. There was little doubt that they would encounter large numbers of armed Soviets along the way. She wanted to get out of the country—as did the dozens of other uncertain and desperate Americans circulating in the lobby. But following this woman would mean turning her back on those people and, if she was caught, potentially even causing the Soviets to take some draconian measure against others in the hotel.

"No," Shirley finally replied. "I'm sorry. You have been a good friend, and I shall not forget." Others approached her with similar ideas all afternoon, the escape schemes growing increasingly outlandish, including a getaway hidden in a hay truck.

As the day passed, Shirley noticed some less-welcome individuals showing up in the hotel. On every floor two men suddenly appeared, sitting behind desks, their faces stony. Shirley wasn't sure whether they were there to help the guests or to spy on them. Other suspicious new faces filtered into the lobby, attempting to blend in.

Shirley pointed them out to another Praguer who had stopped by to check in on her. Shirley subtly gestured to a slim, elegant woman dressed in a camel-hair jacket and matching trousers. "They are strangers," Shirley whispered to her Czech friend. "They wait around within earshot, say little, mix not at all. I think they speak German."

"German, really?" The pupils of the woman's eyes dilated. "Well, I must go now," she said abruptly, and sidled out the door.

Night fell, a dusk-to-dawn curfew kicked in, and Shirley's flow of visitors ended.

THE dwindling food supply made for a short stay in the dining room. Shirley appreciated the one decent meal she had consumed that day and accepted that it would have to sustain her. She let the others, the geologists and their wives, some elderly, take the limited fare that remained. She was distracted from her hunger by the relentless barrage of gunfire, growling tanks, and shrieking ambulances.

A message came through from officials at the embassy: they were trying to get buses in from Austria to help Americans escape. They would send news if they had it—and in the meantime, US citizens were reminded not to leave the hotel. Hours passed without further word. The radio was still broadcasting intermittently, now from various clandestine locations. At around nine p.m., the announcers offered some grim news: "[A] short time ago," the broadcaster said, Dubček, along with three other reform members of the government, was "abducted from the Central Committee building in Prague and taken to an unknown destination."

Later that night, an abrupt burst of gunfire sounded outside the hotel entrance, causing Shirley and the others still downstairs to start. Shirley recalled, "A woman nearby, more daring than I, bolted outside and cried, 'Someone's been shot!'" Shirley followed her out onto the cobblestone street. To her horror, she saw the lifeless body of another woman, crumpled before them in a crimson pool of blood. It seemed that she had shaken a clenched hand in anger at the invaders and taken a bullet in the stomach. A Soviet armored vehicle was already trundling away on Štěpánská Street. It was too late to help.

"Look," said another guest, a heavyset tourist from Miami, holding something in her hand. "It's a bullet! Wait until they see this back home!" Shirley turned away, sickened—the image of the woman's splayed-out body searing into Shirley's memory to remain there for a lifetime. She went back inside and slowly walked up the stairs to her room, "exchanged evil glances" with the pair of strange men still sitting at the entrance to the floor, and locked her door behind her.

Could it really have been just a day since she had fallen into bed with such satisfaction? Back in the close quarters of room 21, her hunger made her woozy. Her hosts had plied her with so many delicacies before the invasion—fresh Bulgarian melon; shellfish; the Czech national liqueur, slivovitz; and more. She should have stocked up. Instead of eating, she washed her hair. At least the water hadn't run out. She laid out her clothing for the coming day. What do you wear to an invasion? She chose the sensible navy dress. She lay down on the bed in her underwear, still wearing her yellow boots in case she had to move fast. "For a long time I lay there, listening to the crackle of gunfire and staring out at my blank wall, musing occasional thoughts of melons, lobsters, and slivovic [sic], and sending lonely and loving thoughts toward my family."

THE next morning, Shirley rose with the sun. She quickly made her way down to the lobby, just as the desk clerk was slipping out the door of the hotel. "I must go," he said, his face drained of the high spirits that she had seen there before the invasion. He shook her hand firmly. "Mrs. Black, I wish you good luck."

She sat in the dining room with a reporter from United Press International, James Jackson. As they sipped their coffee, they could hear the crushing of Czechoslovakia. As Jackson wrote, "The shooting has different sounds. The small arms echo, 'crump, crump, crump.' The heavy ammunition from a Russian truck blown up by partisans goes, 'Whump! whump! whump!' Ponderous and almost rhythmical as the fire sets it off."

Immense cargo planes had replaced the MiG fighters in the airspace over the Alcron, distracting Shirley with their deafening approach. It sounded as if they were going to land on Štěpánská Street, not at Prague's Ruzyně airport. That was not the only sound in the air, however; "Kde domov můj" was everywhere. Someone was constantly singing, humming, or playing the national anthem, which had also been the last thing that Radio Prague played before signing off the day before. By now, Moscow's justification for the Soviet invasion was making its way around the world: "to give the fraternal Czechoslovak people urgent assistance, including assistance through military force." The words were a twisted echo of the brotherly Slavic embrace offered to Gottwald by Stalin in 1945. The Czechs in the Prague streets now saw the true nature of the nationalistic hug from their fellow Slavs and were decidedly unenthusiastic about returning it.

Shirley watched the military vehicles rumble along Štěpánská Street and grimly took note of several soldiers across from the hotel entrance. First had been the German-speaking spies attempting to mingle in the lobby, then the two men watching the hotel landing, and now this: the hotel under armed guard.

At nine o'clock, a Czech pulled up in a station wagon and hurried into the lobby, holding a list of names. Shirley recognized him: it was the same embassy driver who had delivered her to the peaceful world of the Petscheks earlier in the week—which seemed like a lifetime ago. "Mrs. Black, you must come with me to the Embassy," he said, his prominent Adam's apple bobbing in his throat.

"But I understood the Embassy wanted us to wait here for some buses to Austria," she replied. His expression grew mournful as he quietly corrected her: "Madame, that is a dream. We must go now." The geologists and their wives huddled around her. "Smells like a trap," one friend cautioned her. "I'll call the Embassy." They tried dialing but, as usual, had no luck.

Again Shirley deliberated. The car had diplomatic license plates, and she knew the man from her visit to the palace. She decided to take her chances. She grabbed her suitcase and traded embraces with those remaining behind, who either couldn't or wouldn't leave the relative security of the Alcron Hotel. One of the maids openly wept as she approached Shirley to say goodbye. Shirley tried to cheer her, joking that if she did not leave now she might have to stay forever and work there. The woman, her face wet from crying, pressed eight red carnations wrapped in newspaper on Shirley. She took the maid's rough hands in her own—she had always preferred working hands to idle ones—and kissed them.

On her way out, Shirley looked more closely at the newspaper encircling the flowers. It was from June 8, 1968: the date of Bobby Kennedy's funeral. A picture of his widow, dressed in black as she buried her husband, appeared on the page. The image was not a very promising augur for the day.

Shirley exited the Alcron and darted across the road, the staccato of nearby gunfire speeding her step. In the car, she joined two other passengers. The three women waited for a fourth. "Obviously everyone hadn't slept with their boots on," Shirley thought. A massive tank sped along Štěpánská in their direction, downshifted, and crept toward the car. The barrel of the tank swiveled from side to side. It pulled up to them, reeking of petroleum, exhaust fumes, and hot steel. The hatch popped open, and four soldiers leaned out to appraise the silent women. The Soviet soldiers wore overalls and had automatic weapons strapped across their bodies: short-barreled Kalashnikovs, with their trademark long sight posts and ammunition magazines curving out like scimitars.

Their grim faces, framed by their leather caps with earflaps dangling, continued staring. Shirley was terrified. Just when she thought that she couldn't take it anymore, the tank shifted gears and rumbled on down the street. She cranked the window closed, as her pulse began returning to normal. Finally, the woman they had been waiting for exited the hotel and joined them. With that, the car pulled away from the curb.

On their way, they discovered roadblocks all along their route. The Soviets had improvised the barriers, positioning tanks face-to-face across the road. At each of these obstacles, their local driver swore, spun the steering wheel, and swerved down an alternative street. Although none of them had any idea where he was headed, he apparently knew his way.

Scattered clashes were happening around the city, and the sounds of conflict could be heard from afar. They tried to keep very still as the car wended through the maze of the Malá Strana neighborhood. Even on a normal day, it was easy for a visitor to get lost amid Prague's tangled streets. Shirley had no clue where they were.

After about twenty minutes, the car came to a stop in front of an archway puncturing a tall façade of stone and plaster that was flying the Stars and Stripes: the American embassy. Shirley let out a sigh of relief. The driver had been legitimate, thank goodness. She and the others got out, joining several dozen people milling in front of the Schönborn. Four centuries old, it had seen many an invasion in its time: Austrian, Swedish, Prussian, German, and now Soviet.

It seemed that the buses had fallen through for the moment, so Americans and other Westerners who had cars (and gasoline, which was no longer commercially available) were forming a convoy to drive out of the country. In the hubbub, Shirley was ignored by the preoccupied embassy staff—and on one of the few occasions where she wanted badly to be noticed. How was she going to get out of here? Unlike the vehicle owners, sitting in their cars, she had no means of transportation. Lugging her suitcase with her, she cornered a frazzled young official and identified herself. "Why am I going *now*?" she asked. "I have no car."

"Listen, Mrs. Black," he replied, "if there's anyone who wants you out of Prague more than *we* do, it's the Soviets." He pulled her through a vaulted passageway guarded by marines and framed by two ancient caryatids: eight-foot statues of warriors robed in lion skins and holding war clubs. She entered the broad interior courtyard of the embassy as he carried off her bag. On three sides rose the wings of the structure, white walls punctuated by windows set in stone frames.

She leaned against the wall of the old building, feeling forlorn. Above her, thick black smoke poured out of an antique chimney on the roof. The embassy was burning its files, as Toussaint had done exactly forty years before about a block from here. Her solitude did not last long. She was placed in the front seat of a Mercedes, parked directly ahead of a black station wagon draped with a large American flag. It reminded her of a hearse.

"That's the flag car," said a young, cerebral-looking foreign-service officer, his high forehead creased with stress. His name was Larry Modisett. He slipped behind the wheel. "It's got a Czech driver who knows the way. We'll lead to the checkpoint, and he'll take over the lead after that. Let's go." They would head west, to the border with West Germany, crossing at Rozvadov, then continuing to Nuremberg, and home—if all went according to plan. But things rarely go according to plan during an invasion.

The other vehicles at the curb pulled out behind them, one by one.

THEIR convoy "snaked past many troop carriers, armored cars, and tanks, most of them heading toward the center of Prague and all moving fast, usually in the middle of the road. At every major intersection were Russian troops and vehicles. Parked at both ends of bridges and along the railroad track, there were tanks moving, tanks waiting, tanks by the hundreds."

The trip away from the embassy was even more tortuous than the one toward it had been. On three occasions Modisett stopped and vanished to scout out the road before returning and proceeding. They were nearing the outskirts of Prague when he stopped yet again. They had reached a row of vehicles containing Americans and other foreigners that had pulled over on the right side of the road, apparently waiting to join the motorcade. Modisett pulled over at the back of the line and exited the car yet again, walking ahead until he was out of sight.

Five minutes passed, then ten. A full half hour went by as Shirley grew tense with impatience. Suddenly the door opened, and a man told her, none too gently, "Get going!" She explained that she wasn't the driver and wouldn't know where to go. But he didn't care. "Drive it up there, lady," he barked at her, brandishing an official-looking ID card embossed in gold.

Following his orders would require driving on the wrong side of the road in an unfamiliar car to get around the vehicles in front of her. But Shirley was nothing if not game. She slid behind the steering wheel and peeled out of the line of parked cars. Behind her was a jeepload of young GIs. They had been trapped by the invasion while touring and were protecting the convoy while it passed through Soviet lines. When she pulled out, they let out a resounding cheer.

They then followed her, and soon the whole flotilla of cars was trailing behind. "All the convoy was following me like a swarm of lemmings.

I had gone only several yards when a big Czech bus pulled onto the highway, and we stopped again." Grinning at her, the man driving the bus pulled over and onto the sidewalk. Shirley inched past him, waved, and sped off, even though she had no idea where she was going.

The question of their destination was soon answered—definitively so. "Perhaps five minutes later, my problem was solved by two enormous Russian tanks, parked nose to nose across the road. I approached slowly and pulled up to within a car length of one of the tanks, noticing that its cannon muzzle, a big black circle, was looking directly at me through the windshield." Shirley drove the car straight up to the tank. She didn't look at the tank crew, hoping they wouldn't take any notice of her.

On the side of the highway, a debate was raging between a group of Westerners and a knot of Czechs and Russians, some in uniform, some not. Shirley approached her driver, Modisett, and called out to him. He turned around and did an astounded double take. The young foreign-service officer explained to Shirley that "the soldiers were holding us up because we had no official transit papers." He excused himself, and further argument ensued, seemingly to no avail. The tanks did not budge. Finally, a Soviet officer in black boots marched over and ordered the tank to let Shirley's vehicle through. Modisett joined her and she squeezed the car through the opening in the barricade, surrounded by stern faces; the massive tank wheels were within spitting distance on both sides.

The drivers behind her followed. Expanded to include the other parked cars that had been waiting at the checkpoint, the convoy that had left the embassy had grown to more than one hundred vehicles. It included Americans, Canadians, Brits, Western Europeans, and even several dozen Czechs who were not sticking around to see how the invasion turned out. It stretched for more than a mile down the scenic highway, through green fields and rolling hills. But neither Shirley nor the other drivers and passengers had any appetite for sightseeing today. As previously agreed, they soon yielded the lead position to the local driver piloting the flag car. He immediately floored it, the Stars and Stripes streaming behind the vehicle. Shirley, never one for accepting a supporting role, overtook him. She "resumed the lead position and kept it."

SHIRLEY and Modisett alternated driving. She was in the passenger seat as they approached Plzeň at midafternoon, and she was uneasy. They had been warned that the city was showing signs of trouble, with protests and fights lighting up the streets. And their convoy had also fallen two hours behind schedule, thanks to its hundreds of bladders, at least one of which seemed to need emptying every five minutes. Their progress had been a succession of "halt, start, string out, and halt."

At one point, Shirley and Modisett were startled to find that they had gotten too far out in front of the others and had lost sight of them. They pulled over, waiting until two Czech youths on motorcycles passed by. Shirley waved them down and asked if they had seen a long trail of cars behind them. Yes, they had—but they were a substantial distance behind. Over shared cigarettes, the motorcyclists showed them some pamphlets supporting Dubček, issued by the workers at the Škoda arms factory. The bikers parted amicably and were on their way, and before long the convoy had caught up and followed suit.

If they could just make it through this next stretch of highway, the border would be close. But as they paused again by the side of the road for yet another rest stop, a Soviet fighter plane hurtled from nowhere and, flying low, shrieked past their car—the noise hurting Shirley's ears. At the exact same time, a Russian helicopter suddenly rose up from a stand of trees and came straight at them. It stopped, hovering perhaps ten feet above them, a red star painted on its dull grayish-green body, the powerful draft of the rotors causing the grasses at the side of the road to lie flat and shudder. Soldiers stared out of the cockpit, surveying Shirley and her companions.

She felt the eyes of Russians boring into her for the third time that day: the tank crew outside the hotel; the soldiers at the roadblocks in Prague; now, the helicopter. She had been stared at all her life, but never like this.

After a few very long minutes, the small caravan cautiously restarted its journey to the border. Shirley's car was still in the lead, followed by the flag car. The helicopter floated off to one side, remaining stationary in that spot as the convoy slowly passed. It was "like a general reviewing the troops," Shirley thought. She looked back down from the chopper in the sky only to see armored cars and tanks pouring out of side roads and filling the highway in both directions. One stream of Soviet vehicles en route to Plzeň caught up to and passed the slow-moving Western convoy, and another flow of Russian might surged by in the opposite direction, headed toward Prague. They had blundered into the thick of the invasion force.

They continued apace—what other choice did they have?—and the Russian forces gradually fell away once they circumnavigated Plzeň. When they completed their detour around the city, Shirley thought that they were in the clear. Then a giant Soviet tank, trailed by a jeep, sped up onto the highway from the side. It accelerated and "cut in between" Shirley's vehicle and the flag car. "It came thundering along right behind us, buttoned up for action, its muzzle cap off. We were afraid to speed up, afraid to slow down."

Then, as quickly as the tank had appeared, it was gone, vanishing down another side road. The jeep remained, however, and it had two Soviet officers in it. "Don't look now," Shirley told Modisett, "but I think we're convoying a Soviet jeep to the border." The jeep, too, eventually turned off.

Before long a number of Czech military men carrying weapons waved Shirley's lead car down. They shared the welcome news that the convoy was only a mile from the West German border. The vehicles should proceed in the left lane. The troops smiled and waved them on their way.

They soon saw why they had been sent along the left side of the road. There was a bottleneck at the border. Shirley observed that it was "clogged with dozens of autos lined up on the right, doors open, and many people standing around in the sunshine." Shirley and her fleet had been given priority. They followed instructions, remaining in the left lane as they slowly made their way to the gatehouse.

Shirley gave her passport to the Czech guard outside the booth. He carried it inside, where Shirley could see that a Soviet officer was in charge. Both squinted out the window of the gatehouse at Shirley. After an interval, the Czech came back outside and addressed her. "Pass," he said, handing her back her travel document.

The car, with Shirley in the passenger seat, rolled into West Germany.

It came to a stop and she emerged "still clutching the eight red carnations." Shirley was thronged by reporters, American troops stationed in Germany, and military police. She was peppered with questions as she stood in the late afternoon sunlight, a television camera in her face.

"What did you see?"

"I saw many Czech people crying, and it makes me cry too," she answered.

She had come to witness freedom flourish and instead had seen it crushed. She would never forget the dead woman on the sidewalk in front of her hotel. She did not intend to let the people responsible for this get away with it.

And she wasn't giving up on seeing Dubček.

She would be back.

14

A REVOLUTIONARY PRODUCTION

B ACK IN HER SUNNY NORTHERN CALIFORNIA HOME, A SANCTU-
ary among the green hills, Shirley was haunted by Prague. When
she closed her eyes, she saw that woman splayed out in the street. For
Shirley, that nameless victim symbolized all the Czechoslovaks who
had stood before the guns and tanks of the Soviet invaders, peacefully
resisting.

Over and over again, Shirley played the record she had brought back
from Prague of "Kde domov můj," the Czech national anthem, wearing
grooves in the black platter. She put on traditional Czech garb—a richly
embroidered red apron, a peaked peasant cap, and a white blouse—and
attended a demonstration in San Francisco against the Soviet invasion.
She wept as the news from Prague came in: crackdowns, the installation
of hard-liners, the restoration of Stalinist-style rule. Her befuddled family had never seen her like this.

Eventually, Shirley packed her Czech outfit away in her bulging
closet, alongside her collection of costumes going all the way back to her
earliest films. But she was changed. She pored over newspapers and jour-
nals, studying world affairs. She told people that she should have gone
into the foreign service long ago. She wanted to find a way to fight for
people like the dead woman—not just Czechs, but all those whose freedoms were being stolen.

She was a Republican, though a liberal one, and campaigned vigorously for the party that cycle. That and her new determination to work in
international relations earned her an appointment from the just-elected
Richard Nixon as one of the US delegates to the UN General Assembly

for the 1969 session. During orientation, she impressed Henry Kissinger with a smart question about Namibia; he was shocked that Shirley "even knew the word."

She dove into her UN work, crafting resolutions, debating issues, and building coalitions. The other delegates praised her as a "fresh breeze that has gently blown into our midst." The body often divided along Cold War lines, but, despite her traumatic experience in Prague, Shirley was pragmatic in her approach to Communism. When the American ambassador to the UN briefed her on the US policy to marginalize Red China, she stunned him with her response: "Now I understand *how* we're keeping China out of the United Nations. Would somebody please tell me *why* we're keeping China out of the United Nations?"

Shirley was a different kind of Cold Warrior. She was a vigorous opponent of Communism but believed there was room to work with her adversaries, not just fight them. In that, she foreshadowed the détente of her bosses Nixon and Kissinger. That won her widespread goodwill among other countries at the United Nations, even if some of the more vehement anti-Communists who framed American policy might have thought that she was too soft. The no-compromise school had been led by the Dulles brothers—the very same ones who had come to Viky's aid in negotiating with Laurence Steinhardt—when they served in government in the '50s and into the '60s. Shirley's was a more nuanced approach—one that she believed was closer to the democratic values that America had been advocating globally ever since Wilson had made America a world leader in 1918. She did not think America was perfect—just that (like Otto Petschek's long-ago building project) it was pursuing perfection.

After her UN posting ended, Shirley held a series of other government jobs, mostly focusing on international environmental issues (she was ahead of her time as a green Republican, too). The jobs were not glamorous; Nixon believed in dues paying, and she was doing her share. When Gerald Ford assumed the presidency in 1974, she got her reward: an ambassadorship to Ghana. She was among the very first officials whom Ford swore in, taking the oath with another well-known American, the new envoy to China, George H. W. Bush. President Ford was determined to present a fresh face to the world after Watergate. Shirley would have liked to have gone back to Prague, but she was thrilled to serve anywhere. Once settled in West Africa, she quickly won over the Ghanaians, becoming an honorary chieftain and countering Soviet influence. But Ford was struggling to win reelection after pardoning Nixon, and in less than two years he called her back to D.C. to serve as his chief of protocol.

When Ford lost in 1976, Shirley found herself out of a job. She had hoped that President-elect Jimmy Carter might keep her on, but, after flirting with the idea, he wished her well and brought in a protocol chief of his own. She had enjoyed a golden run in government, and she waited for a Republican or a discerning Democrat to win and bring her back into politics.

Twelve years later, she was still waiting. She had been a candidate to head the CIA and for other plum jobs in the Reagan years, but none of these posts materialized. Rumor had it that Nancy Reagan blocked her because Shirley had once kissed "Ronnie" in a movie—and then joked about it. But the dispositive factor may have been that she had backed his primary opponent, the more moderate George H. W. Bush.

To occupy herself, Shirley pioneered a State Department orientation course for new ambassadors in 1981. She had too much energy to simply sit at home. By the time Bush was elected in 1988, she had trained virtually every American ambassador of the previous eight years. She sent hundreds of them on their way, including to Prague. Although it was considered a hardship posting because of the surveillance and harassment by the totalitarian Czechoslovak government, it had its compensations—not least the glorious property that she had visited in 1968, where the ambassador lived. Otto's palace had become famous throughout the foreign service. As one of her Prague-bound ambassadorial students put it, the palace was "prime, prime property for Ambassadors." Otto would have enjoyed the praise, though he surely would have been surprised to learn that US envoys and not future generations of Petscheks were scrubbing themselves in his green-tiled thousand-stream shower. (It might have been some solace that his son, Viky, had finally been paid for the palace in the 1980s, as part of a global settlement with Czechoslovakia.)

In February 1989, Shirley was on a business trip to Seattle when she received a call in her hotel room. It was the White House. Would she hold for the president? Her heart leaped. Then she was on the line with her Ford-era swearing-in buddy, the newly inaugurated President Bush.

After a warm hello, he got right to the point. Would she agree to serve as ambassador to Czechoslovakia?

"I said yes so quickly and so loudly," she later told a reporter, that her startled husband exclaimed, "What have you agreed to?" To her surprise, Bush had no inkling of her history with Prague—that her experience in 1968 had triggered her career in international relations. He just recognized that she was smart and tough and that her charm (and still potent fame) might help accelerate change in the stubbornly brutal regime. Her husband laughed as Shirley got off the phone and began to jump up and down with glee. She was celebrating her return to a police state, one of the more repressive in the world, and one where she had survived great danger, to boot. Nonetheless, she was thrilled to be able to do something to make things better in the country that had set her on her destined path.

⌒

TWENTY-ONE years after she had first seen the palace, almost to the day, Shirley reascended the driveway on the windy, drizzly evening of August 11, 1989. The Roman arch next to the guardhouse was slightly more weathered; the greenhouses beyond it were a little more dilapidated. But as she walked through the interior, she found, atypically, that she could not remember any aspect of its grandeur. She had been so overwhelmed on her first visit that nothing had stuck. She felt that she "came as a stranger."

Outside the palace's walls, Czechoslovakia felt to Shirley like "a Stalinist backwater." The man who had ousted Dubček, Gustav Husák, was still in power, now as president. Hard-line colleagues such as Vasil Bil'ak, who had invited the Soviets to invade, also remained in official positions. They shared the reins with members of an uncompromising younger generation such as Miroslav Štěpán, the Prague party head. The Czech leaders had little affection for the sweeping change emanating from Mikhail Gorbachev's Soviet Union and had brutally cracked down on a series of dissident protests during the past year, using water cannons and tear gas, and beating and arresting demonstrators.

Shirley confronted a thorny problem: how to extract more liberty for the Czech people out of the recalcitrant apparatchiks. Despite the country's commitments (under the Helsinki Accords) to respect freedom of speech, the press, and assembly, the government leaders still openly persecuted citizens who attempted to exercise those rights. Shirley wanted to push the leaders as far as possible. But for all of her ardent commitment to freedom, her experience since her UN days had reinforced her more nuanced approach to Communism. She couldn't just attack; she would have to carefully juggle tough criticism with positive inducement to make progress.

Some of the battle-tempered Cold Warriors working in her own embassy, as well as experts back home, questioned whether Shirley was up to the task. It was as difficult a job as any American ambassador in the region faced. "If Prague were Rome or Paris, it would be easy to see George Bush's decision to ask her to be Ambassador to Czechoslovakia as simply a political reward for long, loyal service to the conservative Republican cause," one journalist wrote. "But Prague is a difficult post that has usually been held by career diplomats with a background in Eastern European affairs." Another reporter was more blunt: "I loved her in *Bright Eyes* and *Curly Top* when I was in grade school, but was not in thrall to her diplomatic credentials." Shirley smiled away such doubts publicly but—privately—was incredulous. She had labored in a series of jobs across the executive branch, served as a successful ambassador, trained hundreds of others, and even been named the only honorary foreign-service officer in the nation's history, by then–secretary of state George Shultz. Yet some still claimed she was not good enough. The criticism was well summed up by the child of one of her embassy officers. He explained that when he told his daughter that Shirley Temple was going to be the US ambassador, she said, "But Daddy, isn't she a little girl?"

President Gustav Husák gave her an unusually quick credentialing date of August 23, less than two weeks after her arrival. Diplomatic protocol forbade her attending public events until she was formally accredited, but that didn't stop her. The twenty-first anniversary of the Soviet-bloc invasion was rapidly approaching, and Shirley and her staff heard that Czechs intended to gather at five p.m. in Wenceslas Square to commemorate it. Miroslav Štěpán, the hard-line party chief, had announced that demonstrations would be dealt with firmly, including with the use of "force in accord with valid Czechoslovak laws." The government had gone so far as to echo the warning directly to the embassy: Czechoslovak authorities could not ensure the security of foreigners, whether they be diplomats, journalists, or casual observers who were "present within the range of unpermitted demonstrations." Shirley didn't care. Inspired by her memories of 1968, she refused to be intimidated by Communists once more.

On August 21, Shirley laced up her sneakers, took Charlie by the hand, and told the palace staff that she and her husband were going to take a walk. She was careful about what she said in the palace: she had been warned that listening devices were everywhere, planted by the regime. Weaving through the nearby Letná Park, a giant swath of green stretching for miles through the city, she told Charlie where they were headed: Wenceslas Square.

Her tall husband, towering over the petite ambassador, genially fell into step. Beneath his thinning gray hair and owlish glasses, Charlie still had the movie-star looks that had attracted her when they first met in Hawaii thirty-nine years before. She had been recovering from her first, short marriage to a would-be actor. Shirley was chagrined when a handsome young veteran whom she met at a Honolulu party didn't recognize her on the spot. It turned out that Charles Black had never seen one of her films. As they spent more time together, she came to appreciate that fact: Charlie saw who she actually was and fell in love with her for that, not for her fame (or her money; he was from a San Francisco social-register family and had plenty of his own).

Despite his patrician roots, Charlie had a bohemian streak; at the time that they were introduced, he was working in the Dole company's executive office but spent his spare time surfing and beach-bumming. He complemented Shirley's own appetite for adventure, and they had had many in their almost four decades together. Charlie was confident in his own skin and accomplishments, including a Silver Star for valor in combat and a string of successful businesses. He let Shirley be Shirley (such as the time that he had trusted her to deal with the armed man at their front door while he called the police). But he could be protective, too, when her appetite for action ran away with her. His lack of macho posturing in combination with his quiet strength made him a good husband for an ambassador—particularly one who could be a little too fond of risk.

As they headed to the square the two of them were struck by how downtrodden the Czech pedestrians seemed. "It was an oppression you could see and feel," Shirley later said. "What I noticed . . . was posture. The posture of the people was as though they were being crushed. You could physically see the problems. And you could see that they were not supposed to talk to foreigners; they didn't even talk to one another. . . . It was spooky. It was strange. Even the children were silent." The Watchers of Prague had become afraid to look—their vision obscured by fear.

Shirley and Charlie entered the vast open space of Wenceslas Square at its northwestern end. A half mile long, gradually rising from northwest to southeast, it was little changed since Shirley had last been there in 1968. The buildings that faced the square on either side were still a hodgepodge of eras and styles, the beautiful miscellany that characterized the Prague streets. A saving grace of Communism was that the regime built relatively little in the city center. At the south end of the square, rising high above it, was the nineteenth-century National Museum, with its metal-and-glass dome. The imperfectly repaired Soviet artillery damage of '68 was still visible on the façade of the museum and those of the buildings around it. Just below the museum was the equestrian statue of Saint Wenceslas, staring straight ahead to where Shirley and Charlie entered the square. The atmosphere was grimier and, Shirley felt, sadder, having accumulated twenty-one years of soot and tears.

Like the Blacks, others were strolling around the perimeter in couples, as well as singly and in small groups. At around five p.m., many quickened their pace, joining pedestrians suddenly streaming in from every direction toward the south end of the square. In what felt to Shirley like a matter of seconds, a crowd of about fifteen hundred people had coalesced at the base of the Saint Wenceslas statue. The protesters soon unrolled a banner: THE BOLSHEVIKS CAME WITH TANKS, WE COME WITH FLOWERS. Arms were raised, fingers pointed skyward in a V—the peace sign. Chants went up: "Long live freedom!"

As the crowd massed, the Blacks stood back a bit. They continued walking and watching from a distance. It was reckless enough to be there at all during the diplomatic limbo before Shirley's credentialing. She dared not get tangled up in the demonstration itself. But she still wanted the regime to notice that she was there and that she was observing them. Lest they miss her, she wore a cap emblazoned with her initials, which were also those of the dreaded secret police: STB.

Shirley and Charlie were not the only observers. The Veřejná bezpečnost (VB), the riot police, soon came as well. They were some-times called *kosmonauti* (cosmonauts), because they looked like space travelers, with their white protective headgear. They appeared almost as quickly as the protesters had. The police marched forward in forma-tion, row after row, holding clear plastic shields and white batons. The crowd was warned to leave. A group of protesters resisted passively, sit-ting down on the pavement. Shirley watched as each demonstrator was lifted by four police officers, one for each limb, and arrested, the officers carrying them into police vans. At that, the crowd began to disperse. The square was completely cleared by about five thirty.

Shirley had mixed feelings as she and Charlie walked home to the palace through the park. She hated that the government showed such open disregard for its Helsinki obligations. However, as she wrote back to Washington, "political activism [was] growing." It was not 1968, of course, when it had seemed to her that the entire population of the city was in the streets. The country still had not recovered from the invasion. But it was something. The resistance was alive.

The next day, she met it for coffee.

ON August 22, Shirley put on a polka-dot dress and welcomed a cluster of Czechoslovak dissidents at the home of an embassy colleague. The group was led by Jiří Dienstbier, one of the founding members of Char-ter 77, the foremost dissident movement. Dienstbier was silver haired and mustachioed, his face weary from two decades of work in menial jobs, including as a furnace stoker on the Prague subway. A former jour-nalist, he was one of the tens of thousands of Prague's reform-minded intellectual elites who were purged in the aftermath of the Soviet inva-sion that Shirley had witnessed twenty-one years prior. Several members of the younger generation of Czech dissidents came with Dienstbier to meet Shirley. Long-haired and lively, they could have passed for gradu-ate students on a field trip with their professor. But the group was much tougher than it looked, having endured daily police harassment, beat-ings, dog attacks, water cannons, arrests, and imprisonment—always reacting nonviolently. These dissenters were not content to passively watch Prague remain in the grip of totalitarianism. They had made peaceful protest into a weapon, if not yet a decisive one.

Dienstbier and the others eyed the new ambassador, sizing her up. They wondered if there was some kind of deep American strategy in giving the job to a former movie star. Regardless, a meeting such as this was "very important" to their cause and even to their physical safety. "It was an opportunity to share information we had collected. And also it offered us a certain protection. It was more difficult to arrest somebody or kill somebody if they were taken seriously by foreign officials . . . And that was a matter of life and death. In our case the question was whether we would be thrown in prison for a couple of years or somehow protected."

The dissidents pulled no punches with Shirley. Husák, Biľak, Štěpán, and the others in power wanted to cling to Communism and their own authority at all costs. To do so, they needed to shore up the economy, including by getting most favored nation (MFN) trading status from the United States. Dienstbier and the others implored Shirley: Don't give it to them lightly. Tie MFN to human rights.

"There was a lot of emotion underneath" the dissidents' words, Shirley felt:

> You knew of their prison sentences . . . the terrible abuse of human rights . . . [n]ot just going to prison, but also, perhaps, losing your home if you were a person of independent thought. Perhaps not having your children be able to continue their education if they didn't think like the party wanted them to. Having your phone ripped out. Having night searches in your house. Everything that could produce stress, heavy stress, on people. And knowing of these abuses made me very sad for the people. They'd been oppressed for so long.

Shirley came to the conclusion that the Czechs wanted change, but they hadn't banded together as a nation to achieve it. As they sat there—the carefully groomed and coiffed ambassador, her grizzled Cold Warrior staff, Dienstbier and his scruffy colleagues—Shirley sensed that change was on its way. The meeting energized her, especially on top of the signs of life that were conveyed by the protest. She emerged certain that something big was coming. "No one knew when it was going to happen, but everyone was talking about it, thinking about it, and hoping."

SHIRLEY was unsure of what reception to expect when she showed up at Prague Castle the next day to present her credentials to President Husák. Her attendance at the protest surely had not gone unnoticed by the secret police. They had undoubtedly trailed some of the dissidents to that meeting with her as well. Would Husák castigate her? He had hung on to power for two decades, most of that as the head of the Communist Party, before his current occupancy of the castle as president. He was a World War II partisan who had been purged from the party and imprisoned during the Stalin years before being "rehabilitated." She tried to read his face during the elaborate ceremony in the Throne Hall of the castle. Tall, white haired, and still powerfully built, he was inscrutable as she handed him the credentials.

She made a short speech in Czech. *"Predavam do vasich rukou pane presidente akreditacni listiny."* ("I am presenting to your hands, Mr. President, my letters of accreditation.") When she finished, she put a hand on her chest, spontaneously telling him that she hoped she hadn't hurt his ears too much. He smiled, replying, "not very much," and everyone in their respective entourages grinned.

The ceremony complete, the two of them went to an adjacent drawing room for a private chat. They took a seat at a table that had been set with refreshments, including cigarettes and matches (they were both smokers). After some friendly banter, Husák explained the speedy credentialing: "I wanted to have you come here and present your credentials right away . . . I wanted to see how you had turned out." He told Shirley that he and his wife loved her old films. Shirley often said, "Shirley Temple opens the door for Shirley Temple Black." Now she thought to herself, "Whatever works." They had a wide-ranging conversation. She reminded him that she had been there in 1968 and told him that she felt that the country had never recovered from the invasion by the Warsaw Pact. He listened politely but noncommittally. Afterward, free at last to talk to the press, Shirley said much the same thing.

Not everyone was as courteous as the president. Three days later, Shirley was cornered at an event by another one of the dinosaurs of '68, Husák's colleague Vasil Bil'ak. He was the chief ideologist of the party and had helped the Soviets depose Dubček. Bil'ak stalked up to Shirley and angrily told her, "I don't like what you said about my country and government."

Feigning innocence, she replied, "Mr. Bil'ak, what did I say that got you so upset?"

Her calm only agitated him further. "The people from [my] government couldn't digest what [you] said about the invasion by the Warsaw Pact armies of Czechoslovakia in August 1968." He said that it was nothing more than an "incident" and insisted, "When you will be here for a longer time, you will see that we were right."

She refused to pass it off as a mere incident. Unflinching, she answered, "I was here in August 1968 and saw with my own eyes and heard with my own ears, what was happening . . . I [have] my own opinion about the *invasion*," she told him, which "I would *never* change." At that, Bil'ak stormed away.

She was more cordially received by the press, which thronged to her in Prague. She welcomed them to the palace and seated them in the library, beneath the tall shelves of multilingual books that Rudolf Toussaint had allowed Pokorný to preserve. With its ornate décor, the house was a marvelous stage for a host—and no one knew better how to command a stage than Shirley. She used the palace and everything in it to fight for freedom for the Czechoslovak people. She let the reporters hold the miniature Oscar stationed on the library mantelpiece, then focused the journalists on the mistreatment of the dissidents. She explained to the press that "the age-old and very useful and important message is that you don't intervene in the internal affairs of another state. But one can certainly urge a government to meet its treaty obligations, particularly in the area of human rights." By agreeing to the Helsinki Accords, the Czechoslovak leadership had assented to minimum standards, and she intended to hold them to it.

Safely credentialed, she also brought a provocative sense of humor to that battle for human rights. Across the street from the palace was a cluster of buildings belonging to the StB. Her bedroom's balcony faced in their direction. Sure that their binoculars were trained on her whenever she went onto the balcony, she took to wearing a T-shirt emblazoned with her initials (matching her hat from the August protest): STB. When it became clear that they were following her Cadillac, she affixed the monogram to the car. When she got a boxer puppy, she named him Gorby after Gorbachev. On one occasion, the Soviet ambassador canceled dinner at the last minute, later apologizing to her at a gathering.

"Oh, don't worry," she replied. "Gorby was there." "Everybody got a little pale," Shirley later recalled. "They asked: 'At the residence?!' So I said, 'And he's still there.' And I let it go at that, because I'm that type."

Over time, she also found that at least one subset of the Watchers of Prague was warming to her. When she'd go walking, she would say good morning to them in Czech—"*Dobrý den.*" At first they would avert their eyes, but then they would edge up to Shirley and extract their wallets. Shirley thought, "What's this going to be, [a] Communist Party card or what?" But then they would slide out a Shirley Temple fan-club card, frayed around the edges, shyly presenting it to her. It happened dozens of times.

These encounters could be deeply moving. One woman told Shirley how much her movies and the books based on the movies had meant to her. It turned out that "she and her entire family were rounded up because they were Jews and they were sent to concentration camps and separated. At the end of the war every other member of her family was gassed and dead. But this woman had one connection to her former life, her Shirley Temple books." The woman wept, and left Shirley and those around her in tears as well.

Shirley did not confuse these small moments of grace with breakthroughs. Communists remained in control. But, just as on her first visit to Prague, a surprise awaited.

⌒

SHIRLEY maintained a steady schedule of meetings with dissidents that fall. As one of the embassy staff noted, "everybody in the embassy had contacts with the dissident community, from the ambassador on down. Everybody in the political section, the economic section, the public affairs section, the consular section had contacts. We would stop by and chat with them. We were conscious of the fact that we were being followed and we worried about the fact that would be causing them trouble, but they wanted that contact with us . . . [I]t gave them a little—maybe a little—protection."

Some of the other embassies questioned this strategy, asking, "Why do you Americans continue to encourage the dissidents by meeting with them in this way? Why not accept the fact that things are the way they are? They have been this way for more than forty years and they're not going to change." But Shirley and her team—her supportive deputy, Ted Russell; her hard-nosed, brilliant political-economic chief, Cliff Bond; her human-rights officer, the compassionate Ed Kaska—saw it differently. Cliff's wife, Michele, also an embassy official, explained, "We maintain connections with them because we think they're right, because we agree with what they're saying. We agree with what they are pushing for and insisting on and we respect them for it." America had had its ups and downs in the Czech lands since 1918—promoting Wilsonian democracy, then turning away; roaring back to help defeat Fascism, only to let the country slip away again, this time to Communism—but the commitment to the dissidents was one that the United States could be proud of. Shirley was.

On October 4, she welcomed perhaps the most important of the dissenters to the palace: Václav Havel. The fifty-two-year-old playwright was the de facto leader of the protest movement. His friend and long-ago schoolmate, the Czech expatriate director Miloš Forman, was in town. Shirley arranged for the two of them to come over to celebrate Havel's birthday, October 5. Havel was relatively recently out of prison and minding his step, so they needed that pretext. What could have been more logical than a small birthday gathering of artists: Havel the writer, Forman the director, and Shirley the actress? Forman thought that the stratagem was splendid and the ambassador "smart . . . clever . . . courageous."

The palace was a familiar destination for Havel. It was where he and the other Czech writers met their American peers who had flocked to Prague to support them. Philip Roth, John Updike, William Styron, Arthur Miller, Kurt Vonnegut, and many more, a living Library of America, had visited. They had long, boozy, smoke-filled dinners with Havel and his Czech peers beneath the intricately carved boiserie, old-master paintings, and elaborate crystal chandeliers. Updike was so taken with the place that he used it as the setting for a *New Yorker* short story:

> The American Ambassador's Residence in Prague has been called the last palace built in Europe; it was built in the late twenties by a very rich Jewish banker whose family within a decade of its construction had to flee Hitler. They had made their money in coal mining. The Americans had acquired the building and its grounds

after the war, before Czechoslovakia went quite so Communist. The whole building gently curves—that is, it was built along the length of an arc, and a walk down its long corridors produces a shifting perspective wherein paintings, silk panels, marble-topped hall tables, and great metallized oaken doors all slowly come into view, much as islands appear above the horizon to a ship at sea and then slowly sink behind it, beyond the majestic, roiling, pale-turquoise wake.

Shirley and a couple of her State Department colleagues welcomed Havel and Forman in the library. The jovial director held forth, telling funny stories about movie making as the group served themselves from platters of thinly sliced delicatessen. Shirley took the measure of Havel. He sat quietly, looking a bit uncomfortable in the fancy Manchester suit that he had donned for the occasion. He had sandy hair and a matching mustache and was not much taller than Shirley, the grand surroundings making him seem even slighter.

Havel appeared tired, and with good reason: he had been doing unflinching battle with the Communist regime for more than two decades. Like Shirley, 1968 had altered his trajectory, launching him from theater into politics. His had been one of those rebellious radio voices during the invasion, and he went on to cofound Charter 77. The regime's brutal response had included a long prison sentence under harsh conditions that led to Havel's recurring lung disease (although his two-pack-a-day smoking habit didn't help). Husák, Bil'ak, and their lieutenants ordered him harassed incessantly, including tailing, wiretapping, and periodically rejailing him. Perhaps most painful of all, they refused to allow his plays to be produced in Czechoslovakia, though he kept writing them and they were staged and acclaimed around the world.

Shirley had met leaders from FDR to Nikita Khrushchev to Richard Nixon, and they all had a tendency to crave the spotlight. Not Havel: he seemed content to sit and listen, munching his deli sandwich. But he soon became the center of attention. "Vašku, you may win a Nobel Prize tomorrow," Forman said, using Havel's school nickname. "They will announce it at 11, we all are waiting for it!" Now Havel couldn't avoid saying something. Everyone looked at him expectantly. He began by apologizing for his English. He explained that he and Forman knew "each other . . . from the days when neither of us could speak English, from school . . . [W]e learnt it together, and he has learnt it better than I."

Havel then quietly answered questions about everything from his time in prison to his thoughts on Czechoslovakia's current problems to whether the United States should have intervened in 1968. He had been treated better than ever before during his most recent prison stay of four months, which had ended in May 1989. "[It] was almost like a holiday," he said. That was a sign of progress. Havel's view was that "more had changed in those four months than during the years of my previous incarcerations. It wasn't just because a lot had changed in the neighboring countries—in Poland, Solidarity was already having a huge influence on the communists, and in the Soviet Union there was perestroika—but mainly because Czechoslovak society had begun to awaken from the anesthesia into which it had been plunged in 1968 by the Soviet occupation."

Shirley felt that same quickening, and they had "a long discussion . . . regarding the pace and direction of political change in Czechoslovakia." Havel cautioned her that the road would likely be a long one. The talk turned to 1968. One of her colleagues told Havel "that he worked at the US State Department, when the invasion started in August '68. And that they had wondered: What should we do? Should we take action, one way or another? How should we act not to make things even worse?" Havel did his best to answer. In truth, he was much more focused on what Dubček and the other Czechoslovak leaders should have done to secure international support before the invasion. He did not know whether that would have been effective, though his instinct was that it promised a better chance of success.

When the gathering finally broke up after two hours, Shirley was sold. She *loved* him. He was a "moral leader" for the Czechs. He may have been quiet, but he was "charismatic." As Havel left, Shirley gave him a hug and, as is traditional in Prague, kissed him first on one cheek, then the other. That first meeting with Havel, she felt, "will always remain in my heart." She had seen a lot of performing in her time, but Havel was the real thing, a worthy heir to leaders such as Masaryk and Beneš. He enhanced her hope that a transformation was coming.

CHANGE continued to accelerate in the region. Poland and Hungary were liberalizing rapidly, including expressing regret for their role in crushing the '68 Prague Spring. In East Germany, protesters flooded the streets, ushering in a more moderate (though still Communist) government that began talks with dissidents. Outside the borders of Czechoslovakia, the political waters were roiling, yet in Prague, Husák placidly received ambassadors at the castle, Bil'ak glowered in the parliament, and they continued to officially applaud the 1968 invasion. Czech Communists looked east for reassurance: to Romania, where Ceauşescu held an iron grip on power; to Moscow, where there were whispers of a possible right-wing coup against Gorbachev; and to China, where Tiananmen Square offered a chilling example of how to stamp out dissent. Observers noted that the Czech "Government's attitude until now has been to refuse to talk with opposition and human rights groups, insisting that any measures leading to political or economic change must be orchestrated solely by the leadership."

Dissidents murmured to Shirley that another major demonstration loomed, on October 28. It was the seventy-first anniversary of the birth of the country, the signature triumph of Masaryk the elder and Beneš. The date had always been a flashpoint. Its celebration had been ecstatic in 1918, then grim in 1938, 1948, and 1968. This year, the dissidents intended to mark it with a massive protest at that magnet for confrontation, Wenceslas Square.

As the date of the protest approached, the Communists bluntly warned Shirley to stay away. The threat came in a meeting with Štěpán, the Prague party boss. He was perhaps the leading hard-liner of the younger generation, sometimes identified as the heir apparent of Husák and Bil'ak. On October 18, Shirley met him in his office at the Federal Assembly, right next to the National Museum in the square. Štěpán was obese, with heavy jowls and thick lips, his narrow eyes set into an oblong head.

After cursory introductions, Štěpán launched into an hour-long monologue, lecturing Shirley on respecting the Czech Communist government and denigrating the dissidents. Then he tried to end the meeting, claiming to have an appointment with the visiting Palestine Liberation Organization leader, Yasser Arafat. Shirley stopped him, telling him that he had spoken and now she would have her say as well.

She told him that "human rights was as much your problem . . . as mine," because "we could not hope for progress in areas like MFN until solutions were found." She "did not understand why freedom of speech could not be exercised in Czechoslovakia." She ticked off the names of specific dissidents who were being persecuted. Štěpán replied belligerently that "he would not play naive and act as if he did not recognize them . . . [W]hen someone publishes a newspaper that failed to respect Czechoslovak laws it should be closed down. Just . . . as a journalist should be stopped who libeled someone." His stance was that if valid Czechoslovak laws were broken, the criminals would be prosecuted.

In terms of their present situation, he cited a law prohibiting demonstrations in Wenceslas Square. He urged Shirley to be realistic and warned that ordinary Czechoslovaks did not agree with the agitators. "We will never permit them to influence the masses to criticize us or deny that our Party had accomplished anything over 40 years." His and Shirley's "relations could follow one of two roads. One was the way of charges and counter-charges. The other was to cooperate."

Back at the embassy after this blunt conversation with Štěpán, Shirley ordered staff to stay away from the protest. Attending was too dangerous. She had no intention of following her own orders, though.

～ɔ

SATURDAY, October 28, was a "grey and bitterly cold autumn day." The demonstration was scheduled for three p.m. At about two that afternoon, Shirley said to Charlie, "I'd like to go for a walk."

"Where do you want to go?" he asked.

"I think the park," she replied. She spoke loudly for the benefit of the hidden microphones. She was confident that the palace was "bugged completely." And her hunch that some of the palace staff worked for the secret police also kept her from speaking freely in her own home.

She laced up her Reebok sneakers. They were yellow, like the boots that she had worn in August '68.

Once out of the compound, the Blacks walked briskly to the nearest Metro stop, Hradčanská. From there, it was three quick stops to the Můstek station on the square. The car was crowded, and surrounding passengers stole furtive glances at Shirley. Shirley and Charlie exited the train in a stream of other couples and strode past the medieval arch embedded in one wall of the station.

As soon as the Blacks emerged onto the huge square, they spotted other marchers waiting for the signal to begin. "Wenceslas Square was filling rapidly with people pretending to look in shop windows, or walking purposefully from one end to the other, in the hope of avoiding the increasingly frequent police checks of identity papers." Shirley and Charlie made their way toward the usual rallying point: bronze Saint Wenceslas, sitting astride his horse at the southeastern end of the square. He was a suitable patron saint for the dissidents under threat from their own government: a legendarily good leader who was assaulted by his own brother.

Just past three p.m., the protesters converged on the equestrian statue. First hundreds, then thousands, of people flowed together, gathering directly in front of the monument to the saint. Two of the protesters "raised a banner bearing the ironical slogan 'We will not allow our republic to be subverted.'" It mocked the authorities, who used the phrase to explain "why they are ready for dialogue with all groups except those that disagree with them." Another sign displayed Masaryk's slogan, *PRAVDA VÍTĚZÍ* (TRUTH PREVAILS). Many in the crowd unfurled red-blue-and-white Czech flags and waved them high, the fabric fluttering. Western journalists covering the event climbed the statue's base and started their cameras rolling. Police began demanding IDs. Shouting erupted, and the crowd, thinking someone was being arrested, began to chant "Let him go, let him go!"

Shirley, her husband in tow, worked her way southeast across the square to the statue. As she did so, a "little short guy came up with a camera trying to get my picture." He was obviously from the StB. Shirley told him firmly that she did not want her picture taken. She tried to turn away. "I really gave that photographer a bad time," she later remembered. But secret-police paparazzi are even more brazen than the regular kind. He managed to capture one shot, which the StB later exhibited with the caption "U.S. ambassador at demonstration."

The crowd swelled—Shirley guessed that there were ten thousand people there. They began clapping rhythmically, the sound "rising, then sinking, then rising again, in volume and intensity." The noise was interspersed with stretches of relative quiet. "Everyone seemed to be constantly monitoring the situation, as if knowing that it would soon be broken up, perhaps violently, along with arrests." Then the thousands of voices joined in a familiar tune, one that Shirley had heard and played, in her head and on her stereo, for two decades: the national anthem, "Kde domov můj" ("Where Is My Home?"). At that moment, *this* was Shirley's home—Prague, on the square, with people who were brave enough to demand their own freedom.

"Suddenly, hundreds and hundreds of riot police marched from the metro station entrances and lined up across the top . . . of the square." The VB arrived on the scene, just as during the August demonstration. "They were wearing white helmets with visors and they were carrying large shields and long white truncheons. It was a frightening, overwhelming show of force.*

Shirley and Charlie were by now quite close to the protest, just slightly off to one side. As they watched, police loudspeakers began to crackle. "The throng of the growing crowd became momentarily hushed as a voice of authority barked through an echoing megaphone. It was impossible to hear the words clearly" through the static. But there was no mistaking the content: the authorities ordered the crowd to disperse. The blurred words were repeated again and again as many in the crowd whistled to show their disdain.

Nevertheless, the enormous mob gradually stirred, the protesters turning and making their way back across the square in an orderly fashion. They waved their flags and signs, chanted "Masaryk!" "Freedom!" and "Havel!" and resumed their rhythmic clapping—an impressively loud sound when made by thousands of hands striking together.

As Shirley and Charlie watched, the anti-riot troops began following the crowd, as if bringing up the rear of a procession. "Their heavy boots clapped against the pavement as they marched and they held their truncheons with both hands in front." Soon they accelerated, pressing into the mass of people, "forcing the crowd down the length of the square." The pressure rippled forward, causing the entire phalanx of marchers to speed up. Then commotion broke out: "[T]he police had broken file and were now attacking stragglers that did not move fast enough to suit them." Their faces impassive behind their plastic visors and shields, "they simply walked into the crowd and hit at random."

"Now we run," Shirley said to Charlie. They turned and took off, heading back the way they had come. The crowd was sprinting in that direction as well, racing away from the police, whose batons were rising and falling, mowing through the back of the crowd like threshers. Shirley put her yellow Reeboks to good use as she and Charlie sped northwest with the rapidly flowing crowd. They blended into the stream of people of all ages and paces. Even in the melee, the Watchers of Prague noticed their American friends. "At one point a Czech student ran by me and said, 'Thank you for coming.'"

As they dashed back across the square, the Blacks looked to the first side street, Krakovská, to escape. But just as they approached, a VB barricade went up, blocking their exit. They kept going, "got across another street and there were barricades" again. The same was true at the next intersection, Opletalova. "Every time we crossed a street, the police were just putting up barricades." They intended to flush out the square, and they did not want people leaking back in from the sides, so they were sealing it off in sync with the advancing line of their white-helmeted colleagues.

Meanwhile, the riot troops continued pushing forward from the back of the crowd, their *pendreky* flailing as they drew nearer. Shirley and Charlie "took cover behind a nearby billboard" as the "crowd swept past." In the chaos, she spotted people heading her way. Two figures had peeled off from the crowd as it flowed by, and they approached her and Charlie. Were they plainclothes police, about to demand her papers? She braced herself as they "advanced on her." Then they spoke. "May we please have your autograph?" She dashed off two quick signatures.

As the two fans took to their heels, Shirley and Charlie saw an acquaintance in the midst of the chaos: Perry Shankle, a congenial State Department inspector on tour in Prague. Shankle did a double take, then asked Shirley, "What are you doing here?" She replied, straight-faced, "Oh, we're out for a walk." They were several doors down from the Hotel Jalta, a Khrushchev-era landmark where Shankle was staying. They decided to take refuge there, on the theory that "it might be better than on the street because the police were starting to use truncheons on heads" nearby.

No sooner did they enter the lobby of the Jalta than the doorman tried to lock the door behind them. Shirley identified herself and insisted that the hotel leave the entrance unlocked to admit other refuge seekers. That point secured, Shirley surveyed the eclectic and sizable crowd forming in the lobby and saw another friendly face: the British chargé d'affaires. The chargé introduced Shirley to the man standing next to him, a London *Times* reporter, Richard Bassett.

Bassett interviewed Shirley on the spot. "Musing on the helmeted riot police armed with shields and batons, the woman who had spent her childhood in Hollywood said that those years had prepared her for anything." She told him about her role in her favorite film, Kipling's *Wee Willie Winkie*, in which she had held off an entire army. That experience "had left her unperturbed by a few riot police."

She explained that she was "no stranger to violence in Prague. In 1968 she had been staying in the venerable Hotel Alcron, on the other side of the square, when the Soviet tanks arrived to crush the 'Prague spring.'" She described the sight that had haunted her all these years, the woman who had shaken her clenched fist at a tank and taken a bullet in the stomach, dead in a pool of blood in front of her hotel. If Shirley looked across the street, she could see Štěpánská Street, where the Alcron was located. She said to Bassett, "Nothing crushes freedom more effectively than a tank."

Shirley wanted a clearer view of what was happening. She made her way upstairs to Shankle's room, which overlooked the square. (He would

Shirley and Charlie overlook the demonstration in Wenceslas Square, October 28, 1989.

later call his wife and tell her, deadpan, that "Shirley Temple spent the afternoon in my hotel room with me.") He had a large window with a ledge. It was filthy, dirty enough that it appeared to be coated with grime from the First Republic, the last traces of the flakes of the Petschek coal that had once swirled up chimneys and through the Prague air. Shirley hoisted herself up and sat on the window ledge—her yellow-shod feet dangling in the air over the crowd.

Shirley saw below that the VB had stopped advancing. They had driven out all those who were ready to flee, clearing the square of all protesters, "but a few hundred refused to be intimidated and just stood there defiantly." They clapped and chanted and sang the national anthem again, along with Masaryk's favorite song, "Ach, synku, synku" ("Oh, My Son, My Son"). "During the singing people held their arms high and made the [peace] sign with their fingers." The VB seized cameras from both journalists and amateur shutterbugs, exposing the film and tossing it onto the road. "People jeered and whistled at the police as they literally dragged vocal citizens away down the center of Vodičkova street."

As she watched, the police surrounded the remaining protesters. They "created a box around the protesters by closing off the square above and below. By lining up shoulder to shoulder, they then proceeded to make the box smaller and smaller . . . [T]he riot police left one corner of the box open, where the faint-hearted could escape if they chose . . . They then proceeded to tighten the noose and moved in on the few hundred demonstrators remaining." Finally, they were completely boxed in, no escape from any side.

Then the beatings began. Shirley watched in horror as the "cosmonauts" launched themselves into the peaceful crowd of dissidents. "These few hundred were beaten up randomly and thrown to the ground before being herded into paddy wagons. . . . Young men in casual dress who were obviously working with the uniformed police seized demonstrators, beating them and dragging them into waiting buses." It took only ten minutes or so for the VB to completely clear the square. Then they dispersed as well, vanishing as quickly as they had appeared some thirty minutes before.

A shaken Shirley, accompanied by Charlie, headed back downstairs to leave. As she passed through the crowded hotel atrium, all eyes were upon her. She tried her best to maintain a neutral expression. Behind the long obsidian bar at the back of the lobby, a white-jacketed waiter called out to offer her a drink before she left. A Shirley Temple. She demurred. Even at the best of times she had no fondness for that syrupy drink. She certainly was in no mood for one now. She had earned a more adult beverage, which was waiting for her back at the palace. She and Charlie slipped outside.

They headed north out of the square in the fading daylight. The sun was sinking, reducing visibility and lowering the temperature. They quickened their step toward the safety of Otto's compound.

But as Shirley and Charlie turned down one of the city center's narrow avenues, they suddenly found themselves cut off. A crowd of marchers rounded the corner and poured into the street, moving directly toward them. The group was evidently heading back to Wenceslas Square. There seemed to be thousands, "chanting 'No violence!' . . . and 'Dialogue, dialogue!'"

The Blacks tried to squeeze forward, but swimming upstream through the dense mass of people proved impossible. They had no choice but to turn and head in the opposite direction—only to see a row of white-helmeted VB coming from the other end of the street, blocking their escape. The demonstrators marched forward and "shouted, 'Gestapo!' and, 'The World Is Watching!'"

Once more, she and Charlie were in the thick of it. They looked around frantically for a place to hide. They were directly in front of a closed butcher shop, slabs of meat hanging in the plate-glass window. Shirley tried to shelter in the doorway, but two women were already filling it, huddling together. So she flattened herself against the glass, as Charlie did his best to shield her.

As the protesters surged by, she thought that she "might get knocked down, and that will be the end of me." She pressed against the storefront and looked at a pig's carcass hanging in the window right behind her. She wondered if that same fate was about to befall her, knowing that she could easily be trampled if she tumbled into the stampede.

But the flood of protesters thinned momentarily, and she and Charlie spotted an opening. They sprinted through the gap, darting around the marchers. Finally, they were through—the street ahead empty, the sound of the masses receding behind them. They maintained a brisk jog for several blocks. Then they slowed down and resumed their course toward Bubeneč, this time plotting a roundabout route to avoid further protests. What should have been a quick walk ended up taking more than two hours.

Back in the palace, Shirley and Charlie collapsed onto a pair of the antique chairs. They had been extremely lucky, and they knew it. Shirley stood up again, only to see that her jumpsuit had left dark streaks on the tapestry-covered seating—the grit from the Hotel Jalta ledge. The black streak was an intrusion into Otto's sanctuary—no less filthy than if a lump of his coal had been smeared over the upholstery.

That night, the city was quiet. The streets were guarded by the People's Militia—back, as in 1948, to defend the Communist prerogative. These were the sons and even grandsons of their bullying forebears, some of whom, now grizzled, were still among them. State television reported that around "250 people were detained." Those included foreigners less fortunate or less careful than Shirley and Charlie; a dozen were to be deported. No numbers were immediately available on how many marchers had been hurt or hospitalized.

In the days that followed, Shirley paid the price for her impulsive decision to protest. Her presence was prominently noted in the Communist press. Together with Radio Free Europe and the Voice of America, she too was among those whom the regime publicly blamed for inciting the dissenters, the general "directing her troops." On Monday she had to face her colleagues in the embassy and explain why, after instructing them not to attend the protests, she herself had done so. She described what happened next to a journalist. He asked, "So you disobeyed your own order not to go?"

"I told you I don't take my own advice," Shirley replied.

"Did you hear from Washington after it came out that you had been there?"

"No. At the next country team meeting, which was a couple days later, I went in and I said that I had disobeyed my own orders and that I was going to punish myself as I would any one of them who had done that."

"So what did you do?"

"Nothing. I didn't put a letter in my file. I forgave myself."

She had needed to feel the pulse of dissent firsthand to do her job. Up to ten thousand people had turned out. It was "Czechoslovakia's biggest demonstration for 20 years," since she had last been there, in fact. The participants were not just prominent dissidents but also ordinary people. The ranks of the Watchers of Prague were swelling again, "even though they were hit on the head and arrested and corralled on side streets and sent to jail." The Watchers had gone far beyond mere observation. That made it "a very dangerous time for them."

Shirley understood that she had a role to play in protecting the people. Her gaze was a form of insurance—and there was much more that she could do as ambassador when the time was right. But whatever happened next, she wanted the Czechs to own it. As she sometimes told her embassy colleagues when they were choreographing her appearances, "There was only one star on the stage." This time, it was not she. So Shirley waited—and watched.

15

Truth Prevails

The Palace; Friday Morning, November 17, 1989

THE PALE DAWN SUN CREPT INTO THE SKY OVER THE PALACE. Its first rays shared the chilly November air with the isolated cries of birds from the bare trees ringing the garden. On the second floor, from the window of the small family dining room, a light shone out into the still-dark morning. Inside, the small room still contained the oval table for six. Once Otto Petschek had sat at its head, tapping out the meter of a mystery aria on its surface as Martha smiled and Viky, Eva, Ina, and Rita listened, heads cocked, straining to guess the tune.

Now just two of the places were occupied. Shirley and Charlie generally breakfasted in a companionable silence. If they had anything of moment to say to each other, they passed written notes, assuming that the room was bugged. That left the secret police listening to the clink of official State Department china, the crunch of toast, and the rustle of the morning newspaper on their eavesdropping devices. Charlie was an early riser, and Shirley joined him. It was a chance while her mind was fresh to think through the challenges of the day—or, as she preferred to consider them, the opportunities.

Her contacts had alerted the embassy that they expected several thousand people to take part in demonstrations that afternoon. November 17 was the anniversary of the 1939 Nazi crackdown on the Czech universities. The occupation forces had responded ferociously to students protesting their reign. Hitler's men had executed the leaders, deported more than one thousand more young activists to concentration camps, and shuttered the campuses. Exactly fifty years later, students were planning to gather on one of the Charles University campuses at four p.m. to commemorate those atrocities.

Would today be the breakthrough that they had all been waiting for? Shirley would have loved it to be—but as she sipped her coffee, she didn't believe that this was the day. For one thing, the anniversary was not a particularly explosive one. It was far less significant to Czechs than the two landmark dates that had previously drawn her to Wenceslas Square: the August 21 commemoration of the Soviet-bloc invasion and Czech Independence Day, October 28. Given the oppression that had defined so much of Czech history, the closing of the universities was far from the most lachrymose event to commemorate.

Then there was the fact that it was an officially sanctioned gathering. It was cosponsored by the Communist-approved Svaz socialistické mládeže (SSM), the Union of Socialist Youth, together with a little-known independent student group, STUHA (Ribbon). The regime apparently thought so little of the risk that they had granted a permit for the event. They hadn't even bothered to crack down on Havel and the other leading dissidents, who likewise didn't expect much of the day. The playwright was at his country house, purportedly to avoid stirring up trouble for the demonstrators (though some of his friends thought that it was to be with a girlfriend).

On the other hand, as Shirley had just asked colleagues, "who could have predicted [East] Germany a few weeks ago?" Countless numbers of people had taken to the streets there, toppling the seemingly eternal hard-line rulers. Thousands had fled the country, pouring into Prague and seeking asylum in the West German embassy just down the block from the Schönborn. When they were finally allowed to leave for the West, Shirley herself had stood in front of her embassy and waved to them, smiling, as they departed for freedom. They were jubilant, throwing their worthless ostmarks out the windows of the buses. A few days later, on November 9, the same German popular energy had collapsed the Berlin Wall.

In the end, Shirley decided to hedge her bets on the seventeenth. She would send observers to the Charles University gathering, just in case. There would be three: Cliff Bond, the political department head; Ed Kaska, who worked the human-rights portfolio; and a young consular officer, Robert Kiene, whose appetite for protests rivaled Shirley's own.

Were it the weekend, she might have gone herself. Her brush with disaster on October 28 hadn't frightened her away from activism—quite the opposite. But more mundane duties called: cohosting a US-Canadian business reception downstairs in the lavish salons of the palace that afternoon. It was an uphill struggle for North American firms trying to succeed in the Communist-controlled economy. She couldn't pull the rug out from under a long-planned event to help them just because she was intrigued by a student gathering.

When she got to her office at the Schönborn that morning, Shirley authorized the embassy trio to attend the protest and gave strict instructions for Bond to call her at the palace if anything interesting happened.

IN the early afternoon, the three emissaries exited the Schönborn, the yellow Renaissance palazzo housing the embassy. As they walked down the cobblestoned medieval street to the end of the block, the sky above was a dazzling blue, intensified by the clear, cold air. At the corner, they turned left, then used the excellent Prague public transportation to make the twenty-minute trip south to the Albertov campus of the university. Cliff Bond had copper and silver Czech coins jingling in his pocket so that he could use the pay phone to reach the ambassador if needed.

The Americans arrived at about three p.m. to find a good vantage point. Hundreds of students, in high spirits on the beautiful afternoon, were already waiting at the center of the campus, a roughly five-acre open space. The buildings framing it included neobaroque architecture dating from Otto's day and reminiscent of his palace. The J-shaped pathology building even had a similar, unusual curve to it, curling around the top of the campus. It was a reminder that if architecture could bend, so could politics.

Like the rest of Prague, the structures were saturated in memory. The pathology institute had served as a reliquary for saints of democracy. It was where the Germans had brought the cadavers of Heydrich's assassins, Kubiš and Gabčík. Their heads were later preserved in the institute, floating in formaldehyde-filled glass jars. And it was here too that the Communists had delivered Jan Masaryk's broken body for examination. The leader of the 1939 protests, Jan Opletal, had been enrolled here until the Nazis shot and killed him.

Cliff and his colleagues first realized that the day would be out of the ordinary by the size of the crowd that was forming. A few hundred became a few thousand, and they kept coming, gradually filling the enormous space. By four p.m., the campus was packed with a throng of nearly twenty thousand students. Their antigovernment sentiments were clear from their homemade signs, black words lovingly hand lettered on the white placards and bedsheets waving above the crowd: ZRUŠTE MONOPOL KSČ (REPEAL THE CZECHOSLOVAK COMMUNIST PARTY MONOPOLY) and SVOBODU (FREEDOM). Another banner bore a slightly altered version of Tomáš Masaryk's motto, PRAVDA VÍTĚZÍ (TRUTH PREVAILS). The protester had added a question mark: WILL THE TRUTH PREVAIL?

After some preliminaries, Josef Šárka ascended to the simple speakers' platform tucked into the curve of the pathology building at the top of the green. Now in his seventies, Šárka had grown up with the First Republic, helping Opletal lead the anti-Nazi protests in 1939 and consequently being deported to Sachsenhausen. He had returned to serve in the resistance in World War II, to participate in the Prague Uprising, and to resist Communism, including signing on to Charter 77. He was a living monument to Czechoslovak defiance.

Šárka had no fear of aggravating the regime, as the watching embassy staff noted. "Students, do not be afraid, I'm glad you're fighting for what we've fought at that time," he roared. The crowd gave their elder an enormous ovation, thousands of voices shouting out, "Freedom!"

The representative of the Communist-aligned cosponsor, the SSM, perhaps alarmed at the tone being set, took the stage next. He tried to speak, but the crowd had been riled up by Šárka. They repeatedly interrupted the man with the same sharp whistling that had greeted the police announcements in Wenceslas Square a few weeks before. When he asked what the government could do better tomorrow, the audience shouted, "Resign!"

As the sun set and the sky turned indigo, speaker after speaker rose to denounce the regime: "We will not merely commemorate this event silently, we have come here for the present as well. University students have fought and will fight against totalitarian injustice." "Oppression is worse than death! . . . We must fight for freedom because you cannot live without it."

A startling rumor spread through the crowd, galvanizing the Ameri-

can observers and the students alike: Dubček was there. As improbable
as it may have seemed—the hero of 1968, who was now living a quiet existence under heavy surveillance in Bratislava, suddenly popping up at a student protest in Prague—it was true. He had been in Prague to meet friends
and learned of the demonstration. With his fedora, topcoat, gray suit, and
neatly knotted tie, he was immediately distinguishable from the casually
dressed, mostly long-haired demonstrators. No sooner did he arrive than
he was thronged by ebullient well-wishers and autograph seekers. Almost
as quickly, plainclothes police swooped in and whisked him away, but not
before his presence had been noticed, electrifying the crowd.

Dubček's name was chanted, flags and banners waved, and the slogans of October 28 shouted again, reverberating off the neobaroque
walls. *"Svobodu!"* *"Masaryk!"* *"Havel!"* New ones were added that bore a
sharp antigovernment edge: *"Svobodné volby!"* ("Free elections!") *"Chceme
novou vládu!"* ("We want a new government!") *"Nechceme Štěpána!"* ("We
don't want Štěpán!") The young, energetic attendees sounded like a large
audience in a sports stadium. They acted like it, too: they were having
a good time, laughing and kidding around. They weren't only chanting
about freedom, they were practicing it.

By five p.m., it was dark. The speakers had finished, and it was time
for the second part of the approved program: a march uphill to the
nearby Vyšehrad cemetery, the burial place of Czech national artists
such as Dvořák, Mucha, and Smetana. There the students would pay
tribute to Opletal and the others who had fallen fifty years ago. The
demonstrators withdrew candles from their coats—seemingly everyone
had brought one. The students marched out of the campus, tens of thousands of small, flickering lights floating uphill to the graveyard, Cliff and
his colleagues following behind. The demonstrators grew solemn as they
filed into the burial ground. The place was one of the lesser-known treasures in Prague's jewel case—more like a sculpture garden than a memorial site, each tomb lovingly customized; the sepulchres as varied in eras
and styles as the buildings of the city.

The head of the procession stopped before the grave of the
nineteenth-century romantic poet Karel Hynek Mácha. He had been to
his generation what Havel was to the current one—its collective voice—
and his words still resonated. Mácha had once been a student at Charles
University, like the demonstrators and Opletal; like Otto and Kafka.

The people observed a moment of silence for all the victims of 1939, for all the losses that had followed, for the freedom that they had grown up without. Then thousands of young voices spontaneously rose in singing the national anthem.

It was about six p.m. The students were supposed to disperse, but the ceremonies had turbocharged their emotions. As they turned to leave the cemetery, the leaders shouted out *"Václavák! Václavák!"*—"To Wenceslas Square!" Where else would they gather to celebrate freedom? Thousands of them headed toward the city's center. Now they were unauthorized, violating the law, but they didn't care. One student carried a sign with an Opletal quote: KDO SE BOJÍ, AŤ ZŮSTANE DOMA, ALE MĚLI BYCHOM JÍT! (LET WHOEVER IS AFRAID STAY AT HOME, BUT WE SHOULD GO!)

Cliff went in search of a phone to call the ambassador.

IN the palace, the US-Canada business promotion was in full swing. The North American businesspeople and their Czechoslovak counterparts mingled with Shirley and her cohost, the Canadian chargé, Rob McRae, in the Wintergarden. Whether capitalist or Communist, everyone wanted to shake hands with Shirley. She was patient with the retail aspect of ambassadorizing: shaking hands, signing autographs, posing for pictures. Laurence Steinhardt's first reaction when he saw the place had been right: the palace was a superb venue for conducting American statecraft, and Shirley made the most of it.

In the middle of the hubbub, one of her aides pulled her aside. Cliff Bond was calling. She strode into the library and pressed the phone to her ear. She liked Cliff, though they did not always see eye to eye. But he was an outstanding officer—as good as they came—and she could take his reporting to the bank. He filled her in: "The crowd of students is very large. We've heard rumors that Alexander Dubček was in the crowd earlier. The demonstration has taken on a decidedly political tone, and now they've broken from the authorized program. The students are heading for Wenceslas Square."

Shirley felt the marchers' energy from across town. They had the same fire as in the August and October demonstrations—indeed, the same spark that she had observed in Wenceslas Square twenty-one years ago before it was so cruelly extinguished. But these youngsters were a new generation. They hadn't seen hope crushed in 1938, 1948, or 1968—their vision wasn't marred by witnessing history. Maybe today would be the day of reckoning after all. She told Cliff to keep her posted.

She returned to the Wintergarden and conferred with Rob McRae. Like her, he was a friend of the dissidents and a connoisseur of the protests: he too had attended the October demonstration and many others. The two of them were not yet ready to say that this was the moment they had been waiting for, but agreed that it bore watching. They resumed their mingling within the serene confines of the palace, but their minds and hopes had turned elsewhere.

⌣

THE embassy trio rejoined the procession as it poured down the hill. When they reached its base, the march leaders prepared to veer right and enter Vyšehradská Street, the most direct route to the square. But as they neared the intersection, they saw that they had company: a phalanx of white helmets. It was the VB, several rows deep, blocking the way, riot shields and batons at the ready.

On this occasion, however, the protesters had the police outnumbered. The authorities had not been expecting twenty thousand demonstrators. As the vanguard of the marchers reached the intersection, the VB attempted to make up for their inferior headcount by taking the initiative. Some launched themselves at the crowd, hauling off some of the ringleaders, including Havel's friend, the well-known anarchist John Bok. His wild hair flying out from his head in every direction, he screamed, "Tell Vašek!"—that is, Havel. "Get a message to him at Hrádeček! . . . Tell him what's happening! Quickly!" A group of officers seized Bok in a headlock and carried him, kicking, into a nearby police van.

The student protesters were unfazed. They knew their nonviolence. They had learned from Havel and other dissidents and from the protests of the recent past. Indeed, they shouted "We are unarmed" and "No violence!" With strength in numbers, they simply redirected, like water flowing past a rock. They avoided the blocked street, instead walking straight on Plavecká Street, toward the river. The outnumbered police made no further effort to stop them—yet.

With the US diplomats carried along, the students turned right onto Gottwaldovo nábřeží (Gottwald Embankment), the brutal Stalinist father of the Communist state now remembered with a boulevard. A stream of people was soon traveling north on the avenue, parallel to the Vltava River. It was a major thoroughfare, lined with restaurants and bars, apartment buildings, and shops facing the water. The view was stunning: bridges spanning the river every quarter mile or so, and on the other bank, Malá Strana, topped by the enormous Prague Castle. In the midst of that postcard panorama, the students were a spectacle. They filled the street, waving flags and protest banners, clapping and cheering. They soon began chanting in unison, "*Češi! Pojďte s námi!*" ("Czechs! Come with us!"), calling out to their peers, parents, grandparents, and even some great-grandparents; to the previous generations of Prague Watchers; and to those who had looked away. The message was clear—time to act.

And that was just what the people along the route did. They threw cash on the tables where they were drinking, asked salesclerks to hold purchases for later, left cinemas and theaters, and emerged from their apartments, running to catch up. Every time a light in a window winked out, marchers cheered: someone else was bundling up to join the seemingly unending parade of protesters. The people of Prague joined by the thousands, then by the tens of thousands, until the human river filled the avenue. Some were noisy, picking up the cheering and the chanting: "Forty years of Communism is enough," and "Warsaw, Berlin, and now Prague." Others were quiet, marching in a daze, as if they couldn't believe what they were seeing.

Cars, trollies, and buses all halted to admire the procession. The drivers honked again and again, signaling approval. Their passengers extended their arms out of the windows to shake hands with the demonstrators or to flash the peace sign. All were dipping their toes in the waters of freedom.

By the time the vanguard of the procession had made its way a mile up the embankment, the numbers had swelled enormously, perhaps to as many as fifty thousand. The demonstrators knew Prague, its winding streets as familiar as their own pulses. And now they were ready to essay another march on the square. The leaders turned right, away from the river, onto Národní třída—National Road. The spot seemed fitting to Cliff and his embassy colleagues. At that corner stood a shrine to the nineteenth-century rebirth of Czech language, culture, and identity: the Czech National Theatre. As the crowd passed before that gold-roofed venue by the thousands, they were chanting and singing. The protesters were so exhilarated that it did not occur to them how narrow and dark the street was or that they could be heading into a trap. Tonight, Prague was a giant chessboard, and the regime—Husák, Štěpán, and the rest—was about to make its next move.

～

CLIFF found a phone, dropped in the silver coins, and placed another call to Shirley. This time the curious Rob McRae knew exactly what was happening when the ambassador was passed a message. She stepped away and listened to Cliff's account: "The students marched north along the Vltava, the crowd is even larger, and they are chanting 'Berlin, Warsaw, Prague.' They are turning on to Národní třída towards Wenceslas Square." She told Cliff to take care of himself and the others, and said she was eagerly awaiting the next update.

Shirley huddled with McRae and informed him that "something really big is happening." The Canadian chargé agreed. But they knew that "something" could be dangerous. They had both witnessed the regime's willingness to use force. They decided to end the reception so that they could be ready to respond to the demonstration, whatever course it took.

The cohosts clinked their glasses to get the attention of their guests. As politely as possible, Shirley and McRae thanked everyone for coming and wished them a good night. The visitors seemed confused but dutifully filed out. McRae departed, too, and Shirley headed into the library to await the next call.

～

ABOUT a quarter mile down Národní třída, the leaders abruptly came to another halt, causing everyone behind them to do the same. The three Americans, farther back, saw the people in front sit down. The street was bisected by a wall of the white-helmeted riot police—rank after rank of them.

The bravest protesters were always at the front. They would be the first targeted if there was a police assault. And they drew on that courage, walking right up to the officers and asking them to let the march pass. The cosmonauts' faces were distorted by two layers of thick plastic: clear face guards that descended from each brim and another transparent riot shield held in front. But up close, the demonstrators could see that many of the troops were young—the same age as they were.

The students tried to meet the eyes of the police, but the officers looked blankly into some middle distance or stared at the ground. The demonstrators told the troops that they were nonviolent. They just wanted to go to the square; then they would go home. They attempted to hand flowers to the VB, a gesture of peace. One slightly overzealous young man, his bouquet refused, tossed it over a shield. It landed on a policeman's hand and he shook it off as if it were a burning brand.

The police did not budge. So the marchers returned to their places and again sat down in the road. They placed lit candles on the few feet of pavement between themselves and the troops, and behind the tapers, flags. They sang the national anthem, interspersed with clapping and slogans against Communism and the regime. They repeatedly called for a government representative to come and discuss terms. All they were asking was to go to the square. Eight-foot-long homemade banners were held up: NECHCEME NÁSILÍ (WE DON'T WANT VIOLENCE) and DEMOKRACIE PRO VŠECHNY (DEMOCRACY FOR ALL). Western journalists were everywhere: reporters holding steno pads or microphones; photographers with multiple Nikons and Canons around their necks, or heavy, shoulder-borne video cameras.

Because marching had stopped, thousands in the long tail of the protest began to drift away. Farther back on Národní, the fact that they had marched at all seemed sufficient, and they slowly returned to whatever they had been doing. When the authorities started using loudspeakers to order the demonstrators to disperse, some of those toward the front filtered away, too, quietly slipping down side streets or out the back end of Národní.

But, just as on October 28, a core resistance group refused to leave. On this occasion, there were thousands, dominated by the students who had begun their odyssey hours ago under the blue skies at Albertov. They took turns sitting and standing, as Cliff, Ed, and Robert observed, now near the front. The candles burned low in front of the leaders, the wax freezing into rivulets in the cold night air, as the minutes ticked away and nothing happened. It was a stalemate.

Cliff took advantage of the lull, stepping away to find a phone and report back to Shirley: "Police are blocking the students' path to the square. There is a standoff on Národní třída." She did not like the sound of that. A similar lull had preceded police action on October 28. But that had been in the bright light of day, and this was on a darkened street, on a cold night. True, Cliff was experienced at what he was doing. Nevertheless, she warned him again to be careful, this time more forcefully.

Cliff concluded the call: "Madame Ambassador, this is not going to turn out well."

When Shirley got off the phone with Cliff, she called Washington, D.C. "State Ops," the voice on the other end of the line answered. It was the State Department Operations Center, the after-hours line for reporting important developments anywhere in the world. She had one.

⌒

ROBERT Kiene, the most junior of the three Americans, used the standstill to take a quick break from the protest. His embassy colleagues knew the first rule of covering protests: "Pee before you go." Robert, newer to all this, did not. He badly needed to use the bathroom. He found an unlocked door to one of the buildings on Národní and entered. In search of a lavatory, he went down to the basement. Instead of a toilet, he discovered that "a ballroom in the basement was filled with young people dressed in tuxedos and fancy dresses, participating in the time-honored Czech tradition of the '*taneční*,' or dancing class." As urgently as he required the facilities, Robert took a moment to watch the youthful couples in formal wear spinning around the dance floor. "They were completely oblivious to what was happening on the street above"—their scruffy peers sitting in, confronting rank after rank of riot police in the harsh fluorescent light and night air.

Robert rejoined Cliff and Ed. The three embassy men, near the front of the crowd, watched as the authorities increased their verbal pressure over the next hour. The police repeated over and over again through their bullhorns that the people should leave. And many, particularly at the back of the crowd, quietly dispersed. By just after eight p.m., the protesters still numbered in the thousands—perhaps as many as ten thousand, though the crush made it difficult to say for sure.

Those who remained had made their minds up that it was their right to pass to the square. They were scared, but they were not *that* scared. One veteran dissident explained the state of mind necessary to stay put under circumstances such as these:

> When you are faced, for the first time, with a solid line of space-helmeted grim-faced young men with their meter-long batons and Star-Wars shields . . . you wish with all your might to be somewhere else. When it happens for the fifth time, and you are still around, and still the same person, give or take a couple of bruises, it starts to feel like something you can take. There might even be a sense of thrill, unwise as this appears. When your instinct is telling you to run for your life, but people next to you, some of them perhaps your friends, don't, your legs do not move either. Increasingly, you draw resolve and encouragement from the shared chanting of slogans, from exchanged looks, from the brush of your shoulder with the one next to you. There is always someone ahead of you who takes even greater risks and who is braver and crazier than you are. And so you stay.

The regime was no less implacable. Štěpán had warned Shirley that the "laws will be enforced." As party leader of Prague, he was following the protest closely. He repeatedly called the police commander on the scene from the comfort of his office, undoubtedly smoking one of the cigars produced by their allies in Cuba, the smell of the tobacco so strong that it almost came through the receiver. Štěpán insisted that the students not be allowed into the square—no matter what. Take *strong* measures, he screamed at the police colonel in charge. The man was hesitant. Wouldn't violence be playing into the protesters' hands? But, under pressure from Štěpán and other government leaders, he finally ordered his men to ready themselves.

At eight thirty, after about ninety minutes of the standoff, the faces of the young police grew grimmer. Their grip on their shields and batons became tighter, their posture more rigid. They "looked hard and angry, almost beside themselves, as if drugged or psyched out."

Cliff and the other Americans felt the change. It was as if the temperature had suddenly dropped. The protesters noticed it, too. They sang "We Shall Overcome" and repeated, "You have to protect us" and

"Our hands are empty." Then there was a disturbance at the back of the crowd. Cliff and his colleagues turned around and saw why. "To our dismay, we realized that the police had cut off the street about a hundred yards back." A second cordon of riot police had closed off the street behind them. Just as on October 28, the authorities had formed a box, trapping protesters between police lines to the east and the west and the buildings on either side.

> Suddenly the crowd realized that it had lost its escape route, and that it was surrounded. All hell broke loose. Many of the trapped and panicky demonstrators began to chant, "No violence! No violence!" . . . Other demonstrators, sensing correctly that they were now at the mercy of the white-helmeted riot police, taunted them with shouts of "Freedom! Freedom!" . . . Once again came the megaphoned order to disperse. The crowd now knew that this was a sick joke, since there was nowhere to go.

The tension had reached an unbearable level. As the senior American present, Cliff "decided discretion was the greater part of valor." He turned to Robert and Ed and said, "We need to get out of here." They moved to the front of the crowd and confronted the police at the street corner. A young, terrified girl trailed them, begging the Americans to take her with them. "We invited her to follow us. The plainclothes security policemen at the corner, all dressed in black leather jackets, were some of the biggest young men I have seen before or since in one place in Prague. We approached a figure of authority, surely an STB officer, and flashed our diplomatic identity cards at him. He scowled, wrote down our names, and motioned for us to leave." The girl's ID was also demanded, but she had nothing to proffer, so the StB official turned her away, extending a finger to direct her back into the crowd. She slumped, reversed, and was soon swallowed up by the sea of people. Cliff watched her go, hoping that she would be safe, as "a giant in leather pushed us roughly into the street, outside the box."

The three Americans looked back to ascertain what they could observe from their new vantage point, but they had been expelled onto a side street with no view. Perhaps another street would give them a better perspective on what was happening. As they raced around the block, they heard an eruption of noise behind them. The attack on the demonstrators had begun.

⁓

SHIRLEY paced the library, awaiting the next update from Cliff. The palace never felt more still than just after a large group had departed, the sudden emptiness echoing throughout. Tonight it was hard to believe that thousands of people were gathered, protesting, within walking distance, through the park and down the hill. Otto had sheltered the palace from the world, wrapping layers of protective insulation around its occupants. The compound's wall, the gardens, the exterior of the house, and the rooms within were like *matryoshka* dolls, each nestled inside the next.

In the library there was an extra barrier: the volumes lining the walls. They represented a lifetime of Otto's reading, a layer of culture that he had believed would somehow shield him and his family, or at least allow them to lose themselves in better worlds. Shirley could not do that tonight—she kept coming back to this one, restless and uncertain about what was happening downtown.

Just after nine p.m., the phone finally rang, slicing through the still air. On the other end of the line, Cliff shouted into the receiver from the scene of the demonstration. There were cries and screams in the background. He told the ambassador that the police had attacked the peaceful protesters. The brutality was far worse than anything that they had seen in August or October. The VB had surrounded and then waded into the crowd, viciously slashing their batons down onto the exposed heads and bodies of the people. Many were knocked unconscious by the first blow.

Even when the victims toppled and passed out, the police continued to beat them. Some students had tried to dodge, but there was nowhere to go, and the police chased them around the confined space, eventually cornering them. Protesters were now staggering about with heads split open, blood streaming from their wounds, or limping piteously from blows to their torsos or legs. Many were weeping, tears mixing with the blood on their cheeks, welts rising from the blows of the truncheons. Not even members of the Western press were safe. More than a dozen had been attacked, their notes seized, their film exposed, their cameras smashed to the ground. And, most disturbingly, Cliff said, "I saw a young mother beaten while holding a child in her arms. Other students shielded her from the police with their bodies, trying to protect them." His voice shook.

As Shirley listened in horror, Cliff described the scene in real time. Now the students were being chased out of the battle zone. They were being pursued by Czech Red Berets. They were the regime's antiterror police, "trained killers," known by their trademark headgear. The special troops wore blank expressions, their faces impassive, showing no sign of exertion despite the fact that they were running. If the riot troops dealt injury, the Red Berets threatened something worse.

Suddenly Cliff realized that the Red Berets were not targeting only the fleeing Czechs. They had locked their eyes on him, Ed, and Robert. They were headed directly at the Americans and closing in fast. In midsentence, he told Shirley, "I have to run, the police are coming," and, dropping the phone, he, Ed, and Robert sprinted away down the street.

He left the ambassador hanging on the line. She listened, the phone pressed against her ear, desperately hoping that her men had gotten away in time. She didn't need to be standing on Národní třída to be fully present. Her memories were still fresh—the butcher's window, the faces of the troops, the sudden bursts of violence against unarmed civilians, their screams. The woman outside the Alcron Hotel, her body broken.

But she saw something else, too. The people were waking up. The Prague Watchers were becoming the Prague Marchers. After tonight, everything would change.

⌇

Not long after Shirley reported into State Ops, she heard from Cliff that he, Ed, and Robert were fine. The Red Berets hadn't been running all out, just enough to flush out Národní třída, and the three embassy men were now duly flushed. They would grab some dinner, and then Cliff would stay up to prepare a cable to D.C.

Shirley also stayed up late that night, taking calls from embassy staff as well as from the press and other sources. As the details of the violence came in, she grew angrier and angrier. But, as bad as it was, she knew that it could get much worse. China's successful crackdown in Tiananmen Square the previous summer had proved that, with hundreds dead and thousands injured. There, massive force had worked, crushing the dissidents. True, Prague was not Beijing. But she could not rule out Štěpán and the rest of the hard-liners unleashing violence.

Starting that night, Shirley fired back with every armament in her diplomatic arsenal. She and her colleagues filed an immediate protest with the government, detailing the abuses and the violations of international law. They urged Main State to cancel an invitation for an upcoming Czechoslovak government delegation to visit America. Shirley pressed D.C. to call in the Czech ambassador for a dressing-down and to publicly blast the regime. The State Department complied, declaring that the Czech government's "senseless violence . . . further damaged their credibility at home and abroad." Shirley also dispatched her officers back to the streets and to the homes and offices of their contacts, to take the pulse of the city. Her staff spread out over Prague, reporting back to her and the embassy, including tallying arrest and casualty numbers. She made sure that up-to-the-minute information was transmitted to Foggy Bottom, a stream of updates flowing over the wires around the clock for the next seventy-two hours.

Finally, Shirley deployed perhaps the most potent weapon of all: her own voice. She was the most famous American in the country and one of the most famous in the world. She discarded protocol to publicly flay the regime. "The government," she told the press, "is scared and out of control, which we deeply deplore." Her words vibrated with fury. The sentiment was genuine, but it was also tactical. She wanted everyone to know that the United States was livid. Let them wonder: If the ambassador was this angry about the initial use of force, how would the United States react to the use of tanks?

For the moment, it seemed to work. On Saturday morning, November 18, Robert Kiene had returned to the square and reported "an uncanny buzz of energy in the air." Over the course of that day and the next, thousands of Praguers took to the streets. The authorities let the crowds roam in and around the square and blow off steam—a lesson learned too late. Perhaps the closest that things came to an actual clash was on Sunday, November 19: several thousand demonstrators tried to cross the river and march up through Malá Strana to the seat of government, Prague Castle. Robert was in the middle of the crowd as it attempted to traverse one of the bridges spanning the Vltava and reported back what happened:

> I walked with the crowd over the bridge, and at its far end, our march was stopped by a line of helmeted police like those on Národní on the 17th. I instantly recalled the events of that day, and realized that in case the police boxed off the crowd as they had done before, there was nowhere to go but over the sides into the cold November waters of the Vltava. Everyone in the crowd seemed to have the same idea at once, and we gingerly retreated from the bridge to the relative safety of the embankment.

In the end, the nightsticks that had split so many heads on Friday were restrained all weekend. Shirley considered that a victory. She hoped that the frenzy of embassy activity, with her and all of them working around the clock, had contributed. But as she laid her head on her pillow in the palace that Sunday night, she knew Monday would bring another major demonstration. The students were calling for a nationwide general strike in a week, on November 27, and were planning a protest to call attention to it. She wondered whether, and when, the streets would again be stained with blood. Her whole body ached. Under the stress, she had broken out in hives.

SHIRLEY was right to worry. Husák, Bil'ak, Štěpán, and their henchmen recognized that they were facing the most profound threat to their authority since 1968. Led by the chair of the party, Miloš Jakeš, they spent the weekend of November 18 and 19 meeting, talking, and thinking about how to hang on to power—including through force. The public statement that resulted on Monday was ominous. The Communists declared that although they "did not want to go via a path of confrontation which the antisocialist elements are trying to force on us," they "could not agree to the violation of the Constitution and the laws of the land," nor would they "watch helplessly activities of those groups which act at variance with the Czechoslovak legal order and are incited from abroad." The jab at the United States, and at Shirley, was unmistakable.

To Shirley, it sounded as if the regime was readying its forces to back the threats. The Prague Watchers reported armored personnel carriers and troops assembling and drilling in different locations around the city. Every district had a sports stadium, and rumor had it that they were being used as staging points. Robert Kiene was startled on one of his fact-finding walks to see the police apparently organizing for an assault in Smíchov, not far from the embassy. He became alarmed that the embassy itself might be a target, though his more senior colleagues assured him that that was unlikely. The regime had also summoned to Prague the hated People's Militia, the paramilitary force that had helped clamp down on freedom in 1948 and again in 1968.

Shirley kept up her diplomatic counteroffensive that Monday. She and the embassy fired off more press statements, another diplomatic note warning the Czechoslovak government, and additional cables that drove Washington to speak out strongly.

And later that day, she decided to take out another weapon from her armory: her yellow Reeboks. She would personally attend the evening demonstration in the square. This time, she made no secret of it—no pretext of a walk with Charlie. She hoped that the StB was listening when she proclaimed in her loudest voice that she was going to the square and that she would meet Cliff in front of the Hotel Jalta there. (An StB agent was in fact monitoring her and dutifully jotted it down in her surveillance record.) She wanted everyone in the regime—particularly the bloody-minded aggressors, such as Štěpán and Biľak—to know that she would be watching.

Shirley was there as the people of Prague emerged by the tens of thousands. They kept coming until it seemed that the enormous space, overseen by the benign Wenceslas with his helmet and spear, could not hold them anymore. There were high schoolers, long hair cascading to their shoulders, their pairs of prized Levi's or Lee jeans from the West laminated to their skinny legs; mothers in their best dresses; fathers in suits and ties; wrinkled grandparents, their faces puckered like the last apple in the barrel. Most had been obedient just seventy-two hours ago. Many were even members of the Communist Party. Now they had been transformed into rebels by the violence against their own children, and against a generation of Czech youth.

The torrent of demonstrators made the crowds Shirley had seen in August and October seem like a trickle. By the time the gathering peaked, she estimated that she was gazing out at two hundred thousand people at least—certainly the largest demonstration since 1968 and one of the largest in Czechoslovak history. The throng took up chants, both familiar—"*Svobodu!*" ("Freedom!"), "*Svobodné volby!*" ("Free elections!")— and new—"*Máme toho dost!*" ("We've had enough!"), "*Masaryk na stovku!*" ("Masaryk on the hundred-crown note!"), "*Demisi!*" ("Resign!"), and the rhyme "*Konec vlády jedné strany!*" ("The end of single-party government!"). In what would become a hallmark of the time, they shouted, "*Už je to tady!*" ("It's finally here!") and shook their keys, the chiming metal symbolizing bells sounding the death knell of the regime, the people unlocking Prague Castle, or one of many other meanings that the Watchers muse about to this day. Whatever the reasons, two hundred thousand key rings jangling in unison was an inimitable noise. For all the unusual things Shirley had witnessed in her eventful six decades, she had not heard anything like it.

The crowd periodically scanned the entrances to the square for the sudden, dreaded appearance of white helmets—or worse, the Red Berets or the green-suited army troops—but they did not materialize. Riot police with water cannons and armored vehicles were stationed some distance away, and they stayed there. The only visible sign of authority was a video camera surveilling the square at the top of a street pole, openly swiveling back and forth to capture images of the protest. A nimble student clambered up the pole. The higher he got, the more the cheers spread. When he finally yanked the electrical cord out of the camera with a flourish, disabling it, thousands broke into applause.

Loudspeakers were set up around the Wenceslas statue and wired to a megaphone. There was not much in the way of an organized program. This was a day for the Prague Watchers to be free. For at least one afternoon, they were in charge of themselves. Most of the crowd could not hear the loudspeakers, given the volume of listeners and the relatively poor amplification. Nevertheless, some students and others spoke, urging support for the strike.

By the time Shirley met Cliff, it was well after dark. The space was illuminated by giant floodlights atop the National Museum. The demonstrators had decided that the authorities were unlikely to flush them out. They were safe, at least for tonight. The throngs were peaceful and cheerful, the slogans funny, the mood celebratory. They greeted Shirley and welcomed her as one of their own. She had always loved parties, and, despite the looming danger, this felt like one—a salute to freedom, the recurring theme of the singsong chants and banners. The tenacity of the Czechoslovak hunger for that virtue moved her as she met Cliff on the steps of the Hotel Jalta. But they agreed that the protesters did not seem to be organized.

That would not be the case for long.

⌣

HAVEL had rushed back to Prague on Saturday, speeding down country roads in his big black Mercedes. Once back in town, the dramatist set to work scripting the revolution—though perhaps staging an improvisation was more like it, given the spontaneous nature of much that followed. He did so in his professional home: the theater. In the evening, as the students announced their strike and protesters took to the streets, Havel and other dissidents gathered at the Realistické Theatre, just across the river from where the massacre had occurred. They argued all night about what to do and who would do it. Havel moderated the group, mostly listening, occasionally offering a proposal.

Their back-and-forth continued Sunday morning at Havel's apartment, followed that night by a long and unruly debate in another theater, the Actors' Studio. Packing the small room, onstage and in the audience, were writers and actors, philosophers and politicians, many of whom had been relegated post-'68 to careers as stokers and custodians, trashmen and night watchmen. Havel let others do most of the talking, quietly intervening when they seemed stuck, and gently—at times obliquely— nudging the group to consensus. In the end, they adopted a script largely written by him: a declaration establishing a new umbrella organization, Občanské fórum (the Civic Forum).

Their headquarters going forward would be in a third theatrical venue, the Magic Lantern. They spent the day on Monday getting organized—melding the various factions into one, dividing up duties. Havel did not barge into the Monday protest on the square. The Civic Forum, his players, hadn't quite gelled. Accomplishing that cohesion was critical if the peaceful revolution was not to dissolve into warring factions. Besides, he respected the audience. Like Otto, he was a Prague Watcher himself, reared in and by the city.

But the leaders of the protests begged him to come to the square on Tuesday. They feared that the regime would otherwise "drown us here like rabbits." He agreed. And, more than that, he would put on a show to remember.

⌣⌐

ON Tuesday, Shirley watched as another massive crowd assembled on the square. Despite freezing temperatures and snow flurries (not to mention the risk of a police attack), it was at least as large as the day before. Czechoslovak flags and signs waved above the multitudes. Ninety-six orchestral musicians rallied beneath a sign declaring, THE CZECH PHIL-HARMONIC ORCHESTRA IS WITH YOU. Even the Socialist Party, officially a member of the government, joined in. Havel needed a place to speak, and the Socialists' newspaper offered the elevated terrace of its offices, in the middle of the square. But how would he be heard? "As if out of nowhere there appeared . . . stagehands, sound technicians and stage managers of various rock 'n' roll bands." They set up huge speakers, wiring the balcony and the square for sound as the people awaited Havel's arrival.

At four p.m., "an enormous wave of thundering cheers broke through the air" as Havel stepped to the railing of his overlook to speak, the snow falling around him. "The sound system was amazingly loud and clear and Havel's careful, dramatic and somewhat gruff voice boomed over Wenceslas Square. *'Vážení přátelé!'*" "Dear friends," he began—even that humdrum introduction drawing an extended ovation. The people could not believe that they were together, two hundred thousand strong, and actually hearing from the long-banned playwright. Some feared that police would emerge on the mezzanine to seize him before he could say anything more—or attack them all.

But no white helmets, Red Berets, or green army uniforms invaded the square or Havel's balcony as he launched into his remarks. He explained the program of the Civic Forum—the script agreed to by the dissidents. They demanded a reevaluation of what had happened in 1968; the exit of those responsible, including Husák, and of their heirs, particularly Štěpán; an investigation of Friday's attack on the protesters; and the freeing of political prisoners. They would also support the November 27 student strike.

Havel was not a great speaker. He was more comfortable at his typewriter or giving cues from the wings. But today he drew ecstatic cheers. His points were things that everyone could agree on—terms that a popular movement could coalesce around. And then, after about ten minutes, Havel did something surprising. He stopped. He thanked the people and turned the stage over to others. It was characteristically generous—the opposite of the Communist stem-winders lasting for hours that were the usual fare at regime rallies. Havel knew that monologues were boring. He was used to entertaining his audiences, and the program that followed proved it. Next came short, emotional appearances by representatives of the universities, the theater, and labor. Then a dissident priest read a statement from Cardinal František Tomášek, the archbishop of Prague. The ninety-year-old prelate had held fast against Communism for decades, many of them spent under house arrest. "The Archbishop exhorted the people to seize democracy now. The crowd went wild and shouted, 'Tomášek, Tomášek, Tomášek!'"

The finale topped even that. The singer Marta Kubišová stepped onto the balcony. She had once been the most famous vocalist in the country—the voice of 1968. She had been banned for her role in the Prague Spring. This was her first public performance in Prague in twenty-one years. In a clear tone infused with more than two decades of repressed hope, she led the entire square of two hundred thousand in "Kde domov můj." Many of the Prague Watchers were openly weeping as together they sang the words:

> *Where is my home? Where is my home?*
> *The waters murmur along the meadows,*
> *The pine groves whisper along the rocks,*
> *In the orchards shine the blossoms of spring.*
> *It's an earthly paradise to look upon*
> *And this is the beautiful land,*
> *The Czech land, my home, my home!*

The American ambassador was moved—and impressed. Havel had staged a bravura revue, whether it had been scripted or improvised on the spot. She believed in the power of performance to knit people together, to give them purpose and strength. She had helped do that for

America during the Depression. Today Havel and his troupe had done the same for the Prague Watchers, now become actors all. But would it be enough to help them withstand the blows, should the regime strike?

⌒

ON Wednesday, a highly placed Communist told the embassy that two factions had emerged within the deeply divided Communist leadership. One was conciliatory. But the other camp was urging extreme measures. Its leaders included Štěpán, who, the informant said, "gave the orders to the police and paramilitary to attack the demonstrators on November 17." He was attempting to secure a tough response to the protests, "pushing for a curfew or possible declaration of a state of emergency." The Prague party leader was positioning himself to take over the country.

Other signs worried Shirley. After Czech TV reported on the massive Monday and Tuesday rallies, the regime had occupied the studio and taken control of the broadcasts. Now "entry is controlled by the police and . . . uniformed security officials are stationed inside the building." The head of Czechoslovak Television went on the air to insist that they had not been taken over. He claimed that "he had invited in security forces to keep unauthorized persons from the studios." No one believed him, certainly not Shirley. Radio staff had been locked out of their building.

Most ominous of all, the army was continuing to mobilize. Rumors swirled that it would soon attack, to the point that Kiene again feared for his own safety. Old hands in the embassy assured him that he need not worry. But it did little for his nerves when two student leaders came to see him, entrusting him with a document: the last will and testament of the demonstrators. They were counting on the embassy—on the power of America and the celebrity of Shirley—to get it out to the world, should any harm befall them.

Shirley urged her team to hit the streets and contact their sources to gather whatever information they could on the military situation, troop movements, and, above all, the troops' loyalty to the regime. The situation was alarming: the special army units "trained to deal with 'public insurrection'" were on high alert, awaiting a signal from the Communist leaders.

If they mobilized, they would secure downtown, evicting students from universities and tightening their hold on the city. Štěpán and his clique were, it seemed, leaving the way open for the Tiananmen solution.

THURSDAY was Thanksgiving in the United States. The day was gray and cold, with snow flurries, but the palace captured what sun there was and projected it within, like a prism. Otto's determination to open rooms to the outdoors, with windows embedded on two, three, or even all four sides, meant that every corner of the palace was bathed in natural light at all times. In the Wintergarden, the embassy families gathered for a mid-morning holiday service. Having done everything that she could think of to help Havel and the Czechoslovak people, Shirley had one last thing to offer—a prayer:

> In 1620 a small band of Pilgrims landed in what would become the United States in search of freedom from oppression. In 1620 Czech noblemen fought at Bila Hora for the same reason.
>
> Today, in 1989, we celebrate the Pilgrims' success with thanks to God. Today, in 1989, our Czech neighbors are locked in a struggle for freedom.
>
> Today we here offer thanks to the God of all people for our good fortune. Today, let us offer a prayer to Czechoslovakia for success in achieving their own freedom.
>
> May our celebration today acknowledge not only our gifts of freedom and peace, but the same gifts for Czechs and Slovaks.

That afternoon, Havel spoke in the square and offered a plea of his own, speaking to the security forces on behalf of the multitudes listening with upturned faces:

> We call on all the members of the People's Militias to not come out violently against their fellow workers and thus spit upon all the traditions of worker solidarity.
>
> We challenge all the members of the Police to realize that they are first and foremost human beings and citizens of this country and only second subordinate to their superiors.

We challenge the Czechoslovak People's Army to stand on the side of the people and, if necessary, to come out in its defense for the first time.

We call on the public and the governments of all countries to realize that our homeland is from time immemorial the place where European and world confrontations have begun and ended, and that in our country it is not only its fate which is at stake, but the future of all of Europe. We therefore demand that they support in every way the people's movement and the Civic Forum.

Afterward, Shirley cabled Washington that "Vaclav Havel gave an impressive performance at the demonstration." The Czech authorities were not so satisfied. The defense minister, Milán Václavík, went on television to respond. He criticized "the submission of ultimatums and unrealistic demands by opposition groups, the inappropriate criticism of what has already been done, the staining of everything that is socialist." He stressed that the army had not engaged in violence against the protesters. Shirley noted in a cable to Washington that his message was ambiguous. Indeed, it was: it left the possibility of military intervention lingering in the air.

Shirley's skepticism was more justified than she could have known. Privately, Václavík conveyed a less enigmatic message to Štěpán and the Communist leaders: "Together with workers, peasants, intelligentsia, we are ready to defend . . . the achievements of socialism, freedom and peace of the Czechoslovak Socialist Republic." The army troops were fully mobilized and prepared to act on the government's instructions. Václavík had handed the party a loaded gun. They would meet on Friday to discuss whether or not to pull the trigger.

They believed that the decision was theirs alone. But Havel had a move of his own ready for the next day. Ever the dramatist, he was planning a surprise.

A few minutes before ten a.m. on Friday morning, Husák, Jakeš, Biľak, Štěpán, and the other members of the Central Committee filed into a party training facility, surrounded by armed guards, to decide what to do. All day long, they leaked bits and pieces of information to the press:

that there would be leadership changes, that the events of November 17 would be investigated, that they were ready to negotiate with the dissidents. Shirley thought that the news was being "dribbled out to the media in a way that seemed designed to produce maximum favorable impact on the public." But, after forty years of Communist lies, who could believe it? The opposite was just as likely to be true.

The Communist leadership was still in session six hours later, with no signs of breaking, as the largest crowd yet gathered to await Havel—about 350,000. It was an ocean of people, and the square could not contain another drop. The Watchers overflowed into the side streets, filling those as well. Shortly before four p.m., Havel emerged from his headquarters in the Magic Lantern theater, a short distance away. He was surrounded by his bodyguards, led by John Bok—the same wild-haired anarchist who had shouted out "Tell Vašek!" when he was arrested at Albertov the previous Friday.

Today Bok protected both Havel and a second man walking in tandem with him. As they worked their way to the square through arcades and rear alleys, the pedestrians whom they passed stopped and stared. Havel's companion was a familiar figure. "He looks as if he has stepped straight out of a black-and-white photograph from 1968. The face is older, more lined, of course, but he has the same grey coat and paisley scarf, the same tentative, touching smile, the same functionary's hat." He and Havel entered the back of the Melantrich building, where the speaking balcony was. They drew more incredulous looks as they made their way to the fourth floor, finally stepping together onto the balcony.

Spotting Havel's guest, a roar spread through the crowd. The people started chanting his name, over and over again: "Dubček!" Havel had brought them the hero of 1968, and he stepped back and let the former first secretary and the Watchers enjoy each other. The cheers were so powerful that they caused the square to quake—for all the volume of the week's events, no one present had ever heard a sound like it. Dubček threw open his arms as if to gather the multitude into an embrace and said, "You know I love you."

Shirley, watching as she had throughout the week, relished the din of elation. Here was Dubček at last! She knew the meaning of an ovation, and this one went on and on: a minute . . . two. Finally, after three full minutes of cheering, Dubček settled the crowd down and spoke. He endorsed the Civic Forum. Czechoslovaks were, as in 1968, speaking out, he said—trying to make their society a better one. He called for the ouster from power of the 1968 generation, Husák and the rest. "Already, once, we witnessed a new dawn," he proclaimed. "Let us act now so that dawn becomes day."

Three hundred fifty thousand people answered, "Dubček to the castle, Dubček to the castle!"

"That," he answered, "depends on you."

As Dubček talked, the last rays of sun vanished from the sky, and the floodlights came on all over the square. He spoke for eleven minutes before stepping back, setting off another round of cheering. Next came Havel, their pairing delighting the crowd, who began to chant "Dubček-Havel." The two men stood there, together, as if they were a presidential ticket.

Afterward, Havel and Dubček returned to the Magic Lantern and held a press conference from the stage. Dubček was still a Communist—still preaching Marxism with a human face. He and Havel were amicably debating when Havel's friend Jiří Černý, a tall, balding music critic, sidled up, leaned in, and whispered into Havel's ear. Černý then took the microphone and said that he had an announcement: "All members of the Presidium of the Central Committee, and all members of the Secretariat of the Central Committee resigned." The last few words were drowned out by a roar as the entire room, hardened dissidents and cynical reporters alike, erupted in cheers. The leadership of the party was stepping down. There would be no military intervention after all. Štěpán and the rest of the hard-liners had blinked.

Havel grinned and made a *V*-for-victory sign as he and Dubček leaped to their feet. The younger man embraced the elder and, laughing, momentarily buried his face on Dubček's shoulder. From the wings, a bottle of champagne materialized—Havel's favorite beverage, one that the regime had prevented him from tasting during the years of his life spent in unjust incarceration. He lifted his drink and toasted to "a free Czechoslovakia," clinking his glass with Dubček's. For once there was no tinge of melancholy on the former first secretary's smiling face.

In the square, the people of Prague, marchers and watchers alike, rejoiced as the news was announced, jumping up and down, celebrating madly. The keys jangled again, this time as a prediction fulfilled.

That weekend, Shirley attended the demonstrations—now too large for the square—which had been moved to Letná Park, a few minutes' walk from Otto's palace. The largest crowds in Czechoslovak history, more than half a million strong, gathered to hear speeches and bands on a stage that had been erected where the world's biggest Stalin statue had once stood. It was only the end of the first act, of course. Now the real work would begin. But it was a start. The Velvet Revolution, historians would call it.

It was not Shirley's revolution—that honor belonged to the Czechoslovaks. But she had played her part. The sounds of the speeches and the music reverberated throughout the neighborhood, carried across the Petschek compound, and echoed in the halls of the palace. Otto would have been astonished at this raucous new addition to the soundtrack of his villa and his city. Rudolf Toussaint would likely have made a wry remark, and Laurence Steinhardt exulted. Shirley loved it.

In the embassy, Shirley lifted a poster from her office wall. It consisted of photographs of the Communist leadership, with their names and titles. She turned it upside down and rehung it that way. Štěpán and the rest stared back at her in their stiff official poses—now inverted. She did it, as she later explained, "so I can say I set the Communists on their head." It remained that way for the rest of her years in Prague, an echo of the saying that was going around: "In Poland it took ten years, in Hungary ten months, in East Germany ten weeks . . . in Czechoslovakia . . . ten days!"

Later, she called her senior staff together: Ted, Cliff, Ed, and the rest of the Cold Warriors. They took seats around the conference table. The Velvet Revolution was the moment that they had been working toward, some of them for their entire careers. "Looking them sternly in the eye, she told them 'I'm only going to do this once, just once.'" She stood, smiled, locked her arms into position, and launched into "On the Good Ship Lollipop," singing and dancing around the room in pure joy. When she finished, her staff applauded—for her, for themselves, for Havel and Dubček and all the dissidents whom they had worked with, and above all for the Watchers of Prague. Freedom was back.

16

"The Past Is Never Dead. It's Not Even Past."

The Palace; January 27, 2011; around 9:00 p.m.

NACHMAN, YOU AMERICANS ARE TOO OPTIMISTIC," MY mother said.

The next day I was to present my credentials to serve as US ambassador to Prague. I was in the palace library and on the phone with my *maminka,* running through my remarks in Czech. I intended to use it in the ceremony and then sprinkle it into my TV appearances.

I asked her whether it was my plan to speak the language of my hosts that was too optimistic—or what I was going to say.

"Both!"

She thought that my pronunciation was deficient ("You sound *zmrzačený* [crippled]") and that my publicly announced goals were excessively ambitious, given the current state of affairs. Things had started out promisingly enough after Shirley Temple Black and Václav Havel relaunched US-Czech relations in 1989. George H. W. Bush had visited Prague to see the miracle, including taking in Otto Petschek's palace; he had been followed by Bill Clinton, who used the sweeping curve of the villa as a backdrop for remarks, then won over the Prague Watchers by playing the sax at a Prague jazz club, with Havel nodding along. Czech accession to NATO had been driven by Clinton and his secretary of state, Madeleine Albright—like my mother, a Czechoslovak refugee from the Communist regime. Albright was a frequent guest at the palace, charming the staff by washing and ironing her own clothes.

Even the Czech split from the Slovaks had turned out fine. The Velvet Divorce, everyone called it, to match the Velvet Revolution—but it really was that soft and smooth. Ever since Masaryk and Beneš had improvised the marriage of the two nations in 1918 (to Otto's and everyone else's surprise), the Slovaks had grumbled about being treated as the junior partner. Like many who had ties to both lands, my mother initially thought that separation was a terrible idea. Havel objected so strongly that he resigned as president of Czechoslovakia in advance of the breakup. But she got used to it, and so did Havel—he came back as president of the new Czech Republic for another ten years.

Everything remained more or less velvet throughout the '90s. Then came a gradual deterioration, starting at the turn of the new century: Czech popular disgruntlement at the inequalities and injustices of restored capitalism; a turn toward nationalism and populism and against liberalism, led by Havel's replacement, the arch-conservative Václav Klaus (upon whom my mom had heaped such disdain during our conversations before I had left the United States); and Czech anger over perceived American slights, most recently Obama's canceling a planned US radar base on Czech soil.

I had a raft of defense, economic, and cultural proposals prepared to address the decline, and I would be advocating for them on Czech TV the next day. A big part of my pitch was the fact that I was living in the palace. If the child of a Czechoslovak Jew shipped to Auschwitz by Nazi Germany could return to Prague representing the most powerful nation on earth and live in a house once seized by those same German forces, then *anything* was possible.

My *maminka* was more pessimistic: "You are taking away the wrong lesson."

"And what is the right one?" I asked.

"Expect the worst!"

We both laughed, but I knew what she meant. She was still tormented by all that she had lost, prone to nightmares and sudden tears. In Israel, she had met and married my father, Irvin (a Polish Jewish refugee who, like her, was denied higher education by his religious family). He brought her to the United States, as she had dreamed. They opened the hamburger stand together, but even here she couldn't escape the trauma that Fascism and Communism had left on her psyche.

I remembered my mom's reaction to the Prague invasion of 1968, when I was about eight years old. Along with my dad, we had watched the Soviet tanks crawl across the screen on the little television above the cash register. This was in south Los Angeles just after the Watts riots, and the turmoil in the streets of Prague was not so far removed from what we had seen in our own neighborhood. My taciturn, compassionate father put one of his big, work-calloused hands on my *maminka*'s shoulder as she wept and cursed the Communists and the Nazis before them. Bastards on the left, bastards on the right—what difference did the labels make? As far as she was concerned, they were all the same.

America had been no picnic for her, either. Like so many immigrant dreamers, she and my father had ended up laboring brutally to survive. Without professions, they were left to eke out a living by working sixteen hours a day, every day of the year except Yom Kippur. They ran their little business together until my dad's sudden death from a heart attack in 1975.

From that low point, however, my mom had turned things around. She leased out the stand and supplemented the rental income by selling women's clothing in an upscale department store. She missed my father but loved the work—surrounded by beautiful garments and appreciative customers, as she had been in her sister's dress shop in Sobrance. She invested her own long-frustrated hopes for an education in me, beaming (and boasting) as I got the diplomas that she had craved but could never pursue. When I made partner at a law firm, she retired, settling into a cozy garden apartment in LA.

Frieda in her home office, Los Angeles, California.

Now almost ninety years old, she continued to read voraciously and follow current events on radio and television (both often on at once). Younger friends helped her get the Czech news on the Internet, and she followed my every move. I insisted that her life had been a success, that she had finally achieved the freedom that she had sought, but she did not see it that way. Still, she was as happy as I had ever known her to be and proud of my career, even if she was not shy with her critiques. She frequently castigated me for my failures. That was particularly true whenever she felt that I had neglected to follow the three rules of the hamburger stand that she had drilled into me all my life and that she had stressed to me before I left for Prague: Always do the right thing. Always be loyal. And always serve the best hamburger you can—do your best work, no matter what.

Tonight, it was my Czech language skills—the lack of them—that fell short of her high standards. We practiced some more, and, when I had to go, she signed off by urging me not to embarrass her on television the next day. (The credentialing ceremony would be covered on Czech news.) I told her that I would try not to.

I was in a reflective mood, thinking about my family's journey to this moment, and my own. Before going to bed, I decided to have another look at that swastika under the table. I made my way to the oval chamber, turned up the room lights as high as they would go, set my nightcap down on the richly colored marble floor, lay down on my back like an auto mechanic, and slid underneath the table.

I saw that hateful symbol again, together with the serial number. But now, with the benefit of a repeat visit and better lighting, I noticed that there was also an older mark, daubed on with white paint aged to ivory. It seemed to be the original Petschek inventory designation from when the house was first opened. And there was another, newer number too: the US government property number, I guessed from when the place was first acquired after World War II. It was repeated on a later addition, a shiny modern label, along with a bar code.

There it was, right in front of my eyes, the story of the past century in the palace, arcing as neatly as the curve of the villa itself: Czechoslovak and Jewish origins, German occupation, American restoration and sustenance. My presence in Prague as US ambassador was the result of the identical trajectory. The underside of that table was a map of the Czechoslovak century, and of my family's as well.

I was determined to learn more about every aspect of those who had come before me in the palace. In the meantime, no matter what my mom said, I believed that that story was an unambiguous triumph for our family.

Things turned out to be more complicated than I thought.

THE next morning, I was a little nervous as I walked down the steps of the palace and climbed into the car for the short trip to the castle to appear before President Klaus. It wasn't just my mom who disliked him. Czech and European liberals and most of the ex-dissidents abhorred him. They questioned how he had secured permission during the Communist years to study as a young economist at Cornell (where he had imbibed his free-market economics). They claimed that, as finance minister in the first postrevolution government, Klaus had rigged privatization to benefit his friends. Then there was the sin that as prime minister he had encouraged the dissolution of the country. His critics said that when Havel retired, Klaus had unfairly tilted the election to succeed the playwright, making shady deals with the electors. As president, he sounded nationalist and populist themes, claiming "business-class Eurocrats" who ran the EU looked down on the "economy-class Slavs," and he urged solidarity with other Slavic lands. Above all, Klaus was said to be too close to the Russians. In fact, his climate-change-denial book had just been translated into their language with funding from a Russian energy company, Lukoil, which had Czech business interests.

I found that demonic characterization hard to square with the pleasantly smiling, grandfatherly gentleman before whom I was soon standing on a long Persian rug in Prague Castle. Lindsay and the embassy staff were lined up behind me, in front of what looked like a fourteen-foot-tall white china salt shaker, heavily tooled with gold flourishes: a fancy rococo space heater. We were in the Throne Hall of Prague Castle, just a few feet from where Obama had first introduced me to Klaus. Saint Paul looked out quizzically from a painting hanging on a red silk brocaded wall. All of Prague was visible through the windows, and I could see the

American flag flying above the highest point of the embassy, with the trees and lawns of Petřín Hill beyond it.

The president had senior officials from his office and the Ministry of Foreign Affairs in a row behind him. He was tall and solidly built, with close-cropped white hair and a white mustache. He wore an elegant suit, dark and tailored to the contours of his body, encasing a slight paunch.

I made remarks in my imperfect Czech. Klaus seemed pleased and slightly amused at my efforts. I forced the last few words out and uttered a silent prayer of gratitude that I had not become tongue-tied. I then walked across the long oriental rug between us and handed him my letter of appointment and other paperwork, which he accepted with a grin. We turned and posed side by side for a gaggle of photographers and other press who had gathered behind a rope, as what seemed like hundreds of flashes went off, a barrage, like the finale of a Fourth of July fireworks show.

He told me about his love of the United States: his Cornell education; his affinity for the conservative Chicago school of economics and the city in general, which he was shortly planning to visit. His affection for America was genuine. We discussed his friendships with US senators (all conservatives) and his public praise for Obama's attempts to reset the United States' relationship with Russia. I couldn't very well disagree with him—that was my president's policy. He hoped that Lindsay and I would be frequent guests at the jazz concerts he hosted in the castle monthly: American jazz, he specified with a smile. I liked him and was willing to give the relationship a chance, no matter what others said.

My mother saw the pictures of the two of us and snorted to me when we next spoke, "I see you have a new friend."

I tried to change the subject, asking her if she had made any progress on planning her trip.

She responded, "Why, so I can meet your new pal?"

I decided that another day might be better to discuss her travel.

⌒

Despite my mom's anxieties, I felt right at home as a Jew living in Europe. The Czech Republic had some of the lowest rates of anti-Semitism on the Continent, on par with Canada and the United States. Czechs were also very pro-Israel—by far the most of any citizens of the

European Union. The Jewish Quarter was a major Prague attraction and welcomed millions of tourists, Jewish and otherwise, from around the world. I went to Sabbath services weekly at its heart: the Old New Synagogue, built in 1270 and now the oldest continually operating one in Europe. During Communist times, secret police harassed worshipers entering through its portals, but I was cordially greeted and given a prime spot among its rough-hewn stone pillars supporting vaulted ceilings. My mom was impressed. "Nachman, our family has been praying there for centuries, but you are the first to have an assigned seat!"

That spring, the Czechs hosted a conference on European anti-Semitism. It was convened by the Helsinki Commission—the same body that had once been so crucial to the dissidents. It was still fighting for civil rights across the Continent. The conference was at the Foreign Ministry headquarters in the Czernin Palace. On my way in, I noticed a bust in the inner courtyard. It was a sculpture of Jan Masaryk, situated on the spot where he had fallen to his death.

That set an appropriately somber tone for the day. Speaker after speaker stood up and described appalling incidents across Europe: a French teen thrown to the ground and assaulted by a gang of more than a dozen, who screamed anti-Semitic invectives; a pedestrian in Switzerland asked if he was a Jew, then brutally beaten by three assailants when he replied in the affirmative; a student leader in the United Kingdom, mobbed by protesters chanting anti-Semitic slogans as he waited to make a speech; and discrimination in public accommodations, in housing, in employment. I heard story after story of the kind of traditional anti-Semitism that my family had long endured, as well as new variants. Denial of the Holocaust that had so decimated us or simply substituting *Israel* for *the Jews* in the old canards, hiding hate under a political veneer; "old poison in new bottles," as a Czech official put it.

He also acknowledged that even the Czechs were not immune: "In countries with small Jewish communities like the Czech Republic, the passion for hate is often manifested by attacking the memory of the dead. . . . Swastikas are painted on tombstones in remote locations, words questioning the largest genocide of the past century are posted anonymously in Internet discussions. . . . It is important to point out that they are being directed not only against the Jewish community but also against the Roma . . . and other groups of victims of Nazism."

The conference made news around the world. It didn't take long for my mom to get wind of it. "So," she said, "did you attend the anti-Semitism conference?"

"Yes, Mom, of course I did."

"Now do you admit I was right?"

"Mom, the Czechs *held* the conference. Whatever else may be going on elsewhere in Europe, the Czech Republic is the least anti-Semitic country in the world."

"I see they admitted they have a problem."

"Trust me, you will be perfectly safe here. Why don't you come see for yourself?"

"Did I say I wouldn't? Be patient—you barely got there."

⟶

THE Israeli ambassador invited me over for cocktails. I accepted, but, when the day arrived, I was tired and tried to beg off. Yaakov Levy, a short, intense sabra in his sixties, had for decades defiantly represented his country in hostile venues across the planet. He was not going to be denied that easily. He replied, sounding crushed, "But we invited a special surprise guest; he's coming just to see you. He'll be *so* disappointed." I had no choice but to relent.

In the car on our way over, I made some comment about how exhausted I was to my mother during our daily phone call. Her reply: "You are too tired to go to a *cocktail* party? Ha, *shvoltegger* [lazy bum]. Try standing in the cold at Auschwitz; then you will know tired." Although she and the ambassador had never met, they had clearly studied Jewish guilt from the same ancient sources.

I was chatting with colleagues at the party when I suddenly felt a surge of electricity flow through the room. There, walking through the door and into the gathering was none other than Václav Havel, with an aide in tow. He was instantly recognizable—the hero of '89. Perfectly turned out in suit and tie, looking every bit the ex-president, he was shorter than I expected. Yaakov came over and whispered to me, "He's really here to talk to you; he can only stay for about fifteen minutes," nudging me forward toward the former dissident the way my mom once pushed me to speak to eligible women at weddings.

Havel was a pleasure to talk to, asking me questions in his low, rumbling tone. He had survived several bouts of the lung disease that he incurred during captivity, and that, combined with his smoking, gave him a deep bass voice. He looked drawn but cheerful as we sat down to chat. He had just finished making his first movie, adapting one of his plays, *Odcházení*. It was the story of a retiring head of state forced out of his residence by a competing official, depicted as a scheming con man and gangster and believed by many to be a vicious caricature of Klaus (although Havel, with a twinkle in his eye, had publicly denied it, and said that the tensions between them were overstated).

After we had been conferring for about a quarter of an hour, he turned to say something to the hovering Yaakov. I assumed that Havel was going to offer some key insight before he excused himself from the party, so I bent forward to absorb every word. I heard Havel ask in his deep growl, "Er . . . Ambassador, do you have any champagne?"

He ended up staying for about two hours as the small group discussed the lessons of history and their application to the present. Havel mostly listened, though he would occasionally interject a question or make a point. It soon became apparent that he loved the United States for supporting him and the other dissidents through their dark decades and for welcoming the Czechs back into freedom. That warmth extended to me personally even though we had just met; I was the beneficiary of the hard work done by Shirley and my other predecessors.

I told him about my ambitions for the job and my family history and even shared my mother's feelings about the palace. He was sympathetic to her, reminiscing that he had once been arrested when leaving the compound. He urged that we in the United States remember its lessons and not abdicate our leadership in fighting for democracy. He seemed to think that America had become too complacent and, although he liked my law-school classmate who was currently in charge of the place, believed that we were a bit naive. His view, as he had stated in an open letter with other leaders to Obama, was that Europe was once more at risk from "the forces of nationalism, extremism, populism, and anti-Semitism," and from "Russia's creeping intimidation and influence-peddling." His analysis was not all that different from my mother's.

Pondering his words, I moved close to him and very quietly asked if he had any advice for me in my ambassadorship. He paused and considered for a minute. Finally he spoke. "You must be a *very* undiplomatic diplomat," he said. I wasn't sure exactly what he meant, but the party was breaking up, and there was no time to ask him.

I couldn't wait to tell my mom about the evening. She loved Havel, in part because he was a living connection to her idol, Tomáš Masaryk. She had grown up under the first president of Czechoslovakia, and I had just encountered the last before its dissolution into two new nations. He represented the intimate, complicated American-Czech bond, and so did I, both as an envoy from one country to the other and as a Czech American. The United States had helped create the Czech state, seen it lost to Fascism and then to Communism, but helped rescue it again from both. Havel seemed to think that it was under threat again. But why, I wondered, did he want me to be undiplomatic?

⌒

LINDSAY, Tamar, and I settled into life in Prague that spring and maintained our efforts to get my mom to pay us that visit. I called her doctors myself to ask if she was up to it. It turned out that they had no objection; they thought it would be good for her. Friends and family were flying over to join us for Passover, and we hoped she might travel with them. The three of us had often spent the holiday with her in the past.

But as we ramped up holiday preparations, shipping in cartons of matzo and crates of wine, she announced that she just wasn't ready. "Passover is when they took us to the ghetto, Nachman. I just can't face it." What could I do except tell her that I understood?

Still, the holiday would not be the same without her, so we tried to make up for that by inviting our favorite Prague friends to the seder in the formal dining room of the palace. As far as I knew, these were the first seders to be held here since the Petscheks had left. The holiday celebrated liberty—the Hebrews escaping slavery in Egypt—and those whom we invited exemplified that virtue. They shared with us a commitment to freedom, in all its forms. There were ex-dissidents and their families; folks from the Czech government, the NGO and business communities, and colleagues from various embassies, including my own. It was customary to invite people of all faiths, and we had issued the invitations irrespective of religion.

Attendees were welcomed by our majordomo, Miroslav Černík, with his neatly combed white hair, dark suit, and red tie. He was our Mr.

Pokorný, so attuned to the palace that he once told me, "I often feel I am a part of the place—that anything that happens to it, happens to me." Although I had never met his legendary predecessor, Pokorný, I felt that I knew him through Černík's love for the house, his knowledge of its most intimate operations, and his care.

In the run-up to Passover, I told him as much. Černík replied, "And you have a lot in common with Otto Petschek, Ambassador." I don't think he meant it entirely as a compliment. For example, I had solicited his and the staff's help in cleaning the house for Passover. It is traditional to give one's residence a good scrubbing, including looking for and removing the bread products, or *chametz,* forbidden on this holiday, when only unleavened matzo is eaten. Every leavened crumb must be searched for and disposed of—a much more daunting task in a home of more than a hundred rooms than in our three-bedroom D.C. apartment, but Černík (and the staff, at his direction) had good-naturedly pitched in with us.

Then, when we were done, it was time for another custom: the ritual search for any remaining *chametz.* Small pieces of bread are purposely hidden throughout the house, and the family looks for them with a candle and sweeps them up with a feather—a nod to the days before flashlights and DustBusters. Then those last pieces of bread are incinerated and, in case any were missed, a special blessing is recited that nullifies any crumbs left behind.

Černík walked in on me as I was preparing the small chunks of bread that would be hidden. When he saw them, he practically jumped across the table to seize them.

"Ambassador—bread is forbidden," he scolded. I explained the ritual that I was about to perform. He looked dubiously at the candle, feather, and, above all, the bread.

"But what if you forget where you put a piece?" he asked.

"Don't worry, Mr. Černík, I will say a special blessing nullifying the *chametz,* so it won't matter."

"Ambassador," he answered, looking at me as if I were a madman, "why didn't you just do that before we cleaned the entire place?"

Notwithstanding that and the many other challenges of the holiday, Černík had outdone himself tonight for this special occasion. His beloved palace gleamed as our guests filtered into the dining room,

Černík standing by and helping me and Lindsay welcome them. The paneling glowed, the cornucopias and garlands sculpted in wood as though freshly transformed from the real thing by some artifice of Magic Prague known only to the Gerstel firm that had carved them in the '20s and the driven patron who had placed the order. The real miracle was that we were doing this in a room that had once hosted the likes of Heydrich, Frank, and other high-ranking Nazis at dinner parties. The space was filled to capacity: more than sixty guests seated around eight tables. I welcomed everyone, and we launched into the Haggadah, the story of the Exodus read at the seder, going around the room, each attendee reciting a passage in the language of their choosing. Hebrew, Czech, English, French, even German, were heard—an echo of Otto's polyglot library at the other end of his curved palace.

Perhaps the most famous part of the Haggadah is the story of the four children: wise, wicked, simple, and *mi she'aino yodea lishol,* the one too young to ask a question. Commentators also spoke of a fifth child: the one who had drifted away from the Jews and so was not in attendance. This year, as it turned out, we did invite the fifth child—many of them. Over and over again, guests sidled up to me and whispered in my ear that they were Jewish or had Jewish ancestry. *Ambassador, my mother was Jewish . . . my grandmother . . . my great-grandmother . . .*

When I compared notes with Lindsay after the first course, I was surprised and amused when she said that the same had happened to her. We had invited our guests because we admired their work for civil rights, for the Roma, against corruption, or for other good causes. But it turned out that, whether by coincidence or instinct, we had unintentionally swept up a disproportionate number of our fellow Czech Jews.

When I spoke to my mother after the seder, I told her about it. I thought it was wonderful. She had a different take: "Nachman, why do you think you didn't know about it—or that they had to whisper? They are hiding it. You think after all that they went through, it is so easy to forget, to take a risk, to be sure the past is not coming back? Have you listened to a single thing I said to you since you told me you were going to Prague? They are scared, too. Rightly so!"

I pushed back. But later, as I took my daily constitutional around the gravel walking path, I wondered if she was right. I had thought that history arced, like the curve of Otto's palace behind me. But maybe I was looking at the wrong feature of his construction. Perhaps, instead, history went around and around, like the oval I was now circling, laid out all those decades ago.

⌒

"NACHMAN, you looked like a crazy man on the Internet."

My mother felt that I had gotten a little carried away in my speech in May at the Roma concentration-camp site Lety. The Romani people (they preferred that term to the more colloquial but demeaning *Gypsies*) had invited me to speak at the annual commemoration of their suffering at Nazi hands. The site was a couple of hours' drive from Prague, in an agricultural area, amid farmland and lush fields. When I pulled into the parking lot and got out of my car, a stench assaulted my nostrils like nothing that I had ever smelled. An overwhelming aroma of decay, sweet and rotten, clogged the air.

"What is *that!*?" I had asked someone.

"There is a pig farm next door," he replied. "They are actually minimizing the smell today."

"*Hrozný,*" we agreed—"horrible."

The reek in the air had been a stark contrast to the pastoral surroundings of the site: long rows of trees, a green field, gently undulating pasture. The original buildings of the camp had long ago been razed. Why hadn't the pig farm been moved? No money to do that, I was told. What nonsense; the government could surely afford it.

The stink had been an affront not just to the Roma but to all the Nazis' victims, my mom included. I cast aside my prepared remarks and spoke frankly, expressing my outrage to the audience (including the prime minister and other dignitaries). The media ate it up and picked the angriest, most hectoring footage from my speech. I had overdone it, my mother said. She believed that her attention to appearances had helped her survive the Holocaust. It made the Nazis think that she would be a good worker, and it made her feel good. She wanted me to be more attentive to my own.

"I . . . lost my temper," I said.

"That's not so bad, under the circumstances," she replied. "Just try to keep your dignity next time."

Still, I could tell she was not that displeased. I thought too of Havel's advice: to be an undiplomatic diplomat. I was starting to see what he meant.

⌣

TENSIONS with President Klaus soon arose, just as my mother had predicted—but the resolution surprised both me and her. Klaus had been nothing but kind after accepting my credentials. As promised, he invited Lindsay and me to his frequent jazz concerts in the Spanish Hall built by the mad emperor Rudolf II, ten thousand square feet of white paneling, gilt edges, and mirrors. It was probably the most magnificent space in Prague Castle (and was also where Obama had signed the treaty with the Russians). I loved hearing it filled with the sounds of an American art form. Klaus generally sat us in the front row, often right next to him, and he was always immersed in the music, tapping his foot and nodding his head. My Czech was getting better, and we would converse in that tongue between numbers or when a musician did something truly spectacular.

I thought it was pretty neat that I was friendly with both Havel, whom I had continued to encounter, and his adversary Klaus. Between them, they encapsulated the entire modern history of the Czech Republic. My mom warned me not to make too much of Klaus's love of jazz. "The Nazis loved music, too—some of the same music *we* loved," she said. I reminded her that the Nazis hated jazz, labeling it as "degenerate." But I had to admit that culture could be morally fungible. Look at where I lived, a palace that had been created by a German-speaking Czech Jew and preserved by a German Wehrmacht general, that had been coveted by both the Soviets and the Americans. But, on a human level, I still couldn't help liking Klaus and bonding with him over music.

So I was caught off guard in May when one of his top aides, Petr Hájek, attacked America's accomplishment of bringing Osama bin Laden to justice. In the wake of that event, Hájek claimed that it was a hoax, "a media fiction . . . a modern fairy-tale for adults—good and evil. Should we want, let's believe . . . I personally opine that Osama never existed. 9/11 as it was presented, explained and fixed, never happened." Klaus issued his own statement about the death of bin Laden, and, though it didn't deny his existence, it was tepid—and said nothing about his aide's bizarre rant. When pressed by the media, Klaus declined to criticize his subordinate and would only say, "I thought very carefully over the wording of my statement."

I could overlook Klaus's lukewarm reception to bin Laden's death but had to take issue with his giving Hájek a pass. I, and the United States, couldn't continue to engage normally with Klaus if he ignored his subordinate's slurs. If Klaus didn't respond—and forcefully—I would have to . . . Well, I didn't know what I would do, but it would be something. I skipped my usual call to my mom that day because I was busy dealing with the furor, but I could just hear her whispering "I told you so."

Hájek was a conspiracy theorist who made his boss's climate-change questioning look mild in comparison. He had denied that smoking injured people, contested whether the theory of evolution accounted for human descent (asserting that he "does not come from the apes"), and intimated that President Obama was not born in the United States. He was an exemplar of the classic European far right: populist and disdaining truth, the press, and liberal institutions. The press speculated that Klaus would not repudiate him.

But, to my relief, Klaus did just that. He stated that Hájek had not consulted with him or his office, that the statement was unfortunate, and that "I want to say clearly that he did not express the view of the President." It wasn't a ringing denunciation (the foreign minister and many others provided one), but it was still welcome. Klaus followed it by speaking at our Fourth of July party at Otto's palace, telling some two thousand guests that the day "is an occasion to celebrate the values enshrined in the wording of the Declaration of Independence, because these are the values, Mr. Ambassador, we share with your country."

Even my mother grudgingly gave me credit when we spoke that night. She had seen the coverage of the party, and she was impressed. We talked about that and Otto's magic wall, which we had retracted to accommodate everyone. The machinery still worked, but the descending frame had to be manually supported by workers in the basement, their hands holding the bottom and sides until it came to rest. The palace looked great, but the interior mechanisms were starting to wear out.

"Just like me," my mother said, chuckling, and pointed out that she had been born at around the same time that work on the palace had begun.

"I think you are both holding up pretty well," I answered. "When are you going to come see the place for yourself?"

Soon, she said. Soon.

⌒

I practiced for her hoped-for arrival by entertaining other visitors. None was more welcome than Otto's daughter Eva. At ninety, she was the oldest living original occupant of the palace. She told me over the phone that she wanted to bring her granddaughters to see her childhood home. I invited her to stay. In an English accented with the same ever-so-slight inflections that I had been hearing my entire life, she declined: "Too painful."

Still, we were glad to have her company, if only for an evening. Lindsay, Tamar, and I were bursting with questions as we awaited her on the shallow front steps of what used to be her home. She exited her taxi, slowly but steadily. She was tiny, my mother's height, and similarly elegant. Her husband, Bob Goldmann, who had also fled Hitler's Europe, was the same height and age—they were as perfectly matched as a pair of vintage pearl earrings. Their twin college-aged granddaughters towered above them, tall and with long black hair. As we ushered Eva and her party through the high front door, the glass framed in ornate black iron grillwork, she hesitated, saying, "My father never allowed me to use this entrance."

"I'm the ambassador," I told her. "I hereby give you permission."

As we walked around the palace, Eva brought its history to life. She told us what Otto was like—stern, yes, but he could be fun, too. He loved to play those musical guessing games, tapping out the rhythm of an operatic score on the dinner table with a piece of his heavy silver cutlery and rewarding the first of the children to guess it. She identified remaining examples of the silver: "That's it," she said, amazed. She was surprised and pleased to see that her father's books were still in the library—particularly the Jewish ones. Eva described her father's obsession with constructing the palace "down to every doorknob." When we came to Otto's bedroom, she told us about his death and how Martha had maintained this room as a shrine, forcing Eva to sit here with her and mourn. "I hated that," she said. "I wanted to mourn him in my own way." She later described the family's escape in 1938. I asked if they really had converted to Christianity, going straight to a global Eucharistic Congress after they left, as was rumored. She gave me the same disdainful look that I so often got from my mom. "Silly boy," she said, "that was the only way we could get a visa." She and her husband had maintained a strong Jewish identity, and her granddaughters spoke fluent Hebrew.

Following that visit, Eva and I became close. We spoke regularly, and I took to dropping in on her and Bob when I passed through New York. She opened up to me about her father, and she showed me how to read the palace to understand its occupants. I would find evidence of them all: Otto's architecture and design books, the marked pages transformed into the components of the villa; a Nazi yearbook left by Rudolf Toussaint, detailing the system that he had turned against at the end of the war; a movie theater that Laurence Steinhardt had put in, trying and failing to use films as a weapon against Communism; the restorations all over the house that Shirley had undertaken while democracy too was being restored. I would eventually befriend the descendants of them all, in my quest to learn the full story of the palace.

Eva's visit made me more determined than ever to get my mom to Prague. I told her all about my new friend. "She was rich," she sniffed. "What did she know about suffering?" But my mother was just as curious about the details of the Petscheks' lives as when she and her sisters had discussed the family in the Sobrance house eight decades prior. I made her promise to tell me all her stories again as well. What better place to do that than right here in Prague? She said that we could talk about it when Lindsay, Tamar, and I came to see her for our summer vacation in August.

As we packed our bags for that trip, I thought that my *maminka* was coming around and close to agreeing to visit the palace. She was proud of the work that I had done to rebuild the relationship between her two countries. She could see from the news that the Czechs were happy. She had to admit that no disaster had befallen me. I thought that I was poised to get her to finally commit to a date to come.

Then everything fell apart.

On Thursday afternoon, August 4, I dropped by my mom's for a snack and quality time—just the two of us. She had set aside some *chalushkes,* stuffed cabbage, one of my favorite dishes.

When I arrived, she waved some printouts from the Internet in my face. "What is this?"

I scanned the Czech headlines. It was Hájek again. This time, he was upset about an upcoming LGBT event that I was supporting. Prague's gay community had asked our embassy for help with their first-ever Pride celebration, including a parade. I loved the idea for any number of reasons, not least of which was the resonance with 1989—when the Prague Watchers became the Prague Marchers. We were quick to say yes and contributed funding as well. As a result, mine was the first of thirteen ambassadors' signatures on the letter endorsing Prague Pride. I was told that it was the farthest east in Europe that any Pride event had ever dared to go.

Now I saw why. Klaus's aide had denounced "the forthcoming gay carnival" as a "serious political demonstration of a certain value vision of the world," referring to homosexuals as "deviant." And he was not alone. A senior official at the Education Ministry, Ladislav Bátora, went even further. He announced that he and the leaders of his far-right political party would be delivering protest letters to two leaders of this outrage: the mayor of Prague and me. The party was called DOST—Enough—and its symbol was a fist crashing down. Bátora represented the recurring dark side of Slavic nationalism, still alive a century after Otto had assumed it would wither away. Like Klaus, Bátora was a champion of Czech sovereignty and a bitter opponent of its dissolution in liberal institutions such as the EU. He declared himself for "Confucius over Rousseau, nation state over civil society, goulash over McDonald's, and the Czech crown over the euro," and "against Europeanism, human rightism, genderism, multiculturalism, feminism, ecumenism, environmentalism and homosexualism." He was infamous for, among other things, fraternizing with neo-Nazis and praising as "great" the anti-Semitic Czech book *The Death of the Slavs,* a rehash of *The Protocols of the Elders of Zion* and other canards.

I attempted to reassure my mother. It was just a couple of members of the lunatic fringe acting out.

"Nachman, they both work for the government."

I told her I was sure that they weren't speaking for the government.

"Well, why are they picking on you? Thirteen ambassadors signed that letter."

"My signature is at the top. The American ambassador is the first among equals—that is why it is such a good job."

"*Milacku* [Dear], how can you be so blind? The Jews, the Gypsies, now the gays—you don't see a pattern here?"

I had been sent to Prague to patch things up with the Czechs, and big public confrontations weren't really in the ambassadorial job description. I wasn't prepared for a huge conflagration, and I was six thousand miles away. Most ominously, looming behind Hájek and Bátora was Klaus. Yes, I had a good relationship with the president, but Hájek had a better one. And Klaus had also publicly defended Bátora in the past, dismissing allegations of anti-Semitism and various other misconduct as political correctness run amok. Klaus was not only the most important politician in the Czech Republic; he also had deep ties with US conservatives, including some in Congress—and he had a trip planned there in the weeks ahead.

As we ate, my mom asked me what I was going to do. We talked about my options: back down, say nothing, or fight back, and the pros and cons of each. She silently considered the choices.

I thought about her reminder to me before leaving Prague about the three rules of the hamburger stand. What, I wondered, was the best ambassadorial decision I could serve up, here? Should I be loyal to the larger relationship between the two countries or to my liberal sensibilities on this issue? What was the right thing to do under these circumstances?

I considered Havel's advice, to be an undiplomatic diplomat. I knew better what he meant now: don't let the conventions of my new trade impede my humanity.

And I reflected on my predecessors in the palace. What counsel would they give if they were sitting here with us eating *chalushkes*? I thought of the indomitable Otto, who had pursued his vision no matter the cost; Laurence, whose daring had salvaged the palace but not, alas, the country; Shirley, shrewdly protecting the dissidents and the revolution; and even Toussaint, with his constant compromises, dwindling morally with every concession, then partially redeeming himself at the last possible moment.

They were fighters, all. So was my mother. As we mopped the last of the sweet orange sauce from our plates with coarse rye bread, she finally spoke. "Nachman, what choice do you really have?" she asked. She looked proud and afraid, all at once. "You have to say something."

The professionals in the embassy came to the same conclusion. That Friday, we issued a follow-up statement: "The American Embassy is happy the Czech Republic is a country in which its citizens can enjoy all human rights regardless of their sexual orientation. It is regrettable that there are people in official positions that hold intolerant views."

I reassured my mother that it would all work out fine. She wasn't so sure. She had long ago lost her girlhood confidence in Masaryk's credo, Truth Prevails. I told her that when this all blew over, and it would, she was coming to Prague. We needed her help in the embassy, I joked.

She didn't agree, but she didn't refuse, either.

SHORTLY before we issued our statement, Klaus put out one of his own. This time he wasn't repudiating Hájek—he was backing him to the hilt. In a press release, Klaus wrote, "I strongly disagree with the demands . . . to distance myself from the statements made by Petr Hájek . . . The statements were not made by me, and I would probably have chosen different words. However, I also feel no 'pride' about this event." Klaus argued that Hájek's use of the word *deviant* to describe the gay community was "value-neutral." He continued, "It is one thing to tolerate something, but it is quite another to give it public support in the name of an important institution."

We didn't know about Klaus's statement when we issued ours, but the proximity led the press to believe that we were directly rebuking him. They were soon reporting that Klaus had taken it that way as well. He was angry and demanded that the foreign minister, Karel Schwarzenberg, do something. I assumed that we were in good hands with Schwarzenberg, Havel's former chief of staff and a leading *pravdoláskař*, or practioner of "truth-and-lovism." Benign, tolerant, and good-humored, he was a high-ranking hereditary noble whom everyone called the Prince. He had a tendency to nap at boring official meetings and had run on the campaign slogan "I fall asleep when others talk nonsense." I admired him—he had even been my guest at the palace for a Sabbath dinner in the *Damenzimmer,* with its green silk paneling and illuminated vitrine displaying a selection of Otto and Martha's little glass, porcelain, and silver treasures. It was less cavernous than the formal dining room and more suitable for smaller gatherings. The Prince had charmed us all at the meal by draining his glass of wine and proclaiming "*Shiker iz a goy,*" an old and impolite Yiddish phrase, to the effect that Gentiles are drunks—one seldom heard from the lips of Catholic nobility.

So I was taken aback when Schwarzenberg publicly chided me and the other ambassadors the next day. He proclaimed that the ambassadors' statement was counterproductive and unnecessary because, in Prague, "No one prevents the relevant groups from enjoying their rights and manifesting them in public." Schwarzenberg also said that it "makes an impression of an interference in internal affairs." That was the cardinal sin of diplomacy—the third rail no ambassador was supposed to touch. Although he benignly added that he supposed that we had meant no harm, the damage was done.

My mother's maiden voyage as a diplomatic advisor was proving a bit choppier than expected. Despite my efforts to dissuade her, on Monday she watched the video footage of DOST marching to deliver their protest missive. Led by Bátora, the party's leaders strode up Tržiště Street to the embassy. Bátora sternly presented their letter to one of our uniformed security men at the front door. The guard tried hard to stay expressionless, but on camera his distaste was evident, as if someone had handed him a loaded diaper. The DOST letter was hard to follow, but the gist was that I had betrayed the legacy of Ronald Reagan by embracing gay rights. I thought that the whole thing was absurdly funny, worthy of one of Havel's plays, but my mom failed to see the humor in it. As with my discovery of the swastika under the table, we each took it very differently. She looked at me, grim-faced.

"Mom, you saw them; they are a handful of cranks."

"Where have I heard that before?" she shot back. I got the historical reference.

As if all that weren't enough, Klaus weighed in again that Monday as well. The Prince hadn't gone far enough for him—Klaus said that he himself would have been even more severe. And he took another jab at me, saying that he couldn't imagine a Czech ambassador behaving this way.

It was time for me to go back to Prague.

I told my mom to remember that she had promised to visit when this all worked out. She made a disparaging remark about my sense of humor, admonished me to be careful, told me that she loved me, and sent me on my way.

⌣⟶

THE flight back to Prague was a long one. I sweated it out, not knowing what would await me upon my return to the palace. But by the time I ascended the formal staircase beneath the tapestry of Jason, the situation had turned 180 degrees in our favor.

The DOST march on the embassy had been the tipping point. Bátora's ultimate boss, Prime Minister Petr Nečas, watched incredulously on television with the rest of the country as one of his subordinates strode up to the embassy of the Czech Republic's most important ally to deliver unauthorized hate mail. Nečas publicly denounced Bátora, saying that Bátora did not represent the government and must behave like an official, not an activist. Nečas mocked the whole controversy, saying that it was unnecessarily dramatized, hysterical, and blown up, the product of *okurková sezóna*—cucumber season. (August was the time of the cucumber harvest, which in Czech lore causes people to behave foolishly.)

The prime minister then upped the ante, demanding that the education minister fire Bátora. The Prince and the cochair of his party joined in, calling Bátora "an old fascist." Not to be outdone, Bátora declared that the Prince was an "old lame duck," and a "sorry little old man" and suggested that he would challenge the Prince to a duel but couldn't, for at least three reasons, which he left unspecified. He was soon demoted, and, not too long after that, he was out of a job.

The prime minister hammered his point home by very visibly hosting a visiting American business leader and me a few days later. The media turned up, snapping photographs of me and the prime minister shaking hands. Journalists wrote that the public conflict between Bátora and me had been the precipitating event that had driven the whole affair forward and a "crucial" moment in the Czechs' confronting extremism. Little did they know that I had been eating stuffed cabbage in LA with my mother at the peak of the conflict.

It emerged that Czech ambassadors elsewhere had endorsed Pride events, putting the lie to Klaus's claim that no ambassador of his country would behave as I had. That, the prime minister's admonitions, and Bátora's behavior, quieted Klaus down. Perhaps he sensed the political winds shifting against him. Whatever the reason, he moved on to other topics. Eventually, my invitations to his jazz evenings at the castle even resumed. He welcomed me cordially, as if the whole controversy had never occurred. It was my job to reciprocate, and I did.

A *New York Times* story about the dispute said that Klaus had been left isolated. It proclaimed the flap to be a victory for tolerance. But the reporter admitted confusion about one thing: why the American ambassador had ended up as a central figure.

My mother, a loyal *Times* reader, phoned me to discuss that.

"The reporter should've called me. I could have told him why!" she said, letting out a little laugh.

"See, it all worked out," I replied. "Truth prevailed! You are a diplomatic genius. So," I added, "when are you coming to see us?"

"Let's pick a date," she answered.

Sources and Acknowledgments

This book is built upon three years of research that I undertook in more than thirty archives in multiple countries after leaving my ambassadorship in August 2014. I also conducted dozens of interviews and explored voluminous secondary sources. I benefited from the extraordinary cooperation of the descendants of each of my protagonists; of scholars and experts in each of the eras I write about; and of my wonderful global team of research assistants. They included native speakers of Czech and German, and the work would have been impossible without them, because my grasp of the former language is imperfect and the latter even more so.

All of that enabled me to write of long-ago events in detail. But there was a downside: notes and a bibliography far too voluminous for full inclusion in the print edition of the book. They can be found in toto at www.normaneisen.com/TheLastPalace/Endmatter. The condensed notes that follow below source all quotations and some critical points. Everything else can be found online. The bibliography and full list of archives are available there only.

An army of people helped bring this volume into being and I am deeply grateful to them all. Foremost among them: my friend Daniel Berger, who encouraged me daily when this book was being written and supported it in every way; Brookings and in particular my colleague Darrell West, who was an early champion of the book (and of me) at that institution; my agent Eric Simonoff of William Morris Endeavor, whose excitement about my rough concept propelled it forward, including landing it in the hands of my wonderful publisher, Molly Stern, and her team at Crown; my first editor there, the incredible Domenica Alioto, who worked with me page by page to find the words to animate the people and their stories, and who remade the book with her suggestion (er, demand) that I weave my mother's life in; Domenica's successor at Crown, Claire Potter, who took over when the first draft was complete and brilliantly polished it into final form; my Crown production editor extraordinaire, Chris Tanigawa, so tolerant of my excessive tinkering; my lead research assistant at Brookings, Andrew Kenealy, whose joyful labors made this book as much his as it is mine; our Brookings research colleagues Kelsey Landau, Carolyn Taratko, and Curtlyn Kramer; my lead research assistants in Prague, Mikuláš Pešta and Carmen Rubovičová, and Forum 2000 and its director Jakub Klepal for providing them and me support; our European research colleagues Petr Brod, Jürgen Förster, Julia Gulatee, Kristýna Kaucká, Friederike Krüger, Susanne (Krüger) Maier, Martina Sedláčková, and Adéla Vondrovicová; Otto's Petschek's daughter, Eva Petschek Goldmann, grandchildren Peter Goldmann and Andrea Klainer, great-grandson Marc Robinson, nephew Robert Gellert and grand-nephew David Spohngellert, whose great help stood out even among the warm cooperation of the other Petschek relations named online; Rudolf Toussaint's grandson Alexander Toussaint, Laurence Steinhardt's granddaughter Laurene Sherlock and nephew Peter Rosenblatt, Shirley Temple Black's son, Charles Black Jr., her daughter Susan Black Falaschi, and Curtis Grisham, all of whom provided truly extraordinary assistance; Lital Beer, Rita Margolin and their colleagues at Yad Vashem in Jerusalem, for their invaluable research help; my family, including my mother, Frieda Eisen, wife, Lindsay Kaplan, daughter, Tamar Eisen, mother-in-law, Anne Kaplan, and cousins Moshe and Mordechai Schiff; and the experts who were kind enough to read and comment on drafts, Hillel Kieval (part one), Igor Lukes (parts two and three), Paul Wilson (part four), Leon Weiseltier (entire book), and Al Kamen (entire book). I am immensely appreciative of their aid, though any errors are solely my own. Thanks also to the many others who helped and who are named online.

The opinions and characterizations in this book are those of the author and do not necessarily represent official positions of the United States government.

Notes

As explained in the Sources and Acknowledgements, the following notes are highly condensed due to space constraints. Full notes and a bibliography can be found at www.NormanEisen.com/TheLastPalace/Endmatter.

Abbreviations

AP6	Department of Construction, Archive of Municipal District Prague 6
BAMA	Bundesarchiv Militärarchiv, Freiburg
BFA	Black Family Archive
BHSA	Bayerisches Hauptstaatsarchiv, Munich
ČNB	Archiv České národní banky, Prague
DEPL	Dwight D. Eisenhower Presidential Library, Abilene, Kansas
EPGC	Eva Petschek Goldmann Collection, Petschek Family Archives
FBIS	Foreign Broadcast Information Service
LOC	Library of Congress, Washington, DC
MFA	Archiv Ministerstva zahrančních věcí, Prague
MRC	Marc Robinson Collection, Petschek Family Archives
NARA	National Archives and Records Administration, College Park, Maryland
NSA	National Security Archive, Washington, DC
PadAA	Politisches Archiv des Auswärtigen Amts, Berlin
PFA	Petschek Family Archives
SFA	Steinhardt Family Archive
SOA	Státní oblastní archiv, Prague
TFA	Toussaint Family Archive
VHA	Vojenský historický archiv, Prague

Prologue

2 **first-generation Czech-Jewish American:** For the sake of concision, I use the adjective "Czech" interchangeably as shorthand to reference Czechoslovakia (as in this instance), the Czech Republic, the Czech lands (including Bohemia, Moravia, and a portion of Silesia), the residents of those lands, and the language they speak.

3 **one hundred rooms:** My count includes rooms on all five floors.

4 **"Truth and love will prevail":** "Living in Truth," *Economist,* December 31, 2011.

4 **"truth-and-lovism":** Michael Žantovský, *Havel: A Life* (New York: Grove Press, 2014), 456.

1 | THE GOLDEN SON OF THE GOLDEN CITY

13   **a thirty-nine-year-old man:** Eva Petschek Goldmann, daughter of Otto and Martha Petschek, interview by the author, New York City, March 14, 2014; Andrea Goldmann Klainer and Peter Goldmann, telephone interview by the author, October 20, 2017. My interview with Eva in 2014 was informed by a number of previous conversations that I had with her between 2011 and 2014, and the citations to it herein incorporate those prior contacts.

13   **After eleven years:** See, e.g., letter, Otto to Martha, n.d., item 38, Marc Robinson Collection, Petschek Family Archives (henceforth MRC). Item numbers for Otto and Martha's correspondence simply refer to the pagination order in the respective collections of the materials presented to me; the letters are not preserved in chronological or other order. Items from the Petschek Family Archive that do not belong to a specific collection are noted simply as PFA.

13   **a remaining slice of wilderness:** Eva Penerova, "The House on Zikmund Winter Street," unpublished manuscript, 3.

13   **accumulated multiple plots:** For details of the family property consolidation in Prague-Bubeneč, see Pavel Zahradník, "Dějiny domu"; Pozemkové knihy Bubenče, entry 36 and entry 379, Prague Cadastral Office; box 427, Soupis písemností "A" Bankovního domu Petschek a spol, Státní oblastní archiv Praha (henceforth SOA); and Penerova, "The House," 3. Unless otherwise specified, all references to documents from the SOA are from the above collection.

14   **He had spent years walking:** Letter, Otto to Martha, n.d., item 174, Eva Petschek Goldmann Collection, PFA (hereafter EPGC).

14   **a model citizen:** "History of the Petschek and Gellert Families," March 1946, PFA, 9–23. For an abbreviated draft of this document in the public domain, see "History of the Petschek-Gellert Family," November 15, 1945, box 8, Bernard Yarrow Papers, 1907–1973 (henceforth Yarrow Papers), Dwight D. Eisenhower Presidential Library, Abilene, KS (henceforth DEPL).

14   **Music was likely running:** Eva Petschek Goldmann, interview by the author; Marc Robinson, interview by the author, New Haven, CT, November 6, 2017.

14   **It was his first great passion:** Robert B. Goldmann, *Wayward Threads* (Evanston, IL: Northwestern University Press, 1997), 134; letter, J. Eger to Mr. Petschek, December 12, 1945, box 8, Yarrow Papers, DEPL.

14   **more than one hundred rooms:** House no. 181, Department of Construction, Archive of Municipal District Prague 6 (henceforth AP6); Eva Petschek Goldmann, "The Otto Petschek Compound," unpublished manuscript, n.d.

15   **a residence befitting:** See, e.g., Karel Kratochvíl, *Bankéři* (Prague: Nakladatelství politické literatury, 1962).

15   **an embodiment of the twentieth:** Eva Petschek Goldmann, interview by the author; Klainer and P. Goldmann, telephone interview, October 20, 2017; Robert Gellert, Otto's nephew, interview by the author, New York City, February 2, 2015.

15   **born in 1882:** Otto Petschek's birth certificate can be found in box 502/2, SOA. Census documents show where the family lived in 1890 and 1910, including all household members' names—all kept at Archiv hlavního města Prahy. The details of Otto's childhood are from Eva Petschek Goldmann, interview by the author. Details are corroborated in Viktor Petschek, interview by Marc Robinson, n.d.; and Eric K. Petschek, *Reminiscences* (Bloomington, IN: Xlibris, 2010).

17   **Watchers of Prague:** The term is my own, but the phenomenon is age old. See

Karla Huebner, "Prague Flânerie from Neruda to Nezval," in Richard Wrigley, ed., *The Flâneur Abroad: Historical and International Perspectives* (Newcastle: Cambridge Scholars, 2014), 281–97.

18   **In the years following:** See, e.g., Kateřina Čapková, *Czechs, Germans, Jews? National Identity and the Jews of Bohemia*, trans. Derek Paton and Marzia Paton (New York: Berghahn Books, 2012).

18   **Anti-Semitic pamphlets:** Livia Rothkirchen, *The Jews of Bohemia & Moravia: Facing the Holocaust* (Lincoln: University of Nebraska Press, 2005), 17.

19   **Leopold Hilsner:** Ibid. For the anti-Semitic and anti-German riots at the time, see Hillel Kieval, *Languages of Community: The Jewish Experience in the Czech Lands* (Berkeley: University of California Press, 2000), 167–70.

19   **The fin de siècle waves:** Petschek, *Reminiscences*, 26.

19   **They decided to flee:** "United Continental Corporation: History and Background," n.d., PFA, 22. For the economic activities of the Petschek family, see boxes 1 and 25, "Bankovní dům Petschek a spol., 1868–1988," Archiv České národní banky, Prague (henceforth ČNB); and boxes 415 and 388, SOA. Unless otherwise specified, all references to documents from the ČNB are from this collection.

19   **Otto took a more optimistic view:** Eva Petschek Goldmann, interview by the author.

19   **He wanted to train:** Ina Petschek, daughter of Otto and Martha Petschek, interview by Marc Robinson, n.d.

20   **"10 days in Vienna":** Letter, Otto to Isidor and Camilla, December 31, 1900, item 64, MRC.

20   **They sent him:** For Otto's matriculation, see Archiv Univerzity Karlovy, Matriky Německé univerzity v Praze, inventární číslo 3, Matrika doktorů německé Karlo-Ferdinandovy univerzity v Praze/Německé univerzity v Praze, (1904–1924), folios 42 and 132. For his other university records, see box 502/2, SOA.

21   **"intellectual sawdust":** Reiner Stach, *Kafka: The Early Years*, trans. Shelley Frisch (Princeton, NJ: Princeton University Press, 2016), 248.

22   **"I had to go away":** Letter, Otto to Martha, July 17, 1912, item 1, EPGC.

22   **She had a kindness:** Sylvia Hoag, granddaughter of Otto and Martha Petschek, interview by the author, La Mesa, CA, December 22, 2015 (conveying information from her father, Viktor); Eric Petschek, nephew of Otto and Martha Petschek, interview by the author, Darien, CT, March 16, 2015.

22   **"Why not marry Martha?":** Letter, Otto to Martha, n.d., item 60, MRC.

23   **"a big realist":** Letter, Otto to Martha, August 7, 1912, item 47, MRC.

23   **"In such moments":** Ibid.

23   **"'Thank God'":** E.g., letter, Martha to Camilla, June 4, 1928, item 183, EPGC.

23   **"By the way":** Letter, Otto to Martha, August 7, 1912, item 47, MRC.

24   **"Encouraged by your best present":** Letter, Otto to Martha, August 8, 1912, MRC.

24   **"My Mama always says":** Letter, Otto to Martha, July 29, 1912, item 4, EPGC.

24   **Prague's affluent Jews:** Helena Krejčová and Mario Vlček, *Výkupné za život: Vývozy a vynucené dary uměleckých předmětů při emigraci židů z Čech a Moravy v letech 1938–1942 (na příkladu Uměleckoprůmyslového Musea v Praze)* (Prague: Dokumentační centrum pro převod majetku z kulturních statků obětí druhé světové války, 2009), 366.

25   **"Madam, would you like":** Letter, Otto to Martha, n.d., item 174, EPGC; letter, Otto to Martha, October 25, 1916, item 10, EPGC.

26   **"It's FLOWING":** E.g., letter, Otto to Martha, n.d., item 76, EPGC.

26 **"HRDLS":** E.g., letter, Otto to Martha, n.d., item 161, EPGC.

26 *der Hund:* Letter, Otto to Martha, n.d., item 109, EPGC, among others.

28 **He wandered the halls:** V. Petschek, interview.

29 **"schlmiel" and "won't listen":** Letter, Otto to Martha, n.d., item 7, EPGC; ibid., item 102.

29 **"They are sitting":** Ibid., item 19.

29 **"the child is born":** Letter, Otto to Martha, n.d., item 62, MRC.

29 **"Much to Papa's":** Ibid., item 68.

29 **"Papa was very surprised":** Ibid., item 7; letter, Otto to Martha, n.d., item 68, MRC.

30 **"No Mama, no Papa here":** Ibid., item 113.

30 **"My dear Burschischi":** Letter, Otto to Viktor, n.d., item 22, MRC.

30 **"A thousand and more kisses":** Letter, Otto to Martha, n.d., item 7, EPGC.

30 **"I finally concluded":** Letter, Otto to Martha, n.d., item 120, EPGC.

31 **"Rip up the letter":** Letter, Otto to Martha, c. September 1917, item 25, MRC.

31 **"was so wet":** Letter, Otto to Martha, n.d., item 16, EPGC.

32 **"I'm having the garage":** Letter, Otto to Martha, n.d., item 62, EPGC.

32 **"Now that the wall":** Letter, Otto to Martha, n.d., item 101, EPGC.

32 **"very imprudent":** Ibid., item 56.

33 **"Please arrange through Mama":** Ibid., item 181.

33 **"Hold me or I am going to jump":** Letter, Otto to Martha, n.d., item 59, MRC.

33 **"Bubeneč has been finished":** Ibid., item 44; letter, Otto to Martha, n.d., item 117, EPGC.

33 **"What is the difference":** Letter, Otto to Martha, n.d., item 147, EPGC.

33 **"high hopes for peace":** Ibid., item 143.

34 **a young Czech journalist:** Zbyněk Zeman and Antonín Klimek, *The Life of Edvard Benes, 1884–1948: Czechoslovakia in Peace and War* (Oxford, UK: Clarendon Press, 1997), 21–33.

35 *mischpoche:* Letter, Otto to Martha, n.d., item 31, MRC.

35 **"didn't realize that young people":** Ibid., item 66.

36 **"the Jewish power":** *Štít národa* 2, no. 22 (December 1, 1921): 4.

36 **"Where these Jews":** "Světová katastrofa uhlím," *Čech,* November 5, 1920.

36 **The anti-Semitism was not confined:** Hillel Kieval, *The Making of Czech Jewry: National Conflict and Jewish Society in Bohemia, 1870–1918* (New York and Oxford, UK: Oxford University Press, 1988), 185–86.

36 **"most serious ideological antagonist":** Tomáš Masaryk, *Constructive Sociological Theory,* Alan Woolfolk and Jonathan B. Timber, eds. (New Brunswick, NJ: Transaction Publishers, 1994), 6.

36 *"mir viln Beneš":* My mother, whose religious family always said grace after meals, recalled this jest.

36 **Both were Enlightenment thinkers:** Zeman and Klimek, *The Life of Edvard Benes,* 11; P. Goldmann, telephone interview, October 20, 2017.

36 **Beneš dined with the magnate:** Penerova, "The House," 20.

2 | The King of Coal

39 **She was firmly opposed:** Eva Petschek Goldmann, interview by the author; Klainer, telephone interview, October 23, 2017; Hoag, interview.

40 **For assistance, he turned:** Box 464, SOA; L. Späth, ed., *Späth-Buch, 1720–1920. Geschichte und Erzeugnisse der Späth'schen Baumschule* (Berlin: Mosse, 1920).

41 **It became an instant:** Hoag, interview.

41 **But the harder:** Barbara Kafka and Doris Kafka, granddaughters of Otto and Martha Petschek, interview by the author, Washington, DC, March 20, 2015.

42 **For his architect:** Martin Ebel and Helena Vágnerová, *Otto Petschek's Residence: Two Faces of an Entrepreneur's Villa in Prague,* Prague, Czech Republic, Exhibition by the National Technical Museum and US Embassy in Prague, November 28, 2012–March 31, 2013; Zdeněk Lukeš, *Splátka dluhu: Praha a její německy hovořící architekti 1900–1938* (Prague: Fraktály, 2002), 182–185; box 14, ČNB.

42 **Spielmann rolled out:** House no. 181, Department of Construction, AP6.

43 **Yet Otto approved:** Boxes 493/2 and 512, SOA.

43 **"FLOWING":** Letter, Otto to Martha, n.d., item 76, EPGC.

44 **He bristled:** Prague City Hall, reference no. III-38533/29, October 3, 1929, House no. 181, Department of Construction, AP6.

48 **Otto confronted Spielmann:** I first heard of this story from John Ordway, the interim chargé d'affaires at the US embassy in Prague in 2010, and it has also survived among the Petschek descendants; details were corroborated by, e.g., P. Goldmann, interview, October 23, 2017. It was also repeatedly shared with me by today's Watchers of Prague during my time in that city. It is, I believe, reflected in the dramatic change in the deflection of the palace at this time and corroborated in part by the existence of models of the palace; see Zahradník, "Dějiny domu," 15.

49 **The ashen-faced architect:** See John Ordway, "Villa Petschek—the American Ambassador's Residence in Prague," unpublished manuscript, June 8, 2011, updated December 30, 2015, 7. Ambassador Ordway questions whether the breaking of the model might be an apocryphal story, and indeed it might; I credit it as authentic for the reasons set forth in the preceding note.

50 **"performed without an official permit":** Boxes 386, 493/1 and 493/2, SOA.

50 **"to immediately apply":** Zahradník, "Dějiny domu," 7–8; House no. 181, AP6.

50 **"Building is continuous in the Bubeneč ":** "Bankhaus Petschek," *Štít národa 6,* no. 18 (November 1, 1925): 4.

50 **"I refused":** Letter, Otto to Martha, n.d., EPGC (this letter was not assigned an item number in the collection).

51 **"[E]ither I don't love someone":** Letter, Otto to Martha, n.d., item 129, EPGC.

51 **Spielmann's signature appeared:** Zahradník, "Dějiny domu," 11.

52 **"trashy literature exchange":** Letter, Otto to Martha, n.d., item 5, MRC.

53 **lists of notes and inspirations:** These lists can still be found in the Zinc Room of the Villa Petschek. Unless otherwise specified, all descriptions of Otto's architectural notes and sketches derive from the originals still held in the Villa Petschek.

53 **The City of Prague:** Prague City Hall, reference no. 21244-III/27, October 26, 1927, House no. 181, Department of Construction, AP6.

53 **why he tore out:** Kratochvíl, *Bankéři,* 244–46. Details about the fortune-teller come from, e.g., Eva Petschek Goldmann, interview by the author.

54 **"You don't treat me like an adult":** Letter, Otto to Martha, n.d., item 130, EPGC.

54 **a musical guessing game:** Eva Petschek Goldmann, unpublished manuscript, July 1985, 4.

54 **"The Hund again":** Letter, Otto to Martha, n.d., item 109, EPGC.

54 **"only taking responsibility":** Letter, Otto to Martha, January 1927, item 66, MRC.

55 *"Römer! Mitbürger! Freunde!"*: V. Petschek, interview.

55 **"Rogue, blackguard"**: These exchanges are jotted in the margins of Viky's copy of a biography in English of Queen Victoria (Lytton Strachey, *Queen Victoria* [London, UK: Chatto & Windus, 1922]) held in the Villa Petschek.

55 **"Ottolini"**: Petschek, *Reminiscences*, 28.

55 **an obscure politician**: Volker Ullrich, *Hitler: Ascent, 1889–1939*, trans. Jefferson Chase (New York: Knopf, 2016), 189, 200.

59 **"I told you so"s**: Eva Petschek Goldmann, interview by the author.

59 **ask them for the money**: Petschek, *Reminiscences*, 56; Gellert, interview, February 10, 2015.

60 **"schlmiel"**: Letter, Otto to Martha, n.d., item 7, EPGC.

60 **"Uncle Nazi"**: Petschek, *Reminiscences*, 31.

60 **Otto fought back**: Eva Petschek Goldmann, interview by the author; Klainer and P. Goldmann, telephone interview, November 2, 2017.

3 | PALACE NEVERENDING

61 **Otto walked up the steps**: Eva Petschek Goldmann, interview by the author.

63 **By October 1929**: Details of the villa's progress by 1929 are from Ebel and Vágnerová, *Otto Petschek's Residence;* Zahradník, "Dějiny domu," 12–16; and Prague City Hall, reference no. III-1835/29, January 1929, House no. 181, Department of Construction, AP6.

64 **managed to dodge**: Robert Goldmann, husband of Eva Petschek Goldmann, interview by the author, New York City, March 31, 2016.

64 **the labor actions targeting Otto**: Marie Čutková, ed., *Mostecké drama: Svědectví novinářů, spisovatelů a pokrokové veřejnosti o velké mostecké stávce roku 1932* (Prague: Mladá Fronta, 1972).

64 **"You say that we are under"**: Klement Gottwald, *Klement Gottwald v roce 1929: Některé projevy a články* (Prague: Svoboda, 1950), 118–35.

65 **"The biggest Czechoslovak capitalist"**: National Assembly of the Czechoslovak Republic, Chamber of Deputies, 128th meeting, June 18, 1931, *Digital Library of the Czech Parliament*, http://www.psp.cz/eknih/1929ns/ps/stenprot/128schuz/s128006.htm.

65 **"Maryčka Magdonova"**: "Maryčka Magdonova" was written by Petr Bezruč. The story of the Petschek daughters comes from Marc Robinson, interview by the author, New York City, October 19, 2017, and is corroborated by his notes of his conversations with them, e.g., I. Petschek, interview.

67 **"Now you will get mad"**: Letter, Otto to Martha, n.d., item 166, EPGC.

67 **"My dear Dumme!"**: Ibid., item 54.

67 **moving into the palace**: Zahradník, "Dějiny domu," 17–18; Prague City Hall, reference no. 49881/30, December 29, 1930, House no. 181, Department of Construction, AP6; boxes 329/1, SOA.

68 **June 1931**: Penerova, "The House," 8.

68 **Otto proudly led them**: Eva Petschek Goldmann, interview by the author.

69 **He and Martha hosted**: All details, unless otherwise specified, regarding Otto and Martha's dinner parties are from Penerova, "The House," 9, 12, 13–14, 20.

70 **"would have killed me"**: V. Petschek, interview.

71 **Otto's forbidding mien**: P. Goldmann and Klainer, interview by the author, New York City, March 25, 2015; Ruth Stein, niece of Otto and Martha Petschek, interview by the author, Washington, DC, February 8, 2015.

71 **"It's relaxing"**: Stein, interview.

71 **no fonder of it**: Zdeněk Lukeš, architecture critic, interview by the author, Prague, August 5, 2016; and, e.g., National Assembly of the Czechoslovak Republic, Chamber of Deputies, 128th meeting, June 18, 1931, *Digital Library of the Czech Parliament*, http://www.psp.cz/eknih/1929ns/ps/stenprot/128schuz/s128006.htm.

71 **$100 million today**: This figure is from Penerova, "The House," 8.

72 **his groans were heard**: Professor Dr. Herrnheiser, "Results of X-ray Examination of Otto Petschek," September 8, 1931, PFA.

73 **The tall, balding, silent Czech**: Penerova, "The House," 15, 16; Jan Hájek and Miroslav Hájek, great-nephews of Adolf Pokorný, interview by Mikuláš Pešta, Prague, November 15, 2017.

73 **sensation returned**: Professor Dr. Herrnheiser, "Results of X-ray Examination of Otto Petschek," November 26, 1931, PFA.

74 **just under seven million**: Zora Pryor, "Czechoslovak Economic Development in the Interwar Period," in Victor S. Mamatey and Radomír V. Luža, eds., *A History of the Czechoslovak Republic 1918–1948* (Princeton, NJ: Princeton University Press, 1973), 188–215.

74 **"The Czech government"**: Čutková, *Mostecké drama*, 43.

75 **Masaryk had returned the favor**: "Petschek & Co.," *Knihy znovunalezené*, September 6, 2016, http://knihyznovunalezene.eu/en/vlastnici/petschek.html.

75 **Otto was asked to represent Czechoslovakia**: "Report concerning the choice of the Czechoslovak member of the Administration Board of the High Commissariat for Refugees by the League of Nations," November 10, 1933, box 926, 3. Společnost národů, II. politická sekce, Archiv Ministerstva zahraničních věcí, Prague (henceforth MFA).

75 **the Nazi Party had become**: See, e.g., Ian Kershaw, *Hitler 1889–1936: Hubris* (New York: Norton, 1998), 497–591.

76 **The floodwaters of Nazism**: Eva Petschek Goldmann recalled that Fräulein Fürst departed earlier in the 1930s; Penerova seems to place it later in the decade. Due to the uncertainty I have placed this event in a freestanding section and not assigned it a precise date.

77 **seems to have believed**: "United Continental Corporation: History and Background," PFA, 40.

77 **Not all the Petscheks**: Gellert, interview, February 10, 2015; Petschek, *Reminiscences,* 75–77; Penerova, "The House," 20–21.

78 **"He already looks like an Englishman"**: Letter, Otto to Martha, c. 1930, item 161, EPGC.

79 **Asperin von Sternberg**: Rita Petschek, daughter of Otto and Martha Petschek, interview by Marc Robinson, n.d.

81 **"[N]o stairs to the basement"**: Prague City Hall, reference no. 379264/34, August 11, 1934, House no. 181, Department of Construction, AP6; Zahradník, "Dějiny domu," 19.

4 | THE FINAL CHILD

82 **"The Petscheks are gone!"**: Quotations and the other details in this chapter are based on my conversations with my mother over many years. I am grateful to Denisa Vinanska of Sobrance for her many exchanges with me regarding the history of the town. To corroborate my mother's recollections of Sobrance, I relied upon Lýdia Gačková et al., *Dejiny Sobraniec,* eds. Peter Kónya and Martin Mol-

nár (Prešov: Vydavateľstvo Prešovskej univerzity v Prešove pre mestský úrad v Sobranciach, 2013).

5 | AN ARTIST OF WAR

101 **The black diplomatic Mercedes:** For the time and destination of the vehicle, see cable, Eisenlohr and Toussaint to the German Foreign Ministry and the War Ministry, Prague, May 21, 1938, 9:30 p.m., *Documents on German Foreign Policy, 1918–1945. From the Archives of the German Foreign Ministry (DGFP)*, series D, vol. 2 (Washington, DC: United States Government Printing Office, 1949), no. 182: 309–11; and Andor Hencke, *Augenzeuge einer Tragödie. Diplomatenjahren in Prag, 1936–1939* (Munich: Fides Verlagsgesellschaft, 1977), 90–92. Germany maintained a *Gesandtschaft* (legation) in Prague. For the make of Toussaint's official car, see memo by Eisenlohr, February 9, 1937, RAV Prag 6, Politisches Archiv des Auswärtigen Amtes (henceforth PAdAA).

101 **forty-seven years old:** Personalbogen, Rudolf Toussaint OP 61643, Bayerisches Hauptstaatsarchiv (henceforth BHSA). This description is based on photographs of Toussaint from the late 1930s, shared by Alexander Toussaint, his grandson: Toussaint Family Archive (TFA). Additional details about Toussaint's appearance are drawn from a lengthy interview with Alexander, conducted by the author in Prague on August 7–8, 2016. That conversation incorporated information from numerous other talks with him in 2015 and 2016; all are collectively cited here as "Alexander Toussaint, interviews."

101 **Limousines were waiting:** Eva Petschek Goldmann, interview by the author; Gellert, interview by the author, February 10, 2015; and B. Kafka and D. Kafka, interview by the author, Washington, DC, October 16, 2015.

102 **He had trained as an artist:** Toussaint defense, War Crimes Trial, October 25, 1948, Prague, LS 804/48, box 881, SOA.

102 **That watchfulness:** Ibid.; Alexander Toussaint, interviews.

102 **hurtling toward conflict:** Igor Lukes, *Czechoslovakia Between Stalin and Hitler: The Diplomacy of Edvard Beneš in the 1930s* (New York: Oxford University Press, 1996), 148–57; Detlef Brandes, *Die Tschechen unter deutschem Protektorat: Besatzungspolitik, Kollaboration und Widerstand im Protektorat Böhmen und Mähren von Heydrichs Tod bis zum Prager Aufstand,* part 2 (Munich and Vienna: Oldenbourg, 2008).

102 **To try to defuse it:** Hencke, *Augenzeuge,* 90.

102 **Toussaint hated war:** Alexander Toussaint, interviews.

102 **He had survived:** Personalbogen, Rudolf Toussaint OP 61643, BHSA.

102 **Toussaint knew that the Czechs:** Letter, Toussaint to supervisor in Berlin, March 26, 1938, RH 22934, 35–36, Bundesarchiv Militärarchiv Freiburg (henceforth BAMA).

102 **Today's Czech military:** Detlef Brandes, *Die Sudetendeutschen im Krisenjahr 1938* (Munich: Oldenbourg, 2009).

102 **If the Czechs:** Peter Hoffmann, *History of the German Resistance, 1933–1945*, trans. Richard Barry (Montreal: McGill–Queen's University Press, 1996), 51.

102 **Toussaint hoped to:** Cable, Newton to Halifax, August 17, 1938, in E. L. Woodward, Rohan Butler, and Margaret Lambert, eds., *Documents on British Foreign Policy, 1919–1939 (DBFP)*, series 3, vol. 2, no. 675, 1938 (London: His Majesty's Stationery Office, 1949), 144.

103 **contacted him frequently:** Cable, Newton to Halifax, November 1, 1938, *DBFP,* Series 3, vol. 3, no. 253–55.

103 **But his transfer application:** "Topographisches Büro to Bayerisches Ministe-
rium für Militärische Angelegenheiten," May 17, 1919, OP 61643 (49), BHSA.

103 **In 1936, Toussaint was serving:** Memo from the Foreign Office, October 13,
1936, RAV Prag 6, PAdAA; memo of the General Staff, October 10, 1936, Rudolf
Toussaint personnel file, Personalbogen 6/371, BAMA.

104 **Like others who:** See Toussaint defense, War Crimes Trial, SOA; Hencke,
Augenzeuge, 148.

104 **Her brother had:** Alexander Toussaint, interviews.

104 **the German legation notified:** Cable, German Foreign Office to the German
legation in Prague, October 8, 1936; see RAV Prag 6, PAdAA.

104 **Toussaint was met with:** Internal memo, German legation in Prague, November 9, 1936, RAV Prag 6, PAdAA.

104 **When the government organized:** Letter, Toussaint to supervisor (name illegible), November 25, 1937, RH 2/2934 (28), BAMA.

105 **In February 1937:** Memo by Eisenlohr, February 9, 1937, RAV Prag 6, PAdAA.

105 **The following October:** Ibid., October 12, 1937, RAV Prag 6, PAdAA.

105 **he had fallen in love:** Alexander Toussaint, interviews.

105 **He worked out a compromise:** Cable, German legation in Prague to German
Foreign Ministry, April 22, 1938, RAV Prag 6, PAdAA.

105 **"situation was":** Cable, Toussaint to supervisor, November 5, 1937, RH 2/2934
(20), BAMA.

105 **Privately, Berlin instructed:** Lukes, *Czechoslovakia Between Stalin and Hitler,*
122.

106 *Ehrenwort:* Ibid., 125–26.

106 **"according to information":** Memo by Bismarck, Berlin, March 16, 1938, *DGFP,*
series D, vol. 2 (1937–1945) (Washington, DC: Government Printing Office,
1949), no. 85: 169.

106 **"knew nothing of such preparations":** Ibid.

106 **This was what:** Letter, Toussaint to supervisor, March 18, 1938, RH 2/2934 (33–
34), BAMA.

107 *"Ein Volk, ein Reich":* Brandes, *Die Sudetendeutschen,* 312–15.

107 **On May 19:** Lukes, *Czechoslovakia Between Stalin and Hitler,* 143–57; Alfred Jodl
diary entry, August 24, 1938, Records of the Office of the US Chief Counsel for
the Prosecution of Axis Criminality, Defense Document Books, Alfred Jodl, JO
14, National Archives and Records Administration at College Park, MD (henceforth NARA); and Affidavit of Infantry General Rudolf Toussaint, April 3, 1946,
Records of the Office of the US Chief Counsel for the Prosecution of Axis Criminality, Defense Document Books, Alfred Jodl, JO 62, NARA.

107 **placards were pasted up:** Hencke, *Augenzeuge,* 87.

107 **he called his contact:** Cable, Eisenlohr and Toussaint to the German Foreign
Ministry and the War Ministry, *DGFP,* series D, vol. 2, no. 182: 309–10; Hencke,
Augenzeuge, 90.

107 **"for the restoration":** Cable, Eisenlohr and Toussaint to the German Foreign
Ministry and the War Ministry, *DGFP,* series D, vol. 2, no. 182: 310.

107 **"provisionally concerned":** Ibid.

108 **At six p.m.:** Hencke, *Augenzeuge,* 91.

108 **Toussaint described:** Cable, Eisenlohr and Toussaint to the German Foreign
Ministry and the War Ministry, May 21, 1938, *DGFP,* series D, vol. 2, no. 182:
309–11; Hencke, *Augenzeuge,* 90–92.

108 **"irrefutable proof":** Ibid.

109 **At 10:50 p.m.:** Cable, Eisenlohr and Toussaint to German Foreign Ministry, May 21, 1938, *DGFP,* series D, vol. 2, no. 183: 311.

109 **Red Defense:** Cable, Eisenlohr to Foreign Office and War Ministry, May 23, 1938, no. 161, Berlin R 29756 (Tschechoslowakei), PAdAA.

109 **Toussaint and Hitler:** Cable, Newton to Halifax, November 1, 1938, *DBFP,* series 3, vol. 3, 253–55.

109 **"the brown-eyed":** Alexander Toussaint, interviews.

109 **As tensions rose:** Cable, Newton to Halifax, November 1, 1938, *DBFP,* series 3, vol. 3, no. 286: 253–55.

109 **On Monday, May 23:** Hencke, *Augenzeuge,* 101.

110 **The ceremony would be held:** See Brandes, *Die Sudetendeutschen,* 157–58.

110 **Toussaint and his colleagues :** Hencke, *Augenzeuge,* 101.

110 **He was ordered:** Vlastimil Klíma, *1938: Měli jsme kapitulovat?,* Robert Kvaček, Josef Tomeš, and Richard Vašek, eds. (Prague: NLN-Nakladatelství lidové noviny, 2012), 21.

111 **Toussaint maintained a military salute:** Photograph, Berliner Verlag/Archive (ČTK Fotobanka: Third Reich–Sudetenland Crisis 1938).

111 **He placed first one wreath:** G. E. R. Gedye, "Fiery Talks Mark Sudetens' Funeral," *New York Times,* May 26, 1938.

111 **"It is not my intention to smash":** Wilhelm Keitel, *Generalfeldmarshall Keitel. Verbrecher oder Offizier? Erinnerungen, Briefe, Dokumente des Chefs OKW,* ed. Walter Görlitz (Göttingen: Musterschmidt Verlag, 1961), 183; William L. Shirer, *The Rise and Fall of the Third Reich: A History of Nazi Germany* (New York: Simon & Schuster, 1960), 365.

111 **"It is my unalterable decision to smash":** Letter, Hitler and Keitel to von Brauchitsch, Raeder, and Göring, May 20, 1938, States Exhibit no. 69, Nuremberg Trial Proceedings, vol. 3, Eleventh Day, December 3, 1945, item 11, 16 English version, *The Avalon Project at the Yale Law School: Documents in Law, History and Diplomacy,* http://avalon.law.yale.edu/imt/12-03-45.asp.

111 **"The situation":** Letter, Toussaint to superior in Berlin, June 1, 1938, RH 2/2934 (45), BAMA.

112 **"Negotiations between the government":** Letter, Toussaint to superior in Berlin, August 17, 1938, RH 2/2934 (47–52), BAMA.

112 **"We must":** Report by Henlein, March 28, 1938, *DGFP,* series D, vol. 2, no. 107: 197.

112 **At the end of the summer:** E.g., cable, Newton to Halifax, August 23, 1938, *DBFP,* series 3, vol. 2, no. 675, 143–46.

112 **"as to how":** Letter, Toussaint to superior, August 17, 1938, RH 2/2932 (47–51), BAMA.

113 **Jodl confided:** "Case Green, August 24–31, 1938," Records of the Office of the US Chief Counsel for the Prosecution of Axis Criminality, Defense Document Books, Alfred Jodl, JO 14, NARA.

113 **Jodl wanted a candid assessment:** Diary of General Alfred Jodl, translation of doc. no. 1700-PS, September 7, 1938, microfilm T84, roll 268, frame 180 (51), NARA.

113 **"judge[d] the Czech situation":** Ibid.

113 **Once back at the legation:** Andor Hencke was the first counselor of the German legation in Prague at the time. His memoir (Hencke, *Augenzeuge*), though it must be treated carefully, is indispensable for describing the atmosphere in the legation in Prague from 1937 through 1939.

113 **"Hitler has established":** Ibid., 148.

114 **"like helpless wild-fowl":** Hitler, "The Final Speech of the Führer at the Nuremberg Party Days," September 12, 1938, published in the *Freiburger Zeitung* 135, no. 249 (September 13, 1938): 1.

114 **"completely broken":** Friedrich-Carl Hanesse, statement under oath, November 28, 1949, Toussaint War Crimes Trial, Abt. IV OP 61643, BHSA.

114 **The next day, Toussaint:** Cable, Toussaint and Hencke to Wehrmacht High Command (henceforth OKW) *Attachegruppe,* no. 356, September 13, 1938, R 29.767, PAdAA.

114 **"We want to return to the Reich":** "Special Announcement of the German News Agency: Henlein's Proclamation to the Sudeten Germans demanding return to the Reich," *DGFP,* series D, vol. 2, no. 490: 802.

114 **The legation was flooded:** Hencke, *Augenzeuge,* 153.

115 **"Spreading of the news":** Cable, Toussaint and Hencke to the OKW, September 17, 1938, *DGFP,* series D, vol. 2, no. 515: 824.

115 **he was more determined:** Friedrich-Carl Hanesse, statement under oath, November 28, 1949, OP 61643, BHSA.

115 **Their reaction to Hitler's:** Lukes, *Czechoslovakia Between Stalin and Hitler,* 211–18.

115 **Nor did they receive:** Hencke, *Augenzeuge,* 151–167.

116 **"Thanks, excellently":** Diary entry, September 22, 1938, Records of the Office of the US Chief Counsel for the Prosecution of Axis Criminality, Defense Document Books, Alfred Jodl, JO 13, NARA.

116 **Jodl hurriedly explained:** Ibid. See also Toussaint's affidavit, which corroborates it. Keitel's memoir also reports directing Jodl to call Toussaint in late September during the Godesberg negotiations. Keitel, *Erinnerungen,* 192. See also Hencke, *Augenzeuge,* 154–55 (describing call but apparently misattributing it to Keitel instead of Jodl).

117 **Jodl was clearly disappointed:** Hencke, *Augenzeuge,* 155.

117 **His and Hencke's warning:** Cable, Toussaint and Hencke to OKW *Attachegruppe,* no. 427, September 23, 1938, R 29.768, PAdAA; Ullrich, *Hitler,* 738–39.

117 **"dead silence":** Quoted in Ullrich, *Hitler,* 738.

118 **"If peace breaks":** Hencke, *Augenzeuge,* 169.

118 **"[a]ll attachés said":** Cable, Toussaint and Hencke to OKW *Attachegruppe,* no. 443, September 24, 1938, Büro des Staatssekretär R 29.768, PAdAA.

118 **He learned through:** Hencke, *Augenzeuge,* 171, 181.

119 **"It's not a question of Czechoslovakia":** Quoted in Thomas Childers, *The Third Reich: A History of Nazi Germany* (New York: Simon & Schuster, 2017), 409.

119 **"itinerant professor":** Ibid.

119 **By now it was unofficially known:** Hencke, *Augenzeuge,* 179–84.

120 **"Calm in Prague":** Cable, Toussaint and Hencke to OKW, September 27, 1938, *DGFP,* series D, vol. 2, no. 646: 976.

120 **The ranks of the career Wehrmacht:** Jodl diary entry, September 7, 1938, microfilm T84, roll 268, frame 13–198, frame 180, NARA.

121 **"There is no way":** Lukes, *Czechoslovakia Between Stalin and Hitler,* 245.

121 **The next morning broke:** Hencke, *Augenzeuge,* 184.

122 **But the details of the Munich Agreement:** Interrogation of Rudolf Toussaint on November 3, 1947, at Pankrac RG 1329/S/1/187, Vojenský historický archiv, Prague (henceforth VHA).

123 **On March 15, 1939:** Hencke, *Augenzeuge,* 309.

123 **As Toussaint had feared in 1938:** Cable, Newton to Halifax, November, 1, 1938, *DBFP,* series 3, vol. 3, no. 378.

123 **Before him alone:** Hencke, *Augenzeuge,* 309.

124 **As Toussaint wound down:** Brandes, *Die Tschechen unter deutschem Protektorat: Besatzungspolitik, Kollaboration und Widerstandim Protektorat Böhmen und Mähren bis Heydrichs Tod (1939–1942),* part 1 (Munich and Vienna: Oldenbourg, 1969) 34–36.

124 **The Petscheks' four-story bank:** Cable, Newton to Halifax, March 31, 1939, *DBFP,* series 3, vol. 4, no. 136.

124 **the highest value:** Krejčová and Vlček, *Lives for Ransom,* 368–70.

124 **One night before:** Penerova, "The House," 23; Marc Robinson, interview by the author, New York City, October 19, 2017.

6 | THE MOST DANGEROUS MAN IN THE REICH

126 **constantly escalating demands:** Ian Kershaw, *Hitler: A Biography* (New York: W. W. Norton & Company, 2008), 480–84.

127 **Although he had been pushed out:** Terry C. Treadwell and Alan C. Wood, *German Fighter Aces of World War One* (Stroud, UK: Tempus, 2003), 120.

127 **Laumann started secretly:** Toussaint defense, War Crimes Trial, SOA.

127 **"reactionary":** Confidential report, December 2, 1939, Dienststelle Ribbentrop R 27179, PAdAA .

127 **On November 8, 1939:** Richard J. Evans, *The Third Reich at War: 1939–1945: How the Nazis Led Germany from Conquest to Disaster* (London: Penguin, 2009), 109–11.

127 **"I cannot agree":** Confidential report, December 2, 1939, Dienststelle Ribbentrop R 27179, PAdAA.

128 **In Berlin:** Diary entry, November 29, 1939, *War Journal of Franz Halder* (A.G. EUCOM, 1971), 2:58; Toussaint defense, War Crimes Trial, SOA.

128 **So he claimed:** Alexander Toussaint, interviews.

128 **Von Tippelskirch passed his findings:** Diary entry, November 29, 1939, *War Journal of Franz Halder,* 58.

129 **"Don't say so much":** Alexander Toussaint, interviews.

129 **"rumors in Belgrade":** Diary entry, November 29, 1939, *War Journal of Franz Halder,* 58.

129 **Von Tippelskirch, finding himself:** Keitel, *Erinnerungen,* 235.

129 **As 1941 began:** John Keegan, *The Second World War* (New York: Penguin, 1989), 180–96.

130 **"I struggle internally against":** Letter, Toussaint to supervising general, May 15, 1940, RH 2/2922, BAMA.

130 **"brown-eyed general":** Alexander Toussaint, interviews.

131 **"great zeal and energy":** Rolf Toussaint personnel file, Personalbogen 6/71086, BAMA.

132 **They dueled at chess:** Alexander Toussaint, interviews.

132 **"[O]ut came":** Penerova, "The House," 23. Some misspellings are corrected in text.

134 **"The Jew":** "Otto Petschek—pražský Rothschild," *Moravská orlice,* January 12, 1941.

134 **"Gestapo Arrest List":** *Die Sonderfahndungsliste G.B.,* 1940, Hoover Institution Archives, http://digitalcollections.hoover.org/objects/55425.

134 **That October:** Cable, Koeppens to Rosenberg, "Tuesday, October 7, 1941,"

Bundesarchiv Berlin, R 6/34a, in Martin Vogt, ed., *Herbst 1941 im Führerhaupt-quartier* (Koblenz: Bundesarchiv, 2002), 63–66.

135 **A picture window:** Kershaw, *Hitler: A Biography,* 624–26.

135 **Hitler was a dedicated vegetarian:** E.g., Henry Picker, *Hitlers Tischgespräche im Führerhauptquartier* (Munich: Hocke Books, 1963, 2014).

135 **"ransom/hostage system":** Cable, Koeppens to Rosenberg, "Tuesday, October 7, 1941," 66.

135 **"All Jews in the Protectorate":** Ibid., 64–65.

136 **"After the war":** Ibid., 63–66.

136 **his new boss:** Robert Gerwarth, *Hitler's Hangman: The Life of Heydrich* (New Haven, CT: Yale University Press, 2011), 14–83.

136 **Like many others:** Perhaps among the issues was Toussaint's relationship with Admiral Canaris, a longtime threat to Heydrich. See note 429 in Jan Björn Pot-thast, *Das jüdische Zentralmuseum der SS in Prag: Gegnerforschung und Völkermord im Nationalsozialismus* (Frankfurt am Main: Campus, 2002), 137, 165; Gerwarth, *Hitler's Hangman,* 272–73.

137 **"temporary transit camp":** Letter, Heydrich to Bormann, October 11, 1941, in doc. 16 in Miroslav Kárný, ed., *Protektorátní politika Reinharda Heydricha* (Prague: Tisková, 1991), 132–36.

137 **On October 15, 1941:** Letter from Horst Böhme, October 15, 1941, in Kárný, *Protektorátní politika Reinharda Heydricha,* 137.

137 **In November:** Cable, Toussaint to OKW, November 13, 1941, 1799 ÚŘP-ST, Czech National Archives, http://www.badatelna.eu/fond/959/reprodukce/?zazn amId=339715&reproId=372871.

138 **The more muted daylight:** Penerova, "The House," 24.

138 **"ordered to write":** Foreign Broadcast Monitoring Service, Federal Communications Commission, March 13, 1942, *Morgenthau Diary,* vol. 508: 164, https://catalog.archives.gov/id/28276963.

139 **Multiple reports:** Gerwarth, *Hitler's Hangman,* 2, 276.

139 **"the Jewish question":** Peter Longerich, *The Wannsee Conference and the Development of the "Final Solution"* (London: The Holocaust Educational Trust, 2000), 4.

140 **"Reinhard's Crime":** Gerwarth, *Hitler's Hangman,* 270.

140 **Toussaint kept:** Photo evidence in a recent documentary shows a cheerless Toussaint at the concert seated with his wife, Lilly, and Reinhard and Lina Heydrich. "Atentát: Episode 39/44," *Heydrich-konečné řešení,* directed by V. Křístek (Prague: Česká televize, 2012).

140 **The next morning:** The account of the events on May 27, 1941, is principally drawn from Gerwarth, *Hitler's Hangman,* 1–13.

142 **"Lackeitel":** in Geoffrey Megargee, *Inside Hitler's High Command* (Lawrence: University of Kansas Press, 2000), 42.

142 **"the active intervention":** Sworn statement of Fromm's chief of staff, Carl Erik Koehler, February 15, 1949, Toussaint War Crimes Trial documents, TFA.

144 **Toussaint was awakened:** There are two accounts presented by Toussaint in his postwar trial. According to one statement, he was called at six a.m. the next day, though at another point in his defense he said that it was the night of June 9. I conclude that the call occurred on the morning of the tenth, as that is corroborated by several other witness statements. See Toussaint defense and Toussaint witnesses, War Crimes Trial, SOA.

144 **"Sir," he told Toussaint:** Toussaint defense, War Crimes Trial, SOA.

144 **"As the inhabitants":** Jan Richter, "The Lidice Massacre After 65 Years," Radio

Prague, August 6, 2007, http://www.radio.cz/en/section/curraffrs/the-lidice
-massacre-after-65-years.

145 **Toussaint moved through the day:** E.g., Brickenstein statement under oath,
February 16, 1949, OP 61643, BHSA.

145 **He found Frank:** René Küpper, *Karl Hermann Frank (1898–1946): Politische Biog-
raphie eines Sudeten-Deutschen Nationalsozialisten* (Munich: Oldenbourg, 2010),
275–78.

145 **"If you only knew":** Toussaint defense, War Crimes Trial, SOA.

145 **"You should judge":** Ibid.

7 | Is PRAGUE BURNING?

147 **Rudolf and Rolf Toussaint were:** Alexander Toussaint, interviews.

148 **An audacious sequence:** Frank, trial testimony, June 10, 1945, Nuremberg, Germany: International Military Tribunal, vol. 104, 31.04; June 20, 1945, 14 in Dono-
van Nuremberg Trials Collection, Cornell University Law Library.

148 **Frank had gone:** Brandes, *Die Tschechen unter deutschem Protektorat,* 2: 121–22.

149 **Early on Saturday:** Roučka, "Saturday, May 5, 1945," *Skončeno a podepsáno,* np.

149 **The Prague Uprising:** Details regarding the Prague Uprising are primarily
from Pavel Machotka and Josef Tomeš, eds., *Pražské povstání 1945: Svědectví
protagonistů* (Prague: Ústav T. G. Masaryka, 2015); Brandes, *Die Tschechen unter
deutschem Protektorat,* 2: 113–46.

150 **"to prevent the destruction":** Toussaint defense, War Crimes Trial, SOA.

150 *schlapper Kerl:* Hans Gottfried von Watzdorf statement under oath on September 1, 1949, SpkA K 1834, Staatsarchiv Muenchen.

150 **Bloody Ferdinand:** Alexander Toussaint, interviews.

150 **"liquidate the uprising":** Quoted in Roland Kaltenegger, *Generalfeldmarschall
Ferdinand Schoerner: vom Kommandierenden General zum Feldmarschall der letzten
Stunde, 1943–1973* (Würzburg: Flechsig, 2014), 123.

151 **"On the order of SS Feldmarschall Schörner":** Cable, Toussaint to subsidiary
sector Beneschau L95, May 5, 1945, British National Archive ULTRA Decryp-
tion File, box HW 1/3758. CX/MSS/T541/24.

151 **He dragged his feet:** Observers reported that in many areas of Prague, Wehrmacht units showed little resistance to Czech rebels. Brandes, *Die Tschechen unter
deutschem Protektorat,* 2: 125.

151 **The dispute between:** "Minutes of meetings between representatives of the
Czech National Council and their military representatives on the one side and
General Toussaint, two officers and headmaster Rudl representing the German
side," Tuesday, May 8, 1945, box 3, Česká národní rada 1945–1949, Vojenský historický archiv (henceforth VHA), hereafter cited as "Minutes of meetings," VHA.

151 **Schörner dispatched five divisions:** Wehrkreis Prague (Military Area Prague),
B-135, microfiche 0129G, 0128, Record Group (henceforth RG) 338, NARA. Biographical information on Schörner derives from Peter Steinkamp, "Generalfeldmarschall Ferdinand Schörner," in *Hitlers militärische Elite,* Gerd R. Ueberschär,
ed. (Darmstadt: Primus Verlag, 1998), 236–44.

151 **Patton wanted to continue:** Igor Lukes, *On the Edge of the Cold War: American
Diplomats and Spies in Postwar Prague* (Oxford, UK: Oxford University Press,
2012), 32–54.

151 **He dispatched one of his:** *Vollmacht* [Power of Attorney], signed by Frank and

Toussaint, May 5, 1945, Německé státní ministerstvo pro Čechy a Moravu (110 AMV), box 109, Národní České republiky, http://www.badatelna.eu/fond/2199/zaznam/984054.

152 **Toussaint's aide:** Rolf Toussaint, interview, "Gebt meinem Vater die Freiheit wieder," *Deutsche Soldaten Zeitung (DSZ)*, March 1960; letter, Rolf Toussaint to Stanislav Auský, October 23, 1977, box 2, Stanislav A. Auský Collection, Hoover Institution Archives, Stanford, CA.

152 **"with a white flag":** Rolf Toussaint, interview.

152 **"Rolf, you must understand":** Ibid.

153 **"*Das ganze*":** Cable, from Pückler, May 5, 1945, in Wolfgang Schumann and Olaf Groehler, eds., *Deutschland im Zweiten Weltkrieg*, vol. 6, *Die Zerschlagung des Hitlerfaschismus und die Befreiung des deutschen Volkes (Juni 1944 bis zum 8. Mai 1945)* (Köln: Pahl-Rugenstein, 1985), 765.

154 **One of his men brought peculiar news:** I reconstructed the details of the meeting among Toussaint, Meyer-Detring, and Pratt by piecing together information from multiple sources, including "After Action Report, April 28 to May 9, 1945," box 13260, entry 427, 616-CAV-0.3, 23rd Cavalry Reconnaissance Squad, 16th Armored Division, World War II Operations Reports, 1941–1948, Record Group (henceforth RG) 407, NARA; Roučka, *Skončeno a podepsáno*, np; Jindřich Pecka, *Na demarkační čáře. Americká armáda v Čechách v roce 1945* (Prague: Ústav pro soudobé dějiny AV ČR: 1995), 77–80; Karel Pacner, *Osudové okamžiky Československa*, 3rd ed. (Prague: Brána, 2012), 246–50; and Bryan J. Dickerson, *The Liberators of Pilsen: The U.S. 16th Armored Division in World War II Czechoslovakia* (Jefferson: McFarland & Co, 2018).

156 **At ten the next morning:** Toussaint defense, War Crimes Trial, SOA.

157 **They had blindfolds:** Machotka and Tomeš, *Pražské povstání 1945,* 19–22.

157 **"stood with his Adjutant General":** Ibid. The sequencing and description of the negotiations on May 8 is primarily from "Minutes of meetings," VHA. I also relied upon the memoir of CNC representative Albert Pražák, *Politika a revoluce: Paměti* (Prague: Academia, 2004), 107–130, reprinted in Machotka and Tomeš, *Pražské povstání 1945;* Roučka, "Tuesday, May 8, 1945," *Skončeno a podepsáno*, np; and John Toland, *The Last 100 Days* (New York: Random House, 1966).

158 **"Do you have enough authority":** "Minutes of meetings," VHA.

158 **"I do not have the authorization":** "Die Tätigkeiten des Tschechischen Nationalrates in Prag zwischen 4. und 9. Mai 1945," MSG 137-3, BAMA.

160 **All eyes turned to:** Letter, Auský to Rolf Toussaint, October 10, 1977, box 2, Stanislav A. Auský Collection, Hoover Institution Archives.

160 **"[Your] son was found":** "Minutes of meetings," VHA.

160 **blow up the dam:** Horst Naude, *Erlebnisse und Erkenntnisse als Politischer Beamter im Protektorat Böhmen und Mähren* (Munich: Fides-Verlagsgesellschaft, 1975), 182.

161 **And for good measure:** Alexander Toussaint, interviews.

161 **Toussaint drew his gun:** Toussaint defense, War Crimes Trial, SOA; "Gedächtnisprotokoll der Unterhaltung mit General Toussaint in München," March 18, 1965, TFA.

161 **But Pückler was not:** Arthur von Briesen, statement under oath, February 17, 1949, TFA.

161 **Toussaint and von Briesen:** Ibid.; Jindřich Marek, *Barikáda z kaštanů: Pražské povstání v květnu 1945 a jeho skuteční hrdinové* (Cheb: Svět křídel, 2005), 204–5.

161 **"Ten hours are left":** "Minutes of meetings," VHA.

162 **Kutlvašr agreed:** Stanislav Kokoška, *Prag im Mai 1945: Die Geschichte eines Aufstandes* (Prague: Univerzita Karlova, 2009), 212.

162 **"Who am I now?":** Toland, *The Last 100 Days*, 581.

8 | "If You're Going Through Hell, Keep Going"

163 **"If You're Going":** This quotation is often incorrectly attributed to Winston Churchill. Its provenance is unclear. "Quotes Falsely Attributed to Winston Churchill," *The International Churchill Society*, https://www.winstonchurchill .org/resources/quotes/quotes-falsely-attributed/.

163 **The Nazi ammunition train:** The account of the refugee train from Lübberstedt that was struck by British bombers on May 2, 1945, was a story that I heard from my mother. It is substantiated by Rüdiger Kahrs, "The Evacuation of the Satellite Camp Lübberstedt in Bremen to Ostholstein 1945," *Schleswig-Holstein History* 36 (1999): 93–96; and further detailed in Barbara Hillman, Volrad Kluge, and Erdwig Kramer, *Lw. 2/XI, Muna Lübberstedt: Zwangsarbeit für den Krieg* (Bremen: Edition Temmen, 1996), 130–35. The events are also corroborated by roughly contemporaneous statements collected by the National Committee for Attending Deportees (DEGOB), https://www.degob.org. See, in particular, statements (known as "protocols") numbers 1236, 1453, 1574, 1801, and 1827.

168 **Many others had lesser wounds:** Geoffrey P. Megargee, ed., *The United States Holocaust Museum Encyclopedia of Camps and Ghettos, 1933–1945* (Bloomington, IN: Indiana University Press, 2009), 1:1, 157–58.

170 **The day after that:** "May 3–9, 1945," *Diary of the 6th Guards Armoured Brigade, Brigade Headquarters,* catalog no. War Office 171/4321-4, National Archives of the UK.

170 **After some initial food shortages:** Union O.S.E., "Report on the Situation of the Jews in Germany: October/December 1945" (Geneva, 1946), 29–30.

9 | "He Who Is Master of Bohemia Is Master of Europe"

177 **"He Who Is Master":** Attributed to Otto von Bismarck, likely apocryphally. For that reason, the quotation takes different forms: see, e.g., Suzy Platt, ed., *Respectfully Quoted: A Dictionary of Quotations Requested from the Congressional Research Service* (Washington, DC: Library of Congress, 1989), 27.

177 **Otto Petschek's palace:** E.g., letter, Steinhardt to Williamson July 28, 1945, box 82, Laurence A. Steinhardt Papers (henceforth Steinhardt Papers), Library of Congress, Washington, DC (henceforth LOC).

177 **The newly arrived US ambassador:** Details on Laurence's life before his time as ambassador to Czechoslovakia are from Lukes, *On the Edge of the Cold War,* 67–80. For a response to Lukes offering a different assessment of Laurence, see Peter Mareš, "History in the Service of a Story: On Igor Lukes's Book 'On the Edge of the Cold War,'" *Czech Journal of Contemporary History* 4 (2016): 157–76.

178 **the Soviets had seized the building:** Penerova, "The House," 24–25; Dulcie Ann Steinhardt Sherlock, unpublished memoir, Steinhardt Family Archive (henceforth SFA), 107.

178 **"some Russian officers":** Letter, Steinhardt to Williamson, July 28, 1945, box 82, Steinhardt Papers, LOC.

179 **He had done the same:** Laurence was recognized by at least one authority for his work to aid refugees as a wartime ambassador. See "Visas for Life: The

Righteous and Honorable Diplomats Project," Institute for the Study of Rescue and Altruism in the Holocaust, http://www.holocaustrescue.com/visas-for-life .html. Others have taken a more critical perspective on his efforts in that period. See, e.g., I. Izzet Bahar, "Turkey and the Rescue of Jews During the Nazi Era: A Reappraisal of Two Cases; German-Jewish Scientists in Turkey & Turkish Jews in Occupied France," PhD diss., University of Pittsburgh, 2012. Laurence's family notes that he was active in aiding refugees, often endangering himself, and that the work was necessarily secret: Steinhardt family, interviews by the author, Washington, DC, November 13, 2015, and Washington, DC, November, 13, 2015. See also Mordecai Paldiel, *Diplomatic Heroes of the Holocaust* (Jersey City: KTAV, 2007), 215.

180 **"camping out in this covered stadium"**: Letter, Steinhardt to Alling, September 19, 1945, box 82, Steinhardt Papers, LOC.

181 **"had hoped"**: Letter, Steinhardt to Schoenfeld, May 21, 1945, box 82, Steinhardt Papers, LOC.

181 **"crawled to the White House"**: Quoted in Walter Ullmann, *The United States in Prague, 1945–1948* (Boulder, CO: East European Quarterly, 1978), 13. Bracketed insertions omitted.

181 **Franklin Roosevelt had dispatched**: E.g., Dennis J. Dunn, *Caught Between Roosevelt and Stalin: America's Ambassadors to Moscow* (Lexington: University Press of Kentucky, 1998), 97–144.

181 **"hoss-trader"**: Steinhardt family, interview by the author, Washington, DC, October 7, 2016.

181 **"a wealthy, bourgeoisie [sic] Jew"**: Dunn, *Caught Between Roosevelt and Stalin,* 107.

182 **"where we have a fighting chance"**: Letter, Steinhardt to Riddleberger, September 1, 1945, box 82, Steinhardt Papers, LOC.

182 **"In the First World War"**: Geoffrey Roberts, "Stalin's Wartime Vision of the Peace, 1939–1945," in *Stalin and Europe: Imitation and Domination, 1928–1953,* Timothy Snyder and Ray Brandon, eds. (Oxford, UK: Oxford University Press, 2014), 249.

184 **"a matter of political wisdom"**: Letter, Beneš to Fierlinger, August 9, 1945, box 987/35, Archiv Kanceláře prezidenta republiky; also quoted in Lukes, *On the Edge of the Cold War,* 88.

185 **"I would not wish to occupy"**: Letter, Steinhardt to Williamson, July 28, 1945, box 82, Steinhardt Papers, LOC.

185 **The Soviets had even taken**: Cable, Klieforth to Department of State, June 21, 1945, *FRUS* 1945, Europe, vol. 4, William Slany, John G. Reid, N. O. Sappington, and Douglas W. Houston, eds. (Washington, DC: Government Printing Office, 1968), 459–60.

186 **"Truth prevails, but it's a chore"**: In, e.g., Matěj Barták, *Velká kniha citátů* (Prague: Plot, 2010), 226. See Marcia Davenport, *Too Strong for Fantasy* (Pittsburgh: University of Pittsburgh Press, 1993), 433, for plans to marry; and Sherlock, unpublished memoir, SFA, 122, for his nickname of "Johnny."

186 **He told Laurence**: Cable, Steinhardt to Department of State, August 25, 1945, *FRUS,* 1945, 4:485.

187 **"What the Soviets have done"**: Letter, Steinhardt to Williamson, July 28, 1945, box 82, Steinhardt Papers, LOC.

188 **"On behalf of Mr. Viktor Petschek"**: Letter, Hollitscher to Williamson, August 28, 1945, box 46, Steinhardt Papers, LOC.

188 **"The answer is 100% no"**: Letter, Williamson to Steinhardt, August 29, 1945, box 46, Steinhardt Papers, LOC.

189 **"The sudden withdrawal"**: Cable, Steinhardt to Department of State, August 31, 1945, *FRUS*, 1945, 4:486–87.

190 **On September 14**: Unless otherwise specified, all details and quotations from Laurence's meeting with Beneš on September 14, 1945, can be found in: cable, Steinhardt to Department of State, September 14, 1945, *FRUS*, 1945, 4:490–92.

190 **"union of the Slavic peoples"**: Roberts, "Stalin's Wartime Vision of the Peace," 249.

193 **"so he will know"**: Letter, Steinhardt to Williamson, September 25, 1945, box 82, Steinhardt Papers, LOC.

195 **"As you know"**: Cable, Byrnes to Steinhardt, November 2, 1945, *FRUS*, 1945, 4:506–7.

10 | LUSH LIFE

197 **"I have received your message"**: Cable, Byrnes to Steinhardt, November 9, 1945, *FRUS*, 1945, 4:508.

198 **"I was, of course, very much astonished"**: Letter, Williamson to Steinhardt, November 21, 1945, box 46, Steinhardt Papers, LOC.

199 **Among those distractions**: Cecilia Sternberg, *The Journey: An Autobiography* (New York: Dial, 1977). Unless otherwise specified, all information about the Sternbergs, and quotations attributed to them and to Laurence while in their presence, can be found in *The Journey*.

203 **The waves of soldiers**: I relied upon Lukes's description of the event in *On the Edge of the Cold War* (pages 110–11), as well as on photos in the SFA.

204 **"General Harmon"**: David Vaughan, "November 1945: Homeward Bound," Radio Prague, August 11, 2008, http://www.radio.cz/en/section/archives/-november-1945-homeward-bound.

204 **the painfully cold winter**: Walter Birge, *They Broke the Mold: The Memoirs of Walter Birge* (Paul Mould Publishing, 2012), 298.

206 **With the diplomatic mission**: Sherlock, unpublished memoir, SFA, 108. Unless otherwise specified, further information about Dulcie Ann's diplomatic adventures comes from her memoir.

206 **She was attending a diplomatic dinner**: Sherlock, unpublished memoir, SFA, 107–8.

207 **"He was still in the prime of life"**: Sternberg, *The Journey*, 27.

207 **"Your Excellency"**: Letter, Sternberg to Steinhardt, September 10, 1945, box 94, Steinhardt Papers, LOC; Sternberg, *The Journey*, 26–27.

207 **"gathered together like cattle"**: Sternberg, *The Journey*, 35.

208 **"could not have cared less"**: Ibid., 28.

208 **"heart-to-heart woman's talk"**: Ibid.

208 **"Do tell me"**: Ibid.

209 **"Godless terrorism"**: Gary B. Nash et al., *The American People: Creating a Nation and a Society, Concise Edition, Combined Volume,* 7th ed. (Upper Saddle River, NJ: Pearson Hall, 2011), 786.

210 **"the country is still living"**: Letter, Yarrow to Foster Dulles, December 26, 1945, box 82, Steinhardt Papers, LOC.

210 **"Your property was taken over"**: Letter, Goodrich to Petschek, January 21, 1946, box 49, Steinhardt Papers, LOC.

211 **"I was informed"**: Letter, Yarrow to Foster Dulles, December 26, 1945, box 82, Steinhardt Papers, LOC.

211 **"The Ambassador suggested"**: Ibid.

211 **"the Communists will be lucky"**: Letter, Steinhardt to Foster Dulles, December 26, 1945, box 82, Steinhardt Papers, LOC.

11 | SMALL SALVATIONS

213 **"Unquestionably there is"**: Letter, Steinhardt to Williamson, May 1, 1946, box 95, Steinhardt Papers, LOC.

213 **Gottwald's goal**: Cable, Steinhardt to Department of State, May 27, 1946, *FRUS, 1946*, Eastern Europe, The Soviet Union, vol. 6, Roger P. Churchill and William Slany, eds. (Washington, DC: Government Printing Office, 1969), 199–200.

214 **"the influence of western"**: Letter, Steinhardt to Williamson, May 1, 1946, box 95, Steinhardt Papers, LOC.

214 **"initiate further action"**: Letter, Yarrow to Steinhardt, May 23, 1946, box 50, Steinhardt Papers, LOC.

214 **On election day**: Lukes, *On the Edge of the Cold War,* 134; George F. Bogardus, interview by Charles Stuart Kennedy, April 10, 1996, *Association for Diplomatic Studies and Training Foreign Affairs Oral History Project* (henceforth ADST), LOC.

215 **"They would come at him"**: Bogardus, interview.

215 **"would be controlled"**: Cable, Steinhardt to Department of State, May 15, 1946, 860F.00/5-1546, box 6570, Central Decimal Files, 1945–1949, RG 59, NARA.

215 **"[I]n spite"**: Cable, Steinhardt to Department of State, May 27, 1946, *FRUS, 1946*, 6:199–200.

215 **"I find no disposition"**: Cable, Steinhardt to Department of State, June 3, 1946, 860F.00/6-346, box 6570, Central Decimal Files, 1945–1949, RG 59, NARA.

216 **"of common sense"**: Cable, Steinhardt to Department of State, July 3, 1946, *FRUS, 1946*, 6:204–5.

216 **"I have every reason"**: Letter, Steinhardt to Foster Dulles, July 23, 1946, box 7, Yarrow Papers, DEPL.

216 **"drive a hard bargain"**: Letter, Steinhardt to Williamson, July 29, 1946, box 95, Steinhardt Papers, LOC.

216 **"smug self-satisfaction"**: Letter, Steinhardt to Williamson, August 29, 1946, box 95, Steinhardt Papers, LOC.

217 **"[T]he important consideration"**: Letter, Steinhardt to Boček, September 26, 1946, box 89, Steinhardt Papers, LOC.

217 **"the palace originally served"**: Letter, Ministry of National Defense to the Ministry of Foreign Affairs, August 7, 1946, box 1, Territorial Departments–Standard, MFA.

218 **"could not be replaced"**: Letter, Steinhardt to Boček, September 26, 1946, box 89, Steinhardt Papers, LOC.

218 **"It has been my practice"**: Letter, Steinhardt to National Property Administration, May 7, 1947, box 49, Steinhardt Papers, LOC. This memo is dated May 7, 1946, but that is incorrect, as is clear from the letter's context, which shows that it was actually written on May 7, 1947.

219 **"beautiful and extremely comfortable"**: Letter, Steinhardt to Therese Rosenblatt, November 14, 1945, box 82, Steinhardt Papers, LOC.

219 **"its opulence and extreme gaudiness"**: Sternberg, *The Journey,* 26.

219 **"interfering with [his] proper duties"**: Letter, Steinhardt to National Property

Administration, May 7, 1947, box 49, Steinhardt Papers, LOC (incorrectly dated; see note above).

219 **"this little mother has claws"**: Quoted in Stach, *Kafka: The Early Years,* 23.

220 **"great obstacles"**: Yarrow's letter is transmitted to Foster Dulles in letter, Riddleberger to Foster Dulles, May 21, 1947, PFA.

221 **"Both Stalin and Molotov"**: Cable, Steinhardt to Department of State, July 10, 1947, *FRUS,* 1947, The British Commonwealth, Europe, vol. 3, Ralph E. Goodwin et al., eds. (Washington, DC: United States Government Printing Office, 1972), 319–20.

222 **"[H]e is now in a position"**: Cable, Steinhardt to Department of State, July 10, 1947, 840.50 RECOVERY/7-1047, box 5720, Central Decimal Files, 1945–1949, RG 59, NARA.

222 **"All Slavic states"**: Cable, Steinhardt to Department of State, July 11, 1947, 840.5 RECOVERY/7-1147, box 5720, Central Decimal Files, 1945–1949, RG 59, NARA.

223 **"[T]he political situation here"**: Letter, Steinhardt to Foster Dulles, October 21, 1947, box 84, Steinhardt Papers, LOC.

223 **"The election campaign"**: Ibid.

223–24 **He reported to Washington**: Cable, Steinhardt to Department of State, October 6, 1947, *FRUS,* 1947, Eastern Europe; The Soviet Union, vol. 4, Roger P. Churchill and William Slany, eds. (Washington, DC: Government Printing Office, 1972), 235.

224 **"with Anglo-Saxon support"**: In Gerhard Wettig, *Stalin and the Cold War in Europe: The Emergence and Development of East-West Conflict, 1939–1953* (Lanham, MD: Rowman & Littlefield, 2008), 110.

225 **"reactionary agents"**: Lukes, *On the Edge of the Cold War,* 192.

225 **"[T]he situation is messed up"**: Quoted in Ullmann, *The United States in Prague,* 147.

225 **"Should the [Socialists]"**: Cable, Steinhardt to Department of State, February 21, 1948, 860F.00/2-2148, box 6572, Central Decimal Files, 1945–1949, RG 59, NARA.

226 **"action committees"**: Cable, Steinhardt to Department of State, February 23, 1948, 860F.00/2-2348, box 6572, Central Decimal Files, 1945–1949, RG 59, NARA.

226 **"There were far fewer"**: Birge, *They Broke the Mold,* 319.

226 **"the embassy receptionist"**: Ibid.

226 **"positively grim"**: Ibid.

227 **"seemed to have aged"**: All quotations and details from Laurence's meeting with the Sternbergs can be found in Sternberg, *The Journey,* 40–41.

228 **"had been subjected"**: Cable, Steinhardt to Department of State, February 27, 1948, *FRUS,* 1948, Eastern Europe; The Soviet Union, vol. 4, Rogers P. Churchill, William Slany, and Herbert A. Fine, eds. (Washington, DC: United States Government Printing Office, 1974), 741–42.

228 **"There was no evidence that Beneš"**: Ibid.

229 **"because of a quarrel"**: In Peter Neville, *Hitler and Appeasement: The British Attempt to Prevent the Second World War* (London: Hambledon Continuum, 2006), 107.

229 **"with a loud thud"**: Cable, Caffery to Department of State, February 22, 1948, 860F.00/2-2448, box 6572, Central Decimal Files, 1945–1949, RG 59, NARA; also quoted in Lukes, *On the Edge of the Cold War,* 195.

229 **Masaryk came to the palace:** Sherlock, unpublished memoir, SFA, 122. All details regarding Laurence and Masaryk's last lunch together come from Dulcie Ann's memoir.

230 **"the bitter criticism":** Cable, Steinhardt to Department of State, March 10, 1948, *FRUS*, 1948, 4:743–44.

230 **"to run down":** Letter, Steinhardt to Vedeler, April 7, 1948, 860F.00/4-748, box 6573, Central Decimal Files, 1945–1949, RG 59, NARA.

231 **"The February storm":** Protocol of the Session of the Constituent Assembly, March 10, 1948, http://www.psp.cz/eknih/1946uns/stenprot/094schuz/s094002 .htm.

231 **"Slavs have come together":** Protocol of the Session of the Constituent Assembly, April 29, 1948, http://www.psp.cz/eknih/1946uns/stenprot/109schuz/s109004 .htm.

231 **"[T]he past three weeks":** Letter, Steinhardt to William Rosenblatt, March 19, 1948, box 93, Steinhardt Papers, LOC.

231 **"What has taken place":** Letter, Steinhardt to Diamond, April 20, 1948, box 90, Steinhardt Papers, LOC.

232 **"return to the United States":** Letter, American Embassy Prague to the Czechoslovak Ministry of Foreign Affairs, July 1, 1948, box 193, GS-A, 1945–1954 USA, MFA.

232 **"What are you doing here?":** Alexander Toussaint, interviews.

233 **"was more successful":** Cable, Steinhardt to Vedeler, April 7, 1948, 860F.00/4-748, box 6573, Central Decimal Files, 1945–1949, RG 59, NARA.

234 **"wooden money":** Sherlock, unpublished memoir, SFA, 107.

234 **"The ambassador's residence":** "Life Visits U.S. Embassy in Prague," *Life*, November 15, 1948.

235 **"I like to be able":** Ibid.

235 **"the Czech State promises":** Letter, Hollitscher to Yarrow, July 2, 1948, PFA.

235 **"unless the Department considered":** Department of State Memorandum of Conversation, Participants Steinhardt, Yarrow, Vedeler, Williamson, Donaldson, Oliver, and Taylor, July 21, 1948, PFA.

236 **"Adolf has an intense sense":** Letter, Steinhardt to Ballance, September 7, 1948, box 58, Steinhardt Papers, LOC.

236 **Operation Flying Fiancée:** All quotations and details can be found in Birge, *They Broke the Mold*, 341–50.

12 | "Never, Never, Never Give In"

241 **"Never, Never, Never Give In":** This quotation is an abbreviated version of a line that Winston Churchill delivered in October 1941. Winston S. Churchill, *The Unrelenting Struggle: War Speeches by the Right Hon. Winston S. Churchill* (London: Cassell, 1942), 274–76.

242 **"Let women be placed":** H. Gordon Skilling, *T. G. Masaryk: Against the Current, 1882–1914* (Hampshire, UK: Macmillan Press, 1994), 128.

253 **"used":** Moshe Schiff, nephew of Frieda Grünfeld, later Frieda Eisen, telephone interview by the author, September 14, 2017.

254 **"the yoke of capitalist exploitation":** Ilya Ehrenburg, "Answer to a Letter," *Jewish Life*, June 1949, 27.

13 | NOTHING CRUSHES FREEDOM LIKE A TANK

259 **Nothing Crushes Freedom:** Shirley expressed variations of this sentiment to multiple journalists; I have adapted it here. See, e.g., Richard Bassett, "Taking shelter in a riot with Shirley Temple," *Times* (of London), October 30, 1989.

259 **The Palace; Tuesday:** Shirley's published memoir about her experiences in Prague in August 1968, "Prague Diary," *McCall's*, 1969, was the most important source for this chapter. In some instances, I have altered the tense of quotations from "Prague Diary" from present to past to improve the flow of the text. The time, the vehicle, and other details from Shirley's trip to the palace on August 20, 1968, are in her forthcoming autobiography, chapter 1. It was generously made available to me by her family. Because the manuscript has not yet been fully paginated, it is cited throughout by chapter, rather than by specific page. See also Julian M. Niemczyk, Air Attaché in Prague from 1967 through 1969, interview by Charles Stuart Kennedy, December 16, 1991, *ADST*, LOC.

259 **"could melt an audience":** James O. Jackson, "Sounds, Sights of a Country Being Crushed," *Evening Star,* August 22, 1968.

260 **Later that afternoon:** See, e.g., Craig R. Whitney, "Prague Journal: Shirley Temple Black Unpacks a Bag of Memories," *New York Times,* September 11, 1989; "Přijetí u ministra dr. Vlčka," *Lidová demokracie,* August 21, 1989; Black, "Prague Diary," 75; and Bill McKenzie, "A Conversation with Shirley Temple Black," *Ripon Forum,* December 1990, 5–6.

260 **she was restless:** Shirley Temple Black, *Child Star: An Autobiography* (New York: McGraw-Hill Publishing Company, 1988).

261 **Stalin-era hard-liners:** Dean Vuletic, "Popular Culture," in Stephen A. Smith, ed., *The Oxford Handbook on the History of Communism* (Oxford, UK: Oxford University Press, 2014), 575.

262 **official Communist writers' conference:** Jaromír Navrátil, ed., *The Prague Spring 1968: A National Security Archive Reader* (New York: Central European University Press, 1998), 5.

262 **Dubček was just eighteen:** Alexander Dubček, *Hope Dies Last: The Autobiography of Alexander Dubcek,* ed. and trans. Jiri Hochman (New York: Kodansha America, 1993).

262 **He wanted to reform Communism:** See, e.g., Kieran Williams, *The Prague Spring and Its Aftermath: Czechoslovak Politics, 1968–1970* (Cambridge, UK: Cambridge University Press, 1997).

262 **"Socialism with a Human Face":** Navrátil, *The Prague Spring 1968,* 92–95.

262 **"The apex of hope":** Niemczyk, interview.

263 **"[T]he television reporter":** Kenneth N. Skoug Jr., Commercial/Economic Officer in Prague, 1967–1969, interview by Charles Stuart Kennedy, August 22, 2000, *ADST,* LOC.

264 **"charmed out of [her] boots":** For this quotation, as well as details on the timing of Shirley's return to her hotel room after her meeting and its results, see Black, "Prague Diary," 75. Further details from Black, forthcoming autobiography, chapter 1. That the meeting occurred on the campus of Charles University is from Anne Edwards, *Shirley Temple: American Princess* (New York: William Morrow, 1988), 264.

264 **"Your meeting with Mr. Dubcek":** Whitney, "Prague Journal."

264 **"a bleak stone wall":** Black, "Prague Diary," 75.

264 **"as those things do"**: Whitney, "Prague Journal."

264 **"seemed very good indeed"**: Black, "Prague Diary," 75; see this also for Shirley's bedtime routine on August 20, 1968.

265 **"it was an appointment"**: Ibid.

265 **"airport"**: Whitney, "Prague Journal."

265 **"Whatever it was"**: For this and all other quotations and further details regarding what Shirley heard and thought throughout the very early hours of August 21, 1968, see Black, "Prague Diary," 75.

266 **"Awake, madame!"**: Ibid.

266 **"Great green tanks"**: Ibid.

266 **"Personnel carriers rolled"**: Ibid.

267 **"disbelief and confusion"**: Ibid.

267 **"Then a small knot"**: Ibid.

267 **"A block away"**: Ibid.

267 **"While tanks continued"**: Ibid., 91.

267 **Bits and pieces of information**: Ibid. Using Shirley's own writing, together with context provided by journalistic accounts, I have reconstructed the morning of August 21, 1968. See Alan Levy, *So Many Heroes* (Sagaponack, NY: Second Chance Press, 1980); Peter Rehak, "Undated Occupation," Associated Press Collections Online, August, 30, 1989; Clyde Farnsworth, "People of Prague Scream Defiance at the Tanks," *New York Times,* August 22, 1968; Robert Littell, ed., *The Czech Black Book* (New York: Praeger, 1969). I also consulted US government materials in the Czechoslovak Crisis Files, 1968, Office of the Executive Secretariat, RG 59, NARA; and US government–intercepted radio broadcasts (captured and recorded by the Foreign Broadcast Information Service [henceforth FBIS], an open-source intelligence arm of the US government).

268 **"Chambermaids, busboys, and guests"**: Black, "Prague Diary," 91.

268 **"Military units are approaching"**: "Troops Near Prague Radio," August 21, 1968, *Prague Domestic Service in Czech,* Daily Report (FBIS-FRB-68-164), FBIS; Czechoslovakia Crisis Chronology, box 1, entry 5193, lot file 70D19, Czechoslovak Crisis Files, 1968, Office of the Executive Secretariat, RG 59, NARA.

268 **"Crowds of citizens"**: "Soviet Troops in Prague," *Prague CTK International Service in English,* Daily Report (FBIS-FRB-68-164), August 21, 1968, FBIS.

269 **"Russian tanks by the scores"**: Black, "Prague Diary," 75.

269 **"one overriding impression"**: Ibid., 91.

269 **"Soviet troops were trying"**: "Fighting Reported," *Prague CTK International Service in English* (Prague), Daily Report (FBIS-FRB-68-164), August 21, 1968, FBIS.

269 **"Nine ambulances wailed"**: Black, "Prague Diary," 75; "1215 Situation Report," *Prague CTK International Service in English* (Prague), Daily Report (FBIS-FRB-68-164), August 21, 1968, FBIS.

269 **"People fled before the shooting"**: "Fighting Reported," *Prague CTK International Service in English* (Prague), Daily Report (FBIS-FRB-68-164), August 21, 1968, FBIS.

270 **"Twenty badly wounded persons"**: "Care for Wounded," *Prague CTK International Service in English* (Prague), Daily Report (FBIS-FRB-68-164), August 21, 1968, FBIS.

270 **"What's going on?"**: Black, "Prague Diary," 91.

270 **Soon a crowd**: Ruth Dorf, wife of geologist trapped with Shirley in the Alcron,

"Impressions of Czechoslovakia Accumulated After a Week of Travel," unpublished manuscript, Black Family Archive (henceforth BFA), 3; "To Serve a Healthy World," BFA.

270 **"Sparkle, Shirley, sparkle":** Black, *Child Star,* 20; Rosalind Shaffer, "The Private Life of Shirley Temple, Wonder Child of the Screen," *Chicago Tribune,* September 9, 1934.

270 **"A large cardboard sign":** Black, "Prague Diary," 91.

271 **"as he presented":** Ibid.

271 **"A heavyset man":** Ibid.

271 **"One boy":** Ibid.

271 **"the talk got around":** Ibid.

272 **"If you look through":** Ibid., 91–93.

272 **"old and tend to worry":** "Shirley Temple Black Wakens to Sound of Prague Firing," *Washington Post,* August 22, 1968.

272 **"Things are deteriorating":** Black, "Prague Diary," 93.

272 **"No":** Ibid.

273 **a getaway hidden in a hay truck:** Timothy Kenny, "Changing Communism: Czech leaders rigid, slow to accept reforms," *USA Today,* October 16, 1989.

273 **"They are strangers":** Black, "Prague Diary," 93.

273 **"German, really?":** Ibid.

273 **"[A] short time ago":** Czechoslovak Crisis Chronology, August 21, 1968, box 1, entry 5193, lot file 70D19, Czechoslovak Crisis Files, 1968, Office of the Executive Secretariat, RG 59, NARA.

273 **"A woman nearby":** Black, "Prague Diary," 93.

274 **"Look":** Ibid.

274 **"For a long time":** Ibid., 94.

274 **"I must go":** Unless otherwise specified, all quotations and details regarding Shirley's escape from the Alcron to the US embassy can be found in Black, "Prague Diary," 94.

274 **"The shooting has different sounds":** Jackson, "Sounds, Sights."

275 **"to give the fraternal Czechoslovak people":** Navrátil, *The Prague Spring 1968,* 456.

277 **Larry Modisett:** Black, "Prague Diary," 94; "Americans Safe, Tell of Turmoil, Tragedy," *Los Angeles Times,* August 23, 1968.

278 **"snaked past many":** Ibid., 94–95.

281 **"still clutching the eight red carnations":** Ibid., 95.

282 **"What did you see?":** David Brinkley and Garrick Utley, "Invasion/Americans/ Border," *NBC Evening News,* NBC, August 23, 1968, Vanderbilt Television News Archive.

14 | A Revolutionary Production

283 **She was a Republican:** Unless otherwise specified, Shirley's biographical information can be found in Patsy G. Hammontree, *Shirley Temple Black: A Bio-Bibliography* (Westport, CT: Greenwood Press, 1998), 143–88.

284 **"even knew the word":** Uri Friedman, "Shirley Temple: Actress, Ambassador, Honorary African Chief," *Atlantic,* February 11, 2014.

284 **"fresh breeze":** "Shirley Captures the UN," *Washington Post,* November 28, 1969.

284 **"Now I understand":** Theodore S. Wilkinson, interview by Charles Stuart Kennedy, January 11, 1999, *ADST,* LOC.

285 **"prime, prime property"**: Niemczyk, interview.

286 **"I said yes"**: Dennis Murphy, "Shirley Temple Black Named Ambassador," *NBC News*, September 15, 1989; McKenzie, "A Conversation with Shirley Temple Black," 5; and Mark Seal, "Shirleyka," *American Way*, April 1, 1990, 92.

286 **"came as a stranger"**: Black, forthcoming autobiography, chapter 1.

286 **"a Stalinist backwater"**: Joy Billington, "Star Turn in Prague," *Illustrated London News* 7102, September 2, 1991.

286 **had little affection**: Žantovský, *Havel*, 277–85.

286 **Shirley confronted a thorny problem**: Cable, Black to Department of State, August 23, 1989, Prague 05736, doc. no. C06406518, MDR. See also cable, Black to Department of State, October 19, 1989, Prague 07303, in Vilém Prečan, ed., *Prague–Washington–Prague: Reports from the United States Embassy in Czechoslovakia, November–December 1989* (Prague: Vaclav Havel Library, 2004), 13–17. I was able to supplement the collection of Embassy Prague cables held in *Prague–Washington–Prague* with nearly sixty other cables that were declassified and provided to me by the State Department in response to a Mandatory Declassification Review request that I filed (US Department of State case no. MP-2017-00697, referred to as MDR).

287 **"If Prague were Rome or Paris"**: Whitney, "Prague Journal."

287 **"I loved her in *Bright Eyes*"**: Dan Rather, *The Camera Never Blinks Twice: The Further Adventures of a Television Journalist* (New York: William Morrow, 1994), 175.

287 **"But Daddy"**: Thomas N. Hull III, Public Affairs Officer in Prague, 1989–1993, interview by Daniel F. Whitman, January 8–9, 2010, *ADST*, LOC.

287 **"force in accord"**: Cable, Black to Department of State, August 2, 1989, Prague 05232, doc. no. C06406504, MDR.

288 **"present within the range"**: Cable, Black to Department of State, November 20, 1989, Prague 08087, in Prečan, *Prague–Washington–Prague*, 92.

288 **On August 21**: Whitney, "Prague Journal"; Clifford (Cliff) G. Bond, Foreign Service Officer, US Embassy Prague in 1989, interview by the author, Washington, DC, June 28, 2017. To describe what Shirley saw during the protest of August 21, 1989, I drew principally upon the following sources: cable, Black to Department of State, August 22, 1989, Prague 05726, doc. no. C0606522, MDR; Oldřich Tůma, *Zítra zase tady!* (Prague: Maxdorf, 1994), 69–71; Jiří Suk et al., *Chronologie zániku komunistického režimu v Československu 1985–1990* (Prague: Ústav pro soudobé dějiny AV ČR, 1999), 80–81; Padraic Kenney, *A Carnival of Revolution: Central Europe 1989* (Princeton, NJ: Princeton University Press, 2003), 267–68; and "Demonstrace, 21. Srpen 1989," video from Ústav pro studium totalitních režimů, https://www.ustrcr.cz/uvod/listopad-1989/audio-video/srpen-1989-audio-video.

288 **She was careful**: Ruthe Stein, "Czechs' Favorite Diplomat: Success didn't spoil Shirley Temple Black," *San Francisco Chronicle*, October 16, 1991; Bond, interview, June 28, 2017.

288 **"It was an oppression"**: Ross Larsen, "Three Extraordinary Years for Temple Black," *Prague Post Magazine*, June 30, 1992.

289 **THE BOLSHEVIKS CAME WITH TANKS**: Michael Wise, "Prague Riot Police Charge Protestors on Invasion Anniversary," Reuters, August 21, 1989.

290 **"political activism [was] growing"**: Cable, Black to Department of State, August 30, 1989, Prague 05959, doc. no. C06406529, MDR.

290 **On August 22**: Black, forthcoming autobiography, chapter 9. The exact date of the meeting is debatable, but the weight of the evidence points to August 22.

291 **"It was an opportunity"**: Alexandr Vondra, "Discussion on the Velvet Revolution," panel with Clifford Bond and Michele Bond, the American Center in Prague, August 2015.

291 **"There was a lot of emotion"**: Seal, "Shirleyka," 93.

291 **Shirley sensed that change**: Shirley told reporters after the Velvet Revolution that she had known that change would come to Czechoslovakia but was surprised by the speed with which it swept the nation. See, e.g., "Czeching It Out," *Los Angeles Daily News,* May 16, 1990; and "Sloboda je najväčší dar," *Národná Obroda,* July 10, 1992.

291 **"No one knew"**: Guttman, "Interview: Shirley Temple Black."

292 **"not very much"**: Whitney, "Prague Journal."

292 **"I wanted to have you come here"**: Larsen, "Three Extraordinary Years for Temple Black."

292 **"Shirley Temple opens the door"**: Timothy Kenny, "Czech Leaders Rigid, Slow to Accept Reforms," *USA Today,* October 16, 1989.

292 **"Whatever works"**: Larsen, "Three Extraordinary Years for Temple Black."

292 **"I don't like"**: All quoted dialogue between Shirley and Bilák can be found in "Prala bych vam to nejlepsi," *Prostor,* June 27, 1992. Emphasis added. Other details from: McKenzie, "A Conversation with Shirley Temple Black," 6.

293 **"the age-old"**: Kenny, "Czech Leaders Rigid."

293 **a provocative sense of humor**: For Shirley's sᴛʙ T-shirt, see Vera Glasser, "From Hollywood to Prague Shirley Temple Black Has Challenging Assignment," *St. Louis Post-Dispatch,* July 31, 1991; for the custom license plate, see Jack Anderson and Dale Van Atta, "Shirley Temple Black—Our Woman in Czechoslovakia," *Washington Post,* April 28, 1991.

293 **she named him Gorby**: Alan Levy, "Ambassador Shirley Temple Black," *Prague Post,* November 26, 1991.

294 **"What's this going to be"**: Sarah Kaufman, "Shirley Temple, Remembering Curly Top," *Washington Post,* December 6, 1998.

294 **"she and her entire family"**: Hull, interview by Whitman; Hull, telephone interview by the author, August 30, 2017.

294 **"everybody in the embassy"**: Cliff Bond, "Discussion on the Velvet Revolution," panel.

294 **"Why do you Americans"**: Michele Bond, ibid.

295 **But Shirley and her team**: I learned about the personalities and roles of the embassy officials in Prague in 1989 through my interviews with them, particularly Cliff Bond, June 28, 2017, and August 1, 2017, both in Washington, DC; Edward (Ed) Kaska, Washington, DC, July 26, 2017; and Ted Russell, telephone interview, August 29, 2017.

295 **"We maintain"**: Michele Bond, "Discussion on the Velvet Revolution," panel.

295 **On October 4**: To detail Havel and Shirley's meeting in the palace library on October 4, 1989, I used Václav Havel, "Rozhovor s. V.H., Hrádeček 15. listopadu 1989," interview by Irena Gerová, in Irena Gerová, *Vyhrabávačky-deníkové zápisky a rozhovory z let 1988 a 1989* (Prague: Paseka, 2009), 146–48; Anderson and Van Atta, "Shirley Temple Black"; "Sloboda je najväčší dar"; Shirley Temple Black, "Those Czech Dissidents Were Not Ignored," *Washington Post,* February 16, 1990; "Czeching It Out"; Michael Ryan, "As Ambassador to Prague Shirley Temple Black Watches a Rebirth of Freedom," *People,* January 8, 1990; and Hull, interview by Whitman. I also benefited from a number of informal conversations with Miloš Forman starting in 2011.

295 **"smart . . . clever . . . courageous":** "Miloš Forman: The Coming of the Velvet Revolution," YouTube video, 1:06, the Arts Initiative and the Columbia Center for New Media Teaching and Learning, posted by "ColumbiaLearn," May 25, 2015, https://www.youtube.com/watch?v=P3GLocNnpCs&list=PLSuwqsAnJM twqVoj_mYRiAmvJvJULztv9&index=7.

295 **"The American Ambassador's Residence":** John Updike, "Bech in Czech," *New Yorker*, April 20, 1987, 32.

296 **He sat quietly:** E.g., Timothy Garton Ash, *We the People* (Cambridge, UK: Penguin Books, 1999), 117–18.

296 **"Vašku, you may":** Gerová, *Vyhrabávačky*, 147.

297 **"[It] was almost":** Václav Havel, *To the Castle and Back* (New York: Vintage, 2008), 52.

297 **"more had changed":** Ibid.

297 **"a long discussion":** Black, "Those Czech Dissidents Were Not Ignored."

297 **"that he worked":** Gerová, *Vyhrabávačky*, 148.

297 **"moral leader":** McKenzie, "A Conversation with Shirley Temple Black," 4.

297 **"charismatic:"** Ryan, "As Ambassador to Prague."

297 **"will always remain":** "Sloboda je najväčší dar."

298 **"Government's attitude":** John Tagliabue, "Police in Prague Move to Break Up Big Protest March," *New York Times,* October 29, 1989.

298 **in a meeting with Štěpán:** Unless otherwise specified, all quotations and details on Shirley's first meeting with Štěpán on October 18, 1989, can be found in the following: cable, Black to Department of State, October 19, 1989, Prague 07303, in Prečan, *Prague–Washington–Prague*, 13–17.

299 **Shirley ordered staff:** Robert Kiene, "The Velvet Revolution and Me," unpublished manuscript, 2014, 6; Edward Epstein, "From Hollywood to the Velvet Revolution, Shirley Temple Black . . ." *San Francisco Chronicle,* April 23, 1995.

299 **Saturday, October 28:** To write the section about the protest of October 28, 1989 in Prague, and Shirley's involvement, I consulted her statements and writings, including cables sent by the embassy and signed by her (in particular: cable, Black to Department of State, October 31, 1989, Prague 07590, doc. no. C06406570, MDR), as well as, e.g., Michael Kukral, *Prague 1989: Theater of Revolution* (Boulder, CO: East European Monographs, 1997), 40–43; Rob McRae, *Resistance and Revolution: Vaclav Havel's Czechoslovakia* (Ottawa: Carleton University Press, 1997), 94–97; Jiří Suk, *Chronologie zániku komunistického režimu v Československu,* 93–94; Epstein, "From Hollywood"; "Sloboda je najväčší dar"; Tagliabue, "Police in Prague"; Michael Wise, "Over 10,000 Attacked as They Demand New Government in Prague," Reuters, October 28, 1989; Bassett, "Taking shelter in a riot"; Seal, "Shirleyka," 46, 48; "Zneužili 28. října," *Rudé Právo,* October 30, 1989; Anderson and Van Atta, "Shirley Temple Black"; Richard Bassett, reporter for the *Times* (of London), Prague Bureau during 1989, telephone interview by the author, June 27, 2017; Robert McRae, Canadian chargé d'affaires in Prague during 1989, telephone interview by the author, July 17, 2017; Ryan, "As Ambassador to Prague"; photos of Ambassador Black and Charlie Black on the hotel ledge on October 28, 1989, BFA; Wilkinson, interview; Ted Wilkinson, "Shirley Temple Black: A Natural Diplomat," *The Foreign Service Journal* 91, no. 6 (June 2014): 93; "Einst Kinderstar, heute US-Botschafterin in Prag," *Blick für die Frau,* 1989, 20–21; and Edward Lucas, "Prague Rally Thwarted as Police Try New Tactics," *Independent,* October 30, 1989.

299 **"grey and bitterly cold":** McRae, *Resistance and Revolution,* 94.

299 **"I'd like to go for a walk"**: Epstein, "From Hollywood."

300 **"Wenceslas Square was filling"**: Lucas, "Prague Rally Thwarted."

300 **"raised a banner"**: Ibid.

300 **TRUTH PREVAILS**: Wise, "Over 10,000 Attacked."

300 **"little short guy"**: Epstein, "From Hollywood."

300 **"rising, then sinking"**: Kukral, *Prague 1989*, 41.

301 **"Suddenly, hundreds and hundreds"**: McRae, *Resistance and Revolution*, 94.

301 **"The throng of the growing crowd"**: Kukral, *Prague 1989*, 41–42.

301 **"Masaryk!" "Freedom!" and "Havel!"**: Ibid., 42.

301 **"Their heavy boots"**: McRae, *Resistance and Revolution*, 95.

301 **"forcing the crowd"**: Wise, "Over 10,000 Attacked."

301 **"[T]he police had"**: Kukral, *Prague 1989*, 42.

301 **"they simply walked"**: McRae, *Resistance and Revolution*, 95.

301 **"Now we run"**: Epstein, "From Hollywood."

302 **"got across another street"**: Ibid.

302 **"Every time we crossed"**: Ryan, "As Ambassador to Prague."

302 **"took cover behind a nearby billboard"**: All quotations and details in this paragraph can be found in Bassett, "Taking shelter in a riot." Seal, in "Shirleyka," confirms that Shirley signed the autographs.

302 **"What are you doing here?"**: Epstein, "From Hollywood." Shirley, in this 1995 *San Francisco Chronicle* interview, attributed this dialogue to a conversation between herself and a "journalist from London." However, this is most likely a misrecollection: (Black, forthcoming autobiography, chapter 9; Basset, interview). Accordingly, I have attributed this dialogue in text to Perry Shankle.

303 **"Musing on the helmeted"**: Bassett, "Taking shelter in a riot."

303 **"no stranger to violence"**: Ibid.

303 **"Shirley Temple spent"**: Wilkinson, interview. Quotation tense changed for flow.

304 **"but a few hundred"**: McRae, *Resistance and Revolution*, 95.

304 **"Ach, synku, synku"**: Kukral, *Prague 1989*, 42, 43.

304 **"During the singing"**: Ibid., 43.

304 **"People jeered and whistled"**: Ibid.

304 **"created a box"**: McRae, *Resistance and Revolution*, 95–96.

304 **"These few hundred"**: Ibid., 96.

304 **"Young men in casual dress"**: Tagliabue, "Police in Prague."

305 **"chanting 'No violence!'"**: Wise, "Over 10,000 Attacked."

305 **"shouted, 'Gestapo!' and, 'The World Is Watching!'"**: Tagliabue, "Police in Prague."

305 **"might get knocked down"**: Anderson and Van Atta, "Shirley Temple Black."

306 **"250 people were detained"**: Tagliabue, "Police in Prague."

306 **"directing her troops"**: Kiene, "The Velvet Revolution and Me," 6; see also "Zneužili 28. října," *Rudé Právo*, October 30, 1989.

306 **"So you disobeyed"**: Epstein, "From Hollywood."

306 **"Czechoslovakia's biggest demonstration"**: Michael Wise, "Prague Police Break Up Pro-Democracy Rally," Reuters, October 28, 1989.

307 **"even though they were"**: Epstein, "From Hollywood."

307 **"There was only one star"**: Hull, interview by Whitman.

15 | TRUTH PREVAILS

309 **Shirley would have loved:** Author interviews with Kiene, telephone, June 29, 2017; Kaska; Bond, June 28 and August 1, 2017; Cameron Munter, Desk Officer, Czechoslovakia, Department of State in 1989, telephone, August 2, 2017; Hull; and Russell.

309 **"who could have predicted":** Black, forthcoming autobiography, chapter 9.

310 **In the early afternoon:** My writing on the experiences of the three embassy men during the evening of November 17, 1989, is primarily based on my interviews with them (Bond, June 28, 2017, and August 1, 2017; Kaska; and Kiene) and on Kiene's unpublished manuscript, as well as on cables sent by Shirley to the State Department: Prague 08082, November 18, 1989; Prague 08087; Prague 08097; and Prague 08109, all from November 20, 1989, and all of which can be found in Prečan, *Prague–Washington–Prague,* 87–97, 101–02. Shirley's experiences in the palace derive from McRae, interview. Other important sources on the events of the day include Kukral, *Prague 1989,* 47–59; McRae, *Resistance and Revolution,* 99–106; Kenney, *A Carnival of Revolution,* 280–89; John Keane, *Václav Havel: A Political Tragedy in Six Acts* (New York: Basic Books, 2000), 338–42; the official investigation into the events: Federal Assembly of Czech and Slovak Federative Republic, "Závěrečná zpráva vyšetřovací komise Federálního shromáždění pro objasnění událostí 17. listopadu 1989," accessible at http://www.psp.cz/eknih/1990fs/tisky/t1236_01.htm; Tomki Němec's photo album of November 17, 1989, *Velvet Revolution,* available online at https://tomkinemec.photoshelter.com/gallery/17-November-1989/G0000z2P2W9C1N00/ (hereafter denoted as photo, Němec); and Milan Otáhal and Miroslav Vaněk, *Sto studentských revolucí* (Prague: Nakladatelství Lidové noviny, 1999).

311 **WILL THE TRUTH PREVAIL?:** Photo, Němec.

311 **"Students, do not be afraid":** "Připomeňte si události 17. listopadu 1989 minutu po minutě," *iDNES,* November 17, 1989, http://zpravy.idnes.cz/pripomente-si-udalosti-17-listopadu-1989-minutu-po-minute-pij-/domaci.aspx?c=A091116_120725_domaci_js.

311 **"Resign!":** Ibid.

311 **"We will not merely commemorate":** Michael Wise, "Tens of Thousands Demand Reform in Prague," Reuters, November 17, 1989.

311 **"Oppression is worse":** "Clamor in the East; Riot Police in Prague Beat Marchers and Arrest Dozens," *New York Times,* November 18, 1989.

312 **"*Svobodu!*" "Masaryk!":** Kukral, *Prague 1989,* 50.

312 **"Havel!":** McRae, *Resistance and Revolution,* 102.

312 **"*Svobodné volby!*":** Kukral, *Prague 1989,* 50.

313 **"To Wenceslas Square!":** Ibid., 51; Bond, interview, June 28, 2017.

313 **"The crowd of students":** Bond, interview, August 1, 2017.

314 **"Tell Vašek!":** Keane, *Václav Havel,* 339.

315 **"Czechs! Come with us!":** Kukral, *Prague 1989,* 51.

315 **"Forty years of Communism is enough":** Cable, Black to Department of State, November 18, 1989, Prague 08082, in Prečan, *Prague–Washington–Prague,* 88.

316 **"The students marched north":** Bond, interview, August 1, 2017.

316 **"something really big is happening":** McRae, interview.

318 **"Police are blocking":** Bond, interview, August 1, 2017.

318 **"State Ops":** Munter, interview.

318 **"Pee before you go":** Kaska, interview.

318   "a ballroom in": Kiene, "The Velvet Revolution and Me," 8.

319   "When you are faced": Žantovský, *Havel,* 284.

319   "laws will be": Cable, Black to Department of State, October 19, 1989, Prague 07303, in Prečan, *Prague–Washington–Prague,* 16.

319   "looked hard and angry": McRae, *Resistance and Revolution,* 104–5.

319   "We Shall Overcome": Keane, *Vaclav Havel,* 341.

319   "You have to protect us": Federal Assembly of Czech and Slovak Federative Republic, "Závěrečná zpráva vyšetřovací komise."

320   "To our dismay": Kiene, "The Velvet Revolution and Me," 8.

320   "Suddenly the crowd realized": Keane, *Vaclav Havel,* 341.

320   "decided discretion was": Kiene, "The Velvet Revolution and Me," 8.

320   "We need to get out": Kaska, interview.

320   "We invited her": Kiene, "The Velvet Revolution and Me," 9.

321–22 "I saw a young mother beaten": Bond, interview, August 1, 2017.

322   "trained killers": McRae, *Resistance and Revolution,* 105.

322   "I have to run": Bond, interview, August 1, 2017.

323   "senseless violence": "U.S. Slams Czechoslovakia for Violence Against Protestors," Reuters, November 20, 1989.

323   "The government": Paula Butturini, "Prague, Czechoslovakia," *Chicago Tribune,* November 19, 1989.

323   "an uncanny buzz": Kiene, "The Velvet Revolution and Me," 9.

324   "I walked with the crowd": Ibid.

324   "did not want to go": Cable, Black to Department of State, November 21, 1989, Prague 08144, in Prečan, *Prague–Washington–Prague,* 108.

326   "*Svobodu!*": Kukral, *Prague 1989,* 65.

326   "It's finally here": Paul Wilson, correspondence with author, November 2017.

328   "drown us here": Žantovský, *Havel,* 301.

328   "As if out of nowhere": Ibid., 302.

328   "an enormous wave": Kukral, *Prague 1989,* 72.

328   "The sound system": Ibid.

328   "Dear friends": "Vaclav Havel's remarks over Wenceslas Square, November 21, 1989," Vaclav Havel Library, http://www.vaclavhavel-library.org/cs/index/novinky/768/utery-21-listopad-1989.

329   "The Archbishop exhorted": McRae, *Resistance and Revolution,* 127.

330   "gave the orders": Cable, Black to Department of State, November 22, 1989, Prague 08171, in Prečan, *Prague–Washington–Prague,* 124.

330   "entry is controlled": Cable, Black to Department of State, November 24, 1989, Prague 08208, in Prečan, *Prague–Washington–Prague,* 146.

330   "he had invited": Ibid.

330   "trained to deal with": McRae, *Resistance and Revolution,* 136.

331   "In 1620 a small band of Pilgrims": Shirley Temple Black, Thanksgiving service prayer, November 23, 1989, BFA.

331   "We call on all the members": "Declaration of Civic Forum Representative Václav Havel on Wenceslas Square, Prague," November 23, 1989, History and Public Policy Program Digital Archive, USD AV CR, KC OF Archive, file Dokumenty OF—copy of the computer print. Translated by Caroline Kovtun, http://digitalarchive.wilsoncenter.org/document/111760.

332   "Vaclav Havel gave": Cable, Black to Department of State, November 24, 1989, Prague 08208, in Prečan, *Prague–Washington–Prague,* 145.

332   "the submission of ultimatums": Václavík's remarks can be found in Milan

Otáhal and Zdeněk Sládek, eds., *Deset pražských dnů (17.–27. listopad 1989). Dokumentace* (Prague: Academia, 1990), 298–99.

332 **"Together with workers"**: Ibid.

333 **"dribbled out to"**: Cable, Black to Department of State, November 25, 1989, Prague 08237, in Prečan, *Prague–Washington–Prague,* 149.

333 **"He looks as if"**: Ash, *We the People,* 94.

333 **"Dubček!"**: Kukral, *Prague 1989,* 84.

333 **"You know I love you"**: McRae, *Resistance and Revolution,* 143.

334 **"Already, once"**: Ibid., 144.

334 **"Dubček to the castle"**: Ibid.

334 **"Dubček-Havel"**: Ash, *We the People,* 95.

334 **"All members of the Presidium"**: Videos of the press conference, with Jiří Černý's announcement, can be found on YouTube; e.g., "Demise komunistické strany Demision of the communist party," YouTube video, 0:46, posted by "Nezapomente1989," February 16, 2009, https://www.youtube.com/watch?v=rkt9biLorew.

334 **"a free Czechoslovakia"**: Ash, *We the People,* 96.

335 **"so I can say"**: Stein, "Czechs' Favorite Diplomat."

335 **"In Poland it took"**: Ash, *We the People,* 78.

335 **"Looking them sternly in the eye"**: "Remembering Ambassador Shirley Temple," US Embassy in the Czech Republic, February 21, 2014, https://cz.usembassy.gov/remembering-ambassador-shirley-temple-black-february-21/.

16 | "The Past Is Never Dead. It's Not Even Past."

336 **"The Past Is Never Dead"**: William Faulkner, *Requiem for a Nun* (New York: Random House, 1951), 92.

340 **"business-class Eurocrats"**: "Vaclav Klaus, an unusually combative Czech," *Economist,* February 1, 2001.

342 **"old poison in new bottles"**: For the text of Jiří Schneider's speech, see Organization for Security and Co-operation in Europe (OSCE), "Summary Report of the OSCE High Level Meeting on Confronting Anti-Semitism in Public Discourse," March 23–24, 2011, http://www.osce.org/odihr/77450?download=true, 22.

342 **"In countries with small Jewish communities"**: Ibid.

344 **"the forces of nationalism"**: "An Open Letter to the Obama Administration from Central and Eastern Europe," *Radio Free Europe,* July 16, 2009, https://www.rferl.org/a/An_Open_Letter_To_The_Obama_Administration_From_Central_And_Eastern_Europe/1778449.html.

349 **"degenerate"**: Albrecht Dümling, "The Target of Racial Purity: The 'Degenerate Music' Exhibition in Düsseldorf, 1938," in Richard A. Etlin, ed., *Art, Culture, and Media Under the Third Reich* (Chicago: University of Chicago Press, 2002), 43–72.

349 **"a media fiction"**: *Parlamentní listy,* May 2, 2015.

350 **"I thought very carefully"**: *MF Dnes,* May 4, 2011, 4.

350 **"does not come from the apes"**: "Klaus's Aide Hájek Says bin Laden Is Nothing but Media Fiction," *ČTK,* May 2, 2011.

350 **"I want to say clearly"**: Václav Klaus, "Prezident republiky o výrocích Petra Hájka a jejich interpretaci," May 4, 2011, https://www.klaus.cz/clanky/2828.

350 **"is an occasion"**: Václav Klaus, "Notes for the [sic] Independence Day Speech 2011," June 30, 2011, https://www.klaus.cz/clanky/2860.

353 **"the forthcoming gay carnival":** Petr Hájek, "Jsem kryptofašista. Doznávám se," *Parlamentní listy,* August 4, 2011, http://www.parlamentnilisty.cz/arena/ politici-volicum/Petr-Hajek-Jsem-kryptofasista-Doznavam-se-204468.

353 **"Confucius over Rousseau":** Rob Cameron, "Uproar Over Appointment of Ultra Conservative as Ministerial Adviser," *Radio Prague,* April 5, 2011, http://www.radio.cz/en/section/curraffrs/uproar-over-appointment-of-ultra -conservative-as-ministerial-adviser.

353 **praising as "great":** "Bátora se před několika lety účastnil neveřejné antisemitské přednášky," *Novinky.cz,* April 30, 2011, https://www.novinky.cz/domaci/232168 -batora-se-pred-nekolika-lety-ucastnil-neverejne-antisemitske-prednasky .html.

354 **"The American Embassy is happy":** US embassy statement, as it appears in Erik Tabery, "In Prague, a Fight for Gay Rights Goes International," *Atlantic,* September 14, 2011.

354 **"I strongly disagree":** Václav Klaus, "Prohlášení prezidenta republiky k dalšímu exemplárnímu útoku na svobodu slova," Press Releases, August 5, 2011, https:// www.klaus.cz/clanky/2896.

354 **led the press to believe:** "Klaus Says Ambassadors' Letter on Homosexuals March Unprecedented," *ČTK,* August 8, 2011.

356 **"I fall asleep":** Dan Bilefsky, "Picture Him in a Mohawk: A Czech Prince Seeks Young Voters," *New York Times,* January 24, 2013.

356 **"No one prevents":** "Klaus Says Ambassadors' Letter on Homosexuals March Unprecedented," *ČTK,* August 8, 2011.

357 **cucumber season:** "Czech PM Says State Official Bátora Must Not Behave Like Activist," *ČTK,* August 9, 2011.

357 **"an old fascist":** "TOP 09 Says Bátora Should Leave Czech Ministry—Press," *ČTK,* August 11, 2011.

357 **"old lame duck":** "TOP 09 Ministers Leave Czech Cabinet Meeting, Want Bátora Sacked," *ČTK,* August 17, 2011.

357 **"sorry little old man":** Brian Kenety, "TOP 09 Stage Cabinet Meeting Walk Out, Demand Batora's Exit," *Ceska pozice,* August 31, 2011, http://ceskapozice. lidovky.cz/top-09-stage-cabinet-meeting-walk-out-demand-batora-s-exit-p2a-/ tema.aspx?c=A110817_155152_pozice_33011.

358 **"crucial":** James Kirchick, "Advocate," *Tablet,* January 19, 2012, http://www .tabletmag.com/jewish-news-and-politics/88591/advocate/2.

358 **A *New York Times* story:** Bruce I. Konviser, "Czech Leader Is Isolated in Opposing Gay Parade," *New York Times,* August 15, 2011.

Full notes and a bibliography can be found at www.NormanEisen.com/ TheLastPalace/Endmatter.

Index